CHARLIE'S TOUCHDOWN

Be open to the Holy Spirit!

In Christ,

Mary Jo Stephen

CHARLIE'S TOUCHDOWN

by

Mary Jo Stopher

Edited by

Henri Forget

ISBN: 1-58820-477-4

This book is printed on acid free paper.

Pictures on pages 70, 75, 77, 78, 80 and 242 represent the
Kentucky Easter Seal Society.

1stBooks - rev. 1/18/01

DEDICATION

I dedicate this book to new parents facing the uncertain future of a child with congenital anomalies. Although you will suffer by watching your child endure physical, mental or emotional pain, it is my desire to share hope and encouragement with you. I pray that you may quickly discover the blessings that God has given you through this child. For those parents that don't have the joy of bringing home their new baby, this hope is offered to you as well. I believe that no child's life is in vain. When a baby dies at birth, you can be sure that she/he is bringing every family member and friend closer to God. All will be drawn to God through prayer for you, the grieving parents. Be open to the power of God working through your tragedy.

I also dedicate this book to my loving husband, Charlie, and to my children: Jackie, Marty, Leslie and Jonathan in memory of their brother Charlie. It is for my grandchildren Becca, Jaycob, and all those yet to be born that they may come to know their Uncle Charlie and his gift to them. This dedication is extended to all future generations to enlighten them as to the power of God.

ACKNOWLEDGMENTS

God has shared many wonderful people with me through the years. I thank all those who have touched me and taught me. My parents, brothers, sisters, in-laws and numerous relatives have all played significant roles in the development of my spiritual life. I thank them all.

A special appreciation is extended to all priests who bring Jesus Christ to me in the Eucharist. Their openness to the Holy Spirit through their speech and actions has given me added strength. Three priests in particular are worthy of mention. The late Rev. Patrick Caster enlightened me as to the love of God the Father. Rev. Bruce Dillman led me to a deeper relationship with God the Son. Rev. Terry Bradshaw opened my eyes and ears to the guidance of God the Holy Spirit. To each of these priests, I offer a sincere thank you.

My gratitude is also extended to Rev. Bill Hammer and Rev. Dan Noll, who gave me their time and compassion during my most difficult trial.

The utmost thanks goes to my spiritual mentor, Rev. Jeffrey Leger, who believed in me and was my avid supporter in pursuing publication. He shared his sensitivity toward Catholic concepts and toward non-Catholic readers so that all may enjoy this story. Additional thanks goes to Sherry Epley who assisted in the pre-editing stage and to Rhonda Becker who shared her computer expertise. I couldn't have done it without any of these people.

Finally, it is imperative to acknowledge every person that has crossed my path of life. If I have met you, I assure you that it has not been insignificant. You have added to my spiritual preparation for eternal life. I may know you well or I may only recognize your face. For some of you, I may only remember your act of kindness. Yet, you have still touched me. Many

vii

faces, names and spirits surfaced as I wrote this book. Most are not mentioned but all are a part of this story. For those not mentioned, I thank you.

CONTENTS

Part I

Part II

Part III

Part IV

FOREWORD

To the reader,

You are being invited on a unique and intriguing journey. The story you are about to read reaches to the depth of my soul where many treasures are stored. Until now, only those closest to me have been allowed to peek at these gifts. Even they have not seen the fullness of the favors that God has bestowed upon me.

Valuable insight was revealed to me over time as I faced difficult trials in raising my son Charlie. Together we were given strength and courage to follow the will of God. The experience that you are about to undergo will open your eyes in such a way that you will see how a crisis in your own life can be a doorway to heaven.

Only by the grace of God am I able to bare my soul in this vulnerable way. It has been my desire to share my blessings with others since I first became aware of God's constant presence and guidance in my life. As events unfolded, I knew in my heart that the value of these graces was too great to bury in the sand. With patience, I waited for the prompting of the Holy Spirit to begin my writing. There was clear purpose in allowing time to pass before putting into words the events about which you are about to read. The purpose was healing. Without complete healing, I would have followed the temptation to hold back the most valuable hidden treasure found within the pages of this book. As it was, however, I refused to give in to my desire to share, without first being inspired by the Holy Spirit. As a result, it took seven years after a great tragedy to be properly healed with God's love. Please enjoy the unfolding of that love as you travel on this journey with me. It is my belief that God intends for me to share this with you.

Mary Jo Stopher

Part I

1

THE EYES OF YOUTH

As a 17-year-old high school graduate in 1971, I had the world by a string. I knew that the future was mine for whatever I wanted to make of it. Up until that point my life consisted of school, boyfriend, household chores, baby-sitting, and church; pretty much in that order.

In contemplating my future, I saw that teaching was the one career that I would be interested in. However, the personal goal that I had in mind at the time was to get married and to raise a family. There was one problem. My boyfriend of three years, Charlie, had not asked me to marry him yet, but it was only a matter of time.

Knowing that my true calling was to be a wife and a mother, I chose not to go on to college. Rather, I decided to get a job and start saving for the wedding that I wanted. The following year we were married.

Birth control was not an issue for us as we were both anxious to have a family. Nine and a half months later, on April 21, 1973, I gave birth to a beautiful baby girl, Jackie. It was on that day that I witnessed my first miracle. She was born on Holy Saturday. Having thoughts of the passion and death of Jesus throughout Holy Week implanted the desire to watch a biblical movie on TV that night called "The Robe." However, due to the total exhaustion of my day of labor, I was unable to stay awake for the movie. Reflecting on the passion, I recall trying to imagine how horrible it must have been for Jesus. My eleven hours of labor was nothing in comparison. The thought of it moved me to tears. Easter Sunday came. I felt elated with the gift that God had given me; the gift of life through the Resurrection and this precious baby.

Being a new mom was exciting. Yet, I was faced with mixed emotions as I looked to the future of our new family. Facing my six-week checkup with the doctor frightened me. Charlie and I had discussed birth control for the first time although we both wanted a house full of children. We were facing a serious dilemma. Charlie was attending college and working full time. I had been working up until the baby was born but now was planning to stay home with her. How then, could we possibly believe that it would be right to bring more children into the world right now? We were torn in our thoughts. We didn't see it as a possibility to have the children we wanted right then. We discussed birth control but didn't like any form. We discussed the Church's stand against it as well as our situation at school, work, and at home. We never came up with a suitable answer.

The day came for my checkup and I still had not decided upon birth control. Conflicting thoughts passed through my mind as to the various methods and as to the Church's stand against it. Thinking of society's expectation for it added more confusion. The pill was a product that frightened me. Charlie and I had talked about the unnatural way that it affected a woman's body by stopping ovulation. The possibility of damaging the eggs concerned me. I had an intuitive feeling that it might cause birth defects in the next baby.

Then I thought of all the people at work who had used the pill and had perfectly healthy babies. Many women I knew were on the pill. In spite of this, my gut feeling about it was not good. Underneath it all was that "Catholic conscience" telling me not to take it.

Upon arriving at the doctor's office, I still did not know what I would say when he questioned me. When the exam was over, sure enough the doctor asked, "What do you plan to use for birth control?" It was obviously expected of me to use something. People in today's society just don't have ten kids anymore. As a responsible adult, at all of nineteen-years-old, I knew I'd better say something. After all, I had had over nine months to figure it out.

So I responded, "I don't know. I really don't like any of them." With this answer I assumed he would understand that I didn't want to use birth control. He would surely offer me some magical solution. He'll tell me that I don't have to use anything. He'll say it's okay to have all the children I want. Then I'll know it's acceptable to do so.

4

However, that was not the response I got. He said, "The pill would be the easiest. Do you want me to write you a prescription?"

"I guess so," I responded. I walked out, prescription in hand, wondering just what had happened.

As I drove home, I thought things over knowing that I had to choose something. I shouldn't be so absorbed with these thoughts about birth defects. It hasn't happened to anyone I know. I'll just be using it for a short time while we get adjusted to married life. I'm sure that what the Pope objects to is the refusal of children, not the spacing of children.

I had just talked myself into believing what I wanted to hear. The prescription was filled and reproduction was postponed.

Life as a new wife and mother was all I expected and more. Not that all was perfect, but I found pleasure in cooking, cleaning, even diapering and in midnight feedings. My days were filled with teaching my baby new things. I sang Disney tunes to her, took her for walks in the stroller and rocked her to sleep.

Charlie would come home from work or school with arms outstretched for "Daddy's Little Girl." He loved every minute with her. She often sat on his lap and helped him with his homework.

Time passed quickly. When Jackie was nine-months-old we talked about throwing away the dreaded pills and hoping for another baby. The conversation was very short. We both felt the same way about it. We didn't care what people would say. The expectations of society no longer mattered.

The next day, I called the doctor to see if it would be harmful to stop taking the pill in the middle of a cycle. My eagerness to do so made waiting another two or three weeks difficult to accept. I was told that it would be okay to stop at any time and it would be perfectly safe to get pregnant. So, in the trash they went. A heavy burden was lifted. I felt free. It was a wonderful thought to anticipate another pregnancy.

The thought of birth defects now haunted my mind again by surfacing from time to time. Ovulation occurred only twice in the next six months. With the second time, I became pregnant.

How exciting. Or was it? The fear became greater, but I kept it to myself. People would think I was overreacting if I shared such ridiculous thoughts. After all, I was only on the pill for seven and one half months. That wouldn't change anything in my body that fast. For up to about five months in my pregnancy I pondered the feeling of something being wrong. I was told at each monthly office visit that everything looked good. There was a strong fetal heartbeat. All was fine. Finally, I pushed the thoughts of birth defects out of my mind. I could become obsessed thinking about it. So, I blocked all thoughts of it from then on.

As time drew nearer to the due date, I discovered another feeling that had been just beneath the surface for a while. I had this very strange feeling that I was not carrying *my* baby. This greatly disturbed me. What kind of sense does that make? I didn't know why I felt this way. I didn't know what it meant. All I knew was that the feeling was very real. I also knew that I couldn't share this thought with anyone, not even Charlie. He'd probably think that I didn't want the baby. What was so strange was that I had forgotten about the fear of birth defects. Yet, this new peculiar feeling was so strong.

Through all of this, I don't recall if I had prayed for a healthy baby. We attended church on Sundays and that was about all I thought of prayer.

When the baby was two weeks overdue, labor was induced. I gave birth to a 7lb., 9-1/2 oz. boy on March 15, 1975. Labor had been a short three hours. His position was transverse and required being turned. Two nurses pounded on my abdomen to help push him out. He was blue for whatever reason and required a minimal amount of oxygen to assist his breathing.

When he was brought to my room a few hours later, I took a good look at him. I recall the white film over his newborn body. His color looked a bit funny. I was still groggy from drugs and figured I was out of focus. Noticing that his feet were turned in drastically, I told Charlie that he must have been lying in an awkward position. His feet would probably straighten up in no time. Together, we observed his long fingers, which looked ideal for a piano player. His hands were turned inward also. Again, I assumed that it was all due to his position for nine months. He

6

had all body parts and I was relieved to have a healthy baby. Charlie still thought his color looked a little odd. Yet, I was convinced it was the way newborns were supposed to look before their first bath. I figured he would look better the next day.

We spent some time together fussing over our baby. That evening Jackie came up to visit her new baby brother. Her grandparents and other relatives came as well. It was an exciting visit for all.

When morning came, I patiently waited for my baby as I watched the nurses deliver the others to their moms. After what seemed like a pause in the distribution system, I called out and asked for my son. The nurse told me that he was being seen by the doctor and would be out shortly. Instead the pediatrician on call came and spoke to me. He said that in looking over my baby he detected a small heart murmur. He said that it was fairly normal and would probably resolve itself in twenty-four hours. Meanwhile, he felt that it would be in the best interest of the baby if we kept him under oxygen as much as possible. He said that he could come out for feedings but should go right back to the nursery when I was finished.

I was startled for a moment, yet relieved that it wasn't more serious. I can handle this, I thought. It's just a minor heart murmur. He says it's fairly common and will be resolved in a day. I placed my trust in what he was saying, having no worries about it. At that time my former negative thoughts returned to me. I suddenly remembered my fears of something being wrong with my baby, feeling fortunate that it turned out to be so simple. I knew that things would be fine.

In the beginning when I held my son, I thought about the feeling that he wasn't mine. I held him close, admired him, and the feeling was no longer there. I knew he was mine. I recall wondering where that feeling might have come from. So, once again, I dismissed it. We would soon be taking him home to blend into the family just as Jackie had done almost 2 years earlier.

Our son was named Charles Anthony Jr. My husband was so proud to have a son named after him. He had dreamed of playing baseball and football with a son. He wanted to call him "Charlie" and nothing else. He was on cloud nine. I enjoyed watching him in his excitement.

That Sunday evening Charlie Sr. took Jackie home so that we could all get plenty of rest. What I didn't know at the time was that Jackie would be up most of the night with an earache. By morning they were both still exhausted. It was early Monday morning when my regular pediatrician, Dr. Greathouse, was back in town from the weekend. He had come to check my baby. I met him in the hallway, anxious to hear him say that the heart murmur was now resolved. However, he suggested that I go back to my room and sit down so that he could talk to me about my baby. I assured him I was fine standing in the hallway, as I couldn't bear to wait another second to hear what he had to tell me. With that, he proceeded to tell me that my son had several heart murmurs. He was certain of two and possibly three. He also said that his heart was on the right side of his chest rather than on the left. I could feel my body tremble. He added that my son needed to be transferred to Children's Hospital right away where they could watch him more closely. He explained that several tests would need to be run. He expressed his shock that Charlie had not been transferred immediately after he was born. He was obviously upset. For the first time, which was two days after the birth, I realized that we were dealing with something very serious. I was told that an ambulance would be there shortly to take him away.

My insides were suddenly in knots. I shook as I picked up the phone to call Charlie. The time was about 9:00 A.M. The line was busy. After several attempts, I realized that he had probably taken the phone off the hook so that he could sleep. I then called my mother-in-law to tell her what was going on. I told her why I couldn't reach Charlie and that he needed to come to the hospital right away. She sent his brother, Ray, to wake him up and tell him to get there fast. When Ray reached him with the news, Charlie was confused. He was only told that he needed to be with me but no reason was given. With that he called his mother and insisted on knowing why it was so important for him to hurry down to the hospital. He was certain that his mother was

8

overreacting. He had talked to me just the night before and I had told him not to hurry in the morning. It was much more important for Jackie to get her sleep first. We had agreed that he should wait until it was convenient for him to come. As a result, he took his time in getting there.

Meanwhile, I waited, being strong all the while. I wasn't going to cry. So, I held it in. It would do me good to walk down to the nursery and look at the other babies. As I stood there observing a room full of healthy babies, a kind, grandmother-type woman stood next to me. Other people were talking among themselves at the window. The woman must have noticed that I was alone. In making a friendly gesture, she sweetly asked me, "Which one is yours, honey?" With that, I burst into tears and struggled to get the words out, "He's in the back." Having absolutely no control over my emotions, I felt sorry for the woman who had asked. I knew she must have felt bad but I couldn't explain to her that I appreciated her kindness. All I could do was cry. I turned away and rushed back to my room. The hallway seemed like it was five miles long. I couldn't move as fast as I wanted, due to soreness. I thought I'd never make it. Shortly thereafter, my obstetrician came in asking how I was doing. Again, all I could do was cry as I explained that I was worried about my baby. He said he was sorry, encouraged me to rest and he'd be back tomorrow.

After crying all the tears that I had stored up, I decided that I would go see my baby while I waited for Charlie to get there. The nurses were kind. One nurse offered to let me hold him before he left. I stood there shaking and feeling very weak. Believing that he was going to Children's Hospital to die, I prayed for Charlie to hurry. I looked at my son under the oxygen hood. His color looked good. I felt selfish for wanting to hold him because I didn't believe he could breathe as easily if I took him out of the oxygen. The nurse assured me that it would be okay for a moment. I still didn't feel good about it. I also felt that it wouldn't be right for me to hold him one last time if my husband couldn't hold him one last time, too. So, I just trembled and watched him in the incubator. My mind was spinning with previous thoughts of birth defects, the pill, the guilt, and the feeling of him not being my baby. Quiet tears flowed down my cheeks. I was completely overwhelmed and helpless.

I watched the doorway for Charlie to arrive. Then I heard the sound of the ambulance. I knew it was for my son. My heart pounded. I couldn't bear it. I returned to my room to be alone in my thoughts. I was aware of my roommate on the other side of the curtain. As she held and cuddled her baby, I felt cheated, but I was mostly disappointed in the fact that Charlie had not made it in time. I believed that neither of us would see our son alive again.

When Charlie finally arrived, I went through the explanation of what had happened. He was still unaware of any of it because his mother and I both felt it was my place to tell him. He could stay only a short time due to the doctor's appointment he had made for Jackie.

By afternoon, we were told the obvious. Our baby was cyanotic due to a low level of oxygen caused by the heart murmurs. His hands were turned in tightly, clubbed with his thumbs drawn inward. This was due to muscle spasms in his forearms and lack of oxygen to the extremities. He also had Talipes-varus, which is a severe clubbing of the feet. The pediatrician instructed Charlie to pay a visit to the cardiologist the next day. Meanwhile, numerous tests were being done. From blood work and x-rays to EKG, EEG, and heart catheterization, it was one test after another.

Tuesday, we learned more. Once the heart catheterization was completed, but prior to sharing the results, the cardiologist questioned Charlie, Sr. about how he intended to pay the medical expenses. Taken by surprise, Charlie suggested The Heart Association. We also had insurance. He was told that it would take a lot more than that. He suggested that we look into some other resources. Money was the last thing on Charlie's mind. He was on edge waiting to hear just what we were facing.

The doctor explained the results of the heart catheterization. It showed that our son had cyanotic congenital heart disease. He had dextrocardia (heart on the right side), common atrium (single upper chamber), common ventricle (single lower chamber), complete transposition of the great vessels (aorta and pulmonary

10

arteries reversed), probable pulmonary stenosis (a narrowing of the pulmonary artery), and compensated heart (the murmurs helped balance the oxygen somewhat by the mixture of red and blue blood).

After speaking with the cardiologist, Charlie rushed back to Baptist Hospital where I waited to hear all that he had just been told. After hearing all this, I asked Charlie if he still wanted to name our son after him. Knowing that it would be unlikely that this baby would ever have children of his own, I thought perhaps Charlie would have second thoughts about passing his name on to him. But, I was wrong. He said that this child would most definitely have his name. The birth certificate was signed accordingly before I was discharged. We left the hospital empty-handed.

My first stop was at Children's Hospital. I was pleased that we were able to go into his nursery and visit. We were allowed to hold him and feed him and found great comfort in seeing him respond in a normal newborn fashion. I had slim hope at that time that he would live.

We then picked up Jackie from her grandparents and went home. Now Jackie was a very inquisitive twenty-three-month-old child. She didn't quite understand all that had been told to her. She knew that Mommy had a new baby. However, she did not understand why the baby didn't come home with Mommy as she had expected. It was necessary to take her back to the hospital so that she could see her baby brother.

As the days unfolded, so did information. A liver-spleen test was performed to determine how they functioned in Charlie. Much to everyone's surprise, there was no spleen. Along with this discovery, Charlie Jr. was found to have asplenia syndrome. This meant that the organs in his body were a mirror image on the right and the left. He had bilateral right lungs (each lung had three lobes rather than two lobes on the left). He had a midline stomach and a midline liver that was located behind the stomach instead of to the right. He had a right and left superior vena cava rather than only a right one as in a normal body. (This is a vessel that brings blood back to the heart from the upper body.) X-rays showed that he also had an extra vertebra in his spine at level L2, which is about waist level.

The diagnosis didn't fit neatly into a particular disease category. He was said to have complicated congenital heart disease and congenital anomalies. The heart problems were naturally the greatest concern.

(From this point on I will refer to my husband as Charles and my son as Charlie to eliminate any confusion.)

One evening when I wanted to visit my son, my friend's mother offered to take me. Charles was working and I had been instructed not to drive for two weeks. There was always a caring friend or relative to watch Jackie. I had been pondering many questions about Charlie's prognosis. Mrs. Wolek drove me to the hospital. After spending time with my son, I spoke to the resident doctor concerning Charlie's life expectancy. Until now, all the doctors had been quite vague. Each implied a short life but never specified what short meant. I needed desperately to know so that I might be able to deal with it.

As I started the questions, the doctor explained. He described Charlie's heart as being equivalent to the heart of a frog. He told me that humans have four heart chambers and live on the average about 70 years. Frogs have only two heart chambers and live much shorter lives, probably a couple of years at most. He said that I had to understand that this was only one of the many problems that Charlie had. "When you add all the other main things that are wrong with this two-chambered heart, you can not expect his life to be that long. Most babies with transposition of the great vessels live only a few months. When looking at the rest of all this, it is not very promising. Given the best scenario, he could live a few months but he could never live for over a year. You can see how blue he is. He is not getting enough oxygen. This will get worse each day because his heart has to work very hard. You can see it's a struggle for him to eat. After drinking only one or two ounces, he's too worn out. We don't know if he'll be able to gain the weight he needs."

He did not want to give me any false hope. He kept implying that if Charlie were to go home, things would most likely get progressively worse fast. He doubted that Charlie would be able to handle room air without oxygen. After there were no more questions to ask, I went out to the waiting room where Mrs. Wolek had so patiently waited.

We went to the cafeteria and talked. I was a bit choked up at all that I had just heard. I told Mrs. Wolek, "I don't understand why God would give me a baby if He was just going to take him right back." It didn't make sense to me. What would be His purpose? Would this be a punishment for my sins? I cried from shame. Mrs. Wolek said to me, "We don't know why these things happen. Only God knows. You don't know how long you'll have him. Only God knows. If you take him home and have him for only one day, you need to make it the best day you can have. If you have him for one week or one month, make it the best week or month. That's what you'll have to do. Then you can say that you did your best. And that's all you can do."

By this time I was so exhausted that I wasn't even sure I'd remember her advice. Once I got home and she had left, I had the opportunity to cry again. I called Charles at work and told him I needed for him to come home. I couldn't deal with this by myself.

In the morning, Charles called Dr. Greathouse and told him of the events from the night before. We wanted his opinion on our son's life expectancy. He had a way of softening a blow. He was angry that the doctor had told us so many negative things. He consoled us by saying that with this being so rare we don't have sufficient statistics to go by. With complicated heart disease, sometimes one anomaly works differently when combined with another. Therefore, no one knew what to expect. He did stress, however, that if Charlie survived the first three months when the most crucial, life-threatening problems occur, he may live one year. He promised to do everything he could and he planned to keep a close watch on him.

I can't say that I felt differently about any of it, but I did feel comforted by his caring attitude. I tried hard to regain my physical and mental strength. When I prayed I asked many questions. I begged forgiveness for all of my sins and those of my husband. I racked my brains, as I would go from room to room trying to figure out why or how this happened. Several doctors had told me that this malformation had occurred in the earliest part of my pregnancy. Each had disregarded my suspicion about the birth control pill causing it. I recalled using a powerful oven cleaner and wondered if the chemicals could have triggered it. I thought of every possible chemical that either one of us had been near. Still, I had no satisfying answer to my questions. When I prayed, I was so focused on my problem and my guilt that I didn't notice if God had even tried to answer me.

After two weeks we were able to take Charlie home. He had spent two days without oxygen and didn't appear to be in distress. We were given a list of instructions and a prescription for Ampicillin as a prophylactic. No heart medicine was necessary. It was highly stressed, however, that if he got a fever to have him seen immediately. There was tremendous fear of infection in the heart lining and, if so, response time would be of the essence. Appointments were scheduled for the heart, pediatrician and orthopedic clinics in one week. This was to become the new routine of my life.

Needless to say, Jackie was excited about having this baby home. As we settled in on that first day home, I found myself thinking about the conversation I had had earlier with Mrs. Wolek. I remembered what she had said about making each day the very best. I held him close and promised him and myself that this would be the best day that he could possibly have. I made a promise that however many days that we might have together, they would be filled with only the best.

Jackie parked her small rocking chair next to mine. As I fed Charlie, she fed her baby doll. I sang and rocked. She sang and rocked. We all quickly adjusted to having our new family member.

2

BLESSINGS IN DISGUISE

In making all the appointments for the following week, I quickly ran into bureaucrats. Getting into the orthopedic clinic was like breaking into Fort Knox. It was next to impossible. I was told that they just couldn't take every baby with clubfeet. It had to be serious and he had to be referred. If we had insurance we needed to go somewhere else. The clinic was designed for those on medical assistance programs. Charles researched organizations that could possibly assist in paying for necessary medical treatments.

Going from place to place, he kept reaching dead ends. Finally, there was one kind lady at the department for human resources who told him exactly how to go about getting the help he needed. He wondered why someone suddenly took enough interest in him to explain the various ways to get help. At the end of his discussion with her, he found out that she was blind. This is why she knew all the answers. She had been there herself. God was sending us help without our being aware of it.

We had to file for Social Security benefits for the disabled. Then we had to verify that he was disabled. Doctors had to confirm that based on his birth defects, he would not be able to grow up and get a job. They had to confirm that there was no surgery currently available to correct the heart problems that he had. This verification from all doctors involved went on for weeks.

Meanwhile, we were told that it was very important to have casts put on both of his feet right away while the bones were soft. This could prevent some extensive surgery later.

We went to a private orthopedic office as suggested, rather than waiting to get into the clinic. He had bilateral casts placed on his feet up to his knees. It being a time of tremendous growth, it was mandatory to change the casts once a week.

Once I had found someone to correct his feet, I asked this same doctor about correcting his hands. He felt, after x-rays, that

15

because it was not the bones in his arms or hands that were causing the problem, there was nothing much to do about it. He suggested that I exercise his hands.

I then asked the pediatrician if there was anything else I could do for his hands. They looked terrible. He told me to get a small rubber ball and get him to squeeze it often during the day. I tried every type of ball and squeeze toy there was. He had no strength in his hands to hold anything, much less squeeze it. So, after a week-long attempt, I called the pediatrician back and asked if a well-known hand surgeon in the area, Dr. Kleinert, could be of some help. Dr. Greathouse assured me there was nothing Dr. Kleinert could do. I found it hard to believe. I felt certain that if a doctor could reattach a hand, as he had been known to do, then he could certainly straighten out a hand that had not been severed.

I got on the phone and called to make an appointment. In taking my information, the technician asked me the question that I feared. "Who referred you?" I knew that I couldn't mention any of my doctors. They had all told me it wouldn't do any good. So, I took my chances and answered, "I did." I was prepared to make my case based on the work he had done for others I knew. Much to my surprise, she said O.K. Then she made an appointment for the following week. Now I was well aware that this would be an all-day event. Everyone I knew who had ever been to this doctor had stated that one generally waited about five or six hours in the office before being seen. The technician was so kind. Knowing that this was a newborn with heart disease, she told me to come around to the back door when I arrived so that they could take me in right away. I was stunned. This was wonderful. I knew then that God was helping me to make my son's life better.

Within just a few weeks, our normal weekday consisted of seeing one doctor or another each day. The heart clinic was an all-day affair. I would pack a bag with bottles and baby food for the entire day. I packed a lunch for Jackie and myself. She would throw in her favorite toys and books. We made the day as entertaining as possible.

Starting at 8:00 A.M., we were led throughout the hospital for a wide variety of tests and x-rays. The most trying was the lab work. Charlie had rolling veins, making them difficult to locate. Even technicians that had been there for years would begin to walk away when they saw us coming. They all knew that he would be stuck numerous times before being able to draw blood. I would hold him as an attempt to comfort him and at the same time assist the lab tech in keeping him still. It was heartbreaking to watch him endure this pain. Eventually, we were able to find a technician who could get it in one or two sticks. We began to ask for her every time. From there it was x-rays and EKG. Each stop we made involved a long wait.

After all was said and done, we would return to see the doctor before leaving. Each time there would be a new string of doctors to come in to see this amazing miracle child. These doctors were all brought in for their input. No one seemed to know what to do with him. I noticed each new doctor that would come, would comment on how good he looked. After reading his history, they expected to find a weak, frail, and pitiful child. They were always amazed to find a chunky, healthy-looking baby. He wasn't sad and pitiful. He was happy and smiling. The doctors often would have group meetings and then one would return to tell me there was no plan of treatment to correct his problem. They frequently left the room shaking their heads. The clinic day was generally over by 4:00-5:00 P.M although, on one occasion when the doctor told us he was going to get another group of doctors to come in, he apparently wasn't able to do so. He failed to tell us and we waited patiently until almost 7:00 P.M. By this time, everyone had cleared out, so we left.

On a second day of the week, we would start our morning by soaking Charlie's leg casts in vinegar water. Then I would be able to unravel the casts to take them off. We'd go to the orthopedic doctor and have new ones applied. The reason for soaking the casts off was to eliminate the frightful sound of the saw used to cut casts, for Charlie. The only difficult part of this visit was the stretching of his feet in the new casts. It was painful for him to have his feet pushed the opposite way they wanted to

17

go. The doctor was very gentle with him, which made it more tolerable.

A third day's visit would be to the pediatrician. He conferred with the cardiologist weekly on Charlie's progress. We went back and forth with antibiotics. He needed something to fight infection but the ampicillin began to cause thrush in his mouth. It was debatable. Do we go on with more problems or do we risk the chance of heart infection? After a long debate over it, it was decided to stop the antibiotics. Again it was stressed to get him to a doctor immediately in the event of even a low-grade fever. I acknowledged my understanding.

The fourth doctor visit each week was to the orthopedic hand surgeon. I was nervous about our first visit with him. In checking him for muscle tone, I was asked if I'd been told that he had or could have cerebral palsy. I was really taken back. This is one condition that had never been mentioned. He said that there was a good possibility of it, but it was too soon to tell. He said that we wouldn't be real sure for a while. It may take six months or a year before we'd know. Nevertheless, he did feel that he could straighten out Charlie's hands by making tiny hand splints that would support his wrists upward. These were made with an extended thumb piece that would pull his thumb outward in a natural position. His thumbs had been drawn inward directly under his forefinger since birth. In applying these splints that were made to the form of Charlie's hands, the doctor massaged his hands and forearms to get them to relax a bit. It took about fifteen to twenty minutes to apply each brace. Charlie cried with the pain of forcing his hands straight. I was instructed to work with his hands in the same manner at home. The braces were to be on twenty-four hours a day with the exception of a one-hour breather three times a day.

With a week full of instructions, my daily routine was falling into place. Jackie was my helper. She stood on a chair and helped me wash dishes. She'd throw the dishes into the sink so quickly that I had to work fast to keep up with her. We'd go from room to room making beds and doing laundry. As much as possible, I scheduled doctor's appointments around naps. Between all of this, we'd take walks in the double stroller, bake cookies, sew new clothes, and prepare dinner for the kids' daddy when he'd come home from work or school. As we were busy with household chores, we often played music. We especially enjoyed The Mouseketeers and "Whistle While You Work" from Disney's "Snow White."

My life was hectic by this time. Considering the children, housework, doctors, husband, and a part-time job on Saturdays, there was absolutely no time left for me. Now this did not disturb me because I was doing all that I had ever dreamed of doing and more. I found that I thoroughly enjoyed doing things for them. My relaxing time was when I would rock the baby to sleep as he was being fed. This is when my mind could rest. As I held my son, I admired his very existence. I looked at his cyanosis and watched as he drank his bottle of milk. My thoughts were filled with amazement realizing the amount of energy he used when nursing. How could he struggle so hard yet look so peaceful? I no longer asked God why He would give me a child that He intended to take back so soon. I was now asking how this child was even living after a few months. I was fascinated by the power of God over medical science. This is something that I had never given a thought to previously. I had always believed in God's power but, until now, I never had an opportunity to see it so profoundly manifested.

A significant factor during this time was Charlie's sleeping and eating pattern that was developing. Due to shortness of breath, he would become exhausted after drinking only two ounces. Therefore, he needed to eat every two hours instead of every four hours in order to get the nourishment that he needed. Just as any new mom, I anxiously longed for the time that he would sleep longer at night. I thought of our getting a good night's sleep. However, with each week that passed, he slept less and less. He was not able to breathe well lying down. Therefore, the more difficult it was to breathe, the less he slept.

My very supportive husband, who was also a proud father, was at my side. Charles worked the night shift and found it enjoyable to stay up with Charlie for a while after getting home from work around 3:30 in the morning. This way I could sleep in until 6:00 A.M. With his help, I could usually get five or six hours of sleep.

As time passed, the possibility of getting any financial assistance in regard to the medical expenses was still pending. It turned out that we were not allowed to apply for disability insurance because we made $20.00 too much per week. This meant that I would have to quit my Saturday job in order to qualify. So, we dropped the matter. I didn't feel right quitting for that reason. The bills were mounting rapidly even after insurance. A number of bills of a few hundred dollars quickly turned into bills in the thousands. After all, the situation was not going away. They would only continue to grow.

Meanwhile, Charles was attending Jefferson Community College with dreams of going to Notre Dame or Purdue University. Acceptance letters were starting to arrive from various colleges. He was accepted to attend Purdue. His heart was filled with excitement momentarily. He realized that this dream could not be fulfilled due to our current monetary responsibilities. He sadly discarded his acceptance letter. We discussed being able to pursue any college at that point. The University of Kentucky seemed like a possibility. Charles was afraid to move because of Charlie's doctors. I assured him that there would be doctors in Lexington. By now, the hand surgeon was the only doctor we were concerned about keeping. I doubted that we would find someone comparable. The office visits were now becoming farther apart as Charlie was now four-months-old. I didn't see it as a problem to drive back once a month for a doctor's appointment. As for the cardiologist, we never got any specific plan from him. He could never give us hope. He could not answer our questions. He seemed stumped each time we went for a visit. He saw that things were getting drastically worse but did not know a direction to take. When I last asked him what we were going to do about the fact that Charlie was more cyanotic and short of breath, he merely shook his head and said, "If he gets any more blue we'll have to do something."

I was not sure what was on his mind. Did he mean heart medication, surgery, or what? So I said, "What will we have to do?" He answered, "Oh, I don't know. But, we'll have to do something."

Well, wasn't this reassuring? I sometimes wondered why we were even seeing a doctor. I surmised that the regular visits would at least give them some basis for understanding Charlie's illness if nothing else.

In discussing the pros and cons of moving to another city, we decided that we needed to take the risk. We would never know if it could work out unless we tried it. We agreed to move back if it looked like it would be in the best interest of Charlie.

During this same time frame, I received a phone call from The Commission for Handicapped Children. I was told that there was now an opening for him to see their orthopedic doctor at the clinic for his clubfeet. Although I was comfortable with the doctor that I'd been seeing, I accepted their offer. My only reason for this was that the doctor bills had become quite overwhelming, but I was sad about the need to change doctors.

Before going to the clinic for the first time, I soaked off Charlie's casts just as I had always done. Upon arriving, I was firmly instructed not to ever do this again. I was told that his feet could lose the correction that had been made. I was assured that the cast saw would neither hurt him nor scare him as I had previously been told. I acquiesced by taking him in the next time with the casts on. As the doctor began to saw off the casts, Charlie began to cry. I held him close and comforted him. I spoke to him, reassuring him that all would be O.K. He, nevertheless, continued to cry as the saw went up one side of his calf and down the other. The doctor did not stop to remove the cast. Rather, he continued to cut the other cast in the same manner. It was heartbreaking to see Charlie so scared of the ordeal. Once finished, the doctor proceeded to remove the casts and unwrap the layer of cotton beneath them. Not until that moment did I realize that he had been cut up and down both legs with the saw.

As angry as I felt, I could not reveal this in front of Charlie or Jackie, who was also with me. I knew with the future we were facing, that it would not benefit Charlie to be afraid of doctors. I simply told the doctor that I would be taking his casts off at home in the future. He saw the obvious anger in my eyes over this and that was enough.

In August of 1975, we moved to Lexington, much to the heartache of the grandparents and other family members. As school was starting for Charles, a new course was being paved for me to doctor's offices.

As instructed, we met with a new pediatrician. The following day, we were sent to the University of Kentucky Medical Center to meet with the head of pediatric cardiology, Dr. Noonan. After the vital signs and weight were taken, I was directed into a room with Charlie and Jackie to wait for the doctor. In a short while, a Dr. Carol Cottrill came in to introduce herself. She told me that Dr. Noonan wouldn't be able to see us due to her busy schedule. Immediately, I thought to myself, I can't believe they've given me someone short of the very best in the business. I bet she has no idea how serious a situation we have here. I felt betrayed. I was certain that we didn't have much chance of ever making Charlie's life better without the number-one doctor guiding us. Once again, I could not indicate my fear or my mistrust of this doctor to either one of my children. It was very important to me that Charlie always felt that the doctor was someone to trust.

Dr. Cottrill instructed us to go get x-rays, lab work, lunch and EKG. After all tests were completed, we returned to the clinic room where we would wait to speak to her. It was approaching 3:00 P.M. By this time she had reviewed the chart and learned more about Charlie. She saw that The Commission for Handicapped Children had been tending to his clubfeet. She arranged for me to leave the heart clinic and go several miles away to the orthopedic clinic. After doing this, I was to return to the heart clinic to discuss all the findings.

It was about 6:00 P.M. before we were finished and back at the hospital's clinic. I was certain that she would not possibly be available to talk to me now with it being so late. I was wrong. She came in to discuss what she had found. Most everything she said was what I had been told. I listened carefully with a bit of hope. As I mentioned previously, I did not believe that this doctor would understand the seriousness of what we were facing. Once again, I was wrong. She shared with me that she was a

22

mother before she was a doctor. She told me of her own daughter who had heart disease and had died just eight years ago. I was moved with empathy for her. I knew then that she would be the perfect doctor for Charlie.

After discussing at length the details of Charlie's condition, I had many questions to address. I wanted to be told the truth about where we stood with life expectancy, and I needed to know just what this "something" might be that the Louisville doctor had mentioned. I needed to know exactly what we were facing. With that, Dr. Cottrill proceeded to explain the possibility of surgery. She explained that there was no surgery option to correct his heart. There was, however, an operation that could improve his circulation, which, if successful, might last about six years. At that point, a second surgery would be done that would probably last half as long as the first. Third and fourth operations may be required and would perhaps give him an additional year or two each. With the most widespread hope, she also made it very clear that it would be extremely dangerous to do the surgery. She wanted me to know that the odds of a successful surgery would be very slim. The very best odds of survival would be a 50% chance.

I was quite pleased to hear this. She assumed that I didn't understand what she was saying. She assumed that by looking at my youthfulness at twenty-one-years-old, that I did not understand the seriousness of Charlie's heart disease. What she didn't realize was that for the first time since he was born, I had a bit of hope. For me, it was a wonderful feeling. A slim hope was far greater than the idea of no hope whatsoever. She also didn't realize how grateful I was for each day and each moment that I had with my children.

It was after 7:00 P.M. before I left the clinic. I was anxious to get home to share this hope with Charles. He shared in my excitement and at the same time, my anxiety over the life-threatening surgery that we were to face. One statement that Dr. Cottrill had made clear was that we would definitely hold out as long as physically possible before attempting surgery. The risks were so great that we did not want to take them before absolutely necessary.

About two weeks later, Charlie began to run a low-grade fever of 100 degrees. He was laughing and playing, not bothered in the least. However, remembering the instructions of the doctor, I called the pediatrician to tell him. He said to take him to St. Joseph Hospital immediately and have him checked. In doing so, the emergency room doctor was quite concerned about Charlie's appearance. After hearing his medical history and seeing his cyanosis, he insisted that Charlie be admitted to the hospital for observation. When I inquired as to why, he couldn't tell me. He couldn't find a reason but wanted to watch him because he was blue. I let him know that he had been blue since birth and, I did not bring him in for that reason. He insisted anyway. He instructed my husband to go have him admitted. I stopped Charles. I asked about getting a room where I could stay with him. He said there was none. Charlie would be in a nursery setting. I asked him to call University Hospital to inquire if I could stay with him there. He became angered and told me there were no beds available there, either. I assured him that if I were to leave my son, he would cry so much that he would be black and blue by morning if he were still alive. (With cyanotic heart disease, crying used up all oxygen. I had made sure that no matter what, Charlie would never lie crying. I knew that it would only shorten his life.)

The doctor then became irate over my protection of my son. He hollered, "Well, you're JUST A MOTHER, and I believe these nurses know more than you do about it." By now, I was steaming. I requested of the nurse to see a "REAL" doctor. I specified a pediatrician.

She called down another doctor, who came in with a chuckle under his breath. He was aware of what had happened. He asked about Charlie's cyanosis. I gave him a complete rundown of the heart disease and assured him that this was his normal color. He saw that I was used to this cyanosis and was not alarmed by it. He saw that I was knowledgeable about the disease in spite of my immature appearance. Upon looking him over, he found that Charlie was developing an ear infection. He instructed me to see Charlie's regular doctor tomorrow if he continued to have a fever. He saw how happy and playful Charlie was and felt very comfortable about sending him home. After this episode, I knew to call the cardiologist first the next time. She was the only one who was not scared of Charlie.

Being new to Lexington, we did not yet know our neighbors. As a young married couple, there were occasional disputes to iron out. One particular day, our voices were raised in disagreement. Following this, Charles and I left our apartment with the children, unaware that the downstairs neighbor, Joanie, had been listening and also watching us as we left. She was stunned when she witnessed me carrying a baby with casts on both legs and splints on both hands and arms. She was convinced that child abusers had just moved in above her. She continued to be cautious of us for some time. Eventually, we became good friends and we were able to laugh when she told me of her first impression. How embarrassing.

Once settled, I decided it was time to look into Social Security Disability again for Charlie. I figured that because I had quit my Saturday job when we moved, that we should qualify. Much to my surprise, I was told that we should have been getting help all along. They had denied me the right to apply in Louisville. I was told that the amount I had been making could have been deducted from the disability check that he qualified for. By now, the medical bills totaled the thousands. There was no reimbursement for disability as we had not officially applied. The doctors were all very considerate by accepting the small payments that we sent monthly.

By now, the world around us was well into football season. As Charles had always dreamt of having a son to watch the games with, that's exactly what he did. Charlie, at six-months-old, was the youngest Notre Dame fan that I had ever known. He would sit on his daddy's lap not for one complete game on TV, but for two games whenever possible. He would follow along with whatever his dad would teach him. Charles talked to him as if he understood every play of the game. Before long, I would hear Charlie shout "Uh-Oh." I'd look in to check on him and find him pointing to the TV. I noticed that a Notre Dame player had just been tackled. This became the ritual every time a player was tackled. Although Charlie was too young to talk, he understood that it was an "Uh-oh" when someone fell down.

As the routine of daily life continued, my prayer life was gradually increasing. It had consisted of church on Sundays, night prayers with Jackie, and prayers before meals, in the past. I found that since Charlie had been born, I had more to talk about with God. I realized that throughout the day I was having brief conversations with God concerning whatever I was facing at the moment. I was not one for patented prayers because I did not get much comfort or understanding from them. I found it far more effective to simply speak to God about what was on my mind. I had learned this in high school and was now finding it most helpful. I say it was conversation as if it were two-way talk. The truth is, I didn't get answers from God immediately. On the other hand, I believed that I was being heard and I felt God's comfort in that. I continued to make the best of each day. This was not in fear of it being Charlie's last day. Rather, it was in gratitude for having that day with him. At the same time, I also greatly appreciated my precious daughter, Jackie. I became aware that life was not a guarantee for old age. I acknowledged the fact that today could be the last day for any of us. Therefore, no day was to be wasted.

In November, Charlie experienced his first hospital stay due to the croup. With prayers, God saw him through. Croup and cyanotic heart disease don't go well together. He could barely breathe and was therefore quite blue.

Of course, seldom do parents have one child sick at a time. This was no exception. Jackie was at home with another ear infection. Although her daddy was with her, I felt it was important for Mommy to be there, too.

Not being able to reach Charles by phone, I called a cab to take me home after I got Charlie to sleep. When I left the hospital around 11:30 P.M., I gave clear instructions to call me if he woke up. I planned to check on Jackie, then return to be with Charlie through the night. The nurse promised to call me if he should wake up.

With little pocket change, I got into the cab and directed him toward my apartment. I told him to take me as far as $3.00

would go and I would walk the rest of the way. I figured that it would be better than attempting to walk all the way.

I asked him to stop about halfway there. Instead, he turned off the meter and offered to drive me the rest of the way. Naturally, he inquired as to why I was at the hospital. He was moved with empathy after hearing about Charlie. I was deeply touched by his unusual thoughtfulness for a stranger. I never imagined that he might give me a free ride. I asked him to wait so that I might go inside to get more money to pay him, but he insisted on letting it go. I walked into the apartment thanking God for sending this generous man.

Charles was surprised to see me. He was still expecting me to call him for a ride. We discovered that the phone had been knocked off the hook, thus explaining why I couldn't reach him.

I was happy to return home for Jackie. I remembered too well the agonizing pain of ear infections as a child. I fell asleep next to her after making sure that the phone was working properly. I knew that the hospital would be calling very soon, as Charlie never slept for long periods of time.

I woke up around 6:00 A.M. stunned to see that the hospital hadn't called me during the night. I lost my faith in nurses that night. I was in total disbelief that morning had arrived. After my thoughts had settled, I decided to give them the benefit of the doubt. I thought that perhaps the medication that he had received had made it possible for him to sleep. I got dressed and rushed back to the hospital.

When I reached his room, I was stunned at the sight of swollen eyes, red face, and a weakened, hoarse cry unlike I had ever seen before on a child. I inquired as to how long he had been crying. I was told that the night nurse said that he started right after I left.

"Why didn't she call me?" I inquired in a rage.

The nurse responded that she had been told that I had another one sick at home and they felt sure that Charlie would fall back to sleep. I explained that I had made it clear that he never sleeps well and that I expected to be called. I was terribly disappointed. I knew that Charlie had felt abandoned. Yet, there wasn't a thing that I could do about it. The night was over. He had been in an oxygen tent and therefore survived in spite of all the crying.

It was times such as this that I could not feel like a good mother. Both children needed me. Both were in different places. I was greatly torn in knowing the right thing to do. I stayed every minute thereafter until he was allowed to go home a few days later.

By now, Charlie had gotten his casts removed and replaced with outflare shoes and a bar brace between his feet. This made him quite confined and miserable. It was difficult to crawl in this brace. With encouragement, he would pursue crawling in spite of it. As parents, we did not give in to obstacles. Rather, we took them as challenges to improve his self-image.

One Sunday, after attending Mass at the Newman Center, I was taken back in seeing Dr. Cottrill there. Being in a mostly non-Catholic city, she was equally stunned to see me. When our eyes met, a spark was ignited. There was a sense of instant comfort in knowing that our faith was the same.

Christmas was now approaching. The anticipation of Christ's birth was most exciting. Jackie was now two and one half-years-old and Charlie was nine-months-old. They were both easily entertained with Christmas stories. Often, as we waited to see doctors, I read about the stories of Jesus and of Santa Claus. When we went to church, only the stories of Jesus were allowed to go with us.

When Christmas Eve came, we got to church fairly early so that I would have an opportunity to show the children the nativity scene and explain what was happening. Once we returned to our seats, we waited for some time for Mass to start. Jackie sat on her daddy's lap and I held Charlie. I found myself thinking about Mary and what she had gone through in preparing for the birth of her son. I pictured the angel Gabriel appearing to her and telling her that she would be carrying a very special child. I imagined how she felt upon hearing this. I sensed a bit of fear, yet calmness in accepting God's Holy will. After all, she was not married. She had a great deal to handle.

I had a flashback of my first intuition that my baby would be other than normal. Although this message did not come to me from an angelic apparition, it was still somewhat similar to what Mary must have felt. The uncertainties that I had, she too must have had. She must have understood what I was going through. I looked down at Charlie in my arms. I felt so blessed to have this special child. I thought of Mary. If I felt this blessed over my baby, how much greater she must have felt over her child. My heart was overwhelmed at the thought. I found myself moved to tears over the greatness of her gift of the child Jesus. As Mass began, I continued to feel this bond with Mary. I thought about no room for them in the inn. I thought of no room for Charlie at the orthopedic clinic. I thought of Joseph being directed by God to move the family to Jerusalem. I thought of Charles being guided to Lexington with our family.

Before long, we had reached the consecration of the Mass. It was at that time that the whole picture came together. I pictured the terrible suffering of Jesus. I pictured the suffering of Charlie thus far. I saw the carrying of the cross. I saw Charlie's cross that was still to come. I heard the words, "This is my body." I saw the horrible crucifixion of Jesus yet to come. I was aware of the suffering and death of Charlie yet to come. Although my heart ached as I pictured the suffering that Charlie had already endured, my heart throbbed at the thought of Jesus's suffering and Mary's pain of watching it. I was moved to tears not only from my eyes but also, from the depth of my heart. The suffering yet to come overshadowed this joyous occasion of Christmas.

I was beginning to see God's hand in all that had taken place so far. I saw that it was God's plan that we move and that Dr. Noonan was not available. It was meant to be that Dr. Cottrill would care for Charlie. I felt comfort in that my prayers to God were all being heard.

After seeing the life of Jesus that Holy Night, I realized that there was no one that could understand better the things I was going through than Our Blessed Mother. All that I had been through as a mother, she too had been through as a mother. I saw her as the perfect mother. She was kind, patient, understanding, and loving. I wanted to be that kind of mother, too. From that day on I spoke to her on a regular basis. I was always asking her how she handled situations. I felt her guidance daily. She had become my true inspiration.

3 ABRAHAM'S SCRIMMAGE

The cold winter weather was very difficult for Charlie. By now, his color was bluer than ever. His oxygen level was mostly in the high 80s at rest. Sleeping was impossible. He could usually sleep for two hours at night before waking up unable to breathe. He needed to be upright. I would get him up and let him play on the living room floor for a while until he was no longer short of breath. Often, I would fall asleep on the floor as we played. It didn't last longer than five minutes I'm sure because when he realized my activity would stop, he would hit me on the head to wake up. My next attempt to sleep would be to hold him over my shoulder in the rocking chair. Although he would fall asleep, I knew he could not stay asleep if I put him down. Therefore, we both would sleep sitting up for a while. When I lay him down the second time, he usually slept for one hour. I was in total amazement that this child could keep going on no sleep. I could barely function myself. My two-year-old helper kept me going. We continued our daily ritual of playing records, singing nursery rhymes and Disney songs, cleaning house, and making doctor visits.

On a visit to the heart clinic in late January, surgery was briefly discussed. I was told that Charlie's condition had become significantly more serious. However, I was also told that the doctor did not want to do surgery until the very last minute due to the serious risks involved with his particular heart disease.

About a week later, I received a phone call from Dr. Cottrill. She said, "Mary Jo, it's time to do it." Stunned at hearing this out of what seemed to be nowhere, I responded, "What? Do you mean right away?"

"Yes," was her answer.

With that I said, "Tell me why all of a sudden. I thought we were going to wait until we couldn't wait any longer."

She responded, "I was praying to God last night about it and He told me now is the time."

31

Feeling an instant relief, I said, "Okay. If God said to do it, then let's do it." I had no reservations about it. I was so pleased to have a doctor who trusted in God. Because of this, there was no doubt in God's guidance and grace upon her.

On the evening before the surgery, the surgeon came in to explain what was to be done. His explanation was fairly brief. I had numerous questions running through my head once he left. I called for the nurse to bring him back. I felt that more needed to be explained. I knew the risks were high. A 50 % chance of survival is all that I really knew and to me, that wasn't enough. He apologized and went through a long list of complications that could arise, as I had requested of him. I explained that if I were aware of what could go wrong, I could be better prepared to deal with it. (One factor that I should mention is that I generally got little respect. This was due to being a twenty-two-year-old mother with the appearance of a sixteen-year-old.)

Picking up on the tension that was building in anticipation of the heart surgery, Dr. Cottrill came in to see me. She said to me, "Remember Abraham." I'm thinking, *what?* Not having truly reflected on the matter, I didn't make the connection immediately. Then she said, "You know God asked Abraham to bring Him his only son and to offer him up to God. Because Abraham so loved God, he brought Him his son. Then when the time came for the sacrifice, God did not take his son, because of his faith." These words were very moving. I realized that I too had brought my son merely because God asked me to. It was because of my faith and trust in God that I was able to submit my son to this life threatening operation.

On the morning of the surgery, Charles and I were in the waiting room. I felt so comfortable with God's plan, whatever it was to be, that I took a nap while waiting. I didn't feel nervous or afraid. I did, however, feel a bit anxious for it to be over.

After an eight-hour operation, the three doctors who were involved in Charlie's case entered the room grinning from ear to ear. Their faces were elated with joy. We were given the report that all had gone well. We were reminded of complications that could still arise but were given strong hope that he would live. I thanked God for the moment.

Three days later, things were looking good. Charlie was about to be transferred from the pediatric intensive care unit to the floor. I was allowed to pay him a brief visit in PICU, when I discovered some twitching in his right eye, then his face, and on down his right side. I called for the nurse. I was whisked out of the room and the surgeon and cardiologist were called in STAT. Waiting outside the door I soon realized that Charlie had had a seizure. A cut was made in his left wrist. This was for the purpose of starting an IV quickly. As mentioned before, Charlie had rolling veins, making it almost impossible to start an IV without several attempts. Needless to say, he did not come out of the unit that day after all.

More tests were performed. A neurologist was called in. There was no apparent reason for the seizure. However, it was discovered that there was a malformation on the brain, which was about a dime in size. It was felt that this was present since birth and there was no indication of any brain damage. He was put on seizure medication and transferred to the pediatric floor the following day.

That night I wanted to stay with him in his room. I was offered a chair to sit in or a pillow and blanket to be used under the crib if I wanted to sleep. Due to the fire marshal code, cots were not allowed. I gladly accepted the pillow and blanket. When Charlie fell asleep, I quickly followed. The next thing I knew, I heard nurses stirring in the hallway. On checking the time, I saw that it was early morning. This scared me to death. Charlie had always awakened after a couple hours of sleep. I knew in my heart as I crawled out from under the bed that I was about to find him dead. Much to my surprise, he was still sleeping soundly. Then I remembered that now that he had more oxygen to work with, he should be able to sleep. It took a while for my heart palpitations to slow down. When he did wake up, he was not in a lot of pain. He sat up in the bed playing cheerfully. We passed the mini football around, sang the U of K fight song, and pretended to tackle. Within two weeks he was home and doing well. From that point on, he slept all night every night. That was a tremendous blessing for all of us.

Oh how I loved having him home again. Our lives were changed instantly. We all started sleeping the entire night. Charlie could now eat three regular meals a day rather than every couple of hours. He did not get short of breath when he ate. This freed up a lot of my time. We began to enjoy life even more.

One day, as I held him close over my shoulder, I noticed that the extra vertebra in his spine was now beginning to bulge out quite a bit. Although I had been seeing some changes in it, I could never seem to remember to ask the doctor about it. We were so concerned about his heart each time we met that it kept getting overlooked. As I was taking him back in one week for his checkup from heart surgery, I figured I'd inquire about it then.

We were given an astounding report on the outcome of his surgery. He was fairly pink now and things looked promising. I mentioned to Dr. Cottrill that his back felt like it had a protruding knot where the extra vertebra was. She was so surprised. She too, had been concentrating so much on his heart that she didn't notice this in his records. The records that were sent from Louisville were extremely thick. Naturally, the heart was the biggest concern.

She immediately ordered x-rays of the spine and called in a neurologist, Dr. James. Upon seeing the x-rays, Dr. James came in looking like he'd seen a ghost. He showed me the x-rays. He sat down and began to explain what he saw. Pointing out that the spine was making a 90-degree angle outward at L1 and the vertebrae below it were twisted completely around backwards, he was dumbfounded. He went on to explain the surgery that needed to be done right away. He also stated that he knew of no doctor in the area that would have knowledge of this type of curve. He explained the fusion that was needed. A second surgery would be needed to install metal rods to keep his spine intact. His greatest concerns were finding a doctor who could do it and the justified fear that it would not stay in place even after surgery. He informed me that it was because Charlie had been sitting up for the past five months. The pressure on his spine had caused it to twist and turn. This could happen again when he sits up after having the surgery. Dr. James was also very concerned that, with Charlie's heart disease, the odds of survival would be

34

slim once again. Without surgery, he would inevitably be paralyzed.

What a blow this was one week after Charlie's return home from heart surgery. I began running through my typical long list of questions as I tried to absorb it all.

Dr. James said that he would be contacting doctors, trying to locate someone who's seen this type of curve. Meanwhile, I was to return home and discuss this with my husband. We were to decide whether to take the chance involved in surgery, assuming that a qualified doctor might be found.

I returned home waiting for Charles to get out of school so that I could share all the good and bad news. We also needed to discuss Charlie's first birthday the following week. What an emotional roller coaster.

As we laid our cards on the table, we examined the situation thoroughly. I recalled a girl for whom I had baby-sat for seven years. Charles also knew her. She had cerebral palsy and was crippled. I told Charles that it was painful for me to watch Couzanne have to crawl through the house and struggle to lift herself into a chair. We both felt that the quality of life was very important. We agreed that if Charlie would die from the surgery that it wouldn't hurt him to go to heaven as a baby, although it would devastate us. We felt it would be selfish of us not to at least try to make his life as normal as possible. To stay on the safe side and not take the risk would only hurt him. We couldn't bear to watch him become paralyzed. We decided immediately to give him a chance.

By now, Charlie no longer needed to wear his hand splints. His hands were normal in appearance. His fine motor skills still needed improvement. The hand surgeon could now say that there was no indication of cerebral palsy as he had once suspected might occur. We were grateful for this reassurance.

His first birthday was not one to be remembered as I had hoped it would be. We were so happy that he had lived a full year, yet we were aware that it may be his last. I noticed that not everyone in the family understood the threat of death as I did.

Ten days later, Dr. James called to give me an update on his finding a doctor. He said he had called numerous places across the United States, Germany and other countries without any luck. He told me of an orthopedic hospital in Toronto, Canada, that he still had hopes of being a possibility. The doctor whom he was trying to reach would be out of town for another few days. He encouraged us not to give up.

Once reaching the doctor, he called me back immediately. He was told that it sounded like a curve that they had seen in their hospital only once before. Dr. James was to send the x-ray for confirmation.

Another few days passed while they waited for the x-rays. It turned out that they had seen this curve once. The particular doctor who had done the surgery was no longer working there. Amazingly, he was in Louisville, Kentucky. God was really pulling strings for us this time. We were all in disbelief.

Right away, arrangements were made for us to meet with Dr. Leatherman. We drove in several times to see him as he studied the case. He explained what this surgery would entail. He said that he would have to make an incision across Charlie's left side below the ribs from front to back. He would need to enter from the front in order to reach the spine at the right angle and be able to do the fusion. This meant that he would have to remove all abdominal organs while doing the surgery. The procedure would leave Charlie extremely sore for an extended amount of time. Ordinarily, he would be put in a body cast. However, because of his heart disease, he could not have his chest confined. Doctors would have to have access to his heart in case of an emergency. Therefore, instead of the cast, he would be fitted for a back brace that would be worn constantly. It would have straps across his chest. After one month of recovering, a second surgery would be performed from the back, placing Herrington rods on each side of the spine and securing the spine with screws. He would have to wear a brace for a long time, perhaps a year. We discussed all the potential risks involved. I posed many questions.

He talked of doing the surgery one time, then backed out the next time. We returned to Lexington for a myelogram to determine the pathology of the spine. After three spinal taps without finding any central spinal fluid whatsoever, Dr. James did not proceed with the dye. This indicated a total block of the canal to the flow of central spinal fluid. By all reasoning, he should have been paralyzed from the waist down.

As with all hospital procedures, Charlie always had some type of complication causing him more pain. On this occasion, his left thigh swelled up and became hardened from the pre-medication. Treatments to relieve this pain lasted three weeks and he was unable to crawl during that time due to the pain.

There was continual contact between the doctors debating over the surgery. Finally, as we were becoming more fearful of paralysis, Dr. Leatherman decided that he simply could not do the surgery. He looked at me and said, "This surgery is extremely dangerous on a healthy person. It is usually done on teenagers after their growth spurt. I've never done this type of surgery on one so small. When I go into surgery I have to have the cards in my favor. The risks are entirely too high and I don't want to lose him." I appreciated his honesty. Nonetheless, I did not feel right about not trying. By now, Charlie was beginning to show signs of paralyzed nerves to the bowel. I came back and reported to Dr. Cottrill what I had been told.

The orthopedic doctor who was treating Charlie's clubfeet at the clinic, had been inquiring about the findings of Charlie's spinal problem. When he asked, I informed him of the situation, including that Dr. Leatherman was unwilling to do the surgery. He became almost hysterically angry at those of us in favor of the operation. He said that none of us understood what a difficult surgery it was and the intense pain that the patient would have to endure. He added that there would be more signs of paralysis such as kidney problems, before Charlie would become completely paralyzed and therefore he suggested that we wait.

I assured him that none of us was taking this lightly. I told him of Dr. Cottrill's feelings on the matter. He said that these pediatricians think that surgery is a piece of cake. I tried to explain to him that neither Dr. Cottrill, Charles nor I thought that. (I was often misjudged due to my calm mannerisms.) I attempted to state our feelings about the quality of life versus the quantity of life. He refused to listen. He saw me as an immature mother who didn't understand.

Abandoning all hope, I found myself speaking very frequently to Our Blessed Mother. The questions I asked of her were most often the same, with only slight variations. I spoke to her about the pain of watching our children suffer. I spoke about the helplessness of protecting our children as the world around us took control of their lives. It seemed as though the life of my son was in the hands of the doctors. I connected this feeling with the way that Mary must have perceived her son's conviction. His life appeared to be in the hands of Pontius Pilate. It was in talking to Mary that things became clearer to me. I felt her reminder that neither Pilate nor the doctors have control over our children. I was encouraged to believe in God's will. "This is so hard," I cried. Putting myself in her shoes, I felt great empathy for her. How I prayed that I could be like her. I prayed to have the strength to endure the pain of my loss to come. I felt her motherly protection with me always.

After prayerful consideration, I felt right in the decision we had originally made. I could not give in to the quantity of life over the quality of life, no matter how tempting it was. I did not believe this to be God's will.

I was being drawn to Dr. Cottrill like a magnet. Although I didn't recognize the Holy Spirit working at the time, I was aware of her great love for God. I trusted that she would guide me to do what was best for Charlie.

I called her and discussed the possibility of going to Toronto to have the surgery done. Dr. James, Dr. Cottrill, Charles and I agreed on this. Each of us felt strongly that this was the right thing to do. Each was fully aware of what we were facing. Charles planned to quit school and his job in order to stay with us in Toronto. We weren't sure how we were going to do this but, because we felt right about it, we were certain that God would direct us.

As Dr. James pursued the doctor in Canada, Dr. Cottrill decided to make one final appeal to Dr. Leatherman. Guided by the Holy Spirit, she phoned him. She poured out her concerns about a young mother having to carry a child for years that could have been walking. She spoke of a young father trying to finish school, having to quit and move his family to Canada in order for this child to have a chance. She assured him that Charlie's heart was in the best shape that it would ever be in as he had just recovered from surgery. She let him know that we were all fully aware of the risks of the surgery.

Dr. Leatherman's concerns were that, even if the operation were successful, Charlie might die within a couple of years. He wasn't convinced that the pain he would have to endure would be worth it if he lived to be only five or six-years-old. Dr. Cottrill rebutted with, "Even if he could walk for only one year it would be a good year and would be worth it." With this outpouring of concern from Dr. Cottrill, Dr. Leatherman replied, "What is this, my conscience calling me?" With that, he agreed to do the surgery.

We were not solely focused on medical problems. We continued our normal fun activities. Being a student at U of K, Charles was able to get football tickets for every game. We went and took the children with us. This family activity was the highlight of our week. The bond between Charlie and his dad was growing stronger daily. They both were so excited over the games. Jackie was more interested in the cheerleaders. We always had a great time.

Charlie also enjoyed playing football with his dad. He could throw the best tight-spiral pass across the living room. Fortunately, nothing was broken. When he wasn't playing football, he was watching it. Notre Dame was his favorite team. He quickly learned their fight song and sang it all the time.

We continued to make the best of each day. Charles and I were careful not to worry the children about the life-threatening decisions we faced. We discussed them privately.

Meanwhile, I had been visiting my friend Kathy when I would drive into Louisville periodically. Kathy was a girl I graduated with in high school. The funny thing about it was that we didn't really know each other in school. We never had a class together. We merely spoke in passing because we recognized each other. Shortly after graduation in the fall of 1971, she had been in a terrible automobile accident that nearly took her life. A mutual friend, Arleen, had informed me of the accident when it happened. She invited me to go with her and some others to visit

Kathy once she got home from the hospital. Arleen recognized how lonely Kathy must have been feeling. She told me how Kathy had lost much of her memory. Our plan was to visit in hopes of helping her to regain her memory. I went along and shared some of the general things that our class had done as a whole. We had a lot of laughs, but it never triggered a memory for Kathy. She enjoyed so much hearing our stories that we began to visit regularly. She learned all about the teachers and the various things that we had done. It was a wonderful experience.

As time passed, Arleen went away to school and the other girls pursued their busy lives but Kathy and I were creating a bond that would last a lifetime. She absolutely loved children and dreamed of having her own some day. The reality was, however, that this would be highly unlikely due to the severity of the damage to her pelvic area as well as the overall toll that the accident had taken on her entire health. Kathy found joy in my children. I saw that she was truly happy for me.

Before long, Kathy had her own apartment. I always kept her updated on the latest situation with Charlie. I would stop in for a visit when in town for a doctor's appointment. After getting the children settled in bed at a relative's house, I'd leave them with Charles. Then, Kathy and I would get together for some good old-fashion girl-talk. She was always up late at night decorating cakes. (This was just one of her many talents that she pursued while she attended nursing school.)

I enjoyed watching her decorate as I learned tips of the trade. She enjoyed hearing more funny high school stories and trying to place herself there. We often laughed so hard that our sides would ache.

We both found it very odd that she could remember the studies but could not truly remember her friends. We would go through the yearbook and I would point out to her the friends that she used to hang around with. We would joke about being friends. She said that she would have to believe anything that I told her because she didn't know any better. So, we laughed and I told her of all the things that we used to do together (although we didn't).

40

On a more serious note, when I shared with Kathy the anticipated spinal surgery, she began to share more about the surgery that she had been through after her accident.

It was after midnight, but we were both engaged in conversation. We sat back on the couch and continued to share. There was some mention of dreams or feelings that something bad would happen. I shared some of my intuition from my pregnancy with Charlie. She offered to share with me a story that would make most people turn away. She had been reluctant until now because she didn't want to take a chance on my thinking that she was crazy. She didn't want to risk the friendship that we had found. I assured her that I was crazy, too. If she could tolerate me, I would be glad to tolerate her. We could just be crazy together. The truth is that we had begun to share some spiritual thoughts. We were both hesitant about being so open. We presumed that most twenty-two-year-olds didn't talk about these things. However, the spiritual force between us made us very comfortable and trusting of each other. I encouraged her to go on with her story.

She proceeded to tell me about one thing that she remembered vividly from high school. She recalled talking about dreams during a psychology class. She told her teacher that she had a dream about being killed in a car accident after high school. She said that in this dream, she was driving an orange car. She couldn't recall exactly what the teacher's comments were. Eventually, she disregarded it.

My first reaction was, "Why in the world did you buy an orange Volkswagen?"

She responded, "Because it was the best offer on the lot." Besides, she wasn't thinking about her dream when she bought the car. She was so excited about buying her first car that nothing else entered her mind.

"Wow!" I exclaimed. "Thank God you weren't killed."

With that, she made me promise not to think strangely of her. She proceeded to say that she had experienced death and that she was brought back to life. I had never heard of anything like it. I said, "What do you mean?"

41

She said that she knew she had died and she watched the doctors bring her back to life.

For some reason, I didn't feel the slightest doubt about what she was saying. I was in awe that it had happened. I was dumbfounded. In my silence, she asked, "Do you think I'm crazy? I don't blame you if you do."

I said, "Not at all." I pleaded with her to tell me all about it. I wanted to hear all the details. I had a lot of questions.

Seeing my excitement and openness, she proceeded to tell me the story. Recalling the accident, she said that she had pulled out of the University campus and onto the busy street. A car hit her from the driver's side, crushing her severely. She was taken into surgery right away due to hemorrhaging. While in surgery, she became aware of feeling her spirit being pulled from within her body. It was as though there was an interior ghostly body that left her through her head. This new body was drawn upward toward the ceiling of the room. From there, she witnessed the doctors working on her physical body, trying desperately to bring her back. It took a moment for her to realize that it was herself that she was watching.

I was appalled. "What was it like?" I was anxious to know. She proceeded to tell me that she passed through a long, black tunnel after spending some time over her hospital bed. There was a bright light at the end of the tunnel. She wasn't afraid. She informed me that there were not words in the English language that could come near to explaining the beauty, the peace, or the tranquility of the experience. The peace was unlike any one could imagine. The sense of pure love was indescribable. There was no love like it on earth. She took me step by step on this journey with her. She told me how God had shown her entire life in a flash. It was as if it were in fast motion, yet every aspect of her life was covered. She was shown every act of goodness and of wrongdoing. She said that she could never have remembered all these things on her own. She knew, without a doubt, that it was God showing these events to her. She shared a time when she was very young and a bit of a daredevil. She loved to walk across the top of the swing set. This scared her mother to death and she was told not to do it again. Yet, she did it anyway. She was shown how her disobedience hurt her mother. Yet, God was all understanding. She felt God's love and forgiveness. She understood that these things were for learning and growing.

She told of a beautiful place filled with the most gorgeous flowers of the most unique colors. She convinced me that even the most vivid imagination couldn't compare this reality that she had experienced. She added that she had no desire to come back whatsoever.

This comment inspired many questions for me. I brought her back to the operating room where they were trying to revive her. I said, "What about your parents? Didn't you want to be with them? Could you see them?"

"Yes, I could see them in the waiting room. The walls became transparent and I could see doctors and nurses walking down the halls. Yet, I still had no desire to come back."

"What about the separation? Didn't it make you feel bad seeing them hurt over you? It seems like it would hurt you tremendously to see them grieve. How could you be O.K. with dying? You were only seventeen. What about your future? What about all the things in life that you would have missed?"

Nothing mattered. It was strange. Somehow God created a separation of emotions for the people she loved. She could see them cry. She could see their hurt, yet she was not allowed to feel any pain for them. She was at peace and no outside force could have any influence on her.

I questioned her again on this. She assured me that it was not possible to feel anything sad. She couldn't explain it. She only knew that it didn't matter. Time didn't matter. Age didn't matter.

With this, she proceeded to tell how the force of the spirit pulled her back into her body. She was taken back the same way that she left. The spirit returned, feet first, into her head and down to her feet. It was made clear that her job on earth was not completed. She understood that this was a sampling of the kingdom of God in heaven.

Although she shared how anxiously she looked forward to heaven, she also stated that she had no desire to die. Kathy said that she no longer felt any fear of death for herself or for anyone else.

43

I asked her about what her mother said when she told her about the experience. She said that she couldn't tell her at first. She was afraid to mention it. She figured anyone would think that she was hallucinating, including her mother. However, after being home for a short while, she found that she couldn't hold back any longer. She asked her mother if she had died during surgery. Her mom told her no, but the doctor had mentioned that "Things had gone bad." She admitted not fully understanding the meaning of this statement. With this thought, they inquired on the next visit as to its meaning. He said, "We did lose her for a while." Kathy was so relieved to know that all of this was not her imagination. She couldn't convince herself that it was anything less than real.

With this story, she let me know that we were doing the right thing for Charlie. She said that if he died, she would only grieve for us. She could not feel less than happy for Charlie because she knew the beautiful place he would be in.

It was after 3:00 A.M. before our conversation ended. With many yawns between us, we decided it best to call it a night. With a friendly hug and farewell, I was out the door. Kathy wished me well with Charlie's operation. She said that she hoped that she could eliminate any fear that might exist toward Charlie's risk of death. I promised her that her sharing had given me only hope. I knew that I could face his struggles more confidently with this vision of heaven that she had portrayed. I pondered what heaven must be like as I drove back to the family.

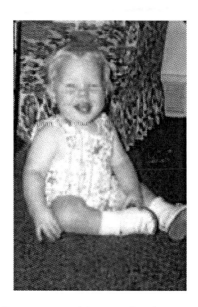

Charlie, one year old - just after heart surgery

4

THE PIERCING SWORD

Surgery was scheduled for the end of October. Because I would be at the hospital with Charlie, I was concerned about missing Halloween with the children. It was an important issue to me.

I planned a Halloween party for the week before surgery. I had run into Dr. Cottrill and two of her children at Kmart when I thought to myself that it would be nice to have her at the party. Being fairly new to the area herself, I thought that it would be fun for her children to do something like this. I wasn't sure how to go about asking her. It was an ethical issue to think about. I knew that I should not even consider asking her. But, something inside of me kept pushing me to do it anyway. I prepared an invitation and wrote a short note explaining that I understood if she felt she couldn't come. It was with ambivalent feelings that I finally put it in the mail. I felt a little awkward at the next doctor's appointment because of the issue, then she brought it up. I told her that I certainly didn't want her to feel uncomfortable about it and that I understood if she decided not to come. She said that she had to go to Cincinnati that day and would barely make it back in time for the party. I took that as a no. Then she added that she would be a little late.

The party began and she didn't come. We waited for a while then continued with the games, not expecting her to show. I felt a little embarrassed that I even had the nerve to invite her. Much to my surprise, there was a knock at the door and there she stood with her two children, both in their Halloween costumes. I felt honored that she had gone to so much trouble to come to my home. By now there was a bond growing between us that could not be explained.

The next day, I began to prepare for the trip to Louisville. Knowing that I would be there a good month or so, depending on the outcome of the surgery, I packed everything from clothes, to toys, to magazines, to needlepoint.

47

Next, I attempted to prepare Jackie for what was to come. She could visit us but couldn't stay. She asked many questions about her brother's surgery. I told her calmly that the doctor was going to fix Charlie's back in order for him to walk. I could only assure her that all would be O.K. I felt it was important not to dwell on what might go wrong. I knew that if things didn't go well, I could deal with it then. As Jackie felt impelled to protect her little brother, she came up to him and offered her consolation. She said to him, "Don't worry, Charlie. The doctor is just going to cut your back with a knife and fix it." At three-years-old, she had no idea what she was saying. Charlie looked at me, puzzled. He knew that a knife was something that we used at the dinner table. He had a very worried look on his face. I assured him that the doctor would use a special tool, not a knife. He would give him some medicine so that he couldn't feel it. It was not the easiest thing to explain to a nineteen-month-old.

Facing this next surgery was far more emotional than the first. The possible outcome covered so much more this time. Life, death, paralysis, severe prolonged pain, back brace, lengthy stay, second phase surgery, possible return of curvature, and who knows what else, were all possibilities. As I began to pray, I told God that I did not know what was best for Charlie. I could not pray that he would live. I could not say if that were truly better for him. I recall saying, "Only You know what is best for him. Whether life or death, I only ask that Thy will be done. Please help me accept Your will, whatever it may be." I placed my son into His hands and trusted in His will. I leaned on Mary for strength and understanding throughout it all. I knew she had faced a similar trial.

Dr. Cottrill and Dr. James both drove into Louisville for the surgery. It was such a consolation to us. When it was completed some eight hours later, Dr. Leatherman came to speak to us. His first statement was, "That was the most tangled-up mess that I have ever seen. I don't know how he was even kicking his feet, much less crawling." He was absolutely amazed at what he had discovered. He added, "I've never seen anything like it. He's stable now but we are not out of the woods yet. The next 24 hours are crucial. We won't know if it was successful or not until he wakes up and is able to move."

I felt a measure of relief. I continued to pray.

The next morning, we were told that Charlie had had seizures during the night. He was still mostly sleeping from the drugs. The extent of damage caused by the seizures was not certain. He would remain in intensive care for a few more days. We were allowed to visit for 10-20 minutes about three or four times a day. He was completely immobile due to the severe abdominal pain he was experiencing. It was determined, however, that he did have feeling in his feet when they were slightly tickled.

Meanwhile, as he was recovering, I stayed with relatives in town. I had been having serious wisdom tooth pain and was forced to see the dentist between hospital visits. The timing couldn't have been better. I had my wisdom teeth pulled while Charlie was in intensive care. This way I could be well enough to care for him when he would be moved into a room on the floor. This turned out to be to my advantage. There was never a time, other than this, that Charlie didn't need me constantly by his side. I was sure that God had allowed this timing of events to make life easier in the long run.

Three days later, Charlie was given a private room where I could stay with him. His only movement was to be logrolled from side to side. Whenever I would speak to him, he began to cry. It was heartbreaking. I tried to get him to say Mommy or Daddy. He would only cry. No matter what I said to him, he cried. At first, I thought that he was crying from pain and would not speak my name because of what I had allowed him to go through. However, after numerous attempts, I told the nurse and Dr. Leatherman that something more must be wrong. Charlie was at the stage in his development that he would repeat anything I asked him to repeat. He had been talking in short phrases. His favorite toy was a football. He would not say football.

I asked Charles to bring in a poster of Mickey Mouse, Charlie's favorite character. He used to call him "Mac Me Me." I felt sure that this poster would break the ice but it didn't.

A test was ordered to determine if he had had some brain damage from the seizures. The CAT scan verified that he had had a stroke. Once again, a neurologist was called in. We were told that his speech control was completely damaged because of the speech center being so close to the affected area of his brain. His right side was partially paralyzed. This was not quickly determined from sight due to the fact that he could not move anyway. We saw that his right hand was now drawn in the way that it was at birth. All of this was devastating to us. I requested that the hand surgeon be notified. He came and ordered a new brace for Charlie's right hand.

I thought that I had prepared for all possible complications. This one had not been mentioned. I was sick with grief over the loss of his speech. I longed to hear him say, "Mommy." I was inconsolable. Every opportunity I had by myself, I cried. I felt a sword piercing my heart and I knew that this was only the beginning. "Oh Mary, help me," I pleaded. "You know how it hurts to see him suffer. You know of his innocence." I watched the pain in his face as he grimaced with movement. His eyes watered as he stared at me, speechless.

As we were dealing with all this, the stroke, the paralysis, the hand and the speech, there was still another major complication to face. His left arm was stretched out perpendicular to his body with his fingers clinched tightly. His arm and hand were ice cold. Under his left arm, there was a huge open sore that covered his entire underarm. This came about because he had been tied down too tightly during surgery. His arm had gone without circulation for the entire eight hours. I could not comprehend why his circulation had not been monitored. There was no justifiable answer to this. A physical therapist had been ordered to come exercise his arm.

We found that whenever someone would touch his hand or arm, he would moan in pain. Upon attempting to exercise his arm, Charlie would scream from excruciating pain. I was forced to ask the therapist to stop. I offered to do the exercise with him more gradually throughout the day instead. This was accepted. However, Dr. Leatherman did not push it when he witnessed what pain Charlie was in.

By now, Henry, from the brace shop, came in to fit Charlie for a back brace. He informed me that it was the smallest brace he had ever made. I was taught how to apply the brace and the proper way to logroll Charlie. Dr. Leatherman was critically concerned about the possibility of damage to the spinal work that had just been completed.

Upon glancing at Charlie, one could see that his right arm and leg were almost completely paralyzed. His left arm was stuck outward with immobility, and his left leg was the only moving part about him. He began to move his leg with an occasional kick. This was a great worry to Dr. Leatherman. He feared that, with movement, the spinal fusion would not stay intact. Therefore, he ordered an additional leg piece to the back brace to prevent movement. As difficult as this was, we did not want to risk losing the correction from the fusion.

In trying to keep Charlie in good spirits, I began to play football with him in the bed. I would toss up the football, catch it, and pretend to fall on him saying, "Tackle." This always produced a smile. We would play for as long as either of us could hold out.

During his stay, I read to him, exercised the three damaged limbs, and constantly combed his matted blond hair. He rubbed tangles into his hair as he turned side to side all day.

I tried various ways to entertain him. Because he was always lying flat, I was limited in what we could do. I once took advantage of a relative staying with him and I went out shopping. I came back with a clown on a unicycle. I strung up a wire across his room and arranged it so that Charlie could pull a string to make the clown go. This was therapy for his hand as well as his spirit. Before long, the room was also decorated with Kentucky Wildcats and Mickey Mouse. I bought toys that would serve as therapy. I always teased with Charlie to make him laugh, being a firm believer that laughter was the best medicine. His dad would come in doing slapstick comedy. Pretending to bump his head into the wall would create the biggest laughs. On occasion, we had to be careful because too much laughter would cause him more pain.

When Charlie would sleep, I kept occupied. I enjoyed creating a needlepoint picture of a little boy, dressed as a cowboy, riding a stick horse. The inscription next to the boy read, "Please be patient...God isn't finished with me yet." I felt inspired while doing it. This quiet time for me was a good time to talk to God and Mary. I found strength to go on. We had a long road ahead of us.

One thing that upset Charlie was the television. I would turn on "Captain Kangaroo" or cartoons in the morning. He would cry because he wanted to watch football. There were no games on that early. He often settled for watching the sports segment of the news.

On Sundays, I would leave to go to church. Charles would stay with him and we would take turns at attending Mass. I never left Charlie by himself. Charles would often bring Jackie in for a visit as well. I missed not being with her more. I knew however, that she was in good hands with her daddy. Their drive from Lexington was about one and a half hours long. Charles had to fit in visits around school and his job. He was there at every opportunity.

The staff had really taken a liking to Charlie. They enjoyed spoiling the only baby patient on the unit. One nurse bought him a huge Tonka tow truck with numerous fancy parts, including a driver named Charlie. Others were playing football with him. They all loved him and it showed.

With all the complications that we now had to deal with, in particular the stroke, Dr. Leatherman said he could not possibly proceed with the second phase of the operation. It was felt that the stroke probably occurred when the blood loss from surgery was replaced. Charlie's blood was very thick because of his heart disease. Most likely, a clot was formed and traveled to his brain to the same area that had been affected before. Once again, the doctors became more frightened of Charlie. We were pleased that he was alive in spite of it all. We, too, weren't feeling too eager to subject him to another risky surgery. We all agreed to buy some time and try to repair some of the damage that had been done.

After a three-week stay, we returned home to Lexington with our list of instructions. Charlie was to remain flat at all times. He could be rolled side to side. He was to wear the back brace twenty-four hours a day. He could only be moved in a horizontal position. He was to have his back securely supported by both arms beneath him, as he needed to be moved from a crib to a wagon. He could be taken from room to room or elsewhere, by use of the wagon. We were told not to carry him any more than absolutely necessary. Any wrong move would possibly cause a fracture of his spine, as there were no rods to secure it.

Once home, an anxious older sister was ready to entertain Charlie. She understood that he was in pain. It was written all over his face. I placed him on the couch. Jackie pulled out her play guitar and sang Mouseketeer songs (with her Mickey Mouse ears in place). A half-crooked smile appeared on his face. He was happy to be home but obviously miserable. Jackie learned to play lying down on the floor next to him. She was a tremendous help.

I did not want his confinement to cause him to miss out on the joys of life. His first trips out were to church on Sunday. We would place him carefully in a padded wagon. We then lifted and rolled the wagon into the back of our station wagon and drove on to church. We carried him carefully into church and laid him in the pew. He seemed to enjoy being with us in our old routine.

It being the Christmas season, we wheeled him through the malls so that he might enjoy the decorations and Christmas festivities. We pulled his wagon near Santa Claus, enabling him to watch his sister sit on Santa's lap. Santa was moved to come down from his stage area and pay Charlie a visit. People everywhere were commenting on what a great idea it was to pull him around in a wagon. Many spoke of how easy life was for this king being pulled in a well-padded wagon. How little they knew. People thought it was a novelty. They couldn't see the brace he wore under his clothes. They had no idea. We simply smiled, acknowledged their observation and went on.

A new daily routine was being established. This consisted of giving Charlie a sponge bath on the counter and diapering under a brace. It meant exercising the stroke-affected right side and making up therapy for his nerve-damaged left arm. It included dressing changes to the open wound under his arm, applying a right hand splint, and wriggling on his outflare shoes. (I had removed the bar to give him some relief.) Constant speech therapy was tried with every waking moment.

Along with this daily therapy, there were still six doctors to see regularly. Dr. Cottrill offered to be pediatrician, as well as cardiologist, to my children. This would eliminate one visit to the pediatrician. I had asked Dr. Leatherman to monitor Charlie's clubfeet so that I could eliminate one of the orthopedic doctors. This was a significant help to me when he agreed. The hand surgeon and neurosurgeon were still needed.

In attempting to correct the damaged left arm, I began to slowly bend his elbow about five degrees. Then I took a long cloth diaper and wrapped it around his arm in a sling-like fashion. I would keep it in that position for about two hours before releasing it. This was done four or five times a day, as time would permit. The neurosurgeon was fearful of major nerve damage and that Charlie might lose his arm. He was monitored weekly for progress. Eventually, the doctor felt safe to say that the major nerve had not been damaged and Charlie would not lose his arm after all.

I continued talking to Charlie all day long in hopes that his speech would return. Months passed without a word from him. It was clear that he understood everything that I said because his response was always appropriate. This was one of the saddest times for me. I wanted so badly to hear his voice again.

After two months, Charlie was able to completely bend his elbow. He was beginning to get some feeling in his fingers although they were still clinched. He started to bite down on them in order to experience the tingly sensation he now felt. During this time his right arm and leg were improving in mobility. I began to make a pallet on the floor for him to play on daily. I would occasionally find him scooting off of it. He managed to pick up a germ of an unknown source. As he bit down on his fingers, this germ was passed on from floor, to mouth, to face, to finger. He broke out in a very strange rash that covered his face like leprosy. This spread onto his fingers and began to spread down his hand. With this latest setback, we were now visiting the doctor on a daily basis to determine if it could be stopped or if he was going to have to have his finger amputated. He was treated for every possible infection and parasite. Eventually, many weeks later, one of the medications worked and the infection stopped. Although several doctors were asked about this rash and its treatment, it was never determined exactly what it was. The threat of losing his finger had now come to an end.

Before long, homemaking was back to what I considered normal life. I was able to make Easter clothes for the kids, as well as bake and clean the way that I used to do.

Dr. Leatherman was pleased with Charlie's progress. X-rays continued to look good. With much pleading, I convinced him to allow me to remove Charlie's brace and give him a real bath in the tub. I promised to take every precaution. I would carefully lay him flat in a tub of shallow water. This was also therapeutic and I thanked God for it.

5 PERSEVERANCE BEHIND THE LINE OF SCRIMMAGE

Spring came six months after surgery. By now, Charlie was becoming tired of having to stay flat all day and all night. He was indicating his desire to crawl. He kept scooting and making attempts to pull himself to his knees. I would have to stop him and tell him that Dr. Leatherman said he couldn't do that. I would be able to reason with him by explaining that his back might break and he'd have to go back to the hospital to fix it. Although he greatly loved his doctors and nurses, the thought of needles was enough to scare him into obedience. He didn't pout or whine. He simply did what he was told. I generally would try to come up with entertaining ideas that he could enjoy in spite of his limitations. I'd get him interested in making cookies or dessert. I lined up ingredients on a covered floor, then allowed him to stir the batter as this was great therapy for his hands.

When Daddy came home, we arranged for horsy rides. Of course, Charlie still had to remain flat. This was manageable with him lying down. He would be a baby only once and we felt that these rides were a necessary part of childhood.

All of us would play football for his entertainment. We played with a lot of noisy spirit, yet tackling had to be done in a soft manner. We pretended to be rough with our actions. He thoroughly enjoyed it. Although Jackie preferred playing with baby dolls, she too would go along with the football game for Charlie's benefit.

Our doctor visits, by now, had stretched to one-month intervals. I promised Charlie that we would ask Dr. Leatherman about allowing him to crawl. However, Dr. Leatherman couldn't bring himself to say yes. He was so afraid of losing the fusion that had been done. He told us that he would possibly allow it next month. To Charlie, another month seemed like forever. Again, he cooperated fully.

With constant daily therapy, he was beginning to move his arms and legs fairly well. The speech was still not there, however. It had already been determined that as the speech had not returned yet, he would have to relearn how to speak by using a different section of his brain. Supposedly, this was considered an achievable task because he was so young when the damage occurred. Because his brain had not been filled with knowledge, as an adult's would be, he could use a portion of his brain that was not intended for speech. I had hope and patience. I worked constantly with him on speech every waking moment of the day. Eight months later, at two-years-old, he was trying very hard to move his lips and follow what I said. Still, no sound came from his mouth.

The one-month wait to crawl turned into three months. Dr. Leatherman was so pleased with the good job I had done in keeping Charlie lying down that he kept delaying his permission. Finally, I pleaded with him, reminding him of his promise to Charlie. I told him how difficult it was becoming to keep him down. The only reason it was working now was because I told Charlie that he would get to crawl for sure after the next doctor visit. It was only out of empathy that Dr. Leatherman agreed, nine months after surgery. Still, he was afraid. He didn't want to say yes. He instructed me that he could crawl and kneel up only. We could also hold him upright for the first time since surgery. Under no circumstances was he to sit down. This was a joyous occasion for us. Once home, Charles and I gradually moved him from his horizontal position to an upright one. We each held him. It was so precious to us to feel that little body snuggled close to our chests. How we had missed those good hugs. Although the back brace was a barrier, it mattered little in comparison to what we felt. That baby embrace was a lasting treasure that I thanked God for. I was grateful for all the progress that Charlie had made.

Next, as Charlie played on the pallet on the floor, he began to scoot, stopping himself. By now, he expected me to stop him. Looking up to me, he was not at all sure what to think when I said to him, "Go on." He looked puzzled, knowing he didn't hear that. Again, I said, "Go on. Dr. Leatherman said that it's

O.K. now. You can crawl." He was so excited. He wasn't sure which way to go. He seemed uncertain if his legs would work. Gradually, he moved about the living room. The freedom he felt must have been overwhelming.

One evening, the family had gone out driving in the car. Charlie was still being transported everywhere in the wagon because he was not to sit up. We were all talking when out of nowhere I heard a little voice say, "Da-da." I was so stunned. I asked him to repeat it. Again, he said "Da-da." My heart was pounding and tears of joy ran down my cheeks. Those were the most exciting words that I had heard in years. From that day on, he began to quickly learn the English language. His speech was slurred as with any stroke victim, but he improved with time and constant teaching.

Once his speech returned, I noticed that he suddenly began using his left hand for everything. This turned out to be because the speech center of the brain adjoined the area that controls hand preference. As he had used a portion on the opposite side of the brain, he would now become left-handed.

He began throwing the football with his left hand. He never quite got the spiral down the way he used to with his right hand. Nevertheless, he was enjoying his learning experiences.

Charles began taking him to the U of K football stadium in the summer, hoping to watch the players practice. He often found a gate slightly ajar. He would squeeze the two of them through the gate. They would go out on the field to kick field goals. Now that Charlie was kneeling, he could hold the football for his dad to kick.

Sometimes Coach Fran Curci would see them, then turn away without asking them to leave. Everyone knew that the public was not allowed in the gates. Coach Curci probably recognized him as the little boy who shouted in church one day, "There's Fran Curci." No one could pass by Charlie without noticing his bright smile.

During this time, I was excited about my third baby due in November. People who were aware of all that I had been through with Charlie were afraid for me. They often asked me, "Aren't you scared to have another baby?" They were flabbergasted with my response. "No. If the next baby should have a problem, I'll deal with it then." I got some very strange looks. They did not know what feelings I had dealt with the last time. By now, I felt confident enough to take on anything, knowing God would lead the way.

Dr. Cottrill and I came to the conclusion that the magnet that was bonding our relationship, was a gift from the Holy Spirit. We were on a first-name basis and felt closer than sisters. This put her in a difficult position from a professional viewpoint. It didn't seem to matter, though. She agreed to be godmother to my new baby.

In making the doctor rounds in September, we learned that x-rays indicated Charlie had fractured his spine at the site of the fusion. Dr. Leatherman was very concerned. This fracture apparently happened from all of his movement, just as he had feared. Sometimes when Charlie would be tired of kneeling, he would have the inclination to sit back on his feet. I was constantly correcting him and reminding him not to do that. Being only two-years-old, it was difficult for him to understand.

With this new discovery, Dr. Leatherman suggested proceeding with the second stage of the surgery now. He did not want to lose all that we had gained. Charlie had recovered from his other injuries and was making progress with stroke rehabilitation at home. Approval from Dr. Cottrill was given. His heart was still in good shape. We agreed to the operation, which was scheduled in October 1977. We felt it needed to be completed soon so that I could return home before my baby was born.

Again, I prayed for God's will and that I could handle the results of surgery, whatever they might be. I also prayed this time that he not have another stroke or brain damage. I was concerned for the quality of his life. I clung to hopes of some normal childhood for Charlie.

Upon arriving at the hospital, Charlie was in a playful mood. He teased with the nurses as they encouraged him to hide from Dr. Leatherman. He hid under the doctor's dictation counter for a while. Then, he crawled into the food cart. Being the only baby on the unit, everyone found him to be a delight to watch.

However, Dr. Leatherman caught up with him and proceeded with the surgery.

Herrington rods were inserted on either side of his spine and screws were secured. Dr. Leatherman had asked our permission to allow a group of doctors from all over the world to observe this operation. They were in town for a spinal convention. Dr. Leatherman had previously taken the study of Charlie's case to Europe to teach them about this unique curvature. We were pleased that they could learn so much from our son. Naturally, we approved.

The utmost precautions were taken to prevent complications. Anticonvulsants were given, as was blood under the strictest observation. The surgery went well and no complications occurred. We returned home the day before Halloween. We allowed Charlie to lie on the dinner table to watch as I carved a pumpkin. In spite of his soreness from surgery, he smiled and enjoyed the preparations for Halloween. I rushed to make a king and queen costume for the children. As people so often referred to him as a "king in the wagon," I thought that perhaps we'd just play along with it. Charles and Uncle Ray took the children to a few houses in the neighborhood. It was Charlie's first time for trick or treating.

Two weeks later, on November 14, 1977, I gave birth to a healthy baby boy. It was uncomplicated and joyful. Charles went home to share the great news with the children. Soon thereafter, he called me at the hospital to ask me to speak to Jackie. He said that she was so disappointed that it was a boy that she was about to cry. We were both aware that she had wanted a girl, but we didn't expect this kind of response.

When she came to the phone, I said to her, "You have a new baby brother. Isn't that great?" She slowly answered, "But I wanted a girl." I assured her that she would be just as happy with a boy. Then she said to me, "Does that mean that he has to stay in the hospital?" I was stunned. She had associated boys with an illness. I promised that this boy would not be staying and that he was healthy just like her. She didn't honestly believe me until I brought baby Marty home and she saw for herself.

Shortly after coming home, I had Charlie and Marty on a floor pallet. As I began to change Charlie's diaper, Marty cried for attention. I informed them both that they would just have to take turns with Mommy. With Charlie just having surgery, wearing a brace, and unable to sit up, I knew it would not be any time soon that I could attempt potty training. They both required a lot of attention. My time with Marty, when he was an infant, was sometimes interrupted with Charlie's needs. However, Jackie did a wonderful job keeping him occupied when he had to wait for me. Not only was she a protective older sister, but she was a great help to me as well.

Life's pace increased once again with the newest addition to the family. The holidays were upon us and numerous expectations were awaiting me. Somehow, Christmas always came and we were always ready. Time was made for visiting Santa, decorating, and shopping.

Charlie recovered gradually, as expected, in spite of the limitations that he faced once again. A new back brace had been made and he was required to lie flat until further notice. Being quite sore, it was not a problem anyway, as he had no desire to move and cause himself more pain. It turned out to be very helpful for him to have a new baby in the house because he could be easily entertained whenever I could set the baby next to him.

Sundays were days that he looked forward to. It was one time, regardless of winter weather, that he was certain to get out of the house. Keeping his back straight as directed, he rode in his red wagon in the back of the car, to church. Maintaining a supine position, he was carried into church by Charles or me and placed gently on the pew. He never seemed bothered by having to look at the ceiling continually. Rather, he was quite content observing the people around him.

As winter progressed and responsibilities of parenting continued to increase, it was becoming more difficult for me to keep in good health. Lack of rest caused the immune system to weaken somewhat. Over the winter, I realized that strep throat had become a regular battle for me, discovering in time that illness was occurring every three weeks. Demands of being a mother prevented me from succumbing to exhaustion. Finally reaching a point where I could no longer function satisfactorily, arrangements were made to have my tonsils removed. With Charlie being over the hump of recovery and Marty now six-months-old, it appeared to be the best time to submit to the surgery. Charles was able to care for the children by using his vacation time from work. The short stay in the hospital and the cut in my throat were only minor sacrifices when given the outlook of being well and functional. I regained physical strength, giving me hope for a better future.

The following summer, Charlie was allowed to sit up for the first time in almost two years. We gradually began to hold him in a sitting position. He was quite frightened by it. With the rods in his back and the brace on as well, he could not maintain his balance. He must have felt as though he was always on the edge of a cliff, about to fall off. His back could not bend and therefore he was totally dependent on others to catch him if he began to lean the slightest bit. It took months for him to get use to sitting. Once I felt that he was more secure with sitting, I began potty training immediately. This was not an easy task with the back brace to deal with. However, it was accomplished.

By now, Charlie had noticed how people would stare at him. This made him begin to feel self-conscious about being out. When I would take him for a walk in the stroller, children would come up looking at him. Other youngsters his age were out walking. He would retort, "Don't see me." When they observed him, they would ask him questions such as, "What's wrong with your legs?" or, "What's wrong with you?" Charlie would be wearing his back brace and his outflare shoes that were obviously different than normal. I tried to explain to the children briefly that Charlie's doctors were trying to help him so that he could walk soon. I had to be very cautious about my wording so as to not make Charlie feel belittled. I told Charlie that they didn't mean him any harm, but they had never seen these braces before. No explanation could take away his embarrassment or humiliation.

I prayed to have the right words to say in difficult times. Later that summer I received a phone call from a U of K student who was doing research on disabled children, for his special education degree. I complied with his request and allowed him to visit. He told me about a special preschool program available that would enable the handicapped child to be prepared for regular school. He asked if I would allow Charlie to attend. I told him that Charlie hadn't even had a chance to be a baby. I couldn't foresee his being ready for school. My oldest daughter would just be starting school for the first time in the fall.

He asked if I would take him there and talk to the teacher before deciding not to send him. Cardinal Hill Hospital and The Easter Seal Society funded the school. There would be no charge for it. To pacify him, out of consideration for his research, I agreed to speak to the teacher.

The school was only a few blocks away. Charlie and I went to check it out. As I spoke to the teacher, Charlie played with one thing after another. Before long, he didn't seem to care what I was doing. He didn't cling to me. He didn't keep his eyes on me to be sure that I didn't leave. I thought to myself, this might be all right. I told Betsy, the teacher there, that I had reservations about leaving him. The only experiences he had ever had away from home were painful. I simply didn't foresee this working. I was impressed with what she had to offer. He could get speech therapy and physical therapy. She pointed out that it would make my life easier if I didn't have to do all of that at home. Being accustomed to this, I didn't have a problem doing it myself. What I liked most about the program, however, was the independence that it offered the children. The purpose of the program was to prepare these children so that they could start kindergarten on time with other children their age.

I had to admit that the stroke had held him back. He would often become frustrated with learning because he couldn't say what he wanted to say.

I made it clear to Betsy that I had no intention of enrolling him when I arrived. However, seeing that he was enjoying something without me, had now changed my mind. I signed the papers for him to start.

Meanwhile, Marty was growing fast. At nine-months-old, he was making an attempt to walk. I didn't want him to, because I feared that Charlie would feel bad about not being able to walk. I was so surprised to hear Charlie shout one day in excitement, "Look. Marty can walk." His face glowed with happiness for his brother. He didn't make a single remark about his not being able to. Not knowing any differently, it didn't bother him.

Soon after school got started, it was time for another surgery. While his heart was still in fairly good shape, it was necessary to operate on his feet. They were so badly clubbed that he couldn't stand on them. He had just begun, once again, to crawl, kneel and sit from the previous surgery. Now, he would be laid up again. The tendons and heel cords in both feet needed cutting to release some of the tightness in his feet. Dr. Leatherman agreed to do this with the help of another surgeon. His plan was to have a surgeon working on each foot at the same time. If two surgeries could be done in the time frame of one, his heart would be better able to handle it and he wouldn't have to be sedated too long.

Complications this time around were not life threatening. However, they were quite painful. His legs began to swell in the casts. Each day, an attempt was made to decrease the pressure that he was experiencing. The casts were trimmed around the toes. A window was cut out about the ankles. Finally, in realizing that the pain was still unbearable, the casts were cut up and down each leg. They were merely loosened and rewrapped with gauze to keep the feet positioned properly. Although I felt more trust with this doctor, I had a flashback of the time when Charlie's legs were cut so badly with the saw.

Once we were back home again, Charlie was suddenly afraid to go back to preschool. Realizing the stares that the public had given him in the past, and the insensitive remarks that had also been made, he did not want to expose himself to anyone. He did not want people to see his casts. He felt different due to his confinement. He was on his back again, which meant no crawling and no sitting. I reminded him that the other children in his class were also limited. Two of them could not sit up. They spent their day on the floor. One walked with braces and a walker. One walked normally. There were only five students in his class, including Charlie. He remained upset over being seen in the casts. So, I saw to it that he wore long pants and socks to hide his casts. I encouraged him to go and see with me. I even offered to stay with him to be certain that he would be all right. I discussed his fears with the teacher. She did a super job at making him feel at home. Once satisfied, I slipped away.

The preschool quickly became a second family to Charlie and to us as well. Betsy insisted on using her first name to make it easier for the children. With only five children, she was like a mother to them. The program was absolutely wonderful. The families got together with Betsy each month to discuss school activities and preparation for regular kindergarten in the future. We were informed about the legal rights for our children. We had an instant support group. The monthly meetings included all family members from two classes. We ended each meeting with a potluck dinner. Many experiences were shared including our faith and love. Betsy was exuberant with her love and concern for our children.

I continued to witness God's love for us by putting such wonderful, caring people on our path. Nothing seemed merely coincidental. I felt certain that all that had happened and all of those special people I'd met were a part of God's magnificent plan. Through sharing I realized that God had sent each friend, doctor, teacher, and acquaintance to see us through our trials.

There were so many more people, other than those already mentioned, that had been sent to me as answers to my prayers.

6

SPRING CONDITIONING

As the school year progressed, so did Charlie's speech and fine motor skills. By springtime, the casts were gone and physical therapy ensued. After wearing casts for so much of his life thus far, Charlie's calves were somewhat atrophied. They were very thin in comparison to the rest of him.

We began teaching Charlie to ride a tricycle at school and at home. This was very difficult to accomplish with such weak muscle tone. I added blocks on the pedals and strapped his feet to each side. I would push his feet down, one by one, until one day he worked up the strength to do it himself.

I began to take his plastic motorcycle to school so that he could ride it from the car to the classroom. Otherwise, I would need to carry him. This way I promoted his independence, increased his muscle tone, and saved wear and tear on my back as well. I also had a two-year-old to keep up with.

Charlie was built stocky. He looked like and thought himself to be a football player. In actuality, he loved all competitive sports. Even the clothes he wore indicated his love for football, basketball, baseball, and soccer.

Dr Cottrill tried to encourage him to play golf. She pointed out that he could play without getting exhausted if he rode in a cart around the golf course. However, it didn't interest him. In his eyes, it was boring. He was so accustomed to contact sports due to the enthusiasm we displayed for football during his illnesses. We'd do almost anything to put a smile on his face. There was a realistic fear that someday he would be greatly disappointed upon the discovery that he would not be able to play these sports. However, there was a mutual understanding between Dr. Cottrill, Charles and me that we should allow him to hold on to this dream while he could.

Charlie also began to take interest in some new TV shows such as "The Dukes of Hazzard" and "The Incredible Hulk." Any toys or clothing along this line would also create a lot of excitement. At four-years-old, he and his brother Marty, now age two, were teaming up to be great buddies.

As therapy increased, The Easter Seal Society provided Charlie with long leg braces. They surprised me one summer day when I went to pick him up. There he stood with the biggest smile on his face. He was in locked braces with the therapist holding him up. It was an ecstatic moment for us all. I had no idea how tall he was. The last time that he stood was prior to his first spinal surgery at nineteen-months-old. I was so used to his lying down that the sight of him standing completely took my breath away.

Therapy aside, we enjoyed our summer months with picnics in the park, swimming, and Jackie's T-ball games. Oftentimes we would go feed the ducks at a nearby pond, or stop to see the horses grazing in the fields near our home.

The children and I frequently visited with Dr. Cottrill and her family. While the children played, Dr. Cottrill and I prepared dinner. Charlie bonded more with Carl, her adopted son with heart disease, because they played at the same pace. This time allowed Dr. Cottrill and I to commonly share our spirituality among other things. On frequent occasions, I left the children with their dad in the evening so that I could give her a perm without interruptions. This was a treasured time for both of us. Until now, I had never felt so comfortable talking about spiritual ideas with another person. (Although we were now on a first-name basis, I will continue to address her as Dr. Cottrill out of respect for her deserved title.)

As my career in motherhood advanced, I learned many ways to cut costs. I could stretch a dollar tighter than a rubber band. I became observant of all the things I could do to save money. My dad had taught me to be creative. With a little imagination, I often found ways to make the things I needed out of materials around the house. My mother had taught me to cook creatively at a very young age. She encouraged me to sew in order to have nice clothes on a shoestring budget. She gave family haircuts to save money. So, I figured that I could learn that, too. I kept my eyes open to save money in every possible way. My mother-in-law was a coupon queen. She taught me how to shop smart and clip coupons. It was a challenge to make ends meet, but it was worth it to be able to stay home with the children.

Eventually, these things weren't enough. Foreseeing the unlimited mountain of bills yet to come, I felt I needed to be working on improving our economic future. Medical bills were constantly growing. Parochial school for three children and the everyday cost of living was something to think about. I thought it best to enroll in college that fall. I arranged my schedule for hours that Jackie and Charlie were in school. My classes fit neatly between Charles' classes. This way, we could meet each other at school and switch off Marty between us. He enjoyed going to college with Mom and Dad.

Charlie's time in the leg braces was gradually increasing. He was gaining strength in his calves from therapy at home as well as at school. Sometimes, he would be put in a standing table. This was a wooden box with a door. It had a tray on it for playing. Ten or fifteen minutes a day there increased his muscle tone.

The next milestone was learning to use a walker. Although very slow at first, he was quite excited about getting to walk like Marty. For some reason, Marty became his inspiration. It was a tremendous struggle for Charlie to use his energy to lift the walker and place it in front of himself. He became short of breath after about eight to ten steps. Charles or I would carry him to his destination and allow him to walk a few steps once there.

When we were out in public, Charlie would have to ride in the stroller. He found this to be humiliating. Being four-years-old now, people always made it their business, saying, "What are you doing riding in that stroller?" "You're too big for that stroller. You should be walking." "Why are you riding and your little brother is walking?" "You should get out and let him ride." It had gotten so bad that I knew each time I would go out with the children, someone was going to say something derogatory. I would generally not respond or laugh it off. However, on one occasion when the attacker wouldn't back off, I responded, "He can't walk." The man was speechless. I quickly realized I had said the wrong thing. Not only was he embarrassed, but Charlie was also hurt by it. He had just started walking with the walker and felt very proud of his accomplishment. He turned to me looking heartbroken at what I had just said. His eyes got big and he stated, "I can too walk." I was crushed for him. I found myself having to explain to this stranger that he uses a walker and is unable to walk very far. I explained to Charlie what I meant.

After this incident, I thought long and hard about what answer I could give the next time it happened. I decided what to say when the next person inquired about why he was in the stroller. I would tell them that it's because we can't afford a wheelchair. That would make them stop and think, wouldn't it? I suppose God was not happy with my new frustrated attitude. He saw to it that no one ever questioned him again. I was never able to use my smart remark.

As Charlie attended school daily, he was unknowingly being observed by Tim Jordan. He was an Easter Seal representative who was searching for nominees for poster child for the upcoming year. Each time Tim would observe the preschool, he found a little towhead smiling, laughing, and full of joy. Upon Tim's recommendation, Mr. Paul Combs, the director of The Easter Seal Society came to investigate further. He too witnessed a joyful child with strong determination for achievement.

Photo by Lexington Leader/E. Martin Jesse

Charlie, four years old, is shown with Wildcat players Felix Wilson (8), Tom Kearns and coach Fran Curci. Also shown is Neil Gossett, a spinal cord patient from Cardinal Hill Hospital.

I was interviewed for approval of photographs and public exposure of my child. With all that The Easter Seal Society had already provided for Charlie, I was more than happy to be involved in their cause. Once all the nominees and their families from around the state were interviewed, we waited for the decision. Within a week, Charlie had been selected. We all found it to be rather exciting. He would get to travel the state and meet many people.

We were informed that for most of the activities planned, Charlie would need to dress in a suit. He was not at all happy about this. Being stocky and short in stature, it was hard to find a well-fitting dress shirt that didn't choke him. Any shirt I bought was going to need adjustments. Nevertheless, as we set out to buy a suit, Charlie informed me that he just couldn't wear one because he had to look like a football player. He was not being contrary. He was quite serious about his appearance. It was important that he portray this image. I tried hard to convince him that when football players go out to dinner, they wear a suit. He was sure that this wasn't so. I suppose at that age he thought that real players lived in their uniforms. He knew I was making it up. With reservations, he cooperated when we went into the department store to look for a suit. He quickly picked out several shirts with football logos, laughing as if he could talk me in to it. "Sorry, son. That's not what we're looking for today," I exclaimed. As I browsed through the racks, there was a blue plaid suit with a label inside marked "Quarterback." It even had a picture of a helmet. I told Charlie, "Look what I found. This is what the quarterbacks wear when they go out to eat." It was the label that saved the day. He believed me. He suddenly loved the suit. I found myself laughing with God on this one. I could see Him working in even the most trivial of situations.

That fall, U of K had donated four 50-yard- line tickets to the Tennessee game, to raise money for Cardinal Hill Hospital. These tickets were to go to the highest bidder. As the preschool was located in the hospital, they requested a representative to be photographed with the football players. Betsy, knowing Charlie's love for football, selected him immediately. He was elated. This was a dream come true for him. He made sure that

71

he took his football helmet with him. He was as close to heaven as any four-year-old could possibly imagine. Upon arriving with Charles, Coach Curci recognized them both. He had seen them at church and in the middle of U of K's field. Charlie felt right at home. He didn't mind allowing the football players to hold him for pictures. Seeing himself in the newspaper made him believe that he was part of the team.

The school year continued. It was very busy for all of us. School, therapy, doctors, work, and meetings to attend absorbed all of our time. Somehow, I managed to make it through the semester at U of K. I enrolled again for the spring term.

Suddenly, our world fell apart. I had taken Charlie to school one February morning. It was freezing cold outside. Frost had covered the windshields of every car. We arrived at school only to find ourselves waiting for Betsy. The later it got, the more we worried. The parents and staff who waited had a sickening feeling in their guts. Linda, the teacher of the other class, began calling hospitals. We discovered that Betsy had been in a terrible accident on her way to school that day. They were taking her to surgery for internal hemorrhaging. Her husband was also in critical condition. We prayed and we waited. No one felt emotionally strong enough to go on with class. By late that afternoon, we received word that Betsy had died. We were all devastated and in disbelief. There wasn't anyone like her to take her place. The children needed her so desperately as did the parents.

We all questioned God. What would be His purpose to take her away from these children? We felt abandoned.

It was a struggle to help Charlie prepare his valentines for his friends. I could only cry when I picked up the one for teacher. I had explained to Charlie that Betsy had died and had gone to heaven to be with Jesus. Initially, he didn't grasp what I was saying. The funeral was held on February 14, 1980. The church overflowed with people. The minister knew Betsy well. He spoke of her childlike innocence and the beauty within her soul. It was a very fitting ceremony. Tears over her death flowed readily throughout the town.

I found myself, from that day on, with my eyes focused on the skies. When I drove, I would look to the clouds of heaven and talk to God, to Mary, and to Betsy. I could feel the love of God beaming from the rays of the sun. I always had the radio on. Almost every song was about loving someone. Frequently, it was about lost love. The thought of Betsy had become a constant one. The words of the songs kept me in tears. I questioned God because I lacked understanding. I begged Him to guide me. The only sense I could make of it was that this was a preparation for Charlie's trip to heaven. I felt that God had placed a *mother* figure in heaven to wait for him. This may eliminate his fear of death. It would be reassuring for me to know that Betsy would meet him when his hour would come. I never thought of us needing anyone other than Jesus, Mary, and the saints. However, I took this to be a future comfort. Driving along, I recited The Lord's Prayer, meditating deeply on "Thy will be done."

In the attempt of getting back to normal, a substitute teacher was brought in. She was a very nice young woman. She was not sent there for us, however. She confided in me a troublesome secret. I realized then, that I was there for her. I saw God's use of every opportunity to save a burdened soul.

Charlie was becoming depressed over the loss of Betsy. He missed her love and affection. He decided that he could no longer walk. This was a tremendous task for him. Without the emotional strength, the physical body just couldn't make it. He told me he didn't want to walk because Betsy couldn't see him. She used to fawn over him as if he were the only person in the world. All five of the children believed they were the only one that mattered to Betsy.

When Charlie was down, I grabbed at another angel that God had sent me. I recalled the after-death experience that my friend Kathy had shared with me. This memory helped Charlie and me to go on. I told Charlie about Kathy's experience. Just shy of turning five-years-old, he seemed to understand quite well what I was telling him. I assured him that Betsy could see him walk. I told him that it would make her so happy to see him try. We made a game out of it. I stood him up and cheered him on with each step that he took. I would cheer and shout that Betsy was so proud of him. Then, I'd give him a big kiss and hug from Betsy. I got more kisses and hugs this way because, I also gave him one from me.

The days got better as far as dealing with the loss of Betsy. However, when night fell, the heartaches surfaced. Frequently, I would hear Charlie crying in the bed. I'd go to him and try to lift his spirits. I kept assuring him of Betsy's happiness in heaven. We knew of Betsy's love for God because of her love for people. I told him that God has promised happiness to those who love Him. We had many heart-to-heart talks about God and heaven. I encouraged Charlie to pray as he fell asleep. This was the only way that I could leave the room after a long talk. I told him to talk to God and to Betsy and they would help him fall asleep.

I, too, was having a difficult time. I cried when I was alone. I began to feel sick daily, and I was tired all the time. With a little more observation, I soon realized that I was with child. I feared that under the circumstances, I would not be able to keep up with school. I was too tired to concentrate. I knew that when God stepped in with His plan that I may as well step out of my own. Knowing that I would not leave a newborn in September to attend school, I saw it best to withdraw from classes until God made it possible for me to enroll again.

A few weeks later, a girl in Charlie's class died from complicated health problems. I couldn't bring myself to tell him so soon after Betsy's death. Linda, the other teacher, told the children that she was gone to another school. We all agreed that it would be too much for the kids to handle. They may become scared that they would die next.

I looked to the heavens with wonder over this. I asked God for the gift of understanding. With that, I gathered that Charlie now had a *sister* figure waiting for him in heaven.

March and April were packed with Easter Seal activities. We traveled across the state for various functions. There were dinners and meetings to attend. There were politicians and celebrities to meet. Charlie was not a bit camera shy. He didn't mind at all being in the newspapers, on TV or on the mailing brochures. He enjoyed all the activity and attention.

74

Photo by Mark Kidd
Major General Billy G. Wellman, adjutant general of Kentucky and commander of the National Guard is pictured with Charlie, at age five, and his parents.

I received my first invitation in public speaking at the annual meeting for volunteers from around the state. It was an elaborate two-day function held at Stouffer's Inn in downtown Louisville. After a full day of conferences, Mr. Combs said to me, "Oh, by the way, I need you to give a talk in the morning after breakfast."

"What? Me?" I replied.

"Yes. I just want you to tell everyone about Charlie's life. Will you do that for me?"

How could I refuse? I warned him that I'd never given a talk before. He encouraged me as if there was nothing to it.

It was 10:00 P.M. before we got back to our hotel room. I began writing what I planned to say. It was too much to cover, so I decided to forget it, go to bed, and leave it up to God in the morning.

In the morning, I jotted down a few notes to keep me on track. The three of us were given seats at the head table because Charlie was the guest of honor. I felt a little nervous, as I looked out at the large number of affluent business people waiting to

75

hear me speak. I was aware that everyone there had donated large sums of money, as well as time, from their businesses to support the Kentucky Easter Seal Society. Now, they needed to see who was benefiting from their efforts.

When introduced, I took a deep breath and began to tell his history. There was complete silence in the room. The focus was on me. God saw me through and I was able to maintain a calm disposition. There was a beautiful tenderness as I spoke in the midst of these people. I sensed their genuine love and caring for those less fortunate, by the look on their faces. They were moved by Charlie's story. Until now, he was a stranger. The effects were mutual for they equally touched me. Getting to know them increased the awareness of God in my life. How fortunate I was to be there. How appropriate, I saw was the symbol of the Easter lily for this organization. Not only did The Easter Seal Society provide new life for the disabled, it was the love and care of others in the bud of the lily. These volunteers resurrected a life that overpowered the limitations of the disabled.

The Easter Seal staff and volunteers always treated us special. They absolutely loved Charlie and he knew it. He could put a smile on anyone's face. Once he was asked to present the (female) president of the National Easter Seal Society with a corsage. He was not about to hand it to her. This was completely out of character for Charlie, as he always did what he was told without hesitation. As I coaxed him into this act, he said to me quite seriously, "I can't give that to her. She's not my girlfriend!" Everyone in the crowd heard and laughed. Thank goodness they had a sense of humor. People were wiping tears of laughter from their eyes.

At times, the grandparents were also included at special dinners. When they came to Cardinal Hill Hospital, Charlie and my mother-in-law enjoyed a good walker race. It was a good way for both of them to laugh in spite of their limitations. (She used a walker because of complications from diabetes.)

Charlie met many special people. He was most impressed with the sports figures such as Coach Joe B. Hall and Sam Bowie. Bo Duke and The Black Stallion also caught his attention. With all due respect, the governor, ambassadors, and

First Lady Nancy Reagan did not rank as high on the five-year-old's list. The clever Director of The Easter Seal Society, Paul Combs, picked up on this. He began to put a plug into the ears of the politicians that Charlie enjoyed football. Anyone could spark a conversation with him if they brought up the subject.

On one occasion, Mr. Combs brought a football with him so that General Wellman could enjoy Charlie's effusive personality. After tossing it back and forth some, he gave it to Charlie to keep. He was so appreciative. General Wellman was put on his list of special people.

Photo by Mark Kidd

Charlie and his mother being interviewed at the Kentucky Easter Seal Telethon in 1980

Photo by Mark Kidd

Charlie with Kentucky Basketball Coach Joe B. Hall

Later, after a picture taking session with Coach Joe B. Hall and Sam Bowie, Mr. Combs let it be known that General Wellman gave Charlie a football. After he said it twice, Coach Hall got the hint and offered the U of K basketball to Charlie. He took him into his office where he autographed the ball. Charlie was absolutely thrilled.

Playtime for Charlie had become quite dramatic with the encouragement of his brother, Marty. They would climb on the arms and back of the couch, shouting "Yee-hah," as if they were in the "General Lee" car from Hazzard. Marty's imagination had no limit. Charlie was determined to keep up with him. Whenever we drove down the country roads, Charles would go fast over the hills, so that the car and everyone in it would bounce up and down. The boys shouted "YEE-HAH," and pretended to be in the "General Lee."

The Incredible Hulk also moved into our lives. The pretending was sometimes scary, but never was it out of control. Charles and I enjoyed watching them grow and develop together.

The more Charlie's character developed, the more changes I noticed in the people we encountered daily. Neighbors witnessed a handicapped child being treated like any other child. They noticed that Charlie didn't think of himself as being any different. They were amazed at the openness in our household. All the children in the neighborhood were welcome into our home. It wasn't unusual to find 10 children playing well together in our living room. Often times, Charles or I could get more done around the house if the children were being entertained. The neighbors enjoyed the break, as well. This kind of normal exposure gave Charlie the self-confidence that he needed to survive.

Strangers were often drawn to Charlie wherever we went. People always spoke to him in the hospitals, clinics, stores, parks, churches, and elsewhere. People offered him balloons, candy, money or other items at times. Cheerful, pleasant comments were constantly coming our way. People were moved just watching this bubbly little boy, often short of breath, get from place to place with his walker.

Generous people would periodically offer assistance or gifts to the family. Initially, these were not easy for me to accept. I reflected on a lesson that was pointed out to me by my dear friend Dr. Cottrill. It is sometimes a greater sacrifice to receive than it is to give. Notice that the gift is not what you have received, but the humility in accepting it gracefully. By accepting, you have allowed someone else to receive the grace for giving. What tremendous insight this woman had shared with me. This was another blessing that God had sent my way, by means of people on my path. Each time someone offered my children or myself gifts, I was witnessing the goodness in them being brought out. It was a delight to witness.

When the day of the Easter Seal Telethon arrived, Charlie traveled by plane to various points across the state, in order to appear on the local segments of the telethon. Charles, Mayor Dr. Harvey Sloane and his son Patrick accompanied him. (Mayor

Sloane was the state representative for The Easter Seal Society.) Charlie was dressed up in his suit labeled "Quarterback." They stepped into the private plane in anticipation of an adventurous day. Before reaching their first destination, Charlie got motion sickness when the plane hit prolonged turbulence. They had some cleaning up to do before he could go on TV. Being on a timed schedule, they operated fast. He recovered from the setback and went on to have an exciting day.

Charlie remained busy with The Easter Seal Society until the next poster child was selected a year later.

The school year was coming to an end and so was a major segment of his life. He was graduated from preschool and we made preparations for his attending kindergarten. It was a sad occasion for all of us. We were breaking some very special ties. Goals of self-esteem had been met. The foundation for his life had been set.

Photo by Lexington Leader/Frank Anderson

Charlie gets a lift from his dad at the Lexington Rotary Club,
founder of the Kentucky Easter Seal Society.

7

Flags On the Play

Keeping my eyes open for opportunities to benefit the family, I came across new housing loans for first time homeowners. I saw that we fit the guidelines for low income. I was so excited at the thought of getting a house. Taking all necessary papers, I went to apply, only to discover that due to medical bills, we would not qualify. I was told that we didn't make enough money for a low-income loan. In spite of having good insurance with major medical back up, along with medical assistance for the disabled, the remainder of the bills not covered was too high to grant the loan.

I was dumbfounded. How could we not qualify for this reason? I tried reasoning with them that we were currently making monthly rent payments and that the house payment would be no different. They refused to listen. I was told that the medical bills would have to be paid off first before consideration. It was useless, knowing that the bills would continue to come in faster than they could be paid. My excitement vanished as quickly as it arose. I was resolved to raise my family in the duplex that we rented.

Finances had been a great struggle over the years. Charlie was qualified to receive Supplement Security Income (SSI) monthly, to meet some of the medical expenses imposed upon the disabled. However, over the last several years I received letters from the Social Security Administration office, stating that he had been overpaid on numerous occasions. I questioned how this could happen time and time again when I so carefully reported every source of income available. I showed copies of student loans and what the money was intended for. The only answer that I was given was that our resources were too high several months of the year and therefore the money allotted him would have to be reimbursed to the government. I pointed out that it was student loan money that was to be considered. It was intended to be used over a six-month period for shelter, food, and clothing for the entire family. Regardless, a large portion of his checks was being withheld until it was paid back in full.

On mornings that weren't spent at a doctor's office, I found myself with the three children, at the Social Security office trying to straighten out the misunderstandings of the SSI. After going over and over the income and expenses with the social worker, he finally and hesitantly told me how the system worked. He must have developed some empathy after seeing me in the office with my children every month. He saw that I was attempting to understand why they were taking back almost every check that they sent me for Charlie. He explained that I should not be putting the student loan money in the bank. By having it there, it was recounted every month as resources available. I explained that it needed to be evenly disbursed for six months to cover our living expenses. He advised me to pay my rent six months at a time in order to spend the money. The rest should be kept in a container in my closet instead of at the bank. I should take out only the amount needed to pay my utilities and medical bills and deposit it when I write out the checks for them. This needed to be done at the beginning of the month to make certain that all checks clear before the end of the month. If I were to write $1000.00 in bills and it did not clear quickly enough, it would be considered money to live on for the next month. This is absurd, I thought. I couldn't believe what I was hearing. I questioned him further, saying, "Even though I've shown you receipts that indicate this money has been spent on rent, utilities, and doctor bills, I am still penalized because I use the bank." "That's right," he admitted. By now, this had been going on for about five years. Most of this income had to be returned to the government. He indicated that he should not be telling me this for fear of losing his job. I thanked him for doing so, as I left in disbelief.

The summer of 1980 was passing quickly. I sensed the financial volcano was about to erupt. Pondering the upcoming school year and the new baby to be born, I feared disaster. I took a careful look at the situation. Charles spent his day at school and work, with few hours left for studying and family. I devoted most of my days to doctor's appointments, physical therapy, and mothering. I searched the classifieds daily for a job that might work into my schedule. It would not be feasible to work during the day. Childcare expenses and doctors' appointments would not allow it. At seven months' pregnant, I could not foresee obtaining an interview, much less a job. The economic future looked rather bleak.

Adamant about sending Jackie and Charlie to a Catholic school, I knew I had to find an answer. The budget was no longer manageable, with more expenses than resources. Exhausting all avenues, I finally prayed. Providence would not come by magic. I ruled out stealing and begging. Reality was that God helps those who help themselves. Weeks passed with no further insight as to how I could do more than what I was already doing. As utilities were being shut off, and my pregnancy advancing, I became totally helpless. Reaching rock bottom, I went to bed one night crying and praying. I pleaded wlth God to guide me. I could not understand why He had not shown me the way. I thought to myself, after trying so hard to go by the rules of the Church, by welcoming children into the world, why then was I in this predicament? I continued crying and praying for what seemed to be hours. Eventually, I fell asleep, my mind exhausted from trying to find an answer.

That night, God spoke to me in a dream. He told me that I could sell something. I told Him that I had nothing left to sell except for my sewing machine. Although it might pay one bill, I did not see that as a permanent solution. Then, He made it clear to me. He told me to go sell Tupperware. Well, that's a good idea, I thought. I questioned the fact that I was now so advanced in pregnancy. He assured me that it wouldn't matter. With that, I agreed to give it a try.

I woke up a little bewildered. Going over it in my mind, I searched my memory for logical reasons for coming up with this idea. There was no logic. I had not been to a Tupperware party for over five years. I saw that my dream was, in fact, an answer to my prayer. I was so excited about my inspiration. I contacted the office immediately. I was told that a manager would be out to see me that day.

When she arrived at my door, she was taken aback at noticing my pregnancy and the children beneath my feet. I feared that she would recommend that I wait to have my baby before starting. On the contrary, she welcomed and encouraged me.

I asked her about the management program. I knew it was going to take a lot of money to make a dent. I started right away. With many phone calls, my calendar quickly filled up.

Charles came home from work in the evenings to take over the parenting, while I headed out to Tupperware parties. We ate dinner together quickly. He got the children to bed and studied while I worked. The timing was perfect.

Over the next few weeks, more utilities were being cut off. Seeing some light at the end of the tunnel, this didn't bother me anymore. I knew it was only a matter of time to improve our finances. I was focused on attaining a manager's position. I was impressed with the meetings starting off with the Lord's Prayer. I understood in my heart that this job was a gift from God.

In reflecting on this, I discovered why it took me so long to find the answer. I had been trying endlessly to find a solution on my own. It wasn't until I had exhausted all means that I asked God for help. He has always said, "Ask and you shall receive." He wanted me to ask. He wanted me to comprehend that I was dependent on Him. It was so simple. The cross was so much heavier trying to carry it by myself. I couldn't do it alone.

My labor began as I was attending an important Tupperware meeting. Feeling safe, I stayed for the duration. That evening, my manager, Mary Ellen, held my party for me so that I could prepare for the birth of my baby. God granted me the time to bathe the children and get them to bed. I instructed them that I would be going to the hospital that night. A neighbor came over to watch them. On September 17, 1980, I gave birth to a baby girl, Leslie. Jackie finally got the little sister that she had been wanting.

Leslie was born with a heart murmur. The nurses were worried after reading my medical history that included Charlie's heart disease. Dr. Cottrill was called in to examine the baby. She put their fears to rest. Although the murmur was there and would remain, most likely throughout her life, I was told not to anticipate a problem or need for correction. It was considered an innocent murmur. She put my mind at ease. I knew that I could trust her judgment.

Leslie was five days old when a friend came for a visit. She had traveled from Wisconsin and, therefore, planned to stay for a few days. As she showered, the water was cut off for nonpayment. This was so embarrassing. It was one thing doing without, but to have it happen in front of a friend was humiliating. She was able to laugh about it, thank goodness. This made the embarrassing moment more tolerable. Knowing that I couldn't afford to take off work to have a baby, I felt guilty. Although I needed to rest, I felt that I shouldn't.

From my bed, I worked on Tupperware business as I recovered from childbirth. I made phone calls and appointments as Jackie assisted me in packaging orders for my customers. I could easily stop in the middle of my work and care for the new baby. In two weeks I returned to my parties each evening. Charles enjoyed his time bonding with Leslie and the others.

During this same time, we were still busy with The Easter Seal Society. I was asked to take Charlie over to Cardinal Hill Hospital so that he could present flowers to Nancy Reagan. She would be arriving on a campaign tour for her husband. This was an important stop because there was current talk of cutting funds to the disabled. It would be important to make a good impression for her to take back to Washington.

It was up to me to get the children dressed for the occasion because Charles would be unable to take off from work. Being two weeks postpartum, I wasn't sure I could get my act together. However, I was aware of the many people whom we had met through The Easter Seal Society. Each had brought so much joy into our lives. It was always well worth the effort to get there. By now, the assembly-line routine of bathing and dressing was well established. The fourth baby just blended right in. Each child helped in whatever way they could. Soon, all were dressed, fed, braces on, and hair brushed. Several trips were made to the car to load up the crew. Jackie carried the diaper bag and the walker. I carried Charlie. Next, Marty climbed into his car seat as Jackie so willingly assisted him. As she helped him, I returned to the house to bring out the new baby. She was buckled in quickly and off we went. I found these family activities such a joy regardless of how much work it was to prepare. The kids were excited and well behaved, enabling me to pursue any adventure.

People at Cardinal Hill were glad to see me and greeted us with a warm welcome. All were raving over the baby including Mrs. Reagan. The other children were equally made over which prevented any thoughts of jealousy.

Once Mrs. Reagan realized that all four of the children belonged to me, she commented about my youth and irresistibly asked my age. Already feeling self-conscious about this, I was not surprised that she asked. I had become accustomed to hearing this question every time I met someone new. At age 27, people still remarked daily that I looked 16. Although most intended this as a compliment, I found it to be morally upsetting when the person asking saw that I had several children. Their thoughts of my youth would imply that I was having children at the age of 9 or 10. Swallowing my pride, I was actually glad to clarify any misconceptions. I found that I was pleased to meet with Mrs. Reagan. Too often the media presented judgmental assumptions about influential people. I was able to discover for myself the caring qualities that Mrs. Reagan had. She was impressed with her tour of the hospital as she witnessed the many opportunities offered to the handicapped child and the adult trauma patient. The visit was indeed another heartwarming event that we were fortunate to be a part of.

The following day as I cleaned house, Jackie came running into the kitchen with a profound discovery. She had been watching T V when she became suddenly enlightened. Dashing toward me with wide-open eyes, she proclaimed, "Mommy, Mommy. I finally figured it out."

"What's that?" I responded.

"I know why everybody keeps saying you look so young," she continued.

"You do?" I inquired with enthusiasm to match hers.

"Yes," she said, "because you use Oil of Olay."

Laughing, I responded to her, "Oh yeah. That must be it. Maybe I shouldn't use it anymore." We enjoyed a good hug. I confirmed my appreciation for her concern as I thanked her for letting me know.

The following fall, Charlie was enrolled in a Catholic grade school, which was a great accomplishment for us. The first month had gone smoothly. The kindergarten had a separate entrance with stairs leading to the second floor. Each morning I held his hand as he climbed up the stairway to the classroom. Handing him his walker and a few words of encouragement, he set off to have a good day.

His teacher was wonderful but fell into the heartache trap. Feeling sympathetic, she often gave in to him when he stopped working. She had questioned me about his limitations. I instructed her that he had none as of yet because he was good at stopping himself when he could go no further. She made a pallet for him to rest on. It was obvious that she was a little intimidated by his cyanosis and heavy breathing.

Before long, he began to take advantage of the situation. He would lie down several times a day. I talked to him and encouraged him to do more schoolwork and not to lie down so much. He had made more progress in preschool because it was expected of him. He was quite capable of learning. I felt it was for his own good to keep up with the class. I didn't want to spoil him. He was not treated like royalty at home, nor was he allowed to have his way because of his handicap. I expected him to do his best and needed for his teachers to expect the same. Knowing his behavior pattern, I could tell whether he was truly pushing himself too much or not. In time, she would know this, too. I had suggested to her that he was probably bored with the assignment rather than too tired. She began to challenge him more and he was happier for it. He began to blossom.

In early November, the mall was offering a contest to select a snowflake court for Santa Claus. In looking at all the attention Charlie had received in the past year as the Easter Seal poster child, I thought Jackie might enjoy something like this. At seven-years-old, she was thrilled at the opportunity. Marty was a three-year-old full of personality. So, I decided to register them both.

The day of the contest, we all went to the mall dressed in our Sunday best. When we stopped to confirm their registration at the office, I heard a sudden outburst from Charlie. "What about me?" he questioned with his mouth starting to quiver. He realized that he was being left out. I was afraid to ask if he could register, wondering what kind of response I would get at the sight of his walker and braces. I tried to smooth it out by saying that I thought he might be too tired of all the attention, as he had been poster child not long ago. He didn't fall for it. He wanted to do whatever his brother and sister were doing. After all, he wasn't any different than they. I sent Charles to inquire if Charlie could still register. I anticipated some way of accepting the response that it was not for the handicapped. After working so hard to build his self-esteem, I hated being the one that would have to tell him that he was different. Much to my surprise, Charles came back and said that he was registered. They did not have a problem with it. The kids were all so excited. They wanted him included as well.

As the contest began, each child was called up individually to speak to the judges. The mall was packed around center court from all angles. We were a fair distance to the back due to the time lapse of registration. When it came time for the five-year-olds, Charles carried Charlie up close to the stage. Staying with the other children, I began to feel horrible knots in my stomach. Charlie was used to the limelight, but that was with The Easter Seal Society. Now he was going to be on exhibit among the "normal" world. I started shaking with fear for him. I knew that when his name would be called, that people would start whispering. I didn't want him to hear it. I was in the back and would not be able to protect him. It was a most tense situation. I couldn't bear to see the public reaction.

"Charlie Stopher," the announcer called. I trembled. I looked around me to capture the expressions of people as they noticed his handicap. The entire mall became dead silent. People stretched to see. Tears began flowing down my face uncontrollably. I sobbed deeply as I waited to hear the chatter start among the people.

Charlie strutted across the stage with his walker. He stopped at each judge and gave a big smile. Holding the walker with one hand, he waved at them with the other. He answered their questions. He felt so proud to be like all the rest. That's why he was smiling.

The sharpness of the silence was suddenly cut with an explosion of clapping and cheering. It lasted for what seemed to be eternity. I could hardly stand it. I turned away with a burst of tears. People not only accepted him, but were moved by his character and perseverance. I watched the crowd. I felt that they must have been appreciating their own children's good health, by their reaction. I thanked God for protecting him from the often cruel world.

Needless to say, Charlie was selected to be in Santa's court. A snowflake crown was placed on his silky blond hair. He was awarded gift certificates and other prizes. He had the pleasure of riding on the fire truck that brought Santa to the mall. He was thrilled with the excitement. He had no idea that anyone even noticed that he was exceptional.

My heart ached now for Jackie. I knew that she had high hopes of being selected. I explained to her that only one member of a family was allowed to win. He was chosen because of the reaction of the crowd. Feeling happy for her brother, she handled her own disappointment rather well.

In December, I had reached my goal to become a Tupperware manager. I was given a brand new Oldsmobile station wagon along with monthly bonus checks. I thoroughly enjoyed meeting all the people on my job. Life was starting to look up for us. We could now pay our bills and afford Christmas gifts as well. The delight of Christmas filled the air. The house was ringing with music and children laughing. The whole family enjoyed decorating, wrapping gifts and baking goodies.

We attended the vigil Mass on Christmas Eve. Charlie stood next to me. Placing my arm around him, I found myself reliving the memory of that first Christmas Mass when he was a baby. I recalled that bittersweet flash of the birth and death of Jesus. Thinking of the correlation between Jesus and Charlie, I felt overwhelmed at the blessings that poured through my child. I imagined Mary when she took her son, Jesus, into a crowd. I assumed that she had to be deeply moved to see the effect that her son had on others.

With the holidays ending, so too was the first semester of school. Charlie had done extremely well in keeping up with his lessons. We were so pleased with his success. The students treated him like all the rest. His teacher was now more relaxed about his health. We couldn't ask for more.

One morning, I received a phone call from the principal. She told me that we would have to find another school for Charlie. She said the school was not designed for the handicapped. I was stunned. I told her that he had done just fine getting around. She added that if anyone were to complain about the access to the kindergarten room, that the school could be sued for not having a ramp. I assured her that I had no intentions of suing. I had already had other instances that I could have sued over, but I didn't. We discussed it at length, but her mind was made up. She said that someone else had mentioned it. It was obvious that she didn't want him there, but I wasn't convinced that it was because of the ramp.

I spoke to Charlie's teacher, who was adamant about defending him. According to her, he made the class special and challenging. An attempt had already been made to allow him to stay. Nevertheless, it was out of her hands.

I was forced to enroll him in a public school with a class for the handicapped. Jackie, however, stayed because she was preparing for her First Communion at the time. As Catholic education was a priority for me, I couldn't see giving it up for convenience.

Always grateful for the diversions from The Easter Seal Society, the letdowns from society were more easily managed. With football season nearing an end, two Dallas Cowboy cheerleaders were in town for a promotion. Pictures were being taken with them as a fundraiser for The Easter Seal Society. Naturally, Charlie was invited to represent the society as he was, by far, the biggest football fan in the city. However, Jackie was even more elated than he at the thought of meeting the professional cheerleaders. When we arrived, Charlie, walker in hands, strutted in to meet them. Marty was equally excited, although he hadn't quite grasped the concept of the sport. The girls, dressed in uniforms and cowboy hats, were drawn to the children immediately, fussing over one, then another. Conversation quickly ensued with each one. They could see that Jackie was one happy little girl to be sharing this time with them. One of the girls asked Charlie if he liked football. Of course, he was elated with the topic and shared his love for the sport. Then he was asked who his favorite team was. Without hesitation, he blurted out in innocence, "Pittsburgh Steelers." Looking stunned at first they cheerfully laughed as they realized his youthful honesty. Leslie, being just four-months-old, did not lack for attention. She was passed between them several times prior to having a picture taken with the group. Then they continued to tease Charlie about his favorite team.

Upon arrival at his new school, I found the room to be dark and dreary. The shades were closed. The atmosphere was cold. The teacher was informative but not particularly cheerful. This was nothing like what he had been used to. For the first time, he was not enjoying school.

Trying to make the best of the situation, I made excuses to Charlie for every justified complaint that he had. I defended the teacher, students, and the school, assuring him that it would just take a little getting used to. As time passed, it became harder to drop him off. I felt sorry for every student in the class. Their personalities were all bland. The classroom was dead. They weren't being challenged. They had nothing to look forward to. Charlie often giggled and was now getting into trouble for his outbursts of laugher. This was his personality not an intentional misbehavior. On several occasions, he came home crying. I realized the necessity to find another school for the following year. Just after turning six-years-old, Charlie began to make attempts to walk without his walker. As he began to do better at home, he did the same at school. The teacher disapproved of this. She forced him to use the walker even when he didn't need it. In talking to her she stated that she was worried that he might fall. My answer was, "So what?" If he falls, he can get up. She didn't agree with my philosophy. I suggested to her that every normal child that I knew falls a time or two in their life. They've had skinned knees, too. If he's ever going to be considered normal, he'll have to handle the falls.

She continued to make Charlie handicapped at school. I continued to make him normal at home. Finally, I decided to send him to school without his walker. He agreed that if the hallway to the cafeteria were too long to walk, he would stop and rest. We were a team fighting the system. Off he went without his walker. His teacher was quite upset. I apologized for upsetting her but not for the absent walker. I merely told her that he never uses it anymore. I was determined not to allow her narrow-mindedness to stunt his growth. We won. I could see with this latest trial that we would probably always be fighting the schools over Charlie's handicap.

The end of the school year was exciting for us all. Jackie had made her First Communion. Charles was to be graduated from U of K with a degree in chemistry. Charlie was getting away from his confining school. I was succeeding with my Tupperware career. Marty and Leslie were adding joy to the household.

Meanwhile, Dr. Cottrill had experienced some close calls with her son Carl. On Easter Sunday he had fallen into a deep, frightening sleep while at church. She carried him out and tried desperately to wake him without success. She was convinced that he was dying. Eventually, however, he woke up as Mass was ending.

We kept in close touch with each other, as his health became more critical over the next few weeks. Due to his advanced congestive heart failure, there was no surgery to help him. In spite of all that she had done for Carl, it was frustrating as a cardiologist and a mother to feel so helpless.

When his time to return to God was very near, I took Carl a snapshot that I had taken of him while playing at my house. It wasn't long before he went to heaven. I understood immediately that God had now placed a *brother* figure in heaven to wait for Charlie.

It was the end of June when I received a phone call from Tim Jordan with The Easter Seal Society. He had recently moved to Louisville and we had not heard from him in a while. Much to my surprise, this time it was not for publicity. It was to inform us that our dear friend and The Easter Seal Society Director, Paul Combs, had died from a heart attack. What a shock. Another person so close to Charlie had died. Mr. Combs was like a grandfather to Charlie. He spoiled Charlie just as a grandparent would, making sure he always got special treats. I was beginning to wonder, who's next? The heavenly family that God was gathering was rapidly growing. My heart was broken. We would all miss him and his playful way with Charlie.

All these recent deaths were people directly related to Charlie. Without him, we would have never known any of them. Although I feared that these events were happening too fast, I recognized that it was all an adaptation for my own separation from Charlie.

8 THREE DOWNS TO SCORE THE MOST

Charles had sent job applications out in Louisville and Lexington. By August, he accepted a job as a chemist in Louisville. At this time, a lot of decisions had to be made. We needed to search for a new parish, new schools and a house. I would need to transfer my job. As a Tupperware manager, I would be required to work twice as much in order to get reestablished in a new city. This would require recruiting and training a new team in order to keep my manager car and the full-time income. Most importantly, there was Charlie's health to consider.

At the most recent heart checkup, we were told that his first cardiac shunt was no longer holding up with his growth. Charlie would be facing another heart surgery soon. Once again, it would be quite risky. We would wait until absolutely necessary.

I thought long and hard about my options. I had so many things to consider. The need to work and the need to be home were constantly balanced in my mind. Again, I had to find a way to do both without giving up my limited time with Charlie.

Driving into Louisville, we quickly found a house, a parish, and schools for the children. Jackie was enrolled in the third grade at St. Gabriel School. For fear of rejection, we didn't inquire about Charlie. It seemed best that we should accept his limitations and locate a school for the handicapped. Hawthorne Elementary offered a program that we believed to be appropriate. He would be taking a bus to and from school, getting home around 4:15 P.M. He could receive speech therapy at the school as well.

I considered his schedule and his upcoming surgery. I questioned myself about what I should do. I presented the facts to God. I knew the seriousness of the pending operation. I wanted to be home with Charlie as much as possible. If I were to transfer my Tupperware job, I would be gone more. With his getting home so late, I would only have, at most, two hours a night with him before leaving for work. This was not satisfactory to me. I valued my time with my children more than anything else in the world.

Considering all possibilities, I recalled an offer I had the year before. I had a hobby of making specialty cakes. I had taught myself this by way of a booklet and tips from my friend Kathy. My sister had convinced me to make her wedding cake. As I had never made one before, I advised her that it was a foolish request. Ignoring this, she persisted until I agreed to learn how to make it. Once the challenge was presented to me, I was motivated. We were carried away with ideas and the result was a huge, four-tier cake with a fountain of water flowing above the second tier. She loved it. I was pleased that it didn't fall from the vibration of the band playing. Even the caterer who cut the cake was impressed. She had asked me to go into business with her at the time. I couldn't very well do it because I lived about eighty miles away. She instructed me to call her if I ever moved back to Louisville. Bingo. "That's what I can do." I said to myself. I'll start a career in cake decorating. It's something I greatly enjoy plus I can work out of my home.

Giving up Tupperware, however, was not an easy decision. I had earned many gifts along with my income. Driving a new car was a luxury resulting from the job as well. After one year, I had caught up on all medical bills from the time of Charlie's birth. I knew that I would be abandoning a good thing and taking a gamble on the unknown. When I looked at the total picture, Charlie was all I could focus on. My time with him was so precious, that nothing else mattered.

We moved at the end of August. Charles started his new job. Jackie and Charlie started school. Marty helped me unpack as Leslie was kept occupied watching all the activity. She was a content and happy baby who was very easy to please.

Right away, I contacted the caterer. She told me that she was no longer in the business since her divorce. Hearing my disappointment, she gave me some pointers on starting my own business. She encouraged me to go ahead with my plans.

With time being the most valuable asset I had, I didn't want to waste any of it. I had business cards made. I planned a "Cake and Candy Tasting Party." I invited everyone I knew. I told them to bring all their friends. People thought I had lost my mind. They never heard of a party like this before. I instructed everyone that there would be nothing at this party to buy. They were to come see my work, eat all kinds of goodies, win door prizes, and take home my business cards for future use. They searched for a catch, but found none. So, they came. And then more came. They continued to come until the house was full. Every room and hallway was occupied. Everyone mingled, laughed and had a great time. They ate cakes, confections, and peanut brittle, to name a few offerings. When they left, my cards went with them. My name was now known throughout the city. Calls started coming in regularly. My business grew overnight. I had also donated a few cakes to the schools and the bus drivers to assist in spreading the word.

I was so thankful to God for allowing me to be home with the children. I thought it was wonderful how He had prepared me for this with my training in Tupperware. Once again, I was introduced to many people. Again, I noticed how touched people were when they came to my home and saw my children. They were drawn to Charlie. He was so full of expression and joy. They watched how he moved about in his short leg braces. Their hearts were touched.

Being new in the neighborhood, Jackie set out with Charlie and Marty to meet the children across the street. They were invited to swing in the back yard. Upon reaching the gate, the boy stopped Charlie and said that he couldn't come in. With disgust, Jackie propped her hands on her hips and demanded, "He can too come in. He's just like you and me. If he can't play then, we aren't playing either." With that the boy backed down and let him inside the yard. In no time he became a close friend of Charlie's. He no longer noticed his handicap.

As time passed, Charlie was beginning to notice that Marty could run quite fast. He would come in with his mouth dropped saying, "I wish I could run and play football." I assured him that he could play football. The neighbors often came over and got a game started. He was always included. Then he added, "I wish I could run like Marty. It broke his heart because his desire to play was so great. In his mind, he knew every play. If only his body could play the way his mind knew the game, he would be a pro player in training.

That fall, he was deeply involved in watching Notre Dame. He cheered them on by himself one day, as Charles was out cutting the grass. Charlie would run to the door and give an update to his dad. Then, suddenly, Notre Dame fell behind. He was in total disbelief. At six-years-old, he had never seen Notre Dame lose. He was devastated. He went to the door sobbing uncontrollably. Charles rushed in to see what was the matter. Charlie could barely get the words out of his mouth. Finally, he gasped, "Notre Dame lost." We felt crushed for him. His dream of becoming quarterback for Notre Dame was shattered. I didn't think he'd ever get over it. He didn't understand the concept of losing because he'd never seen it happen to his team before. We talked to him about the joy of the game and that losing was okay. Losing creates a challenge to improve. He listened with a broken heart. It would obviously take time to heal.

Back at school, things were going well. He enjoyed the challenge and his new teacher. Unfortunately, she needed to take a maternity leave after Christmas. We anticipated a sad loss.

By January, Charlie became short of breath far more often than usual. He struggled to get around. He used his wheelchair more and walked less. At home, he crawled up the three steps from the family room to the kitchen, in our tri-level home. Charles and I always toted him around piggyback to conserve his energy. At bedtime, all the kids got a piggyback ride or two up the stairs. It never failed that by the time the fourth one made it to bed, one or two slipped downstairs to take in another ride. Charles and I didn't mind at all. It made bedtime fun.

Although we encouraged Charlie to do much for himself, we were carefully observant of his health. We were cautious to never let him become over exerted. We either carried him or pushed him in his wheelchair for distances. There was a constant awareness to conserve his energy. Once within boundaries, he set his own limits. It was not unusual to see him stop and rest.

Winter was always hard on Charlie. Cyanosis, shortness of breath, headaches, and chest pain were increasing. It was obvious that he couldn't hold out much longer without surgery. It didn't come as a surprise when Dr. Cottrill scheduled it for February.

Charles and I discussed with the children Charlie's need to have surgery. It was presented simply and encouragingly.

I explained to them that Charlie was always short of breath. He was exhausted even from walking within the house. Marty, being as fast as he was, found it a little difficult to understand. So, I told him to go outside and run as fast as he could until he was so tired that he couldn't run anymore. Then, come back inside and we'd see how short of breath he was. This he did. When he came in huffing and puffing, I could point out to him that this is how Charlie feels all day. It gave him a better understanding of how Charlie felt. He was well aware of his heavy breathing. It could always be heard throughout the house.

Jackie carried her thoughts about the surgery one step further. At school, in the third grade, she was assigned to draw pictures of the seven sacraments. Her pictures were similar to the rest of the children's with one exception. It was on the sacrament of Extreme Unction. This being the sacrament of last rights for the sick and the dying, most children drew an elderly person in a hospital bed. Not Jackie. Hers was a picture of a 10-year-old boy, Carl, in a casket surrounded by beautiful flowers. (Carl was the adopted child of Dr. Cottrill's who died of heart disease the previous year.) This picture prompted much discussion. Jackie had a very real feeling of death. She shared her thoughts and questions about Charlie's heart disease. If Carl died of heart disease, then so would Charlie. I had to explain the differences of the two diseases they shared. We discussed what was the same about them as well. As complicated as heart disease is for adults to understand, I wasn't certain that she understood what I was saying. God was always there for me, giving me the words to relate to my children. When our conversation ended, I was pleased to be able to answer her questions. Jackie was scared for her brother, but she had hope after we talked.

One day Charlie struggled up the steps to the kitchen and said, "Mom, I can't wait to go to the hospital." I couldn't believe what I was hearing. I asked him why he was anxious to go. He said, "So I can feel better." I just hugged him and suppressed my tears. I was obligated to be strong, for his sake. He had to depend on my strength and I knew it. He trusted that all would be better. I wasn't so certain.

As time drew near, Doris and Polly (his bus drivers) presented Charlie with a Bible Storybook. They both had become very fond of Charlie. I saw that Doris was holding back her tears when she dropped him off on his last day. Polly said her good-bye and moved to the back of the bus. My heart went out to them. I was moved to see that they cared so much.

We drove back to Lexington for the surgery. It was difficult leaving the other children behind with relatives and friends. Not only did I need to be with Charlie, I felt a need to be with them as well. I wanted to be there for them when they had questions, but it was out of my control.

Once we were admitted, Dr. Cottrill and Dr. Todd explained, in detail, the plan. They intended to place a systemic to pulmonary artery Gortex shunt, which would allow more red blood, or oxygenated blood, to circulate.

Once again, I prayed for God's will. Knowing the uncertainty of his future, I couldn't begin to guess what was best for Charlie. It was much harder to trust in God's judgment now than it was in the past. There were more children involved. There were more people to be hurt if God decided to take him. I was very uncomfortable about leaving it up to Him without adding my own will.

I prayed long and hard to Our Blessed Mother for some spiritual motherly consolation. I prayed for her to guide me through this suffering of my son. I prepared for the moment that Charlie would be taken away from me, into the hands of the doctors. I pictured the closing of the doors to the operating room, where I would be separated from him. I asked Mary what it was like for her to watch her son being taken away.

Each time I asked her a question, I knew that her suffering and her son's suffering were far greater than what we were facing. Her son was not sedated. Her son did not have the comfort of drugs and a hospital bed. Mary did not even have her husband next to her. I felt she was answering all of my questions.

She answered me with love and compassion. She showed me how blessed we actually were, even in this time of suffering. We had good doctors trying to save Charlie, not soldiers trying to kill him. The doctors were going to be doing everything possible to make him comfortable with medicine; not everything possible to cause him pain with torture. She didn't point these differences out to belittle Charlie's surgery and suffering but to make it apparent how much God loves us. She manifested to me that just as God the Father was with Jesus and with her, so too would He be with Charlie and our family in our suffering. She truly understood. She comforted my thoughts. She encouraged me to continue to pray for God's will. This would be the only way that I could understand whatever was to take place.

The evening before surgery, Dr. Todd spoke to us about having a 50% chance of survival with surgery. Without surgery, there was no chance for survival. We were as prepared as possible. We tried to remain strong and give assurance to Charlie that God would take good care of him. He remained hesitantly cheerful. We played together and prayed together. Charles and I told him that we would be waiting for him while he was in surgery. Being brave, he refrained from crying. However, tears gently fell from his eyes as he spoke of his fear of the operation. He wanted to be sure that he wouldn't die. I reminded him that God helped Dr. Todd to save his life once before when he was a baby. I spoke to him with positive expectations and he was consoled. He was never fully aware of the risk involved. After our talk, he believed that God would protect him because "Mom said so." He had the advantage of youthful innocence. He believed what he was told and didn't dwell on his suffering.

In the morning he became worried that he might have to miss "The Dukes Of Hazzard" TV show on Friday night. Dr. Cottrill promised him that he would be out in time to watch it.

He had another fear of the mask used to put him to sleep. To make him happy, he was sedated by injection. He had complete trust in all involved.

Charles and I said our good-byes to Charlie in the pre-op area. Charlie fought the medication to stay awake as long as he could. He was determined not to miss out on 30 seconds of time with us. He had a strong will that carried him through the most difficult times. We kissed him good-bye and wiped our eyes as we left the room.

Charlie was never left alone with a stranger in the hospital. By now, he was well known by all the staff. The U of K Medical Center was our second home. Suzanne, the patient care coordinator, was always at his side when we were not allowed to be with him. She teased with him just as we would. She made him comfortable. He never cried for Mom or Dad. It was her consolation that gave Charlie the strength that he needed when we weren't around. As parents, we were comforted by the helpers that God had sent us.

Once the surgery was complete, we were given the typical report that was fairly consistent with each of his other surgeries. He was doing well. Things looked good as far as we could tell. We were told that the next 24 hours would be critical. We never knew what complications might arise. Charlie had been treated prophylactically for possible seizures. Fortunately, it worked. We didn't encounter any this time. When we were allowed to see him, we noticed that all looked well. He remained on the respirator and oxygen as expected while coming off of the anesthetic.

The next morning, we visited him in the Intensive Care Unit. On observation, I noticed how blue he looked. Charles agreed. I reassured Charlie of our presence and gave him encouragement to hang in there. Leaving the room with Dr. Cottrill, I said to her, "He looks more blue now than he did before surgery." She agreed by saying that they had just discussed the same thing. They planned to take him back to the cardiac lab for another heart catheterization. They needed to know what was going on. They suspected that the shunt that had been put in had clotted off.

Dr. Cottrill invited me to go to noonday Mass with her. I recalled all the weekday Masses that I had gone to daily with my parents as I was growing up. It sounded like a good idea. I found that I enjoyed being with her at Mass. Our prayers to God were united. I felt strength in being on the same team. It gave me hope. I was only able to go because Charles had waited at the hospital with Charlie. Knowing that he was with him eliminated my fear of leaving. When we returned, a peace was with us.

The catheteriaztion was done that afternoon. Their fears were confirmed. It was explained that Heparin had been given at the start of surgery, to prevent clotting. Then, upon finishing, a reverse medication was given to stop the bleeding. It was felt that his system could not handle the normal amount of medication. To correct the problem, a repeat surgery would be necessary. Dr. Todd would need to evacuate the clot, then redo the surgery. This was now scheduled for the next morning.

I called home several times to check on the children and to update the relatives on what was happening. It wasn't easy, once again, to make a major setback sound like a minor one to the children. Trying to mother them from a long distance was the most difficult part. Their emotions fluctuated along with ours when they heard that their brother had to go back to surgery. I told them to keep praying for Charlie. I told them how important it was because the prayers of children are God's favorite prayers. I trusted that God would guide me with words that they would understand. I believe He did.

The next morning came. Charlie had been kept moderately sedated from the last surgery. Our good-byes were one sided that day because he was unable to respond. It was an awkward feeling.

Surgery ended sometime after 1:00 P.M. Suzanne came to get Charles and me in the waiting room. We were asked to go to Dr. Todd's office for a consultation. Realizing that it probably sounded critical, Suzanne assured us that Charlie was O.K. However, there was a problem that needed to be discussed. Sensing my escalating emotions, she hugged me. All three of us choked up as we attempted to lighten the air. Why should we be surprised to hear that there was a problem? Charlie didn't seem to know of another way. We contemplated what unforeseen complication he might be experiencing this time. He never went by the books. We agreed that he must have not been getting enough attention. The three of us laughed and cried and hugged. We proceeded down the endless hallway with the knots in our stomachs.

We waited briefly for Dr. Todd to come and share the latest. He said that this time he gave the smallest dose possible of the reverse medication to stop the bleeding. In doing so, he clotted off immediately in the same place in the shunt. He would not be able to live like this. Therefore, he needed to repeat the surgery again. Because there was no smaller amount of medication possible to give, he planned not to give any. This meant that Charlie would either hemorrhage or he would stop bleeding on his own, the latter being most unlikely. There was no real choice in the matter. Whatever the consequences, one thing was certain. He couldn't live with this clot in the shunt. It was a must to start the procedure again.

We did not waste time making a decision. We knew what had to be done. Again, we signed consent forms for surgery. Dr. Todd directed us to the doctors' lounge for greater comfort while we waited.

The third operation began. We made a few phone calls to inform the family. It was becoming more and more difficult to talk. As I dialed the numbers, my throat became so tight that I couldn't speak. I'd hang up and try again later. Only after numerous attempts, I was finally able to keep the phone to my ear and pass the information to my parents. Charles was able to reach his parents. That's all we could do.

Charles and I consoled one another. Mostly, we were silent. Our thoughts were held in mainly because of the pain. Words would not come out. As I reflected on Charlie's life, I thought of all the wonderful people we had met through him. I saw the smiling faces of strangers, of neighbors, of relatives, of acquaintances. I envisioned the reactions of others. Most everyone I visualized smiled as a response to Charlie's bright disposition. Endless faces crossed my mind. I saw the good brought out in not-so-friendly people.

I pictured Charlie's success. All that he had learned in such a short time brought a smile to my heart. I felt so blessed at his accomplishments. Each and every thing he learned had made him into a happy child. I thought of his love for life itself in comparison to those who miss it. He had been blessed in spite of his suffering. Being a part of his life was a blessing for me as well. I thought of the special family that God had prepared for him in heaven.

I spoke to Jesus for a while in prayer, meditating on His passion. I noticed that Charlie was following His path. Charlie had just fallen for the third time with the weight of his cross over the last two days. The question was: Would he be able to get up again after this third operation as Jesus did after His third fall? Were we near the end where the crucifixion would take place? This ultimate result appeared inevitable to me. I had no idea when it might take place. I understood that I would not know the day or the hour.

With the outcome looking so uncertain, my parents came to be with us. The waiting was becoming more unbearable. We received word that he was out of surgery late that evening. Dr. Cottrill had come out to tell us and console us. We waited for word from Dr. Todd. At 10:00 P.M., he shared the news that Charlie was now hemorrhaging. Dr. Todd addressed his concerns as we listened helplessly. He explained that if he were to give the medication again, he would obviously clot off again. This would only put us back where we were earlier. Thus, it was not an option. He was bleeding quite a bit. Dr. Todd did not expect it to slow down enough for it to make a difference. He went on to explain that he was now forced to consider a fourth operation. He had begun these last three surgeries with an incision through the sternum. This next one, however, would require him to enter from an incision made across his side. He needed to get to the other side of the heart and attempt a completely different operation. He voiced his concern about this because, if he did this operation, it would definitely be his last one. This surgery would ruin any chance of correction in the future. He stated, "We have to take what we can get now." Charlie was in there bleeding to death and we all knew it. Dr. Todd instructed me to call into the operating room in a half-hour. His partner was at Charlie's bedside keeping a close watch on him. I was to ask him if the bleeding had slowed down. Dr. Todd looked wiped out. He said he was running home to eat dinner and would return with the intention of going back to surgery. If by some miracle, the bleeding slowed on its own, he would not have to go back in.

He left. Dr. Cottrill looked at me and said, "Mary Jo, I'm going home to pray. There's nothing else I can do here." I walked her to the door. We hugged then she left. Sick with grief, I sat down by myself and spoke to God. I said to Him, "Look at all the people whom Charlie has touched in his short life. You know, we've just moved into St. Gabriel's Parish six months ago. We're just now getting to know some people there. With a parish as large as this, I find it hard to believe that Charlie's time would be up now. Just look at all the people there that he could have an impact on. I know he could bring more good out of them if given a chance." I spoke more about the progress that he had made. As if He needed reminding, I mentioned, "Charlie has only been walking on his own for a year now. Couldn't he have some time to play? He's talked about playing T-ball. He loves sports so much. He thrives on the desire to play sports. Couldn't You give him some time to be normal?" At the same time I pondered these questions in my heart, I realized the fearful reality of the near future that I might be asking for. I pleaded with God, "Please don't let him have another stroke. That would be such a horrible setback." I begged repeatedly at that point for God not to allow that to happen. Reality reminded me that his life would be so different if brain damage should occur. I found myself back where I started with my prayers. Knowing that my desires may not come about even if he should live, I prayed for God's holy will. I asked for the strength to accept His will, understanding that He knows best.

I began to pace the floor. My mind had become almost numb. I had said all that I could say to God. Now, I must wait. I was shaking. My complete mind and body were subdued with anguish. Tightness in my throat and a twisted stomach controlled me. Very suddenly, I was hit with a profound bolt that flashed through my body with sharpness and clarity, from my head down to my toes. As it passed through my heart, a message was left there. The message was, "He will live." This whole event lasted probably about a second. A peace came over me. I knew, without hesitation, that it was The Holy Spirit answering my prayer. It happened so quickly; I wasn't sure what it meant. I wanted Him to come back and tell me more. I found myself asking God,

"What does this mean? Does it mean he will or won't be having another surgery? What about a stroke? Is he going to be okay when it's all over? Will he be bedridden?" I was more confused now than ever, but I was certain of having heard that one powerful message: "He will live." There was such peace in my heart. The knots in my stomach disappeared. There was tremendous relief. With that, I knew that whatever happened, God would help me to deal with it. I didn't mention to anyone what had just happened. They would think I was hallucinating. People had always wondered about how I handle crisis situations so calmly. They were not aware of my prayer line with God. This was a personal thing with me that I didn't feel comfortable sharing with others.

Knowing that in one half-hour a decision would be made for surgery, my mother suggested that we pray the rosary. I couldn't. During the most stressful times I could never say any type of patented prayer. I had to talk things over with God. I felt a desperate need to spend time alone with Charles. I knew I should tell him what I had been told. We left the room and walked down the hall a short way. My parents stayed behind to pray.

After a short distance, I stopped Charles to tell him. I didn't know how to say it because I had always kept these things to myself. We embraced. I told him simply that I felt God tell me that Charlie was going to live. I'm not certain of the words I used. The Holy Spirit helped me, I'm sure. I do recall saying that although God told me he would live, I wasn't at all sure about the next operation or what complications we still had to face. I remember trying to word it carefully so that he would feel the comfort that I felt. I said that the only thing of which I was certain was the message that he will live. I sensed some hope from Charles.

We returned eventually to the waiting room. At 10:30 P.M., I called the operating room as instructed. I was told that he was still hemorrhaging a great deal. Reluctantly, they decided to give him another half-hour.

Charles and I held hands and supported each other. My thoughts were on what was to come. At 11:00 P.M., I called again, afraid to hear that things had not changed. I was right. He was still bleeding too much. Something was holding the doctors back. "Let's try another half-hour," I was told.

This happened at 11:30, 12:00, and 12:30. Each time, they agreed that he was bleeding too much. Each time, something was holding them back. Finally, at 1:00 A.M., the doctor on the phone said, "I think he's going to make it." I felt that the words had come from heaven. They agreed to let us come back and see him. With all that had happened, I knew that my prayers had been answered.

We went back to see him. He looked terrible and he looked wonderful. He was pale and full of tubes, IVs, and respirator. Yet, he was alive. That was all that was promised. I was so moved by the course of events from the day.

In reflecting on my experience with the Holy Spirit, I realized that I had never thought to pray to Him before. I recognized Him instantly. Until then, I had no idea of His tremendous power within each of us.

This acknowledgment opened a new prayer line to heaven for me. I came to know The Holy Spirit and began to include Him in my prayers giving equal regard to each of the three Divine Persons of the Most Holy Trinity.

After visiting with Charlie and seeing that he was stabilized, we went to Dr. Cottrill's house to get some rest. The morning came. No calls from the hospital had come in. Dr. Cottrill called for reassurance of his condition. All was well. Charles and I went to visit him every time we were allowed, which was about every four hours. At noon, Dr. Cottrill and I went to Mass. It was so comforting to know that God was there for us. We began going together whenever possible.

With all the stress over the past few days, it didn't astonish me when I began to feel ill. I was unable to eat well. I hadn't rested enough. My immune system was understandably not up to par. I was so nauseated that I couldn't function. I had to get well fast so that I could be there for Charlie when he got better. My friend Judy determined that I might be pregnant. I was certain that wasn't the case. I got a prescription for nausea and tried to regain my strength.

As Charlie became more alert, he was weaned of the respirator. Once removed, his throat was extremely sore. He told me of his pain in a factual manner, then immediately returned to his smiling face.

He was beginning to receive cards with gifts of money. He asked me if he could leave the hospital to go to the store. He wanted to get something for himself and for Marty. I offered to go for him, as he was still in intensive care. He sent me on a mission to find him a robe so that he could go watch "The Dukes of Hazzard" as Dr. Cottrill had promised. He wanted to get one for Marty, too. His disappointment was written on his face as his mouth dropped saying, "I don't have enough for Jackie." I consoled him and assured him that Jackie would understand. Jackie already had a robe anyway. He asked me to pick up some candy for her with the rest of his money.

Venturing out, I found a Spiderman robe and a "Dukes of Hazzard" robe for the two boys. Charlie was thrilled. He couldn't wait to put it on and get out of the bed. With chest tubes in place draining, as well as other paraphernalia, it didn't look like he'd be going anywhere soon. That Friday morning, Charlie reminded Dr. Cottrill that "The Dukes" were coming on tonight. Now, there was no television in the PICU (pediatric intensive care unit). The original plan was to have one operation and be out of PICU by Friday. We did not explain to Charlie that he had had three major heart operations and nearly died. His mind was set on living.

Dr. Cottrill pulled me to the side and devised a plan. Knowing that he was not well enough to leave ICU, she would try something else. Officially, he was Dr. Todd's patient as he was the surgeon. However, being the conservative doctor that a surgeon needs to be, he would probably not go along with taking Charlie out of PICU early in order to watch a TV show.

On the other hand, being mothers, we knew that this would be a wonderful healing tool. So, Dr. Cottrill ordered a nurse to sneak Charlie through the back hallways over to the clinic that evening. There were TVs in the waiting area and the clinic would be closed.

It was a great adventure. Each of us carried IVs, monitors, or drainage containers and pushed his bed from PICU over to the clinic. We laughed all the way. We were instructed to hurry right back before Dr. Todd finds him missing. Charlie had so much fun. We pretended the bed was the General Lee car. I must admit we were a little nervous that a serious problem might surface while over there. Charlie's record for strange complications put him at great risk. It was a relief to the nurse and to me that we made it back without incident. Dr. Cottrill called to make sure we made it back safely, as well. She was glad that our mission to raise his spirits had been completed successfully.

Charlie went on to recover from his surgery. Charles returned to Louisville to care for the other children. When he arrived at home, he notified the friend who was watching the children. He was told that Marty had broken out in a rash. Arriving at their home, he discovered Marty's body was covered with whelps, redness, swelling, and itching. He was told that the children had been taken to a place in the park and were allowed to wade in the creek.

Immediately, he rushed Marty and Jackie to the doctor to determine what they had been exposed to. Being a chemist with great environmental interests, he was well aware of the horrifying parasites and other oddities found in creek water. He insisted on every sort of test to be ordered. Marty was given steroids and Jackie had parasites taken off of her body. Fortunately, Leslie had not been taken into the water.

Hearing this news while in Lexington made me feel helpless and somewhat guilty. The forces around me were constantly testing my motherhood. Naturally, I wanted to be with all the children. Yet, I could see what a good father the kids had and felt great comfort that he could handle these trials.

Several days later, Charles brought the kids to Lexington to visit their brother. Marty looked ghastly to me with his little face so puffy and his body covered with whelps. Charles assured me that he was looking better. My imagination could not comprehend how horrid he must have looked a few days earlier.

Within two weeks, Charlie was doing well enough to come home. Needless to say, everyone was excitedly looking forward to resuming our routine.

After getting settled in, I decided to check my calendar to see if it was possible that I may be pregnant. The thought had stayed with me since Judy had mentioned it. Sure enough, my nausea and weakness were explained. Maybe I wasn't stressed, after all. I was just pregnant. I laughed to myself. Looking up to heaven I said, "I guess we can do it."

Part II

9

THE HOME TEAM

Recovering rather well from surgery, Charlie's mind quickly turned to his upcoming birthday. Hearing how anxious he was about seeing his friends, I decided to have a party for him. It was important to go all out for this party because it was a celebration of life as well as of a birthday. The likeliness of his recovery going so well was not anticipated after the string of events in the hospital. Making goody bags and planning games were a pleasure.

The joy that I experienced in preparing for the party was a testimony of my gratitude for another day of his life. A special "Dukes of Hazzard" cake was placed in the center of the table. Every child in his class was invited, along with his former teacher and new baby. A parent came with each handicapped child. One mother revealed to me that her child had never been to a birthday party for a friend before. Our discussion led me to understand that most of the other children had not been to parties outside of their own families, either. Young faces filled with such excitement were a delight to watch. It was obviously a rare opportunity.

Charlie soon returned to a half day at school. Doing well after a week, he moved on to a full day. The year was about over when I realized how far behind in school he happened to be. He had not learned how to read as I had expected. Not only had he lost about six weeks of school due to surgery, but also the substitute teacher was not trained for special needs. She tried hard but did not understand that the children were capable of doing more. Therefore, without the challenge, they did not progress much. It was hard on her and the children. It became apparent that Charlie was not prepared for the second grade. Yet, I hated to see him repeat the first. After years of preparation, I had hoped that he would be up to par.

Plans for summer were underway as his former teacher, Mrs. Lewis, insisted on tutoring him weekly. Concerned about his falling behind, she taught phonics and reading from her home. Because she lived about forty minutes away, I took the other children to the park while we waited for the completion of his session. She was a tremendous help. We also began speech therapy at the Easter Seal Society office downtown that was forty minutes away as well. Each week, we reviewed the concepts at home in order not to lose ground.

In contemplating the next school year, I decided to approach the principal of St. Gabriel about the possibility of Charlie's going to school with Jackie. Until now, I thought that he would be turned away because of the attitude of the Catholic school in Lexington. However, after this setback, I was no longer shy about asking. He needed to be more challenged.

I notified the principal, Mr. Huelsman, to explain the circumstances and found him willing to give it a try. We were all looking forward to experiencing a normal year with all three of the children in one school. Life would be less complicated and the family unity would be stronger by sharing school activities together.

With the start of summer, life had to include more than studies. My neighbor invited me to sign Charlie up for T-ball at her Baptist church. I thought that this would never go over because of his braces and the fact that he could barely run. Insisting that everyone was just terrific with the kids, she assured me that he would be welcome. She even went so far as to talk to the person in charge and explain the heart disease and the short leg braces.

In spite of it all, he was invited to join. What a tremendous breakthrough. I thanked God for giving him the opportunity to play. Charlie was so elated. You would think that he had been accepted on a pro team by the way that he acted.

Charlie took sports seriously. Although he was always laughing, he wanted to make sure that things were done just right. He had watched enough sports in the last seven years that he knew exactly what he should wear. Proper attire was required to set the mood. He could not agree with wearing shorts to play ball because he had never seen a "REAL" ball player in shorts. He needed white ball pants, which we were able to find at a consignment shop. Next, he recognized the importance of wearing a batting glove, so that he could hit the ball farther. We ordered one right away from a bubble gum wrapper special offer. He planned in his mind how to play most effectively to win the game. Knowing that he could not run fast, his only hope was to hit the ball as far as possible. Immediately, he realized something was missing when he got up to bat. Batters should be cautious about getting hit with the ball. All the "REAL" players wore batting helmets. Therefore, we picked up one at a yard sale to make his dream come true.

When Charlie got up to bat, he was the most determined child that I had ever seen. Taking a tip from his dad, he learned how to hit down the third baseline in order to allow himself more time to get on base. He swung the bat with all of his might, skillfully hitting the ball toward third base. With a wide smile he took off running at full speed. The corrective shoes, with braces up to his knees, did not hinder the effort. He did not allow his partially stiff right leg to deter his will. The fact that this leg had been drawn up into his hip since the spinal surgery didn't matter. The imbalance of having one leg shorter than the other did not extinguish the fire in his soul. Running with a limp was insignificant. His short, stubby feet with high insteps provided a constant pain that was momentarily forgotten. The coach, seeing him struggle, pulled the base in closer for him. When he reached first base, everyone cheered, even the other team. The coaches then huddled and agreed that it would only be fair to bring all the bases in halfway when he would get up to bat. It was obviously going to take him twice as long to go the distance than it would any other child.

Knowing how much energy this was taking from him made it more difficult for me to watch. Yet, the smile on his face made it all worthwhile. Being preoccupied with eyes on Charlie, I wasn't aware of the crowd. Someone pointed out the parents of the other team to me. They gave him a standing ovation. A dad got up and left the bleachers wiping his eyes. People were touched. I was touched by witnessing the power of God working. Charlie didn't get it. He figured everyone was simply cheering because of the great play that he had made. He didn't notice that he was different from any other players. Rather, he was proud to be like the other kids.

This normalcy enhanced his character all the more. The more normally he was treated, the more normal he felt, and the more he stood out among the rest. Strangers witnessed his determination to keep up with the other children. Being treated as such kept him happy. Self-esteem and inner joy were deepened, bringing about a bright smile and sparkling eyes, inevitably attracting people to him.

The summer was too short. Frequent outings with the kids to various parks made the time go too fast. Between our adventures, I continued making wedding cakes and party cakes, and kept my business actively growing. Weekends were spent mostly enjoying our home together, relaxing after cakes were delivered. Then, occasionally we ventured out as a family to explore historical sites in Kentucky. Boredom never struck the household.

Each year, we saved our pennies for an all-day vacation to Santa Claus Land in Indiana. This having become a family tradition, the children eagerly looked forward to this occasion. With vacation not being in the budget, the children were all willing to help with a yard sale to raise money for the event.

As August closed the summer fun, the children found school registration to be particularly exciting this year. Jackie was now a fourth grader whose motherly instincts had never diminished. She sensed a responsibility to her siblings, and was always ready to protect them. It was obvious that she would enjoy being the oldest in the family at St. Gabriel.

As we passed through the registration lines and met with the teachers, I could see that Charlie was delighted at the chance to be there. Being accepted in this school reinforced his sense of normalcy. Nothing in the world thrilled him more than being accepted, not even football.

Although Marty would not turn five until November, it was obvious that he was ready for structured learning. I gathered this from watching his mind work at home. One day he was inspired to take a fan apart to determine what made it work. He was quite fast and was able to do this while I was working in another room.

With this type of readiness to learn, he was enrolled in kindergarten as the youngest in the class.

Getting adjusted to everyone's leaving home was not easy for Leslie. Jackie and Charlie began first. Then, after a few days, kindergarten began. She cried in disbelief when we dropped Marty off for the first time. There was no one her size left at home to play with. A little reminder that she would soon have a baby to play with was helpful.

Prior to school's starting, I had inquired about the possibility of their taking the school bus. The bus route, however, traveled along the outskirts of our subdivision. Knowing that it was impossible for Charlie to walk the distance, I gently pleaded with the company for consideration. I pointed out a way to change their route so that the bus could pass by our street. They were reluctant to make changes and denied my request.

I had searched for a possible carpool to no avail. The anticipation of my daily routine once the baby came was overwhelming, as I was not looking forward to spending much of my day in the car. Without transportation to school, I would be driving back and forth three times a day; taking Jackie and Charlie at 8:00 A.M., taking Marty at 12:00 P.M., and picking them all up at 3:00 P.M.

I devised a plan. Charlie had a so-called "extra" wheelchair that was extremely lightweight. It looked like a large umbrella-type stroller, which proved to be convenient and compact. However, I didn't care to use it because it was humiliating to him. Therefore I only brought it out in desperate situations. After speaking with Jackie, she agreed to push him home from the bus stop, which was a good distance away. This would eliminate my concern for taking the baby in and out three times a day. She jumped at the opportunity to be a helpful sister, thinking it would be fun. So, I called the bus company and asked permission to put the stroller on the bus. It must have made them a bit uncomfortable because after careful consideration, they decided to alter the bus route. They agreed to come down the main street passing my house, if I promised to get Charlie to the bus from the court. This was absolutely wonderful because I really did not want Jackie to have this responsibility, anyway.

God's assistance was plainly seen by the way that He persuaded some and protected others. This one kind deed affected so many people. All the children were being protected. Jackie would not be responsible for Charlie and the safety of Marty. Charlie was spared humiliation. Leslie would not have to be awakened from her nap to pick up everyone. The baby, due in October, would not be spending the day in the car. My cake business would have fewer interruptions. Finally, Charles would have less stress worrying about how I was managing while he was at work. In actuality, the ripple effect was even greater, I'm sure. The feeling of God's protection and providence was sensational.

Our house was two from the corner, which was too far for Charlie to walk. He would generally get quite short of breath at one house length. Therefore, we found it best for him to ride his bike to the bus stop and I would bring it back home. An occasional push along the way would keep him from getting too exhausted. We found this to be convenient as well as less humiliating than the wheelchair. Children often asked why he used training wheels. A simple explanation was given about the metal rods in his back. Being unable to bend, he could not keep his balance. This answer always satisfied their curiosity and prevented any temptation to tease him about it.

Mostly, people did not notice what he was incapable of doing. Some thought it was a novel idea. The routine stimulated his self-confidence. I always told Charlie that if we looked hard enough, we could find a way for him to do the things he wanted to do. I would not allow him to give up easily and therefore, we made accommodations in every situation.

When he arrived at school, an eighth-grade boy would piggyback him from the bus to his classroom. After school he was helped again. The principal, the teachers, and the bus driver were each conscious of conserving his energy and were very caring toward him.

The school year soon began with everything falling into place. I found myself in a good daily routine and I was drawn to attend daily Mass more and more. Marty and Leslie went with me and I frequently discussed the gospel stories on the way home. I was attracted to the soul of the pastor, as were many others. Fr. Caster spoke to the school children with such love; it amazed me. He spoke to the parents about the gems that they had been given. His love for children was so profound that his words touched my heart deeply. I was so greatly moved by his insight that I anxiously looked forward to attending Mass the next day.

With the Bread of Life within me, I was able to face the challenges of the day. I began by filling cake orders. Baking began early. From there, I raced through the bathing of children, cleaning house, doing laundry, fixing lunch, taking Marty to kindergarten, preparing dinner, shopping for groceries, and running other necessary errands. Cakes were in and out of the oven throughout the day. The children enjoyed watching me decorate cakes and getting ready for the new baby. Joyful music continued to inspire me as a mother, wife, and homemaker. In the afternoon Leslie and I would walk to the corner with Charlie's bike, and we would meet the kids at the bus stop.

With coaxing, the children shared their experiences from the day. A light snack and homework followed. Marty observed my helping the others with their homework. Once, he asked me to explain his assignment. As I began to read the instructions on the paper, he suddenly withdrew his request saying, "Oh never mind, Mom. I forgot. You didn't go to kindergarten." He figured that I would not know how to do the work. Those funny things that the children would say would often make me reflect on Fr. Caster's teachings. He frequently referred to children as treasures. I could see it right before my eyes. I had a house full of treasures and one on the way.

On October 18, 1982, our son Jonathan was born. The children couldn't wait to get home from school on the day he was expected home from the hospital. Their hearts and eyes gleamed with joy as they took turns holding the baby and fussing over him. Such a tremendous blessing it was to have another baby in the house.

On the contrary, it seemed as though the world around me thought otherwise. Opinionated people informed me that I was irresponsible, inconsiderate, immature, or selfish in having so many children. Comments came from all directions when I was pregnant. Some joked about my being crazy as they wondered how I could take care of all these children and deal with Charlie's constant needs as well. Others felt that I was irresponsible by not using birth control. A few people thought I was inconsiderate of my husband by imposing all these children on him. Still others implied immaturity, because I was not thinking of the future of my children. There was one person who said I was being selfish. She commented that just because I loved children, didn't mean it was right to have so many. This person thought that I should stop having babies and get out and get a job to pay for them all.

This could have discouraged me, but I found it interesting that the people whom I attended Mass with felt just the opposite. Positive, supportive remarks came from those who knew me best. As I reflected on the differences of opinions, I recalled a recent time when this was bothering me a great deal.

Late one night just prior to Jonathan's birth, I found myself restless. I crawled out of bed and began to write a poem so that people might understand how special my children were to me. This would become our birth announcement. Knowing the assumption that we were planning our children, I knew that I had to be clever enough to stop the curious from asking and inform the others that we may still have more children. By putting a twist in the wording, the wise would understand that we remained open to God's will. I was determined to let everyone know that we were very excited about our latest addition. God was doing the planning in our marriage and we loved it.

Going on about my business, I found that church, parenting and cake decorating intermingled with the routine of school and doctors. Life was flowing smoothly with minor bumps along the way. I managed to attend Mass two or three days a week now with the three little ones at my side. Fr. Caster continued to reinforce all that I believed. Gaining tremendous strength from his homilies, I understood that our children were putty in our hands. We were to mold them and put them on the path of God. Those who were attentive could feel his love for people pouring into the church. His words came from The Holy Spirit. This profound truth inspired me to attend daily Mass.

After church, I would socialize with the other parents. A moderate number of young parents attended Mass because their children frequently participated in special ways. This was a beautiful, constructive form of family interaction involving faith. Many new friendships were established here through God. This lifted spirit enabled me to start my busy day, as it would become a constant game of "Beat the Clock."

As school progressed, Charlie required a lot of assistance with homework. Due to the stroke, completing a task was a strenuous job. Nevertheless, he always got it done and looked forward to school the next day. After explaining to Mr. Huelsman before school started that I wanted Charlie to be challenged, he was given every opportunity for growth. He was treated as were the others and he loved it. It was hard for him, but it increased his self-esteem.

His social life being important, Charlie attended every activity offered in the school, from skating parties to football games. Although he could not skate with the others, he was there to socialize. We learned to accommodate his needs wherever possible. He was given the same amount of money as the other children. They used theirs for skating while he used his for video games. During the skating session his friends were constantly coming up to play with him. As long as he was with his friends, he wasn't bothered by the fact that he couldn't always do what they were doing.

Charlie also attended various school programs. When the kindergarten class prepared a Christmas presentation he was eager to watch Marty perform. As we walked toward the cafeteria, a teacher passed by. Approaching the door, smiling at the children, she noticed how dark Charlie's lips were. She said to him in a playful voice, "Have you been eating a popsicle?"

He replied, "No."

Knowing that it was cyanosis that she was observing, I decided it best to let him answer. Then she persisted in a friendly manner; "You've been eating something purple, haven't you? Did you have a sucker or something?"

Charlie thought very little of it and answered "No," once again.

Then she looked at me and said, "I know he's had something grape." She was just trying to make friendly conversation, but I felt obligated at that point to tell her that he had heart disease. This is why he looks blue. She was quite embarrassed and I felt embarrassed for her. It was obvious with her apology that she felt like crawling under a table. I attempted to assure her that it was an innocent mistake.

His blue lips caused great concern to many people. Once the truth about his heart disease surfaced, faces were often overcome with sympathetic expressions. I found myself wanting to protect those who unexpectedly discovered this.

Our next visit to Dr. Cottrill's office shed some hope for a brighter future. She said to me with enthusiastic spirit, "Mary Jo, I have an early Christmas present for you this year."

"Oh really?" I said surprisingly. Unable to hold back any longer, she informed me that a new operation had been discovered that could almost repair Charlie's heart. She added that they couldn't fix everything, but they could make it so that he would be "pink forever."

This was so encouraging to hear. I sensed her great love for me. She had a great desire to protect me from losing my child. She added that she was not ready to try it on Charlie just yet because it had only been attempted three times. She felt it was too soon and too risky for Charlie's complicated disease. It needed to be performed more times before trying it on such a complex case as Charlie's.

This gift offered me hope and comfort. Yet, hidden beneath the surface I questioned if it would really work for him. Charlie was well known for developing complications after his surgeries, so I had legitimate concerns.

As time passed, Charlie's feet began to hurt more. Walking became a harder task for him. More seventh and eighth graders were helping him to get around. Before long, he was tiring out more quickly as well. Nearing the end of December, he was looking more cyanotic. I tried to be observant of his activity and his color, frequently looking at his lips and nails for color changes. He was always happy, so it was difficult to tell if he felt bad. He never let on, if he did feel bad, for fear of missing out on something.

His next cardiac appointment was scheduled for mid-January. Shortly after returning to school from Christmas break, I received a phone call from Mr. Huelsman. He informed me that several teachers had noticed some changes in Charlie's appearance. His color looked worse and he was also getting short of breath more often. They noticed that he stopped to rest far more frequently than ever before. With sincere gratitude for calling, I told him of his upcoming appointment, which happened to be that week. I expressed how important it was that he had confirmed what I believed to be true because it was sometimes difficult to determine whether he was actually getting worse or if it was my imagination. This information from him shed more light when we went to the doctor.

Arriving at the heart clinic, we began our normal procedure. It had been a couple of months since our last appointment. Dr. Cottrill immediately noticed the changes in his appearance since the last visit. I had called her earlier to inform her that several people had reported the same observations. By now, he was quite cyanotic and short of breath with the slightest exertion. He was using a wheelchair whenever possible. When walking, he struggled with every step and was constantly looking for something to lean against in order to rest.

After speaking to Dr. Cottrill, we proceeded with x-rays, EKG, Echo and lab work. Being the most frightening for Charlie, the lab was saved for last. He would cringe at the thought of it and dreaded the sight of it. The hemoglobin and the hematocrit were the most needed information and therefore made the lab work impossible to avoid. Although brave and cooperative, he could not hide the fear from his face and voice. He would pray that it would only take one stick.

Once all the tests were complete, we went to lunch. On our return to the clinic, we were told that it appeared that the shunt, which was put in place the previous year, was no longer functioning. His hematocrit was rising and oxygen saturation had dramatically decreased, thus causing his stamina to decrease. He was in need of surgery again. The problem was that he needed it immediately. This was a frightening thought after what he had been through only 11 months earlier. None of us was prepared for this so soon. We had hoped that the last operation would last about three years.

At this point, I was glad that I had left the other children at home with relatives. I had a gut feeling that this would not be a typical clinic visit. It was imperative to perform a phlebotomy at once. He was taken into a room set up for the procedure. I stayed with him and comforted him the best that I could. Due to the thickness of his blood, it was apt to clot quickly. This meant that a very large needle was necessary in hopes that the blood would flow easier. With a history of rolling veins, the only appropriate option was to use the carotid artery in his neck. When Dr. Cottrill pulled the needle from the package, I was stunned at its size. In my eyes, I related it to the size of a key. I'm not certain whether the fear exaggerated my perception of this or if it really was that large. Needless to say, this was a painful procedure and he cried throughout it. Dr. Cottrill and I would try our best to distract him from the pain as we talked and joked with him. At some point, his crying became false. It was as if the pain was over, but he didn't want us to know it for fear of losing some attention. The cry turned into a fake noise, which was similar to that of a tired child. Dr. Cottrill was pleased that he continued the crying noise because it helped the blood to flow faster with every whining breath. Once it was over, he was a new, pinker child.

With the phlebotomy completed, we could now buy some time before facing the next surgery. Time was needed to absorb and prepare for this. With complications from the previous operation being so critical, we were not at all eager to face it again. Each of us had a great deal of preparation to do.

The new surgery that was devised for serious, complicated heart disease was not something to try just yet. Dr. Cottrill and I both were fearful for Charlie and his history of complications.

I was to go home and break the news to Charles. With careful consideration, we needed to make these life-threatening decisions again and relay the conclusion to Charlie.

Leaving the clinic, Charlie and I went to visit a few friends before going to Dr. Cottrill's house for dinner. She and I discussed what God was allowing to happen. I expressed my disappointment. I questioned why so soon. This was becoming harder and harder to understand. She promised me that she, too, had plenty of questions for God. There was so much suffering of innocent children. When is enough enough? I had thought of this myself each time I was in the hospital for Charlie. Often, I found myself thinking of all the children that we had encountered in one day. I tried to picture these suffering children in the right perspective. I imagined the number at the hospital on a given day. As I peered out the window, my mind carried me to every hospital in town, in the state, throughout the country, and, finally, throughout the world. This was a phenomenon far greater than I could possibly imagine. It was a realistic part of life and most people were not even aware of it. I felt such empathy for all of them. I thought of all the young families that I knew, both friends and relatives. I thought of what their normal day was like. Most of them probably don't have a clue as to what suffering is going on in their own towns. So, why are some exposed to so much and others to none? I was in awe over the thought of this. Dr. Cottrill and I shared a heartwarming talk before I headed back to Louisville. There was so much to absorb and so much to understand. I felt her compassion for us.

Once home, Charlie shared with his dad all the experiences of the day. He showed him the empty IV bottle that was once full of plasma. Then, with typical excitement, he told him that we drove around the football stadium before leaving. (This was a common ritual with every trip to Lexington.) Once the excitement died down, Charles and I put the children to bed. Then I told him the shattering news. He was in disbelief. We hugged and consoled each other as we discussed what we were facing.

10
BETWEEN THE GOAL POSTS

When I went to church the following morning, I felt drained, confused, and lost. I prayed and asked God to help me understand this picture. At the time, I didn't recognize that God was answering me. However, in my distress, I developed a desperate need to speak to someone. I didn't feel drawn to talk to family or friends because none of them had ever been through this type of experience. Most people whom I knew seemed to view life differently than I. So often I witnessed others being annoyed by children. I needed someone who appreciated children and who identified with my feelings toward them. It was Fr. Caster on whom I needed to depend for help. He was the only person in my mind who saw the depth of treasure in a child. He would be able to relate to the threat of losing this treasure.

I tried to settle the knots in my stomach as I knocked at the rectory door. My face was sickened when he answered the door and I had to speak. It was difficult for me to ask, "Have you got a few minutes? I need to talk to you about something. I need some spiritual guidance." He obviously sensed my troubled heart. His smile disappeared as he allowed me to enter. "Yes, come on in," he offered. He guided me to his office and offered me a seat. I couldn't help noticing the large box of tissues on the table. I thought to myself, I bet people come in here crying all the time. Fighting desperately to control my emotions, a force from within pushed the words from my lips.

I began by briefly explaining Charlie's history, going on to give the details of last year's surgery. I described the events of the hemorrhaging episodes and the resulting three consecutive operations. He understood the reality of how life threatening it was. In recounting the events, I told him of how I prayed for Charlie to have some time. I spoke about getting to know the people of St. Gabriel and how I believed that Charlie could perhaps make a difference in their lives. Addressing this, I shared my experience with the Holy Spirit. This caused me to

131

choke up as I cried out to him, "Why didn't God understand me? When I asked God for some time, I meant TIME. I meant TIME to play, TIME to be normal, TIME without operations, TIME to be a child, TIME without suffering." I broke down uncontrollably. Father offered me a tissue. I felt embarrassed for not restraining my emotions. I felt angry. I said to him, "I thought that God understood me. I don't mean to be unappreciative, but one year is not what I had in mind. Why didn't He know that? It doesn't make sense to me that God would misunderstand me." I felt betrayed. I felt that I had been naive to believe that God would grant him more time simply because I had faith that He would. I was beginning to feel upset with myself for having faith. Yet, I also knew that it was because of my faith that I had already been blessed with the time that we had been given. Then I felt greedy and selfish for even asking God for more. My mind was spinning with emotions, confusing love for God with love for my family. I felt such a stabbing in my heart as I spoke to Father. I sobbed and fought desperately to regain control of my emotions.

Fr. Caster listened intently and understood my feelings. He shared with me the loss of a nephew that had drowned as a young child, explaining how deeply this affected him. He confided in me how he prayed daily to his nephew, sharing with me the strength that he had drawn from this small boy. He expressed his sympathy for the family and how puzzling it was that this drowning should happen. Yet, because of the faith in the family, all were able to work through it with God's grace. "Often times it's hard to understand why things are allowed to happen," he admitted. "However, we must trust that God knows what is best." Going on, he attested that God did truly understand my prayers. "These things are happening for another reason. You must continue to pray and trust in God's will."

"I feel like God is playing tug of war with me," I said. "Every time it looks like he'll live, God starts tugging again to pull him back. I don't like playing games with God. I know He's always going to win." Another perception of all of this was sensed. I said, "It's as though I'm a baby-sitter. God keeps coming by to pick him up, but I'm not ready for him to go home yet."

Acknowledging what I was saying, he said, "That's an interesting way of looking at it. Basically, that's what it is. Our children don't really belong to us. They are loaned to us, for us to nurture." I understood that my most important job as a mother was to prepare my children for heaven. His words gave me strength. They were sincere. He knew that I recognized the treasures that had been given me. As we parted, he offered consolation and prayers for my family.

I left feeling uplifted. I was no longer confused or angry. I needed to move on and accept whatever I was facing. God would be with me even if things didn't go my way. My faith had not been shaken and shattered, merely tested.

Returning home, I resumed my motherly duties with my mind and heart on God.

Life continued in a normal fashion. Charlie went back to school and worked hard. The eighth-grade boys continued to piggyback him to the bus. They all seemed to love doing things for him. David, a regular helper, took a special interest in Charlie. He even offered to baby-sit for my five rowdy kids because he enjoyed being around Charlie. We took him up on the offer but suggested that his sister come along to lighten the load.

Charlie became well known around the school because of his special needs. He stood out among the others because of the braces on his legs and his unsteady gait. Of course, being the only child to receive regular piggyback rides also made heads turn in his direction. At lunchtime, the cafeteria workers suggested that someone help carry his tray for him if he had soup. Charlie felt embarrassed by this, but the workers always joked with him to make him feel more comfortable. So many people in the school found themselves giving Charlie a hand.

When we attended school functions, picnics, conferences, church, or meetings, we observed that dozens and dozens of people, young and old, noticed Charlie. It was a constant "Hello, Charlie."

He asked me one time, "Why does everyone know me and I don't know them?"

All I could say was, "Because you're so special." He didn't understand why. I knew that it was because people are naturally drawn to those in need. The braces and the shuffled gait would catch their attention. In watching him for a moment, they would quickly notice the shortness of breath and the determination on his face to get where he was going. This is why they knew him. They admired his strength.

Oddly enough, the young children didn't seem to notice the braces and the walk as something to sympathize with. They saw him as another student. His dearest friend, Robby, would go home regularly and tell his mother about Charlie. He told her that he had to get Charlie's lunch box down for him because he was too short and could not reach the shelf. As he talked about him daily, he also asked if Charlie could spend the night with him. His mother agreed to allow it as soon as she had an opportunity to meet us. Soon thereafter, we both attended a parent/teacher meeting at school. The boys were so excited when we met because they had been hoping for the chance to spend the night. The mother, Bette, was quite surprised when she met Charlie. She told me that Robby had never mentioned that he wore braces. She only knew that he was short. She was impressed that her son had overlooked the appliances and commented that it would be so nice if everyone thought like a child. She did not withdraw her promise to Robby because of the braces. Rather, she asked me to show her how to apply them in the morning, feeling confident that it would not be a problem for her. I instructed her and also warned her of how badly deformed his feet were. She convinced me that she could handle it and for me not to worry.

This was a dream come true for me. His peers and their parents were accepting Charlie. I had feared that he would always be looked upon as different, not expecting him to be invited places by other children.

Bette and I soon developed a special bond as we encouraged each other in faith. Before long, she was attending daily Mass as well.

Still trying to absorb the news of the needed surgery, I took my concerns to God. It was springtime and thoughts of losing

Charlie were constantly on my mind. The second graders were preparing for their First Communion. I kept thinking to myself that if I hadn't put Charlie back in the first grade again, then he too could be making his First Communion. I had hopes that he could experience this great joy of receiving Jesus before facing Him at the hour of death. Being so close to death last year made me wonder if he might encounter the same type of experience again with the next operation.

I continued to pray and attend Mass as much as possible. One morning, after a Mass where the school children attended, Charlie's teacher, Mrs. Dutton, came over to me. She asked me if I had ever thought about having Charlie make his First Communion before his surgery. I was stunned that she mentioned it. I said, "Yes. I had been wishing that he could, but the second graders would be making theirs next week. He couldn't possibly be prepared by then. Besides, I doubt that Fr. Caster would approve because Charlie is in the first grade."

She said to me, "He's eight-years-old, isn't he? He knows enough that I believe Father would go along with it. I've been thinking of what a great help it would be to him. I think that if he makes his First Communion before surgery, he'll have more strength to make it through the operation." She believed that his chance of survival would be a sure thing if he could only receive Jesus. She spoke with conviction in her voice. I was impressed by her faith. She offered to speak to Fr. Caster for me. That very day she called me and said that he, too, thought it was an excellent idea. I was to call him and arrange a date. We agreed that Charlie didn't need to do this with the second graders.

I called Fr. Caster. Without hesitation, he suggested that Charlie make his First Communion on Easter Sunday. This was only two weeks away. Under the circumstances, the priest thought that this would be the most appropriate day for the occasion. I addressed my concern about his ability to learn everything in two weeks. He was adamant that with Mrs. Dutton, Mr. Huelsman, and himself helping, that Charlie would be prepared. He reinforced his desire to celebrate the sacrament on Easter. Upon ending our conversation, my heart throbbed with gladness. Instantly, I became elated, shedding tears of joy. I shared the wonderful news with Leslie, now two and one-half-years-old, and Jonathan, now five-months-old. They were the only ones home who could share in my excitement. They were both very happy because Mommy was so excited. It didn't matter that they didn't understand.

Immediately, I dropped what I was doing to run out and get invitations for the occasion. I began cleaning faster than ever. Planning food for the event was a joy. It gave me the opportunity to be creative with an Easter theme as well as First Communion.

When Easter Sunday came, I was overwhelmed with joy. I thought of Mrs. Dutton's belief that Charlie would survive the surgery. A sense of relief overcame me that he could experience Jesus now before getting so close to death once again. However, the strength of my faith and the constancy of my hope did not allow me to believe that he was invincible. God's will would be our answer to deal with when the time came. I was so grateful for the mentors sent my way. They gave me hope and enabled me to persevere. Teachers, family, and friends joined us in the celebration.

Moving toward the end of the school year, all remained normal with the exception of the underlying knowledge of the imminent surgery. Dr. Cottrill had agreed to hold off as long as possible once again. It appeared as though he could possibly wait until June or July.

Sign-ups for T-ball were being announced at church and school. I knew that it would not slip past Charlie very easily. He was so excited when he heard about it. He came to me with his bubbly smile and eager anticipation. "Come on, Mom. Me and Marty can both be on the same team this year. And Robby's dad is gonna coach."

I couldn't bear to tell him no. That would put him back in that category of being abnormal. He would know it. It was a fine line between building self-confidence and protecting his health. Yet, my foremost thought was on the quality of life. My only way out of this was to inform him that I needed to ask the doctor. His smile turned upside down. I could sense his great disappointment by the look on his face. The final decision was up to me. I didn't want to hurt him physically or emotionally.

I called Dr. Cottrill and spoke of our concerns. We went back to that idea of quality of life. It was important that he be allowed to be a child. She was well aware of my faith. We both felt that God intended for Charlie to be exposed to the world rather than be isolated from it. She asked me if he wasn't setting his own limits anyway. "Doesn't he stop and rest when he gets too tired?"

"Well, yes," I responded. She added that kids at this age usually do. Therefore, she suggested that we go on and let him play.

Charlie waited nervously for me to get off the phone. A look of fear, anticipation, and hope was written all over his face. Hanging up the phone, I said with a smile, "She said okay. You can play."

"YES!" he shouted, as he ran through the house quickly to tell Marty the good news.

Oddly enough, although this type of excitement alone would cause his heart to beat twice as fast, I still wanted him to play. In spite of the conflict between my own mind and heart, I felt good about these decisions. Sometimes logic and facts were not worth listening to, even with the risk of life. Life is a gift meant for enjoyment. Protecting him from the world in order to keep him with us longer would only rob him of the joy that he deserved. His jubilant expression validated my decisions.

Charles was always willing to trust my judgment when it came to choosing limits related to Charlie's health. We thought alike in most things but particularly in this area on the quality of life. He wanted as much as I did for Charlie to enjoy his time as a child. Considering all, we took the plunge and signed him up to play.

Prior to the season starting, I had the opportunity to speak to Robby's dad, Bob, about Charlie playing. Having the bases brought in halfway for him was discussed. I explained to him how this had worked at the Baptist church last year. Agreeing to this, it was explained to the opposing team's coaches before each game. They did not have a problem with it. On the other hand, some of the parents did. Not many, but some would holler out that we were cheating. Charles and I watched the other parents' reaction when Charlie got up to bat. Sometimes there was arguing among them over bringing the bases in closer. One person would oppose, while another would defend him. They soon realized that he was incapable of running. He walked as fast as he could and still some objected. We were in disbelief over their callousness and ignorance.

Charlie, at age eight playing T-ball at St. Gabriel prior to heart surgery - friend Robby about to run

In preparation for surgery, a heart catheterization was scheduled for June. His dad and I took Charlie to Lexington for the procedure, leaving the other children with relatives for the day. Once completed, Dr. Cottrill confirmed the need for surgery as expected. While Charlie lay resting afterward, Dr. Cottrill invited me to go to the Newman Center with her. We needed to talk and share our perception of God's love and support during these difficult trials. As mothers, our hearts understood each other's pain.

His dad stayed with Charlie while offering me some time to be with her, realizing how important our friendship was. We no longer had many opportunities to be together since I had moved to Louisville. Besides, this sharing would shed more insight on the subject. Thus, when I returned, I was better able to discuss every known detail with Charles, sharing my spiritual understanding of the issue as well.

The relationship between Dr. Cottrill and me continued to deepen in spirituality each time we were together. Arriving at the Newman Center, the two of us slowly walked into the chapel, carrying the heavy burden of the next surgery within our hearts. We sat quietly in the pew about three feet apart. Reflecting on the knowledge of Charlie's complicated heart disease, the problems of the past, and the risks of the future, my mind was somewhat paralyzed in thought. Looking at the tabernacle, I set aside all my thoughts of Charlie. Blocking these worrisome thoughts of the unknown, my heart was drawn to Jesus. I enjoyed just sitting there in His presence without a care in the world. My cares were outside at the moment and did not cause any disruption in my peace. As I sat there looking straight ahead, I felt a hand resting on my right shoulder. The light pressure distracted me for a moment. Knowing that Dr. Cottrill was a few feet away, my peripheral vision verified that it was not she who had her hand on my shoulder. Who could have entered the chapel without my hearing them? I shifted slightly in my seat and glanced to the right, knowing that I would not see anyone else there. I was right, thus confirming whom I thought it was. Turning my eyes back to the tabernacle, the pressure did not leave my shoulder. It was then that I felt the confirmation in my heart. I felt the words "I am with you." I felt comfort and great consolation. It didn't seem to matter what trials we were facing. It was clear that I would not be facing them alone. Enormous support from family and friends was a mere fraction of comfort in comparison to what I was feeling at this moment. I sat without thought and absorbed the graces that were being bestowed upon me. We stayed for a while before returning to the hospital.

Charles and I were forced to postpone our discussions until after we were home, so as not to frighten Charlie. He was aware of the pending surgery, but we were very careful not to elaborate on any particulars that might cause him worry.

Leaving the hospital together, we immediately drove to the football stadium. Whenever Charles was with us we would stop the car and get out to walk around the Wildcat stadium. This was

Charlie's favorite part of the trip. By looking forward to this, he could usually block out the scary thoughts of the hospital. His spirits were lifted at once as he and his dad reminisced about kicking field goals at the stadium.

Driving home was always enjoyable. It was a good time to talk and share the various events in our life. With surgery being an obvious issue to address, we questioned Charlie about exerting himself too much. The slightest suggestion about cutting back on T-ball would instantly crush his spirits. So, the topic was dropped. It wasn't worth it to take the joy out of his childhood. We managed to smooth out the issue by saying that if he felt okay he could continue playing.

Eventually, as we neared the end of the season, Charlie could no longer walk fast. I became more and more frightened that he would pass out or experience a heart attack from pushing himself too much. He was not about to quit. Charles and I discussed our concerns. Charlie's barrel-chest indicated the strain on his heart, knowing the workload that his heart muscle bore. We suggested that he have a pinch runner, as the professional teams do. With great elaboration, we were able to make it sound like a terrific idea to Charlie. He bought it with the understanding that it would spare his energy for the next inning. The last couple of games, Robby stood next to home plate as Charlie hit the ball. As Robby ran hard around the bases, we all called out, "Go Charlie." He thought this was pretty funny. We continued to call Robby "Charlie," when he was taking his place. The last game was played two days before his surgery.

Meanwhile, we had just closed on our first house on July 6, 1983. Feeling that this was a time to celebrate, we took the family out for pizza. Ordinarily, Charles and I would go out to dinner alone on our anniversary, July 8. However, we decided to incorporate the two events and treasure our time together with the children.

There was so much to do at this time. The closing and move took place only two weeks before the now-scheduled surgery. I was concerned about leaving the children again. Normally, they would be split up among family and friends while I was in Lexington with Charlie. This time, as I dreaded making the arrangements, I prayed to God about the care of my children, for I hated leaving them. The separation anxiety was always as bad for me as it was for them. It wasn't their physical well being that disturbed me. Rather, it was the inability to be there to console them and answer their questions. Feeling that routine would make it easier on them, I pondered some way of keeping them together at home. It would be hard enough having their mother and brother gone, much less complete separation from each other. Except for the baby, the others were aware that Charlie would be having another difficult surgery. They remembered the year before. Their dad would be gone, too. He would be at the hospital first, then at work. If only I could have been in two places.

The day after we moved in, I began to search for possible ways that my children could stay at home. At least, there could be one routine thing about their life instead of having it completely upset. As I prayed, it occurred to me to call the Committee of Concern at St. Gabriel. I knew that this was out of the ordinary, but perhaps there would be a way for it to work. I called to inquire about what the committee actually did for people. What I was looking for was not anything within their normal service. Explaining what we were going through, I asked Norma if there were volunteers that could watch my children during the day while I was away. My husband could tend to them in the evenings after work. This way, they could feel some sense of security in their own home. I explained to her how the constant uprooting of the family concerned me. She said that she had never considered a request such as this before. The committee had been used mostly for those in financial crisis or to prepare food for a funeral. Norma offered to check around to see what kind of response she might get. No promises were made.

Being pushed from within, I strove to make the hospitalization the least upsetting for everybody. Much to my surprise, Norma called me back within a few days with a list of people willing to give up a day to watch my kids. It was unbelievable. I didn't really expect it to unfold so easily. I assumed that I would be saying to myself, "At least I tried." Yet,

God was seeing to my every need. It was moving to feel His love right with me.

With uncertainty about God's game of tug-of-war, I sensed that perhaps more people were needed on my end of the rope. As God had the power to jerk the rope away from me at any time, I should gather a team to help me. I placed a note in the church bulletin asking for prayers for Charlie's upcoming surgery, hoping that with greater numbers and more faith from those numbers, God might have mercy on us and loosen His end of the rope once again.

Mrs. Dutton also realized the power of prayer. She informed me that she was having a Mass said for Charlie on the day of the surgery. She intended to call all the children in Charlie's class and invite them to Mass with their parents on that day. I was amazed at her love for us. She told me that God especially loves the prayers of children and felt strongly that He would be most pleased with this idea. I agreed wholeheartedly.

My emotional comfort was improving, knowing that so many people would be praying for Charlie. I felt that if he should die during this time, it would be obvious to me that it was God's will. Yet, the numbers gave me hope as I continued to pray for acceptance of His will.

As time drew nearer, my prayers turned to pleading. Starting with my husband, I envisioned the emptiness of future football games. Jackie, who always mothered Charlie, would be devastated as though he were her own child. Marty would be totally lost without his buddy. How could he face going outside or going to bed at night without his brother? Leslie wouldn't understand where her brother went. She surely wouldn't be able to remember him. Then there was Jonathan. He was just a baby. He would never even know his brother. This final thought caused me to cry countless tears. I lay on my bed praying, pleading, and trying to reason with God, speaking to Him about my request for time. As I prayed, I repeated my concerns for all of my family, begging endlessly for Him to allow Jonathan to get to know his brother. I wanted so badly for all the kids to have time with their brother. I wanted them to have memories of fun, memories of laughter, and memories of playing together before he would be taken away. Another request was made for Charlie to have some time without life-threatening surgeries. I asked for the children to have some good memories without the constant separation of the family for hospital stays. I went over these things daily at Mass and throughout each day.

The day came for us to leave. Charlie, his dad, and I headed toward Lexington once again. The children were being well cared for by people in the parish. This trip was more pleasant than expected. We joked and laughed along the way, ignoring all thoughts of our destination. Once there, a lump came to my throat. As we waited in the admitting area, my mind wandered into thoughts of why we were there. Charlie was still playing and full of trust. I forced myself to smile and stay calm. After settling in our room, preliminary blood work needed to be completed. As in the past, I instructed the nurse to call for the best person on the IV team, for I would not allow over two needle sticks. After these things were done, Charlie received a visit from his uncle Ray. The guys were soon playing football in the limited space of the semiprivate room.

A doctor who was assisting the surgeon came in to speak to us about the surgery. He was going over a list of complications that we could be facing. Speaking right next to Charlie's bed where he could hear every word, I thought to myself, he surely won't be saying too much in front of Charlie. On the contrary, he proceeded to tell all. Now, I was well aware of all of this after having spoken to Dr. Cottrill and Dr. Todd previously. I also was acutely aware of the seriousness of the surgery after having experienced the trauma of the year before. Remaining very calm as he spoke, I hoped that Charlie would not realize what he was saying. I trusted he would be cautious with his wording. Because I remained calm, this doctor became irritated with me. He took it as though I was making light of how serious things were. Although I stated that I understood everything that he was saying, I could sense the tension building in his voice. It looked as though he wanted to shake me when he finally shouted; *"Don't you understand? He could die in the morning!"* With that Charlie about jumped out of the bed. His eyes as big as quarters, he responded, "What?   You mean I might die tomorrow?" He was scared to death. I asked the doctor to please step into the hallway to finish this conversation.

I turned to Charlie and told him not to worry. "You're not going to die in the morning," I said. "This is not the doctor who is doing your surgery. Dr. Todd knows what to do." I told him to wait just a minute while I finished talking to the doctor. I gave Charles a look that he knew meant for him to reassure Charlie until I got back. I could hear Ray trying to play with him as I left the room.

Once in the hallway, I told the doctor again that I understood, relaying to him that I really didn't want Charlie to be scared. He could finish his spiel away from the bed. Although I remained perfectly calm on the outside, I was about to burst with anger on the inside. Yet, I didn't want to cause a scene. Instead, I wanted to end the conversation as quickly as possible so that I could get back to the room and patch up things.

Upon returning to Charlie, I saw great fear in his eyes that I hadn't seen before. He said, "I'm not going to have any operation tomorrow. I don't want to die."

He questioned everything that I said. His trust in all of us had been shattered. I hugged him and assured him that he would not die in the morning, thinking to myself, what gives me the right to say this to him? Knowing that God would be making the ultimate decision, I felt as if I was lying to him. At the same time I realized that God was giving me the words to say. Certain that God did not want Charlie to be afraid, I felt justified in saying what I did. If things did not go well in the morning, God would again give me the words to say to him. I knew that I was not to worry about this. My main concern at this point was to eliminate the fear of an eight-year-old, and guide him to trust in God.

I reminded Charlie that Dr. Todd would be performing the operation. "I know that he will do a good job," I began. Do you know why I know that? I know because he has God helping him. Before he even starts in the morning, he will ask God to help him. As you know, last year Dr. Todd stayed with you and continued working with you until you made it. It wasn't easy but he didn't give up. He'll do the same thing tomorrow if he needs to. He won't quit until he knows that you'll be O.K. He saved

144

your life before and he can do it again." Although I realized that I should be saying that God saved your life, I also understood that Charlie would be able to relate to what was more concrete at the time. I felt it was important to communicate in kids' terms in order for the fear to subside. I knew that God understood my thoughts.

It was apparent that he wanted to trust the things that I was saying. However, he continued to have reservations. Those words, "He might die in the morning," were still haunting him. "Is that other doctor going to be there?" he inquired.

"Absolutely not." I answered. "I'm going to go talk to Dr. Cottrill about it right now. She'll make sure that he's not there."

"Good, because I don't want to die," he said sadly.

"Do you think that we would let you go into surgery if you might die?" I retorted. That sounded so presumptuous. I didn't like what I was saying, yet I knew that I needed to say exactly what I did to put him in the right frame of mind for surgery. "We don't want you to die, either. I'm sure Dr. Todd will do a good job. He's real good about saving lives. Besides, all you have to do is ask Jesus to take care of you and He will. Do you know that Jesus is still inside of you since your First Communion?"

He smiled, "Yeah."

"Then ask Him to help you. He loves you very much and He wants to help you."

I kissed him good-bye and looked to Charles to keep him in good spirits.

Charlie had complete trust in Dr. Cottrill. After all, she had been caring for him since he was a baby. Before leaving him, I needed some reassurance that his fear was gone. To get a response, I burst out with "It's a good thing THAT doctor isn't doing your surgery."

"Yeah," he said. He smiled at me with a renewed trust. I suggested that he play football or whatever else with his dad and Uncle Ray. I would be back shortly.

Immediately, I phoned Dr. Cottrill and asked if I could come speak to her. She invited me over without hesitation.

It took all of eight to ten minutes to walk to my car and drive around the corner to her home. I was still fuming at the thought

145

of what had just taken place. Still in disbelief over the "bedside manners" of the doctor, I was anxious to unload on Dr. Cottrill. She could handle the situation appropriately as well as understand the position I was in as a mother.

My thoughts were also focused on the things I said to Charlie, recalling the words that I had used. I prayed that I had not spoken out of line, being a bit afraid that I might have made things sound too good or too presumptuous. I had not been given any strong indication from God that would lead me to believe the result of surgery would be good or bad. Reflecting on the purpose of my words to Charlie, I saw the point was not about living or dying. It was about faith and trust in God, whatever the outcome. Deciding that I was okay with it, I believed that I was able to reduce his fear and restore his faith as well.

When I arrived at the door, Dr. Cottrill noticed the troubled look on my face. She inquired as to what was wrong. I proceeded to tell her what had taken place. She listened. She apologized for him, and promised to speak to Dr. Todd in the morning about the incident. I knew I didn't have to worry about how it would be handled. My purpose was not to get someone in trouble, but to teach this doctor a lesson so that it did not happen to another person.

We proceeded to enjoy a deep, personal conversation, comparing how God had been working in our lives through our children. Eventually, our conversation led to a time before our "special" children were born.

Reminiscing on our pregnancies, we each recalled that there was something very different about our pregnancies compared with that of our other children. Neither of us had health problems. Neither had any physical evidence that our babies would be different. However, both of us sensed that something was not quite the same. It was more like a gut feeling. Neither of us could determine what it was exactly. We both felt that something wasn't quite right. She thought this meant that she was going to have a girl versus another boy. I thought that this meant that something was wrong with my baby. Neither of us imagined the possibility of heart disease.

Finally, when most on our minds had been said, she added with a sense of shame, "Mary Jo, I felt like this wasn't even my baby." I couldn't believe what I was hearing. I could never admit that to anyone. Yet, she said it to me with complete confidence of understanding. I said to her, "Carol, that's exactly the way that I felt." We both thought that there was something wrong with us. We both had been harboring feelings of guilt as if we didn't want these children because we felt that they weren't ours. We came to realize in our conversation that they really weren't ours. They were God's children on loan to us. They were each sent here with a special mission to draw people closer to God. This was a profound discovery. Although we both had seen what our children had done for others and for us, this hidden guilt would probably never have been revealed or understood had we not talked.

Seeing the reality that Charlie and Crissie (her daughter) really weren't ours removed the guilt that Satan had originally put upon us. God allowed us to sense this in our pregnancies so that we would understand family relationships in the right perspective. None of us belongs to another. We all belong to God in a family far greater than we are capable of comprehending. This reality enables us to love God more than those in our earthly family.

The insight that we shared together was uplifting. I returned to the hospital late that night with a feeling of such tremendous love for God and from God that I could not think of the reality of tomorrow. I thought to myself, What will be, will be. God will guide the way.

11

INTERCEPTED PASS

Charlie's face showed great anticipation when I returned. He needed to hear that Dr. Cottrill would take care of everything, as he had trusted she would. My smile and calmness reassured Charlie. With confirmation that the tactless doctor that had scared him would have nothing to do with the surgery, Charlie's remaining fears had now subsided. Emotions settled and we conversed briefly before Charles and Ray left for the night. Hospital rules allowed only one parent to stay overnight, which meant that the separation could not be prevented. We each kissed Charles goodnight, then settled down to sleep.

Speaking to God from my cot, I anticipated what the morning would bring. It was scary, yet I didn't feel troubled. I was relaxed and aware that God would get us all through this. Reflecting on the comments that I had made to Charlie, I prayed that the right words were spoken. Understanding that it was more important, at this time, for him to strive for the will to live rather than to fear the possibility of death, I was comforted by God that I had done the right thing.

As I lay there, I missed my children at home, wanting so badly to kiss them goodnight and share some thoughts about praying for Charlie. At the same time, however, I hoped that the distance between us would spare them from useless worry.

The next thing I knew, morning had come. Charles returned early to be with us. The nurse entered the room to administer the pre-op medication, which would help Charlie relax. I had slept well and peacefully. Getting up to console Charlie, I ignored the sudden knot in my stomach with a smile and a joke. Charles was also there with a smile, yet I sensed the fear from within him, as well. We both had to be strong for Charlie's sake.

Being the fighter that he was, Charlie was determined not to allow the medication to put him to sleep. He was adamant about staying awake to see what was going to take place. If he could help it, he tried not to miss anything.

149

His dad put Charlie on the stretcher and the three of us went down to surgery together along with the transport personnel. We were allowed to go into the holding area for a few minutes and were able to speak to the anesthesiologist briefly. Charlie was dozing but fighting sleep. When the moment came for our departure, Charles and I kissed him good-bye and offered words of encouragement.

Our spirits were low as we left the room, holding hands. We embraced in the hallway. The pain of our love for each other was difficult to bear. The thought of what Charlie was about to endure stabbed at our hearts. Slowly, hand in hand, we walked to the waiting room.

Shortly thereafter, Dr. Todd entered as we expected. He was to go over the final synopsis of the surgery about to take place. After reviewing the plan, he stated, "He has about 30% chance of survival….We're going to do our best." He explained his intentions for surgery and offered us a chance to ask questions.

By now, I could hardly open my mouth to speak. There were no questions. As he turned and walked away, I had a strong desire to walk into surgery and take Charlie off the table. Charles and I hugged and remained too choked to speak. Finally, Charles commented on the 30% chance. It sounded so frightening. We were both tempted to go in there and get him before it was too late. Yet, we both knew that wasn't the answer. Without surgery, he was certain to die. As threatening as the odds were, they were better than no odds at all. We had to pray. We had to trust.

The time was shortly after 7:00 A.M. I was thinking of the Mass that was being said for Charlie and I wondered if some of the children in his class might attend. It being a summer weekday, I envisioned almost everyone sleeping in late. My thoughts were of all the relatives and friends that were surely praying for him. Remembering the request that I had placed in the bulletin gave me comfort. Perhaps others remembered to pray. I said to God, "I trust in Your will. I know that You know what You're doing." Personally, I had no clue or indication as to what God had planned for the day.

Charles and I sat down and waited. Shortly after 8:00 A.M., Dr. Cottrill came into the waiting room. I sensed trouble right away because she was supposed to be in surgery. She took us to the side stating, "We have a problem."

"Why am I not surprised?" I questioned.

Acknowledging that Charlie has always been an exception, she smiled and continued, "We have him open and prepared to start the procedure, but we can't find the four veins that we planned to use." She continued by drawing a diagram of what they found. Explaining this, she added that everyone has four pulmonary veins that lead from the lungs to the heart. "This is how the oxidized blood returns to the heart for distribution in the body. However, in Charlie, we can see the veins leaving the lungs, but we're unable to determine where they are going. We don't know how the blood is getting back to the heart except for this one vein, which is leading to a left superior vena cava." (The normal body does not have one of these on the left.)

I questioned why we didn't know this before the surgery. Why didn't the catheterization show it? She explained that it couldn't be seen by the catheterization. Also, because it was his first operation from this side of the heart, it had not been discovered before.

Continuing, she offered some options. "We could do another Gore-Tex shunt like we did last year."

"No," I interrupted. "We can't go through that again. It's not worth the risk. We'll be right back where we started. He'll never survive it."

Next, she suggested a modified Glenn shunt. She proceeded to draw a diagram of what she believed might work. Basically, she devised an operation specifically for him, with various adjustments to accommodate his unique heart disease.

The plan now was to make an attempt to separate the oxidized blood from the unoxidized blood. To understand somewhat, one needs to realize that the job of the superior vena cava is to return the unoxidized blood from the body to the heart. On the other hand, the pulmonary vein, which was attached to this on the left, is taking freshly oxidized blood from the lungs to the heart to be distributed to the body. The problem that Charlie was dealing with was that this good blood was being mixed with the used blood, causing him to be cyanotic and making the heart unable to distribute newly oxidized blood. Keeping this in mind, the plan was unfolded to us.

The way that Dr. Cottrill figured, if the persistent left superior vena cava, along with the single vein, was blocked and if the Gore-Tex shunt was also blocked, then the surgeon could construct a new shunt by using a modified Glenn procedure. He would do this by connecting a right superior vena cava to the pulmonary artery. In studying the map of the heart, which she drew, I could see where the procedure would force the blood flow in a different direction. This would indicate a path where the oxygenated blood would be directed eventually to the heart in such a way that it would be able to be distributed through the aorta as it should.

This was an overwhelming concept to absorb. To compare the normal blood flow to Charlie's unique heart was a straining thought process. I studied what she was saying and I asked questions, looking at the outline which she had drawn. Charles asked me what I thought about it. I concentrated on the paper before me. I said, "It makes sense. Let's go for it." With that, Dr. Cottrill went back into surgery. Charles and I studied the paper again. As complicated as it appeared, it also looked clear. We sat down to begin our wait once again.

I was unable to pray at this point. Having already said all that I could, I felt it was important to wait patiently for God's answer. He understood. Placing the situation in His hands, I chose to let go of it and depend on His final decision. So, the two of us mostly sat quietly. Eventually, we walked downstairs to the chapel, to reflect.

After meditation and time alone, we reluctantly strolled into the cafeteria. We had no appetites and were tempted not to eat. However, we forced ourselves to set a minimal selection on our trays, in hopes of having some strength to face the hours to come. Eating was more of a chore than a pleasure, as neither of us had a desire to put the food into our mouths. We shared our concerns about the risks being taken with Charlie's life.

Our hearts drew us to the chapel once again. As I had left word with Suzanne as to where we would be, I had no fear of Dr. Cottrill's being unable to find us. We sat and absorbed God's comfort and consolation before returning to the surgery waiting room. The day was seemingly endless.

Eventually, the surgery was completed. The report came from Dr. Todd that Charlie was doing well. We wouldn't know if it were truly successful until he awakened and was weaned from the oxygen.

That evening, Dr. Cottrill came in to report that he was looking good and was able to respond upon hearing his name. She confirmed that he was far pinker than he had ever been before. Everyone was amazed at the outcome. She was as overjoyed as we were and was pleased to grant us a brief visit with him per Dr. Todd's approval.

Upon hearing our voices, he strained to open his eyes. It was a delightful scene watching him respond. The emotional moment made it difficult for Charles and me to keep from crying. He looked great despite the respirator, IVs, chest tube, catheter and monitors.

I was anxious to call home and spread the news. Once notifying the family, my next thought was to call Fr. Caster. After our talk and all the prayers being said, I knew he'd be waiting to hear from me.

He received my call with great enthusiasm. I explained how the course of events took place throughout the morning. When I described how the problems started so early, in particular, the news shortly after 8:00 A.M., he was in awe. He said to me, "Mary Jo, I have to tell you something."

"What is it?" I exclaimed with curiosity.

He proceeded to say, "This morning, as I was walking out of the rectory to go over to the church, I noticed that the parking lot was full of cars. I didn't think much of it. I figured that there must be a meeting of some sort going on over at the school. I went on in to get dressed for Mass when I heard some noise in the church. So I peeked out. I was shocked. The church was packed. (It being a weekday, there would normally be about fifteen people in church.) It scared me to death. I thought that it was a Holy Day that I had forgotten. Then I saw a number of children. It was then that I realized that these people were all there for Charlie. I was deeply moved."

Hearing this touched me more than I can express. He went on to elaborate on the power of prayer. The special power of children's prayers was discussed. When we correlated the timing of the message from Dr. Cottrill with the Mass beginning at 8:15 A.M., we were both deeply affected. Considering the previous anxiety and the request for prayers, as well as the 30% chance of Charlie's survival, we could feel only blessings poured upon us. This was indeed a miracle.

I asked him to relay the message to those who asked. He went one step further. The following Sunday Fr. Caster spoke about the power of prayer in his homily. He told the parish about the success of the surgery thanks to all of those who prayed. I was unaware of this at the time because we were still in Lexington. People were soon talking about the miracle that had taken place.

The next week went by quickly. Charles returned home to Louisville to work and to care for the kids, as I kept in touch with them by phone. Parishioners came daily to stay with them. Food was even being brought in for their dinners. Everything was falling into place. The people from St. Gabriel had been a godsend.

I couldn't thank God enough for all that He had done. Not only did Charlie survive the surgery, he was also pinker than ever. That meant he would feel better than ever once he recovered. That meant he could play easier. He could do more. He could be closer to normal than he ever had been. Without a doubt, God had answered every single portion of my prayers with mercy. The feeling of God's love was breathtaking.

Only nine days later, Charlie returned home. It's hard to say who was more excited, Charlie for being home again, the brothers and sisters for having him home, or Charles and I for watching the reunion.

As Charlie began his recovery, I began to unpack from our move. Curtains needed hanging, shelves needed to be placed on the wall, and general organization was needed.

School would be starting in just a few weeks. Uniforms and supplies needed to be found or bought. Cake orders had resumed.

The frantic rush of daily life had returned the minute I walked in the door. It was most welcome.

On Sunday, Charlie wanted to go to church. We agreed to take him because we thought it would do him good to get out. After church, friends and acquaintances approached Charlie and welcomed him back. Everyone was so excited to see him. A number of people confirmed that they had been praying for him. It was a grand, uplifting reunion.

We anticipated that Charlie would be starting school late this year after recovering from surgery. However, when it came time to register, Charlie was too excited to stay home. He had been up and walking around normally, going to church on Sundays, and beginning to go outside to play. He had more energy now than I had ever witnessed. There was no holding him back. He was eager to start school with the others.

So, we agreed to allow him to start with the rest of the children. The only condition was that if he became too tired, he was to come home early. His teacher, Mrs. Stivers and principal, Mr. Huelsman agreed to watch for signs of exhaustion. They were both wonderfully caring people. I felt complete trust in having Charlie in their care.

Being in a new subdivision meant that the children would be on a different school bus. A neighbor gave a forewarning that the bus driver wasn't very friendly. She said she barely speaks and never smiles. She was concerned that Charlie might have his feelings hurt by her. I assured her that I would be at the corner with Charlie, helping him on and off the bus every morning and afternoon. Charlie smiled all the time. Therefore, I didn't foresee anyone taking that away from him.

As the school year began, Charlie rode his bike to the corner as usual. I walked alongside him with Leslie, Jonathan, Jackie and Marty. He waited for the bus on his bike so that his feet would not become tired. When the bus arrived, I handed the baby to Jackie in order to lift Charlie to the step. With a jovial smile, he held onto the rail with one hand, and raised the other to wave to the driver. "Hi," he said.

His smile was contagious. She smiled without hesitation and said, "Hi," in return.

As the bus pulled away, I turned to my neighbor with raised eyes. "How about that?" I said. "She smiled."

"I can't believe it. I've never seen her smile," she said.

"Well, people can't help it. Charlie makes them smile." I added. We walked back to our homes, she in disbelief.

It turned out to be unnecessary for Charlie to come home early. He held up well at school. He was excited and he worked hard. He was proud of his accomplishments because it made him like the others.

Football season was upon us once again. Charlie and his dad were intent on going to all the Trinity High School games. Marty found it more exciting to stay home and play outside or play with his GI Joe's. The only game that Marty was really interested in, as a first grader, was the Trinity - St. X game. That was the intense rivalry in town. The stadium would be as packed as any college game imaginable. The whole family would be going to this together and we played it up all week long. The day of the game, Charlie got on the bus as usual after school. Grinning from ear to ear, he proclaimed, "St. X stinks."

Ordinarily, the driver wouldn't stand for this. However, unable to hold back her smile, she said, "All right, Charlie. Everyone for Trinity in the back of the bus. Everyone for St. X in the front."

Not being aware of what was going on when the bus returned after school, I couldn't help but notice a lot of commotion when the bus stopped. Everyone was laughing and having a great time. They were shouting various things about the Trinity Shamrocks and the St. X. Tigers. Once I helped Charlie off the bus, I inquired as to what was happening. The kids were all laughing. Marty jumped in saying, "Charlie started a riot." The neighbors that got off the bus were also chiming in to tell the story. They proclaimed that they had never had so much fun on the bus before. The funny thing about it is that the bus driver was still smiling after several weeks. It was enjoyable for me to watch Charlie bring out the life in so many people.

By evening, the car was decorated in green and white for Trinity. Another neighbor, who was a St. X graduate, painted the words "St. X" on the back of our car with shoe polish. This caused a little delay while we washed off the offending message. We paid them back, after Trinity won the game, with a well-decorated front porch in green and white. The rivalry made the competition all the more fun.

The rest of the season belonged to Charlie and his dad because the family couldn't tolerate the weather. When it came to cold, wet nights, we chose the warmth of our home instead. Although I enjoyed football, I dreaded taking the little ones out in bad weather. His dad continued to take Charlie to the games, no matter what. They both took great pleasure from it. Sometimes an uncle might go along for added company. No matter what, the two of them went to a game every week. I sometimes worried about Charlie's getting too cold. Charles assured me he would be in good hands. They took blankets, hats, scarves, and gloves. I knew in my heart that even if it wasn't good for his health, it was good for his spirit. I could never tell him to stay home. After all, I had prayed for Charlie to have time to be normal and this was it. I loved watching the two of them have such a great time together doing what they both loved the most. With kisses good-bye and a "Have fun. Be careful," farewell, I saw them out the door regularly.

School continued smoothly. With extra help in the evening, Charlie did fairly well keeping up with his work. In time, an announcement was made searching for acts in the talent show. I agreed to help Charlie and his friends to practice their act. The boys had planned an act playing football. Two were on Trinity's team and two were on St. X's team. They would each act out football while singing their school song. They began working hard on it that fall even though the show would not be held until spring. After practicing, a group of friends would meet out front, equipped with helmets and shoulder pads, for an impromptu game of intense football. Charlie and Marty wore their favorite Pittsburgh Steelers helmets and brought out a box of other helmets for their friends who didn't have one. They didn't stop until the sun went down.

Meanwhile, Charlie had been having serious trouble with his feet. They hurt all the time. They had gotten worse because his heart had gotten better. Feeling better meant more time on his feet. Although he had had surgery on them at three-years-old, he still had several more phases of surgery to face before they would be comfortable enough for walking. With the tendons in the heel cords and arches cut previously, his ankles now had a tendency to touch the floor on the inside of his feet. This caused severe pain when he walked. He was still wearing the brown orthopedic shoes with short leg braces.

With the severity of pain increasing, it became more difficult for Charlie to keep up with his friends. Frequently, the smile on his face would drop and become overshadowed by pain. He could not stand very long without extreme discomfort.

On our next visit to Dr. Leatherman, we told him about the severity of pain that Charlie was experiencing in his feet. Looking at them, Dr. Leatherman stated with a frown on his forehead, "Charlie, just looking at your feet makes my feet hurt."

I knew with this comment that he understood that Charlie was dealing with a lot of pain. He told us that he had heard from Dr. Cottrill concerning Charlie's latest heart operation. He smiled a glowing smile of excitement as he expressed how pleased he was with the outcome of the surgery.

He said, "She tells me that you are in better shape now than you've ever been. She feels that now is a good time to proceed with the next operation on your feet."

Although Charlie was not excited about the idea of more surgery, he was excited about getting rid of some of the pain when he walked. His ankles had been sore for some time. Holes had already been cut in his shoes to relieve the pressure. Foam padding had already been used to prevent the breakdown of his skin. It was decided that surgery was necessary. Charlie had a lifelong dream to be able to run like Marty and to play football. He was determined to do anything to make this dream come true.

After taking x-rays, Dr. Leatherman commented that Charlie's back was healing very well. He always spoke proudly when Charlie's successes with health were seen. It became apparent that he was beginning to appreciate the quality of life concept. He began to speak of plans for surgery, as it had become obvious that Charlie could no longer tolerate the foot pain.

12

FIRST DOWN, QUICK TO SCORE

Our visits with Dr. Leatherman were days that we always looked forward to. The children enjoyed playing with the wooden cars and trucks in the waiting room before Charlie was called to a room. After another period of waiting, Dr. Leatherman came in beaming with delight. His greetings were like a reunion of old friends, full of excitement, smiles, and hugs. The examination, x-rays, and evaluation followed. Discussing the need for surgery, we agreed to admit Charlie into the hospital on November 11, for preliminary work and testing to determine the exact plan. His feet were so malformed that the solution was not a simple one. Charlie's first fear was the thought of missing Marty's birthday on the 14th. However, this would be a short two-day stay, as the actually surgery would not take place on this admission.

As always, Charles adjusted his schedule to go with us to the hospital. After a day of testing, the three of us began to relax in Charlie's room and we discussed the agenda for the next morning. We were almost enjoying this stay due to the fact that it was one of the few times in the hospital that were not painful. That evening however, we were distracted by a phone call from the emergency room. The voice on the other end stated that Jonathan, who was now one year old, was having difficulty breathing. I told Charlie that we needed to check on his brother. Having become so accustomed to hospitals by now, it did not worry Charlie to be left alone. Rushing nervously to the emergency room, we discovered our baby in the process of receiving a breathing treatment. With typical infant behavior, he instinctively tried pushing the nebulizer treatment away from his face. His grandmother held him, trying to convince him that all was okay. Upon spotting me entering the doorway, he looked to me for instant salvation, only to discover that I, too, cooperated with the nurse. I comforted him as he received the rest of his treatment.

159

Feeling much better afterward, he was able to go back home with his dad for the night. (It was not unusual for someone in the family to need medical attention whenever Charlie was in the hospital.) On Charles' way home with Jonathan, he picked up the other children so that they could all be home together.

The following day all tests were completed and a plan for surgery had been made. Dr. Leatherman, being cautious and concerned about Charlie's heart, felt it best to make the length of surgery as short as possible.

He had a special place in his heart for Charlie. His decisions showed how much he cared for us. Anesthesia added potential problems that he hoped to avoid. Therefore, in an attempt to lesson the risks, he offered the suggestion to have his partner assist him in the surgery. If Dr. Kotcamp, who specialized in feet, was to perform surgery on one foot while he did the other, he could save half the time under the anesthetic. Dr. Leatherman felt more comfortable with this, having never forgotten the terrible experiences of the stroke and the complications that so greatly affected Charlie's life. We had to agree that it was an excellent idea. Surgery was then scheduled for the end of January, allowing us time to enjoy the holidays.

Although it was difficult to watch Charlie in pain when he walked, it was good for him not to be hospitalized during the Christmas season. Often, we noticed good times to be a distraction from his pain. Facial expressions would frequently change from smiles to grimaces but most always ended in silent acceptance of his physical pain. He had learned by now that when it became unbearable, he could sit down wherever he was. If there was no chair, he sat on the floor or the ground for temporary relief.

After Thanksgiving, the entire family made the traditional trip to the toy store. The purpose of this was to expose the children to the many interesting toys available. They needed to see that there were options besides the most expensive toys that were advertised on TV. We spent an entire afternoon walking up and down each aisle inspecting most every item. Charles and I were able to observe their reactions and interests. Silently, we stored a list in our minds of the less expensive toys which they

160

found to be pretty "cool." The children knew never to ask for anything or the adventure would be ended. They were to use this exploring event to assist them with their list for Santa Claus. Having taken in more than their minds could hold, they were totally confused by the time we left the store. They discovered that they liked so many items. As a result, they would forget what they wanted the most and we were able to inform Santa of the best buys. We would tell them that they didn't need to remember what they liked because Santa was watching and he already knew. This practice eliminated disappointments and distracted the kids from thoughts of themselves. They were taught trust, which freed them to focus on giving. The exciting part about Christmas was choosing and wrapping gifts for each other. This special day with the family put everyone in the Christmas spirit immediately.

Once the holidays were over and the Christmas tree and decorations had been put away, the process of preparing for surgery began. This meant finding sitters and deciding where the children would be happy. Knowing that four children would be a hardship for any one person meant locating three or four sitters. After all, people had their own families to care for.

We saw a new advantage to this upcoming surgery that we had not experienced since his first operation at eleven-months-old. We would now have the luxury of living in the same city as the place of surgery. Our lives would not be disrupted nearly so much as in the past. Charles would be better able to work and care for the children in the evening. He could also bring them to visit Charlie and me more often by being in town. This was a source of security for all of us, which greatly lessened the stress of the circumstances.

Relatives and friends were happy to watch the children. Support from people at St. Gabriel was forever present, as many were willing to help. Having never fully understood how well the children adjusted within another family, I noticed that all was not simple in a child's mind. Although they managed quite well, there was one thing that Marty found to be disturbing. He liked staying with Robby but couldn't help noticing the minor differences between our families. Everyone in our family had

161

blond hair, whereas Robby's family all had black hair. One wouldn't expect this to become an issue. However, when Bette (the mother) went to assist Marty in washing his hair, he stopped her with much concern and said somewhat frightened, "If I use your shampoo, will my hair turn black like yours?"

Holding back the outburst of laughter she felt, Bette answered him with confidence, "No honey, it won't turn your hair black."

These customary daily activities were actually of great importance to the children. Frequent uprooting for hospitalizations was not easy. Each had to adjust to the routines in someone else's home.

The night before surgery a young doctor, who was fairly new in Dr. Leatherman's practice, spoke to us about the operation. Upon seeing Charlie in his Kentucky Wildcat sweatshirt, the doctor instantly informed him that U of L was the better basketball team. This fired up a reaction within seconds as Charlie expressed his strong support for U of K. Neither of them would back down as a playful argument broke out between them. Sports topics were often used to deter the painful parts of his life. By the time he left the room, Charlie was no longer thinking of the surgery he faced. On the other hand, he was trying to devise a way to prove to the doctor that U of K was better.

Compared to previous surgeries, a considerably shorter time was spent in the operating room. Surgery on both feet was completed in just three hours. The technique included the breaking of bones and lining his feet up straight. Dr. Leatherman discussed with us the removal of a bone that was causing serious problems, but it was decided that it should not be done at this time. Removing this bone would cause his feet not to grow much more. It was too soon to consider this because they were already too small for his size. The procedure needed to be reconsidered in the future after he was fully grown. It was best to perform the corrective surgery one step at a time in his case. Surgery ended with metal pins inserted through the tops of his feet in the direction of his heels, keeping in line the work that had been corrected.

Charlie returned to his room with bilateral casts on his feet and legs. The doctor who had teased him came in pointing to a U of L sign made of casting material that was lying between Charlie's legs. He informed me that he was tempted to mold it into the casts on his legs. Instead, he thought that just having it in his bed would be enough to get him stirred up.

Charlie dozed off and on throughout the day, just long enough to see that Mom and Dad were at his bedside. That evening he woke up enough to discover the U of L sign. It made him laugh and more determined to get back at the doctor.

The following day, as his toes and casts were being monitored, it was noted that his left cast was increasingly saturated with serous or watery blood. Charlie didn't indicate that this foot was bothering him in any way. On the other hand, the right cast was white and dry. As he was more able to squirm a bit in the bed, he periodically cried out with pain in his right foot. This was inspected very closely. It was thought that because the right foot was not draining that there was an increase of pressure building up.

The next day was not any better. In fact, by then he was in constant excruciating pain. He was afraid to move an inch in the bed because the pain was intense. If anyone so much as barely touched the bed, he would scream out in agonizing pain. Upon seeing this, Dr. Leatherman felt it necessary to look further into the problem. X-rays indicated that the pins were still in place, thus leaving unresolved questions. It would now be necessary to remove the casts with hopes of visualizing what was causing him such anguish.

Consistent with his concern for Charlie, once again Dr. Leatherman offered to sedate him in order to avoid mental trauma from fear. He invited me back into the operating room to be with him. Knowing that I had seen so much in the past, he felt comfortable having me there. I was honored that my presence in surgery would not disturb him and was grateful for the opportunity to be with Charlie.

Standing by Charlie, I held his hand as the anesthesiologist placed a mask over his face. Becoming anxious to see the cast removed, I anticipated what might be found. As Charlie fell asleep, a terrible feeling came over me. Looking at him so helpless and lifeless was an eerie sensation. It didn't look like he was sleeping. It looked like he was dead. I watched his chest rise and fall with each breath. Nevertheless, he appeared dead. My eyes, my knowledge, and my heart were playing tricks on my mind. I became lightheaded and dizzy. Turning to look for a chair, I was forced to admit that I wasn't feeling well. The room encompassed me and provided a feeling of claustrophobia. A nurse directed me to a seat. Not wanting to hold things up any longer, I could plainly see that the sensation was not going away. I kept thinking that this is what he will look like when he dies. I was given the opportunity to stay or step outside. With my history of fainting in the past, I knew it would be wiser to step out. In spite of my great desire to stay, I realized that I had absolutely no power over my dizziness. Mind over matter, I believed, trying to convince myself that I could move beyond this feeling. However, it was out of my control and I knew it. I agreed to be escorted to a chair outside the door. It was a very humbling experience for me to acknowledge my internal weakness after projecting a strong image to others.

Once in the open air, I came back to focus. The picture of Charlie's face stayed on my mind. Death was a fact that my eyes had not imagined for him before. This was the closest to seeing what it would eventually be like. I couldn't bear it.

Sitting outside the door, I still wished that I could see his foot and what was causing him such pain. Patiently waiting, I reflected on what had happened and why. I spoke to God, inquiring as to why I reacted as I did. I was quickly guided to Our Blessed Mother once again for comfort. I pondered what it must have been like for her as she watched her son die, realizing that she, too, had felt this way at one time.

When Dr. Leatherman came out, he first asked how I was feeling. He just smiled and said that sometimes the smell of the anesthetic will cause people to get lightheaded.

As for the foot, the problem turned out to be that the pin had worked its way out the heel about one eighth inch. Thus, with the slightest movement, the pin would hit against the cast, causing severe pain to shoot through his foot and leg. It was explained that the body naturally tries to reject foreign objects; this is why it was working its way out. The pin was trimmed at the heel with the reasonable expectation that it would suffice until the casts were removed permanently. The blood-soaked cast on the other leg was also changed while he was under anesthetic.

Charlie was like a different child again when he woke up in that he was laughing and playing without concern for his condition. Once this complication was behind him, he was soon ready to leave the hospital. As we planned to leave, we noticed that his personal wheelchair would not be feasible due to the fact that it did not have leg rests to elevate his feet. Therefore, I phoned Tim Jordan from The Easter Seal Society and inquired about borrowing one from them. He was able to locate one and returned my call within minutes. Once again, God's helpful servants were just a phone call away.

His dad and I had discussed plans for taking Charlie home. We agreed that it would be best for Charles not to take time off of work. I was certain that I could manage okay, as he could not afford to miss work. On the morning that we were to leave the hospital, I looked up only to discover Charles entering the room. Surprised as I was, I asked, "What are you doing here?"

He said, "They let me go."

"Why?" I inquired. "I thought you were going to work anyway."

"I did go to work," he added. "But, they said they don't need my services anymore. I've been fired."

"What?" I said with astonishment.

"Do you remember last year when my boss asked me if Charlie was going to have any more surgeries?" he asked.

"Yes," I responded.

"Well, they found out that Charlie was in the hospital, so they let me go."

"How can they do that?" I asked angrily.

"They can do whatever they want. You know they don't have to give a reason to fire someone. If you remember, they sent a letter to Dr. Cottrill asking if Charlie was going to have more heart surgery in the next year."

"Yes, I remember," I replied.

"Well, this is going to make their insurance rates go up. They are a small company and they can't afford to have their rates go up on account of Charlie."

"I can't believe this. Isn't there something that we can do about it?" I pushed.

"There really isn't a thing I can do. If I mention it, they will just deny it. They can simply say that they don't need me any more."

"Well, I think that you should look into it, call the newspaper or something," I insisted.

Charles continued, stating that if he caused any publicity over it, he would never get another job because no one would hire someone who caused trouble. Nor would anyone hire him knowing how often Charlie was in the hospital. No company would willingly take on those kinds of medical bills. "There's nothing I can do except collect unemployment and start looking for another job."

We embraced and comforted one another. Charlie looked on, asking questions. We made every attempt to inform him that it was nothing to worry about, not wanting him to take on guilt for his medical expenses.

We left the hospital in different cars as we had both driven. Charlie was put in my car, lying down in the back seat. Charles and I kissed good-bye and went our separate ways. Upon leaving the parking garage, my mind and heart were heavy with disgust and irritation. Unable to fully concentrate, I attempted to entertain Charlie with conversation. Having driven down Chestnut St. all my life, I suddenly had not given it a thought that it was a one-way street. Seeing no traffic coming toward me, I proceeded to make my left-hand turn from the right lane, turning directly into the car beside me. I couldn't believe what had happened. How could I have possibly forgotten that the street was one-way? It became obvious that my stress level had adversely affected me. Fortunately, no one was injured. After resolving the situation with the other driver, I resumed the ride home, in disbelief over the course of events. I knew that life would go on and we would get by. At this point, we were happy to be going home.

Being the typical child that he was, Charlie was embarrassed to be seen in the casts. To cheer him up, I reminded him of how much he liked his Kentucky Wildcat socks. Of course, they would be stretched out if we attempted to put them over these thick casts. So, I offered to draw Wildcats on the front of his casts, so that people would think they were socks. Taking my limited talent from cake decorating, I was able to create the image. He was thrilled. He thought his casts were fairly awesome. I found that by boosting his self-image, he didn't focus on himself and his many adversities.

In no time he was back at school. He was fortunate to have another caring and wonderful teacher. One problem that had to be overcome was using the restroom. This was not an easy task for a boy unable to stand. It was a perfect setup for humiliation and embarrassment among classmates. Mr. Huelsman suggested that he use the teachers' restroom, which was in the office. His teacher, Mrs. Stivers, would wheel him back there, assist him out of the wheelchair, and help him to kneel on a stepstool in front of the facilities. At that point, she could step out to allow privacy. This procedure spared him from being teased or belittled by classmates.

As parents, Charles and I felt grateful that the school staff willingly went out of their way to help. We were well aware of how heavy he was to lift, with the weight of two casts added. Yet, Mrs. Stivers and others always served him with a smile. Never was it implied that he was too much trouble.

Throughout this period of recovery, Charlie used the wheelchair daily, which was easily loaded into the back of the station wagon for school. The inconvenience of it was never an excuse to keep him home, as I did not believe in giving in to obstacles.

By this time, I had adjusted to having the five children. Often, when I took them to the park, the mall, or the doctor, Jackie and Marty helped by pushing the double stroller or the wheelchair. Their assistance was an important factor in making it possible to do things together.

As a general rule, I took the children with me to the doctor's office or clinic when Charlie had an appointment. I did this for several reasons. Numerous appointments made me aware that if I had always gotten a baby-sitter; it would appear to the other children that Charlie got more attention. However, by having them with me, all the children received the same amount of attention. It also made the kids aware that although Charlie frequently attracted strangers and appeared to be so lucky, his life was not about being special and receiving gifts. It consisted of many tests, procedures, and needle pricks that were highly painful. The reality of his life needed to be experienced by his brothers and sisters if they were to learn from his perseverance. It was simply a family affair to do anything. Having witnessed many people less fortunate than they, each of them became aware of the dignity of others. They interacted with patients and families while waiting on doctors. Although they were sometimes taken aback by appearances of children with deformities, or without hair due to cancer treatments, or wearing strange braces or appliances, they were able to see beyond these superficialities. They may have asked questions but always accepted the answers and moved on. These experiences taught them many lessons about appreciating life.

Through it all, the children developed a close relationship with each other. They were sensitive to Charlie's abilities and disabilities by all that they had witnessed. They made sure that he was treated fairly and always included in activities.

Charlie was sensitive to their desires as well. Whenever someone gave to him, he in turn shared it with his brothers and sisters. Material gifts that could be controlled were always dealt with fairly. Yet, the physical gifts from God were often beyond our control. At times I would hear the words, "It's not fair." coming from one of their mouths.

In Charlie's case, he would occasionally remark how badly he wanted to play football. He would say that all he wanted was to be able to "run like Marty." "It's not fair." he'd exclaim.

"You're right, Charlie," I'd answer. "And it's not fair for Marty that you brought home a stack of presents from the hospital and he didn't get any."

"But he can play with them, too," he'd retort.

"Yes, he can play with them, but people didn't give them to *him*. He sees how people are always giving to *you*."

In the very same instance, Marty came to me privately and said, "It's not fair. Charlie is always getting presents. I wish I could break my leg so somebody would bring me presents."

"You're right, Marty. It's not fair. It's also not fair that Charlie has to go through pain that none of the rest of us have to deal with. It's not fair that he has to get blood drawn regularly, or have heart operations. It's not fair that you can run and he can't." He listened to what I was saying. I added, "Don't ever expect life to be fair, Marty. It never will be. There will always be people who have more than you, and there will always be people who have less than you. God does not make us the same nor does He give us the same. Each of us is given a different life with different abilities. The important thing is that you take whatever you've been given and you make the best of it. You can run and play and you need to be glad of it. Think about being stuck in a wheelchair not being able to keep up with your friends. You can use your energy to help Charlie get around. Be glad when people give Charlie toys and gifts. He always shares them with you. Do you know how happy he is to bring things home to you? Look at Jackie, Leslie, and Jonathan. They should be saying that it's not fair. When people give Charlie gifts, they are always boy toys. He feels bad because he has nothing that would interest the girls. With Jonathan being a baby, even the boy toys are not for him."

Marty listened carefully to what I had said to him. He seemed to understand. He gave me a kiss and a hug and went on about his business.

By March, Charlie's feet were giving him discomfort again. The casts had been worn for about six weeks and were becoming irritating. He complained from time to time about his legs itching. Occasionally, he would use various tools such as pencils, folded paper, etc. to scratch his legs beneath the casts. One night he complained of such pain that I was forced to take him to the emergency room. He informed me that it was serious pain, not just itching that he felt.

When the casts were removed, two things were discovered. A thick piece of folded cardboard (scratching tool) was found deep beneath the cast. Besides this, the pins were beginning to extend from both heels. The doctor, who was one of Dr. Leatherman's assistants, removed the pins and applied new casts. Because of Charlie's medical history, he was admitted for anticipated complications.

The unfortunate timing was such that he was in the hospital on his ninth birthday, March 15. He had been dreaming of a U of K basketball for some time (since Christmas actually). Charles and the kids came with a gift to help celebrate. It made his day to see that it was a U of K basketball. Within the hour, Tim Jordan came by with a birthday present, which happened to be a U of K basketball, as well. He had obviously let it be known around town how badly he wanted this. Immediately, he exclaimed that now he had one for Marty, too. The excitement and laughter intensified. Once the furor died down, his uncle Ray came by with a present. Much to our surprise, it was a U of K basketball, also. We couldn't believe it. There was no doubt where Charlie's heart was. However, he now faced the problem of hurting someone's feelings if he returned one to the store. To relieve his anxiety over this, I offered to take mine back and let him pick out another gift.

During his stay, Charlie had called some of his friends on the phone and apparently had asked them to come see him. When he called Richard and invited him over, he failed to mention that he was in the hospital. Therefore, Richard's mother drove him to our house assuming that Charlie was just gathering his friends together as he often did. When Richard discovered that Charlie had called from the hospital, his mother had to come back to get him. They both laughed at Charlie's nonchalant approach to his hospital stay.

Mrs. Stivers had all of his classmates decorate and sign a long birthday banner. She had many of the teachers sign it as well. Charlie was so elated when Robby and his parents brought it to him, knowing that all of his friends had made it. Its festive appearance expressed to all who entered the room that it was a

170

special day. In spite of his being in the hospital, Charlie's birthday could not have been celebrated in a better way.

The school talent show was normally held on March 17, St. Patrick's Day. This year, however, with Mrs. Kern being aware of Charlie's desire to be in it, it wasn't held until the end of the school year.

After several more weeks in the casts, Dr. Leatherman finally removed them for good. Charlie was put back into the brown orthopedic shoes with short leg braces. Once again, we traveled to the brace shop to be fitted. He would go sock footed until they were ready the next day. A brown, leather T-strap was fastened to the shoes to give him added support.

Due to his inability to bend his back, Charlie required assistance in putting on his shoes. He could not comfortably reach his feet. It was also necessary for me to stretch his feet outward prior to putting them on. This exercise was intended to increase flexibility. Once his feet were in the shoes, they were stretched some more until the fit was just right. From there I moved on to tie the strings and buckle the straps on his shoes and braces. It was so good for him to be able to wear shoes again. Progress walking came rather slowly, as his feet were quite sensitive to standing. Charles or I continued to carry him frequently when the distance was greater than the length of a small room. With time, Charlie became more comfortable and was able to take more steps.

To help promote his independence in church on Sundays, the family had been sitting near the front. Prior to the surgeries on his feet, he was able to walk to receive Holy Communion by himself if it were only a short distance. However, since the surgery, he had been using his wheelchair and the distance didn't matter. Now, his casts had been removed and he had a strong desire to stand for Holy Communion once again. Charles would carry him up the aisle, then stand him before the priest. After receiving Communion, Charles lifted him into his arms again. Although it was necessary, Charlie felt embarrassed in front of his friends.

Then, one Sunday, he was determined to walk to receive Communion on his own. Without saying a word, the pain in his feet was plainly visible on his face. He proudly limped up to the priest. After receiving Communion, he turned to walk, and fell down. With assistance, he got back on his feet and continued back to his seat. I detected some embarrassment from his reaction. His mouth quivered and he was about to cry. I praised him for what a good job he did walking, but he quickly pointed out that he fell. I assured him that no one could see him fall because there were people standing in the way. With that, he swallowed his pride and knelt down to pray.

From that point on he pushed himself daily with great anticipation of going through the First Communion ceremony with his classmates in the upcoming weeks. Although he had already made his First Communion the year before, Mrs. Stivers, Mr. Huelsman and Fr. Caster felt that it was important that he participate with his class as well.

In preparation for this special day, Charlie worked hard at being able to walk about half the distance of the aisle, though with much suffering. When the day came, the First Communion recipients would be walking from their classroom to the church. Then they would form a procession into the church and up the long aisle to the front. Charlie's desire to make it was so strong. Charles offered to carry him to the doorway, but Charlie wouldn't concede. He needed to do this the way everybody else did. He didn't want to stand out. I feared for his embarrassment if he should fall again. Inside, I was anxious to protect him. Outside, I was giving him encouragement to make it happen. I began to tremble as I watched him walk up the aisle with the others. Knowing the obstacles made it that much more meaningful. I observed his limp, his right leg remaining somewhat stiff from the stroke. It concerned me that he could not fold his hands close together like the other children. His barrel-chest and stockiness made it a strain for his hands to meet. The congenital defects of his hands were still visible to my eyes. Yet, despite it all, his heart was glowing so strong with joy, that it showed all over his smiling face. He continued walking all the way to the front with his class. The ceremony was beautiful. He remained stoic and reverent throughout the Mass. Afterward, he walked back the length of the aisle again, feeling very good about his accomplishment. Many friends showed their support for him by acknowledging his achievement. Then, we took pictures of him with his friends and spent some time visiting.

The Stopher family poses with characters prior to climbing aboard the float in the Derby Parade - left to right; Charles, Marty (age six), Charlie (age nine), Leslie (age three) and Mary Jo - second row: Donald Duck, Mickey Mouse, Jonathan (nineteen months) and Jackie (age eleven)

Next, we went to Robby's First Communion party, being as Charlie had already celebrated his.

As for the talent show, it was held during Charlie's recovery. Although he was encouraged to participate even with his casts, Charlie could not bring himself to do it. He insisted that football players would not be playing with their legs in casts, and I had to agree with him. He decided to wait until next year to perform an act.

Never lacking for attention, Charlie was invited to represent The Easter Seal Society on a float in the Kentucky Derby Parade. A new cable TV station in town was gathering a few special children to ride on their float in honor of Donald Duck's 50th birthday, as a promotion for the Disney Channel. Both Mickey Mouse and Donald Duck would be flying in from Disney World for the occasion. Each of the three children would represent a different organization for the handicapped.

Naturally, Charlie was thrilled to have the opportunity to ride in the parade. Having experienced the excitement of the Kentucky Derby each year, he was quite familiar with the event and wasn't the least bit hesitant to accept. A visit to the studio provided instructions and free gifts, including a Mickey Mouse watch. Weeklong activities enhanced the Derby Festival in ways far greater than any participation in the past.

Any event that involved Charlie involved the whole family. We attended the judging of the floats, which gave us the chance to meet Mickey and Donald. We spent several hours enjoying the company of these vibrant characters. Having never visited Disney World, this was a totally new encountering for them.

During the judging period, we were able to mingle among the people and the floats, which provided a rare closeness to a main event. His dad and Charlie climbed aboard the cable TV float, as the parade was about to begin. They sat on a couch as if they were watching Mickey and Donald on a large TV. The rest of us waved them on. At that point, the children and I began walking to the car with plans to meet them at the end of the parade route. After this daylong affair, I had four very tired youngsters. Jonathan, at eighteen-months-old, became heavy rather quickly as I carried him down the street. Leslie, at three and one half-years-old, was worn out after a few steps. So, I carried them both and rested about every fifty feet. For some reason, I had failed to bring the stroller with me.

We could not have missed Charlie's debut on the float. So, we rushed as quickly as possible to the end of the route. By this time it was beginning to seem like an eternity before the parade caught up with us.

I experienced new realities of life that day by being in the crowd at the end of the parade. It was quite obvious that my small family was in the minority as we stood among a massive crowd of blacks. Although the atmosphere was amiable with everyone enjoying the parade, I couldn't help but reflect on how it must have felt only twenty years earlier when a black family would stand in the midst of hundreds of whites. I doubt that they could feel safe and trusting of the person next to them. A sense of sadness came over me that prejudice was so prevalent in the world. Empathy filled my heart as I recalled past news coverage of riots in the streets. Yet, to see these people enjoying activities alongside the whites gave me hope for a better future of acceptance toward all. It was the same type of acceptance that the handicapped communities of crippled, blind, and deaf people were thriving for in their life.

When the Disney float came passing by, it was obvious who was worn out from the ride. The dads and boys managed to smile but were struggling to wave. Yet Mickey and Donald were going strong as they danced and moved about the float. We followed them to the pickup point where those in the parade let out sighs of relief.

As we drove alongside celebrities, the children took pictures and waved to them in disbelief of being so close to special people. The event enlightened us all with a new experience in life.

The Kentucky Derby always gave way to spring fever. The brightness of the sun enticed everyone to enjoy the outdoors as much as possible. Trees and flowers were irresistible to watch as they bloomed into beautiful buds. The children took advantage of the longer days by playing kickball in the courtyard. Parents were once again drawn outside for neighborhood conversations. With summer just around the corner, everyone anxiously counted down the days for school to end.

13

HE AIN'T HEAVY

Our continued activity with The Easter Seal Society gave the executive director the opportunity to invite Charlie to summer camp. Mr. Miller had been trying unsuccessfully for several years to entice him to attend Camp Kysoc. It was first brought to our attention when he was five-years-old. At that time Charles and I felt that he was too young and suggested that he attend when he got older and was better able to handle the separation. Mr. Miller understood our hesitancy at the time, but now believed that Charlie was ready. He could see that Charlie had become less dependent over the years.

Mr. Miller was very proud of The Easter Seal Society and the many opportunities that they offered the handicapped. He wanted to share this with Charlie because he believed that every child should enjoy as much as he/she could in life. This is why the society and many volunteers put so much effort into it.

After further persuasion, Charles and I discussed it and encouraged Charlie to go. Despite the fact that we would miss him greatly, we believed that it would be a unique opportunity. He had been spending the night at his friend Robby's house on several occasions and did not get homesick. He never met a stranger so I couldn't imagine that he would get scared. As a nine-year-old he trusted others and established confidence in himself. We perceived this to be an enjoyable way to develop more independence.

When the brochures came in the mail, Charles and I pointed out all the exciting things that were available. There was swimming, boating, fishing, horseback riding, crafts, and much more. Charlie was not totally convinced that he wanted to go. It was then that I realized that his self-confidence was not what it appeared to be. When I was with him, he believed that he could do anything, but knowing that I wouldn't be with him, he had great doubts about himself. He reminded me of his fear of swimming. He might drown. He might fall out of the boat. He had never ridden a horse before. He might be scared. It seemed that the more I mentioned the more negative response I got. This was all the more reason to push him, I thought. He's obviously becoming too dependent on me.

I thought of my original goal for him, which was to normalize him as much as possible. I couldn't baby him or smother him. Although my motherly instinct wanted to keep him home and protect him, my motherly responsibility forced me to be strong and promote his independence.

The program was well planned with numerous activities. However, I knew that come nighttime, it would be difficult. It always happened that if things weren't going well or if he got too tired, he would go to bed crying over Betsy. Periodically, he was overcome with sorrow over missing her. In the months following her death, he cried most every night. Now, four years later, this happened every few months, usually lasting two or three nights. Many times I sat at the edge of his bed and talked about Betsy and God's love. He was full of questions concerning heaven and what it must be like for her.

It bothered me that I wouldn't be able to do that at camp. It was disturbing to think of his being in bed, crying, with no one there to comfort him. I was as torn about his going as he was about leaving.

My gut feeling told me that it was right to send him. All problems would work themselves out. Charlie was not allowed any reason to think that he might not have a fabulous time. I talked positively as we made the arrangements.

When the day came to leave, we piled the children and the duffel bags into the white Chevrolet station wagon. Charles tied the wheelchair to the luggage rack on the roof of the car. Then off we drove to camp about 90 miles away. It was hard not to think about the separation which we were facing. We played travel games and listened to music to distract our thoughts.

On arrival, we toured the grounds and sleeping quarters. Next, we were directed to the camp nurse to whom we gave Charlie's medications and instructions. We said our good-byes and turned away with some trepidation.

It was hard to simply turn around and leave. So, after pulling out of the campgrounds, we drove across the street to General Butler State Park. As a family, we frequently visited state parks in the summer; so it seemed the perfect place to stop. The children spotted the miniature train station and quickly ran over to it. As Charles and I watched them play, we walked slowly around the park. Our hearts were with Charlie.

I didn't like having only four children to watch. It was no relief for me not to be pushing a wheelchair. I felt that we were missing a link in the family. I looked at Jackie and Marty and saw a gaping hole between them. They seemed so far apart. Charlie should have been with us. This was no respite for us although it was meant to be one of the promoting factors of camp. I began to wonder why I had agreed to it.

The more I watched the children, the emptier I felt. Charles and I walked hand in hand, each feeling the other's emptiness. This must be what it will be like when he's gone, I thought; empty. I couldn't bring myself to say such a thing. But, my feelings were one with Charles'. I knew he sensed my loss with the consoling warmth of his hand in mine.

Little did I know at the time that Charlie's trip to camp was not to promote his independence from me. Rather, it was to prepare me for my independence from him. God knew my ways of thinking and knew just how to prepare me for what was to come.

The next two weeks seemed like an eternity. The house was strangely quiet with Charlie's absence being so obvious. It was actually uncomfortable. To help pass the time, Charles and I loaded the car with the children and took them to a fundraising concert for The Easter Seal Society. There was a moderate crowd in attendance. We ran into several people that we knew including Mr. Miller and his wife. He told us that he had talked to the camp counselor and spoke of what a terrific time that Charlie was having. Mr. Miller had gone there himself to take pictures and see how things were going. He told us how Charlie just laughed the whole time he was there. Believing this was easy because that's exactly how his personality was. Speaking with Mr. Miller lifted our spirits as we were not allowed to call or visit him at camp. This rule was to spare the children from getting homesick.

The day finally came to pick up Charlie. I couldn't tell you who was the first one in the car. We were all anxious to go. He had been sorely missed. The drive was exciting. When we arrived, we were directed to Charlie's cabin. A young volunteer was pushing him in his wheelchair up the pathway to meet us. We could see him smiling from ear to ear even from a distance. It seemed we couldn't reach him quickly enough. As we met, I reached out to give him a great big hug. Before I could get to him, he burst into tears. My heart throbbed at the sight. We all hugged and greeted him. The volunteer was stunned at his sudden tears. She said he had not cried the entire time he was there. When I asked him what was the matter, he proceeded to tell me that he had fallen out of his chair yesterday on the trail to the boat ramp. In doing so, he fell back and bumped his head. The volunteer told us that he didn't experience any injury from the fall. From the look on his face, it was obvious that the crying was not from the fall. He had been brave and strong as always and now he could finally break down. He had missed us so much that the sight of us tore at his heart. We spent a few minutes with everyone hugging before we walked back to the car. A sense of guilt came over me for forcing him to go.

In an attempt to distract him from his heartache, we prompted him to share some camp stories. He was very excited about the fishing competition and catching his first fish. Then he proudly pulled some crafts from his duffel bag, explaining how he made them. It was good to see him do things that he had not done before. The entire week was a great learning experience. They were mostly fun, but just as I had suspected, the nights were hard. One good thing about it was that the children were so tired by the end of the day that they didn't spend much time longing for family before falling asleep.

That summer I began witnessing a new inspiration at daily Mass. New assignments in the archdiocese led another priest to St. Gabriel. Fr. Bruce soon made himself comfortable in the surroundings of the large parish. In a very short time I became attracted to his sensitivity and gift of understanding. When he spoke at Mass, I felt that his words were coming directly from Jesus. All that he said was clear and personal as though I were the only one that he was talking to. Yet, as people conversed after church, I heard that he was speaking personally to them as well. Each had different trials to undergo. Nevertheless, his statements delivered messages to each one of us in profound ways. It was amazing. I felt drawn to his spirit. A realistic feeling of being in the presence of Jesus struck me. This was different than Holy Communion. This was an experience of Jesus's working through someone else in a clear and distinct way. Although I had heard many times that we should see Jesus in everyone we meet, I can't say that I ever recognized it until now. I saw goodness in everyone, yet I never felt the presence of Jesus like this before. Now it was real. I became more anxious to be at Mass every day, which made it easy to get up when the alarm went off. Between Fr. Caster and his tremendous love for children and Fr. Bruce, whose words seemed directly from Jesus, I was quickly moved to a deeper relationship with God. It was magnificent, glorious. I was now getting the most that I could out of daily Mass.

After Mass one day, as Father Bruce was trying to get to know some of the people in the parish, he asked me about my family. He questioned me about Charlie, having noticed that he had a physical disability. I gave him an overall update on Charlie's birth defects and surgeries that he had endured, and ended with the last operation on his feet. I commented on the pain he went through when the pin in his foot had worked its way out through the back of his heel. He turned without hesitancy toward the front of the church and pointed to the large crucifix that hung there. "It's just like Jesus. See the nails in His feet? Look at how he is being used." He said that Charlie was being asked to suffer in very much the same way that Jesus did. Telling me to look at what God asked of His son, he encouraged me to take a look at what God was asking of my son. He spoke of how very similar they were. He added that Charlie was a very special child that God has chosen for a special task.

I was touched by his wisdom and saw very plainly what he meant. Returning home with this in mind allowed contemplation of our conversation. At my kitchen window, I stood washing dishes, all the while meditating on the suffering of Jesus Christ. I began to see that Fr. Bruce had pointed out recognizable facts. In reflecting on the matter, I went back to Charlie's birth. I could see the correlation between every pain that Charlie had endured in the past nine years and that of Jesus Christ. As my mind focused on the crucifix in church, my thoughts carried me from the moment of Charlie's birth to the present. Memories surfaced of Christmas and my previous reflections of Mary's trials as a mother. It was not hard to see how Charlie was quickly put on the cross with Jesus. I pictured his small arm and hand splints stretching out his hands in pain when he was a few weeks old. This thought transferred to Jesus's arms and hands being stretched out on the cross. Short legs held down in casts or braces were similar to Jesus's legs being pressed against the wood of the cross. Picturing the pinholes in the feet that I washed each day reminded me of the radiating pain that Charlie experienced when the pins protruded through his heels. Instantly, the image of Christ's feet came to mind. Such shattering pain must have been felt when those nails were driven through.

Fr. Bruce had offered me an opportunity to reflect and meditate on this portion of Jesus's suffering. As busy as I had been with my responsibilities as a mother, I had overlooked this last message that God attempted to share with me. I realized that there were times that I was too wrapped up in my own busy life to absorb what He offered. However, I had to chuckle because I knew that God sent Fr. Bruce to awaken me. Just as God comes to each of us over and over again through various people, He tried again with me. He would not allow me to overlook this. My conversation with Fr. Bruce made me realize how important it was to meditate on Christ's suffering.

I continued with meditation and reflection as I completed washing the dishes. I saw the incision in Charlie's chest from heart surgery along with the final gash from the spear of the Centurion guard. I observed the serous (watery) blood that flowed from the chest tube along with the water and blood that flowed from Jesus's chest. I pictured the scars from the incisions around Charlie's side and back from the two spinal surgeries. I

182

thought of the lashes from the whips on Jesus's back. Recalling the seizures and the stroke that affected his brain brought forth meditation on the painful crown of thorns pressed upon Him as they mocked the self-proclaimed King of the Jews. Charlie's suffering was a mere sampling of the amount of suffering that Jesus endured for all of us. Yet, I found it amazing that Jesus so willingly would go through it again and again through each of us as we suffer. I was fully aware that Charlie did not suffer alone. Part of this awareness was due to the fact that I was suffering a great deal for him out of my love for him. His dad was suffering in the same way. His brothers and sisters all suffered, as well as every relative and friend that knew him. In varying degrees many people were hurting out of their love for Charlie and the family. In reflecting upon these observations, it was easy to understand that Jesus has suffered along with us. It is because of His great love for us that He experienced every physical and emotional pain of Charlie's life. Far beyond our comprehension is the pain that He feels each day for the millions of people in the world.

Continuing with my reflections, I pondered the hundreds of needle pricks that Charlie had endured for years. This was the hardest procedure for him. It happened over and over and over again. There was no getting away from it. Even during his more healthy times, tests were still being done. I thought of the long night of torture on Good Friday that Jesus endured. The continual pain inflicted upon Him during that terrible passion, was an unbearable image. The thought of this brought to light the depth of His love for us. Then I saw the perseverance that Charlie had while accepting whatever pain we put him through. He did not resent the doctors. He did not complain or refuse an operation. With trust, he willingly accepted whatever was expected of him. I thought of Jesus's persecution and how He persevered to the bitter end. He didn't hate His persecutors. He loved them in spite of the pain that they put Him through, even asking the Father to forgive them.

As my thoughts continued, I began to make sense of the question "Why?" So many people wonder why God would allow bad things to happen to the innocent. I saw that it is only through the suffering of the innocent that we are connected to Jesus' suffering. Who is more innocent than Jesus was? No one, as He was without sin, but a baby is the most innocent of all His creatures. When we witness great suffering, we recall what Jesus suffered for us. It is then that we appreciate how much He loves us. I felt I was being given many graces with this knowledge. I saw that God needed Charlie and many others such as he scattered across the world so that all might witness God's love through them. I felt blessed and honored to be given such an opportunity to witness God's love. This enlightenment put an end to any questions I once had.

By the time T-ball started in the summer, Charlie's feet had improved enough that he could tolerate the discomfort a little longer. Nothing would keep him from playing ball. Although he was nine-years-old, his physical disabilities prevented him from playing baseball. This didn't matter to him because all of his friends were eight-years-old and still playing T-ball. The coach, Robby's dad, allowed him to play despite the rule of age, which was six to eight. It wasn't as though he was going to play better or run faster than the eight-year-olds. It was unanimous that he would not be a threat to the other teams.

In just a matter of time, however, a mother of a child on another team objected to him playing. She insisted that he was too old and it was not fair. Making an issue out of it to her coach, it was then brought to Mr. Wheeler's attention. He not only coached, he was also in charge of the T-ball program. He stood his ground and insisted that Charlie's age would not give him an edge over the rest. Therefore, there was no more discussion of it. He was allowed to play.

It turned out to be a great year. Being on the same team as his brother Marty meant a great deal to Charlie. He proudly took his position and kept his eye on the ball. When he hit the ball, he ran with all his might. The bases were still being brought in halfway, and the talk on an occasional opposing team continued. Although the Reds had another winning season, it was not because of Charlie's skill. After all, it was difficult for him to catch a ball with the stiffness in his back. He always missed the grounders because he couldn't bend down low. At best he would jump to the ground to get it. Despite his inability to run properly, his unyielding spirit overcame all obstacles and inspired his teammates.

The last game of the season was truly special. A fly ball was hit straight to Charlie. His eyes were fixed on it. The ball fell right into his glove and he hung on to it. His heart was pounding with disbelief. His face was glowing. He felt like the hero. The entire team, including parents, raved over him. In three years of T-ball, it was the first time he was able to catch a fly ball. His dad and I were thrilled for him to have finally had this experience, knowing that this would probably be the last year for him to play organized ball.

Going on through the summer, we did our normal activities such as swimming and going to the various parks. On an occasional weekend, I packed a picnic lunch and the whole family would go to visit a historical site in Kentucky.

When fall crept in, Charlie was entering the third grade. His teacher, Mrs. White, spoke with willingness to help Charlie get through the year. In the beginning, it was more difficult than she had imagined as Charlie always started off slowly. It didn't appear as though he would be able to keep up with the class. Mrs. White was excellent, however. She could see that Charlie did fine in understanding concepts. His difficulty was with finishing all the work in a given amount of time. She concluded that if he was given half of the work, he could grasp the concept without all the unnecessary busy work.

Math was not a problem. Charlie loved it and understood it well. By the third or fourth problem it was plain to see that he had mastered it. Given the advantage of working ten problems rather than twenty problems, took the stress out of learning for him.

Spelling was a little more difficult because the stroke had made phonics uncorrelated with his speech. Even with therapy, his speech remained somewhat slurred. Often times, I saw that he was spelling words the way that he spoke them. His brain was obviously having a struggle with this, which was potential frustration. Extra time was required on spelling lessons, which also incorporated lessons in patience. Most evenings required three hours of homework simply because of the extra help that was needed. Feeling the importance of making Charlie believe in himself, meant seeing to it that he understood all that was covered in class. Whenever he doubted himself, I was quick to point out that he was smart enough to do the work, making certain that he understood that time was not an issue. Jackie and Marty would usually find some homework questions for me, as well. They didn't want three hours of work, but they certainly wanted a fair share of my help.

Not long after school started, there were signups being held for soccer. Charlie figured that because he couldn't play football until the fifth grade, that he would sign up for soccer now. He was always putting me to the test. My constant encouragement sometimes backfired on me. He pleaded with me to allow him to play. I pointed out that it would require a lot of standing on the field, which would be very hard on his feet. I indicated that he would have to run a lot and it would be stressful on his heart. None of this mattered. He was determined to play at any cost. By now, Charlie believed that he could do anything that he set his mind to. I felt that this was a good attitude to have; yet, I was afraid of setting him up for disappointment. Sometimes I would fill him with words of wisdom and encouragement to strengthen him, then turn around and wonder why I did. I often turned to God when this happened. I felt that God wanted me to nourish him with spirit. These words could make him strong even if he failed. It was important that he learn trust and faith. He would have to believe in himself because in failure he could see his limitations. With perseverance, he could often overcome the obstacles. This quality that he learned often taught others not to waste their abilities.

His intention to sign up for football in two years was no secret. I dreaded the thought of breaking the news to him that he would not be able to play. Yet, I couldn't destroy the only dream that he ever had. Knowing that there were only two more years before the reality would have to be faced, I began praying more to the Holy Spirit. I prayed for Him to lead me, to guide me, to teach me what to say and do in fulfillment of God's will. It was because of my faith in this prayer that I let things go as they happened. I trusted God's guidance in the words I spoke even when I questioned them. Trusting that I should not worry about the football, I knew that God would direct me on how to handle it when the time came. It was important for Charlie to have this dream as a youngster. It gave him something to enjoy and to live for during all of his trials. I put aside my fears regarding football and took a closer look at the soccer program.

Charlie was bouncing with enthusiasm over the thought of being on a real soccer team. He began to believe in himself. The need to be part of a team was about to be filled. The coach will see what he is capable of doing. Charles and I discussed it and agreed to let him sign up on the condition that he sit out if he got too tired. Happily, he agreed.

As the season began, the coach was quickly touched by his persistence. Charlie hung around him until he was put in to play. After a short time, it was plain to see that he could hardly stand up any longer. He was pulled out and he rested on the ground. Once he caught his breath again and the pain in his feet subsided, he was seen pacing near the coach again. He was put in and pulled out more often than any other player. Once again, as in T-ball, his skills did little for the team. Being a member of the team did more for his spirit and his spirit, in turn, did more for the team. It was truly a rewarding experience for all.

The fall breeze was not the only thing nipping the air. So, too, was the football on Mosswood Lane. Each evening after homework and chores were done, Charlie headed outside with Marty to gather all the boys in the neighborhood for a friendly game of football. Sometimes they played with only a few boys available. Other times the yard was filled with boys. Mostly they played with Jamie and Tony Combs and Scott and Tony Jolly. When the other boys got tired of playing, Charlie shuffled on down the street to play with Trevor and Todd O'Neil. These boys were a bit older, but they never intimidated Charlie. He looked up to them because they both played on the school football team. They generally agreed to toss the ball around with him. After they became tired, Charlie frequently sat on their porch waiting for them to begin a second round. In spite of his shortness of breath, he never wanted to quit playing. His determination seemed to wear out everyone else on the street.

Sometimes, the boys were inspired to play something different. If they rode bikes, Charlie would be asked to mark the finish line when they raced. This way he was included in the action. If they wanted a little more exercise, they would race around the block while he sat on the porch and waited for them to come back. Oftentimes, the children played in the back yard. Together, they made forts on both sides of the creek and enjoyed frontier battles. How I loved watching them play from the kitchen window. It was clear that God was answering my prayers. Charlie was being given TIME to play and TIME to enjoy the normal activities of youth.

A small wooded area stretched a short distance behind our house. It was a struggle for Charlie to walk in the woods because of his unsteady gait over the uneven terrain. As I watched from the window, I noticed how he often waited for the other boys to return from an adventure. Marty's imagination promoted much fun for all the boys. I frequently witnessed him compromising with Charlie, trying so hard to include him as much as possible. Knowing that Marty had the fastest feet in the neighborhood and Charlie had the slowest, one could appreciate the unlimited patience that Marty had with his brother. Many times I watched Marty and his friends assist Charlie over the creek. They were always patient with him. Generally, the group would run ahead and one of the boys would help Charlie until they caught up. When I looked out one day and saw Marty helping him, the song, "He Ain't Heavy, He's My Brother" came to mind. The words of the song reverberated in my head over and over again. It was such a good feeling to see that neither Marty nor his friends found Charlie to be burdensome. Witnessing this brotherly love was a reward in itself, one which brought tears of joy to my eyes.

Occasionally, Charlie would just find it too exhausting to keep up with the activities of the others. Choosing to conserve his limited energy, he would come in bored and longing for something to do. Mostly, he sat at the table and lined up miniature football players on an electronic field or the table itself. He could do this for hours as he arranged numerous plays. His imagination and his knowledge of football enabled him to have a great time by himself. Score was kept, but most often his favorite team won.

During these moments, he filled me in on all the statistics of football, sharing his knowledge of every player and team. The Pittsburgh Steelers and Notre Dame Irish were tops on the list. Charlie also took this opportunity to talk to me about his strong desire to play football on a team. I told him he could have his own team any time that he wanted it. All he had to do was call his friends from school and invite them to come play football with him. I stressed the fact that playing in the yard was far more fun than playing on a school team. He would have the advantage of playing as much as he wanted and resting whenever he needed. He agreed that it would be more fun and quickly asked when he could plan a game. I told him that any Saturday would be fine for such an event.

By the end of the week, I had forgotten our conversation. I woke up early as usual on Saturday morning. After attending Mass, I stopped to do several errands before coming back home. On my return, I discovered a yard full of boys playing football. Some had come from a fair distance away. I greeted them, then went in to ask Charles what was going on. He said that he woke up discovering parents dropping off their children. He informed me, "Charlie said that you told him that his friends could come over to play football."

"Oh." I replied. "I guess he's right. I did say that." I looked outside only to see his face gleaming with excitement. I couldn't dare correct his way of going about it. So, I waited until all the boys had gone home. Then we had a brief discussion about checking with one of the parents just before inviting his friends the next time. It then became a regular event.

As fall progressed, the holidays came quickly. Halloween was a struggle for Charlie due to the fact that he was not able to walk door to door like everyone else. He would be short of breath by the first house. So, in alternating years Charles and I took turns pushing him in his wheelchair while the other stayed behind to pass out candy. Charlie didn't like using the wheelchair for Trick or Treating, but if he could talk Jonathan into sitting on his lap, he would enjoy it more. He didn't especially care about the candy, but participating in the event with his siblings gave him great joy. Although it was strenuous pushing the wheelchair through the grass and up the hills, it was worth the joy that it brought him. Content in going a short distance, he was happy to return home early. At that point he passed out the candy while the others went back out for more.

Thanksgiving was traditionally a very special time for reflection. Thinking back over the accomplishments of the past year gave us so much to be thankful for. Not only were we given a beautiful family and tremendous faith, but Charlie had lived an entire year without the threat of losing his life. The activities of daily living were beginning to look almost normal. It had been ten months since his foot surgery and there was no surgery pending at the present time. We were very grateful.

As the days became shorter and colder, more time was spent indoors. The family had gotten hooked on Bruce Springsteen music. The children all loved it. They would set up a stage in the living room and play their toy or makeshift instruments along with the music. Charles and I were well entertained by them. One day a phone call came from Charles' sister who offered us two Bruce Springsteen tickets for a concert in Lexington. We felt very fortunate to be given this fantastic opportunity. We gladly bought the tickets and looked forward to an evening out together. The children were crushed that they couldn't go with us. So, I told them that if he were to come to Louisville in the future, we would take them. This satisfied them. Little did we know that the very day after the concert, it would be announced that he was coming to Louisville in January. Now we were stuck. We had made a promise that would be very difficult to keep. With Christmas around the corner, it didn't seem even remotely possible. Pondering the timing and our promise led us to buy four tickets and put them in the stockings of the three oldest children and Charles'. Meanwhile, I encouraged the kids to save their pocket money in hopes of buying their own ticket. They began to do extra chores around the house to enable them to reach their goal.

When Christmas came, they were stunned to see that Santa had left them tickets. Naturally, they were each concerned about Leslie, Jonathan and my not having a ticket. Telling them that it would be too cold and too late for the younger ones to go helped them to understand why Santa had not left us tickets, as well. They were pleased that they had saved a few dollars that could now be used for spending money at the concert.

Meanwhile, I had ordered an electric cart for Charlie to get around in. Medicaid approved this because it would promote his independence. On the day of the concert the Tri-Kart arrived. Its delivery was bad timing, which caused them to be late for the concert.

The Tri-Kart that was delivered was made for an adult. Charlie was only nine-years-old, short and stocky. He obviously could not sit back in the seat and reach the handlebars. Observing this, I questioned its size. The deliveryman suggested ordering a different handlebar that would reach inward toward the seat. This way he could grow into the size of the Tri-Kart for future use. He informed me that Medicaid would only pay for one. If he outgrew it, he would not get another one. Therefore, he strongly suggested that we keep the adult size to allow for growth. After being convinced, that's what we did. I could only shake my head in disbelief that he could not have been better fitted for the Tri-Kart.

Charles and the kids went on to the concert. They got there just as the show began, missing part of the first song. It was obvious that the children had the best time as they came home laughing and singing. They couldn't wait to turn on the stereo and blast the house with Bruce Springsteen music when they came in from the concert. They sang with more excitement now. In the following weeks, there was no diversity of music heard. The Disney records had been relegated to the back of the cabinet. The kids sang and danced as they did their chores. They couldn't resist throwing their fists in the air and singing "Born In The USA." As always, music created the harmony of winter indoors.

In the following weeks, Charlie was getting used to riding the Tri-Kart in the house. He had to sit on the edge of the seat because it was much too big for him. It turned out that the new handlebars, which were to be exchanged, were going to cost money that we didn't have and it was going to be more awkward to deal with as well. We decided to pass on the handlebars and wished that we had insisted on a child's Tri-Kart. However, Charlie decided he liked having the big Tri-Kart because someone could ride with him that way. Every child in the neighborhood was fascinated by the novelty of it. They all wanted a ride with Charlie.

When the weather was nice, he took it outside and was able to go wherever the other boys would go. He no longer sat on the porch when the boys rode their bikes. He discovered his independence. He gleefully rode down the street and up the hill to play at Scott's house. Seeing the neighborhood from a new perspective brought a new excitement to his summer. The limitations of staying in the court were lifted. It was the greatest gift that he could have received.

By February, Charlie and Marty had their minds set as to their act for the upcoming talent show at school. They invited their friends Robby, Adam, Jason and Michael to be in their "E Street Band" as they performed "Born In The USA." All but Robby joined in. Being a bit shy, he declined the offer. The others began coming over regularly after school and on weekends to practice their act, which was a great deal of fun.

March 15 rolled around quickly. It was Charlie's tenth birthday. We planned a big party to celebrate another year of life. On this particular birthday, I received a phone call from Dr. Cottrill, in Lexington. She said that she was just thinking about Charlie, and added, "Who would have ever thought that Charlie would be here for his tenth birthday?" She was just in awe that he had come such a long way since birth. She expressed her great appreciation of God's gift of time for Charlie. Together we reminisced about the past ten years. It made me feel wonderful that God had not only given me this time with Charlie, but that He had given me such good people to share his life with. I felt so blessed and fortunate to have been led to Dr. Cottrill, not only because of her professional knowledge, but because of her friendship. When I was with her, I didn't feel reluctant to talk about God as I normally would with most people. It was probably because of the personal trials in her own life that she was aware of my dependence upon God. For whatever reason, the sharing of our love for God drew us closer with each year that passed. As I hung up the phone, I could feel her spirit with me as I prepared for Charlie's party.

All the boys in his class had been invited. Jason was quick to let us know that he would be here despite the fact that his mother was in the hospital about to deliver a new baby. After playing a few games and receiving prizes the boys began an exciting game of football, leaving little time for cake and ice cream before parents came. A football cake had become Charlie's traditional request for the past several years. However, getting a little bored with it myself, I was able to convince Charlie that a different style would be nice for a change. He agreed. So, I made him a "Ghostbusters" cake, as that was popular at the time.

Once the crowd left, Robby, Jason and Adam stayed for the night. They celebrated the birth of Jason's sister, then laughed and frolicked until the wee hours of the morning. Of course, Charles was right in there with them. He would say anything to keep them all hyped up. Each told jokes and stories and played indoor basketball as well as any other activity to keep from going to sleep. Charlie's laughter could be heard throughout the house, as he was easily entertained and difficult to quiet down. In fact, he frequently laughed till he cried and his ribs became sore.

By morning, we were all exhausted. We lounged around after the boys left and spent the day playing with Charlie's gifts.

When it came time for the talent show, the boys were ready to go. I painted Jason's skin brown so that he could play the part of the saxophone player, Clarence. Each boy dressed as Bruce would dress, in a white tee shirt, blue jeans, and a kerchief tied around his head. Each had a ball cap tucked in their back hip pocket as Bruce did on his album cover. They were so excited. They had worked hard to prepare for their turn in the spotlight. As the show began, Marty was center stage with Charlie and Michael on each side. Adam kept the beat on the drums in the back along with Jason on the saxophone. The music began. Marty led the way with rhythmic leadership. They all sang loud and hard and were very effective with their motions. Upon ending, they felt good about pleasing the crowd. As second and third graders, this was a great accomplishment. Charlie, especially, glowed with excitement. He grinned from ear to ear with an obvious sense of belonging. It was this sort of situation that helped Charlie to forget about his differences, such as his braces, his limp, his speech, and his short stature. These were the furthest things from his mind, yet those watching could not help but see the obstacles he overcame.

Before long, the school year ended and summer was upon us. Mr. Miller, from The Easter Seal Society, now wanted Charlie to attend Camp Green Shores. This was a more modern camp than Camp Kysoc and he was certain that Charlie would enjoy it immensely.

Charlie, however, was reluctant to go to camp again because he missed home so badly the last time. Knowing it was a good experience for him, I encouraged him to give it another try. I pointed out the differences that would make camp more enjoyable this year. So much was being offered in sports, fishing, boating, horseback riding and other activities. Modern facilities, such as the air-conditioned cafeteria, would provide more comfort. He would also know more people because of meeting them at previous events.

He remained reluctant. Contrary to my conviction that he would have a positive experience once he got there, I really didn't want him to go, either. Remembering the pain of missing him made me truly want to maximize my time with him. Mr. Miller stressed the opportunity to give parents a break. Again, I had a hard time looking at it this way. Never did I find it a burden to put on braces or lift the wheelchair in and out of the car. These activities were as ordinary as tying my shoes or brushing my teeth each morning. To me, they were not extraordinary duties.

In the back of my mind I felt an obligation to teach Charlie to be independent. It was so tempting to want to do everything for him. Although I wanted to protect him, I did not wish to promote his dependency on others. Therefore, I encouraged him to always try and to believe in himself. Making certain not to baby him, I kept in sight my original goal for him to be as normal as possible. I taught him to accept help when he needed it and to do for himself whenever he could. I had to train myself to do the same. Often, I held back when my heart was intent on doing it for him. The hardest part about raising him was my own self- discipline.

The camp issue was a real struggle in my heart. I spent some time reflecting on what was best for Charlie in the long run. As a result I was more insistent about his going this year. In spite of how difficult it was last year, I believed it was good for him. No matter what I said, Charlie was not convinced that it would be fun.

The night before leaving for camp, I had a large cake order to fill for St. Gabriel Church. Fr. Bruce would be leaving the parish and a special party had been planned. Four full-size sheet cakes were to be baked, which would feed 400 people. The decorating on the main cake was very time-consuming, which entailed staying up most of the night completing it.

The following day, after a short nap, I proceeded to take Charlie to camp. Charles had to work so his mother and sister offered to ride along with me. They were concerned about my making the long trip alone with five children. So, off we went together.

By the time we arrived, my hand was in severe pain. It had been aching since decorating the cakes the night before. Nighttime had fallen and I had been unable to really look at my hand while I was driving to see what the problem was. Once I stopped the car and turned the light on I observed why I had been hurting so badly. My hand had swollen to an enormous size. The sight of it shocked me. There was nothing I could do about it but bear the pain.

We said our good-byes to Charlie. Each of the kids gave him a kiss and a hug. Smiling all the while, my heart was broken at the thought of leaving him. I knew that he was feeling the same way, but we all put on our stoic faces and parted ways.

The trip back was not nearly as enjoyable. We were all tired. My hand was now throbbing and my heart was with Charlie. I suddenly felt as if I had made the wrong decision again by insisting that he go. For some reason, I wasn't convinced at the moment that his independence was all that important. Thoughts of his future life came to mind. I couldn't picture him ever being totally independent anyway. So why, then, was it even important? Feeling eager to talk to God about all these things, I was anxiously looking forward to some private time with Him. I would not be able to reflect as I drove home due to a car full of people. Having them in the car, I was naturally drawn into conversations. Because they felt responsible for keeping me awake, I realized that this time with God would have to come later.

I pondered many thoughts over the next few weeks, realizing that supposedly good things are not always good. As wonderful as the camp was, maybe it wasn't worth it for Charlie. I decided never to push it again. He was getting older and knew by now how he felt about leaving.

The letters Charlie wrote at camp indicated his homesickness, especially at night. This made the two weeks extremely long. The end of the camp session seemed so far into the future that it appeared unreachable. When the day finally came, the children and I eagerly left to pick him up. It so happened that he did have a good time after all. He fell in love with one of the counselors, which made all the difference. She obviously enjoyed working with him and was apparently greatly moved by his enthusiasm. Her caring mannerisms made him feel special, which was an added consolation to me.

Another child who needed a ride back to Louisville returned with us. After dropping the girl off, we directed our path toward Mosswood Lane. Charlie shared a few stories on the way back about his camp experiences. Mostly, the children were dozing off, as the trip had exhausted them. Once home, Charlie perked up instantly upon seeing his dad. He was greeted with a big bear hug. He shared the fun events that he participated in. It was a happy moment when he told of receiving the award, "Cowboy of the Year." In the midst of his excitement, he surprised me by acknowledging that he had no desire to go again because he missed us all immensely.

Anticipating a new summer of baseball, Charlie was looking forward to playing at the next level without using a batting tee. Getting older meant that he could advance in his skills. Yet, the problem remained that he could not run like the others. This would be expected for baseball, whereas in T-ball he could get by. In researching the leagues, I discovered a new team being started that very summer for handicapped players. It was not in our neighborhood, but we felt it was worth driving the distance. The distinction of the team allowed for players from other vicinities. This is perfect, I thought. We signed Charlie up immediately. A special day was planned for all the teams in the Okolona League, starting with a parade and ending with the recognition of the teams. The coaches were excited about the novelty of including special athletes. A meeting was held to explain the game plan. At the first practice, I could see Charlie's great disappointment even before he spoke. The coach took a softball and placed it on a batting tee as she explained how the game would be played. Upon seeing this, his mouth dropped. He had anticipated a year of advancing, not regressing.

The team was primarily designed for those in wheelchairs. A parent would push the wheelchair of their child around the bases. Although Charlie used a wheelchair frequently, he preferred not using it unless he had to. He used determination to get him around the bases. Practicing with the team that day, he chose not to use his wheelchair. He walked up to the tee as he had many times before. Disappointment was expressed on his face as he focused on the softball. This was not the image that had lived in his heart. He expected a pitcher throwing a baseball. The hour-long practice was interminable.

On the way home, he let out his frustration. He almost cried thinking that he wouldn't be able to play *real* baseball this year. Thoughts had been scurrying through my mind as to how I would console him for his loss of another dream. I began by talking up the joy of playing baseball at home with brothers, sisters, and neighbors. I pointed out that many children don't get to play the way that they dream of playing. I shared stories of my own childhood as I explained the sadness of sitting on the bench. The one or two on the bench always feel that they aren't good enough. They feel left out and embarrassed. Being on an organized team was not always full of wonder and glory. It was no secret to him that he couldn't run fast. He knew that he would be the one left on the bench. We talked as we drove home planning a way to enjoy baseball the most. One of his concerns was being able to play on a baseball diamond. I agreed to take Charlie and his friends to the park regularly so that they could experience the feel of a baseball diamond.

That summer, after the chores were done, I loaded up the car weekly with as many kids as we could find and headed to the park. The station wagon came in handy for piling them in. This break away from home was helpful in adding diversity and kept Charlie from getting bored.

There were times that we discovered well-kept football fields around town, too. As he spotted them on various school properties, he easily coaxed me into accommodating his plans for the next day. All it took was to hear the excitement in his voice. Witnessing his joy was well worth all my efforts, even in the heat of summer. Knowing that the girls and Jonathan (being so young) would not get nearly the enjoyment out of it, I discovered alternative ways to spend time with them while the boys played. Cheerleading worked for a while but soon got old. Sometimes we had a picnic or played a game.

One day when it could not have been cooler than 95 degrees in the shade, I found myself on the sidelines cheering on the boys, thinking I was going to suffocate from the stale heat. However, I was determined to smile and go along with Charlie, hoping that one of them would suggest that they had played enough. Time was not a factor and I wasn't about to destroy his enthusiasm. It was very important for him to know that he could count on me. It was vital that he have something to look forward to. This gave him a will to live, which is why I found it so easy to go along with these absurd plans that he came up with. Any time that he found something impossible to do, I offered a different way to make it possible. He had learned not to give up on his dreams. Rather, he was to search for other ways to make them happen. I strongly reinforced in him the philosophy, "Where there's a will, there's a way."

Later that summer, I met with Fr. Bruce for the Sacrament of Reconciliation. By now, he had come to know much of Charlie's history. As we talked, he asked me if I believed that God made Charlie this way because I took the pill. My response, after having these years of observation and spiritual growth on the matter, was this: "No, I don't believe that's 'why' it happened, but I do believe that's 'how' it happened." With some elaboration, I could explain that I did not believe that God inflicts punishment on us by hurting our children. I could clearly see that Charlie was a gift to me and in no way a burden. God had used Charlie to bring many people close to Him. He has shown His greatness through Charlie numerous times. Therefore, it could not be a punishment. However, I did believe that from a physical standpoint, the components within the pill at the time caused changes in my body resulting in damage to the fetus.

As for the gut feeling that I experienced prior to giving birth to Charlie, I believed it was the deceit of evil. Guilt comes from Satan, not from God. It was an opportunity for guilt to consume me and remind me of my unworthiness. I could have made many wrong choices at that youthful age. I could have had an abortion or I could have lived with guilt forever. My marriage could have been torn apart. But none of those things happened because God was more powerful in my life. When God sent intercessors starting with Mrs. Wolek telling me to make the best of my time with Charlie, I was able to listen. The spiritual rewards have been so great that Charlie's life was clearly meant to be as it was. I told Fr. Bruce that I now believe that had I taken the pill or not, Charlie's life would still be the same. Whether it was due to the pill or a chemical that passed by me during pregnancy or a strange fluke of nature, I may never know. It no longer mattered to me. But through this experience I have been made aware of the power of Satan and the greater power of God.

14 STRENGTHENING THE TEAM

Preparing Charlie for the fourth grade was, admittedly, a fearful time. Having been through this transition with Jackie, I was aware of all the changes that Charlie would be facing. Instead of having one teacher, he would have four. Classes would move from room to room requiring good organizational skills. The change would require more mental and physical demands. Nevertheless, I wasn't about to give in to my fears. I was determined to stand with him and see him through. Together we survived the third grade and this would simply be a greater challenge.

The first two weeks of school turned out to be more difficult than I had imagined. Charlie always started off behind the rest. He seemed to lose more during the summer than most kids do. It was apparent by the way he came home from school very frustrated. He would say that he was "dumb." He felt terribly inadequate. Every time the teacher would call on him, he didn't know the answer. When he did know, she wouldn't call on him. I could relate to his embarrassment. I remembered times in school when I was not always prepared for class. At times the teacher would call on me again and again when I didn't know the answer.

My heart went out to him because I knew his pain. I realized, of course, that my experiences of humiliation were my own fault for not being fully prepared. Charlie, on the other hand, worked hard in spite of his limitations. The effects of the stroke were catching up with him now. Not only was his speech still slurred, he also had trouble retaining too much at one time. The undamaged portion of his brain apparently was unable to accommodate all that he needed to learn. His thought process was slow, thus requiring deep concentration. It was hard for Charlie to grasp new topics quickly. Therefore, he steadily fell behind his classmates as the days passed.

He began to come home more frustrated every day. He saw how the other children were learning at a greater speed. This was intimidating to him. The more they learned, the more inadequate he felt. I offered encouragement and prayed for words of wisdom, knowing that God would lead me in the right direction. I had no idea what to expect, but I was certain that there was an answer somewhere.

Upon entering the front door after school one day, his mouth dropped and words of defeat poured from his lips. I hugged him and listened to his expressed pain. That evening, as he was unable to avoid thinking about school, he went to his room in great despair.

My heart was heavy with sadness as I fought back the tears. I followed him to his bed where he lay sobbing. I had never seen him so devastated. I promised him that we would talk to his teachers and work something out. If necessary, we would find another school that would better fit his needs. In defeat he said, "There are no schools for me. They'll all be the same. I'm just dumb."

"No, you're *not* dumb," I insisted. "You had a stroke when you were a baby. Your brain just has to work differently. It has to work harder. You have no control over it. That's why you became left-handed after your stroke. Your brain has to use a different part for learning." I tried desperately to help him understand. He cried. I leaned over beneath the top bunk and hugged him. He said he wished he were dead. He cried out with tears flowing down his cheeks, "Maybe I'll just run out the back door and jump over the balcony. Or, I'll get in the car and run it down into the ditch. Or maybe I'll just get a knife and throw it at my neck." I allowed him to continue, listening intently to the pain in his words. I knew with certainty that he had to get away from the high expectations of the learning environment that he had been living in. With my arm around him, I continued to hug him and soothe his anger. I spoke calmly and promised him again that we would speak to his teachers and work out a solution. He was overwhelmed with helplessness and insisted that it wouldn't help. I suggested alternatives to speed up his learning, such as my reading to him to save time. He had a stack of work that could not be finished by bedtime even with my assistance. I saw that no matter how much I helped, or how much he tried, neither of us could repair the damage done by the stroke he had as a baby. This slow learning process was going to be a pattern for him for the rest of his life. "You will not have another day like this," I promised. "In the morning, you'll stay home while I try to work something out." I could see no point in pushing him further now.

The following day, I met with his teachers and the principal after school. It was no secret that there was a problem. They had already discussed it and offered the suggestion that Charlie go to another school with a program for the learning disabled. Sharing with them his previous experience in the first grade, I explained how he had lost out on so much when he was capable of learning more. I stated that he needed the challenge, yet the frustration level was far beyond normal. In a form of rebuttal, I asked if his workload could just be decreased as it had been in the past. Their response was that the class might believe they were playing favorites if less was required of him than of the others. I pleaded that the students would not have to know. I offered to work with him at any length each evening but to no avail. They felt strongly that it wasn't fair to Charlie to spend five hours a night on homework. Each of them believed that he should not be frustrated and that he needed playtime as well. It was agreed that these were important factors in a child's life. At the same time, however, I grieved at the thought of taking him out of St. Gabriel. It was important to be in the same school as his friends, brother and sisters. From a social aspect, leaving would be detrimental.

In the end I submitted to their decision, thanking them all for their time and effort. Disappointment enveloped my soul. Yet, I knew that it was best for Charlie to be out of this stressful learning environment.

The children had been hanging around the school waiting for me. Charlie was anxious but scared to hear the verdict. I couldn't bear to tell him, especially in front of the other children. Once we were home, I began by sharing with him that everyone agreed that another school would be easier for him. He burst into tears

203

and ran, with his wobbly gait, into his room, exclaiming, "See, I told you they couldn't do anything."

I immediately went to his room to comfort him. I noticed how quiet the other children were in the other room. They were probably listening, not knowing what to make of it all. Charles had not come home from work yet. I knelt on the floor next to Charlie as he lay on the bottom bunk in distress. While slowly stroking his back, I promised him that we would find something more appropriate for him. "Maybe another school would be better. We're going to look into some other options because St. Gabriel is just too hard for you. You should be enjoying school, Charlie. You don't need to be spending all evening on homework." Consolation did not come easily due to his conviction that he could no longer be happy.

He doubted it and responded, "What if it's like that at another school? It's just going to be the same anywhere. I know it."

Discussing his fears, I assured him that we would check out different schools together. After looking at them we would agree on the one to try. "When we find one, we'll try it for a few weeks and if it doesn't work, we'll find another one. If means going to ten schools, then that's what we'll do." I encouraged him not to be afraid or to worry about it. Believing in this promise was difficult for him, as he could not imagine any school to be right for him.

Then came the next heartache, his friends. He cried some more over the thought of leaving his friends. They were his life. We discussed having them over to play. I encouraged him to invite his buddies to a movie or to the park. Whatever was necessary, we would do to keep the ties of friendship alive.

He moved from one issue to another, from friends to family to being in a Catholic school. He liked going to school with Jackie, Marty, and Leslie. He looked forward to Jonathan's going to "his" school. All these factors reminded him of just how much St. Gabriel meant to him. He enjoyed seeing the ladies in the lunchroom, who were always so cheerful with him. He appreciated the older boys who helped him on and off the school bus.

I then suggested that he play with Marty for a while as I prepared dinner. Noticing his sluggishness, I sensed that I had only lifted a small fraction of the weight that he was carrying inside. My thoughts were with him as I worked over the stove. Never had I experienced more emotional pain than I did at that moment. Feeling his heartache and acknowledging his valid concerns were some of the heaviest crosses I had to bear.

It hit me hard when I reflected on what was happening to Charlie's life. First, the summer was not as good as I had hoped it to be. The disappointment in baseball indicated that a part of his childhood had ended. Now, the school that he loved so much would no longer be the same in his life as it always had been. It was another ending. Although I wasn't certain what God's plan was, I was aware that He was leading the way. The dreams that I had for Charlie were slowly being abandoned. I was determined, however, not to allow Charlie to become defeated. Whatever obstacle he faced, we faced together with God.

Hearing the emotional rage of suicidal thoughts coming from this child, who had always been filled with joy and confidence, touched my soul in the most devastating way. Yet, I found strength to console him in his hour of distress. God was constantly there for me with the right words to say. He guided me so that I could relieve Charlie's anguish. As much as it hurt me, I did not give in to fear, for I knew that it was not from God.

When Charles came home from work, we ate dinner and shared with him the results of the meeting. That night, when Charlie went to bed, I tucked him in and gave him my full support. A great load was taken off of his mind knowing that he would not have to go through another day of humiliation. At the same time, he was not at all certain that I could fulfill my promise of finding a good school. He kept asking, "What if?" questions.

I said to him, "Charlie, I don't know the answers to your questions. All I can do is take one day at a time. We'll look tomorrow and see what we can find for you. Meanwhile, as you're going to sleep, I want you to ask God to help us. He knows what kind of school you need and He'll show us where to go." This type of ending would always settle him down. He had a lot of faith and trust and realized that he could depend on God. In the past, whenever I would stay and pray with him, he would ask countless questions about whatever the topic of the day might be. Sometimes the conversation seemed endless. I found that by leaving him alone with God and his thoughts, he would eventually fall asleep without more distress.

The next morning I pursued a list of schools with various special needs programs. It was an eye-opening experience to sift through the phone interviews. It was difficult to classify Charlie into the designed criteria. There were programs for the physically handicapped or the mentally handicapped. Although he was physically impaired, he only used a wheelchair for distances when he became short of breath. He didn't use it because he couldn't walk. Therefore, the physically handicapped program wasn't what he needed. His learning disability was due to a stroke, which was mental but not to the degree of the programs we found. They were mostly for the severely mentally challenged.

I spoke to a lady, over the phone, who was excited about inviting Charlie to observe her class. She went on to tell me that her class was designed to help the children concentrate. She blocked out distractions. The children all had both learning and physical disabilities. Each learned at their own level. As hesitant as I was, Charles, Charlie, and I went to see the school. I told Charlie just to watch, be quiet and not say anything about the school until we leave. I told him to remember that we were just looking. He was not to be afraid because he would not be going anywhere that he didn't like. We planned to discuss our findings once we left.

Upon investigation, we saw that the teacher indeed blocked out distractions. She had each desk enclosed in a large cardboard box. The children were far more mentally disabled than she had described. Some required the use of helmets so as not to hurt their heads. This was not the right place for Charlie. I put his mind at ease as soon as we walked out the door.

I had eliminated most of the other schools after talking with counselors about what they offered. One class had mostly behavioral problem children. They were suffering scholastically due primarily to their turbulent home life. Another was for normal, healthy children that had dyslexia. He couldn't fit in there, either. Still others had all physically challenged students with some of these being mentally challenged as well. Now Charlie was able to walk and needed social stimulation. That ruled this class out. There was one left to check into. It was a small, private school named Ursuline-Pitt that was Catholic by religious orientation but was open to children of any faith. It was run by the Ursuline nuns and named after Monsignor Pitt, who believed in a Catholic education for all Catholic children regardless of learning difficulties. The school was designed for children to learn at their own level and own pace. Some children had mild retardation and the others had a variety of learning disabilities. Class levels ranged from preschool to high school. It was worth a try, we decided.

Upon visiting the school, we found the academic organization to be perfect. Each class was grouped according to academic level, which considered ability and age. Although the age range was fairly widespread, the children were roughly on the same level. The classroom setting was similar to what Charlie was used to. There were religious items such as crucifixes and statues throughout the school, which enriched his sense of belonging due to the familiar Catholic surroundings. We were shown the gym where students were learning gymnastics at the time. Charlie was quite impressed. Sports were offered and every child participated in the Special Olympics. The trainer for the soccer team was Sr. Regina Marie, the principal of the school. She had a warm smile that came straight from her soul. She was a sincere person who obviously enjoyed working with the children. We were all impressed so far. Continuing the tour, we were taken to a ceramics room. Every student learned ceramics. I was astounded to enter upon such an impressive room. The artwork was amazing. Charlie spotted numerous items that caught his attention, especially a Kentucky Wildcat. He was beginning to show a little enthusiasm for the school. We believed that we had found the right place for him.

There were, of course, a few obstacles to address. The location was about twenty miles from home. The tuition was expensive. And then there were the stairs in the school. Being in an old building with high ceilings, the stairway was steep. Charlie's class would be on the second floor, which meant that he would need to climb the stairs before and after school and again for lunch. I knew that physically, it would be too hard on his heart because he would be short of breath after climbing a few steps. I spoke to Sr. Regina about how he got around at St. Gabriel. I told her that the eighth graders would piggyback him to and from the bus. She believed that a high school student could help him get up the stairs. By now, Charlie weighed about seventy-five pounds. The thought of having a student responsible for carrying him upstairs troubled us a bit. With careful consideration, along with strong persuasion from Sr. Regina, we agreed to give it a try. We worked out the tuition and the transportation to get him started.

As my routine required, I saw Jackie, Marty and Leslie off to St. Gabriel in the morning. Then I loaded Jonathan and Charlie into the car for the half-hour ride to school. Once there, we all walked into the school and started up the stairs. Charlie would walk up one step, as I would stoop down for him to climb onto my back. After a slight shuffle and a deep breath, we headed up the stairs with Jonathan close behind carrying his backpack. I let Charlie off at the top of the stairway and into the classroom he went.

He adjusted easily to the latest change in his life. His acceptance of the school was obvious when he began coming home happy again. His teacher, Sr. Raymunda, gave him the encouragement that he needed. He began feeling proud of the work that he accomplished and began feeling good about himself. Charlie experienced great satisfaction when he brought home good grades. He no longer felt inferior in the classroom. Completing an item in ceramics class allowed him to be creative, which also enhanced his self-image.

In time, the reality of cost for his education kicked in. Looking closely at the matter, I saw that driving this distance to school was costing me about $5.00 per round trip. Doing this twice a day amounted to $200.00 a month. It worried me a little when I looked down the road to our already dire financial situation. I began searching for ways to cut expenses. However, knowing that this was the right place for Charlie at this time, I was convinced that God would help see us through.

I called on public transportation for the handicapped. There was a bus that would take him to school, but there was a very long waiting list. I applied for Charlie to be put on the list in hopes that he could secure a ride for the following year. Meanwhile, things continued as they were.

To remain connected with his friends at St. Gabriel, he joined the soccer team once again. At the same time, he played for Ursuline-Pitt as well. Preparing for the Special Olympics proved to be quite exciting. The time and effort spent by Sr. Regina made it apparent that she cared about the balanced life of each child.

Although he was mostly happy again, some circumstances about his new situation remained difficult. He missed being with his friends on the playground at St. Gabriel. So, on his days off, Charlie asked if he could go to St. Gabriel for lunch. I decided that it wouldn't hurt to ask, knowing that Mr. Huelsman could only say yes or no. Charlie was prepared for the possibility of a negative answer. Upon making the call, I was pleased to tell him that Mr. Huelsman gave the okay for Charlie to spend lunch and recess with his friends. Hearing this, he burst out with a loud "YES!" and a fist in the air. He was so excited that he could barely wait to get there. On arrival, his friends were thrilled to see him. After recess, I picked him up and learned he had a wonderful reunion. He looked forward to going back again.

The next trial he faced was learning to deal with a boy at his new school who took pleasure in teasing him. This boy knew that Charlie was easily frightened. He had been assigned to help Charlie with his belt buckle after using the bathroom because Charlie's fine motor skills were too weak to perform the task. On several occasions the boy would get tired of waiting on him. He then turned out the bathroom light and left, leaving him alone in the dark. The fear caused Charlie to scream and he had heart palpitations. It being an old building, there was no sunlight streaming in the bathroom. It was pitch black. He couldn't find the latch to get out of the stall. Feeling trapped and extremely frightened, he struggled to get out. His voice was filled with fear as he told the story. His teacher felt that it was not purposefully done, but agreed to have an older child assist him in the future.

The mental anguish caused by the boy became a regular event. The clever child had a variety of pesky tricks to pull on Charlie. These were addressed to the teacher when the issues came up. I could see Charlie's frustration building. We talked about ways that he could avoid being with him. For the first time, I saw Charlie wanting to get revenge for the injustice that was taking place in his life. We discussed how God would want him to handle it. Charlie, however, couldn't understand why this child was picking on him in the first place. He had never witnessed this type of behavior before from anyone at St. Gabriel. I told him that the boy was obviously feeling threatened by him. He had been used to getting a lot of attention in this small class. Now, there was someone else to compete with. Charlie didn't understand. We talked at length about it, reminding him of the attention that he had received at St. Gabriel. I suggested that maybe the boy had been getting "similar attention until you came. He might be afraid that you will take his place."

Listening intently, he tried to understand but could not, for he did not see the competition. Finally, I said, "No matter what the boy does, don't let him cause you to sin. Getting even only makes God twice as sad. It doesn't make you feel any better about it, either. It would be best if you would just be nice to him and walk away when he starts trouble." This was indeed a difficult challenge. I instructed him not to get mad. If he did feel mad, he was not to let the other boy know it. "Try to think of something nice to say to him. When you speak nicely to him, it makes it harder for him to be mean to you."

Before long, he came home smiling again. He'd tell me of how he followed my advice and the boy started being nice to him. Still he remained a bit cautious and avoided being alone with him.

During this time, I seldom got to daily Mass. By the time I drove back home in the mornings, Mass was over. Before long, I lost the desire to go. I became focused on trying to make ends meet. My cake-decorating career was ended due to the excruciating pain in my hand and arm when overused. I missed it immensely. The creativity that it allowed me had been such a joy. Realizing that more household income was needed, I started selling Tupperware again. My heart was only halfway in it this time because what I really wanted to do was go back to school. Financially, however, it was not feasible.

My days were now tremendously overloaded. Many hours were spent in the car, taking kids to and from school, volunteering at both schools, going on field trips with the different children, attending Tupperware meetings and planning business, visiting doctors, cleaning house, cooking dinner, and taking the children to their practices for sports teams.

Soon, I began missing that experience of daily Mass. I decided to make the effort to go on Saturday mornings when I could. Yet, I didn't expect to be as undisciplined as I was. Although I wanted to go and would set my alarm on Friday nights, I soon discovered that come Saturday morning, I just couldn't pull myself out of bed. More time passed and only occasionally was I energetic enough to get up and attend Mass. Whenever I did, I felt so good that I longed to go again. This longing gave me the boost to attend sporadically.

As any autumn would unfold into winter, so too did the everlasting spirit of football. His dad was forever taking Charlie to the games. Weekly, Charles invited the family to go, but Charlie was the only committed one despite the cold wind, sleet, or snow. Dressed warmly, with blankets in hand, the two of them set out to the games.

I often worried about Charlie's being out in the cold for so long. In spite of this, I held back on my motherly instinct to make him stay home. It disturbed me that he would quickly become short of breath in the inclement weather. However, I also realized that he was a boy who loved football, and loved sharing it with his dad. The quality of life always became a consideration whenever I desired to protect him. My heart wanted to say, "Let him go." My instinct warned, "Make him stay."

It was important that he be allowed to live. Smothering him and protecting him would never have brought out the smile that always covered his face. I knew that God would care for him. He gave him a wonderful dad to see to his needs. Mostly, Charles would tell how Charlie sat on his lap and kept them both warm. If his uncle Ray was with them, they passed him back and forth to keep everybody warm. Charlie came home glowing and shouting with excitement. It was worth every freezing moment to him.

After a Friday night game, he was psyched to play football all day Saturday. Charlie was able to talk anyone and everyone into playing football. He'd call on Scott Jolly and his brother, Tony, to come over and join neighbors Jamie and Tony Combs for a game in the front yard. Marty was always right there with him, helping him with shoulder pads and helmet. These games were serious, yet so much fun. It was a joy to watch them. Sometimes Jason would ride his bike over to play with them as well.

The holidays quickly approached. The exciting part about preparing for Halloween was creating a different costume. All the kids eagerly anticipated this event. We brainstormed, then pieced together costumes made of old clothes, construction board or cardboard boxes, scrap materials, or items from the thrift store. With five children, the ideas were infinite.

Charles and I took the children to the haunted house at school. This year, Charlie was trying to be brave and agreed to go into the haunted house after refusing to do so for the past several years. Smiling, but nervous, Charlie entered into the dark hallway along with the rest of the family. I was concerned about how he would do, knowing how easily he became frightened. Charles watched over the two little ones while I held Charlie's hand. Sure enough, barely making it around the second bend, there was a live scene of a mad doctor cutting off the leg of a patient. It was difficult for Charlie to separate reality from fiction. He became so frightened that he almost hyperventilated. He ran past the scene and headed for the exit as fast as he could. Naturally, I felt bad about his reaction. The younger ones were slightly frightened, but did not associate reality to the scene the way that Charlie did. We sat in the cafeteria for a while as he gathered his composure. This was the first and last time that he ever experienced a haunted house.

The weeks passed quickly as fall moved toward the next holiday. Thanksgiving Day was always special. I prepared a feast, as usual, with all the trimmings. The table was set with china. Reflections went deeper than the grace that was said. Each of us shared his/her personal thanks for what God had given us. When I gave thanks for my family, I felt a sincere appreciation for the gift of life. My thoughts were with each child and my husband, realizing that God could take any of them at any time. The awareness of Charlie's unpredictable health made me equally aware of accidental death that could happen at any time to any of us. I was pleased that God made me mindful of this because I was able to enjoy each of my children fully. I wanted to be prepared for the day that God would call any of us. It was this recognition that encouraged me not to waste the gift of time. Despite the probability, never did I feel that I had the knowledge that Charlie would be called to heaven before the rest of us. Therefore, time was not wasted dwelling on his impending death. We focused instead on living. I was overwhelmed with gratitude over the years already given to us.

Traditionally, I looked forward to relaxation after dinner. This meant kicking back on the couch and enjoying the movie, "Miracle On 34th Street." Being already in an emotional state, I found this movie to be spiritually therapeutic. Stories of love and faith would always inspire me.

Heading full speed toward Christmas was exhilarating for all of us. The Christmas music began once Thanksgiving was over. The following Sunday, Charles and I repeated the traditional toy store scene with the children. They left with their lists for Santa once again.

In the days ahead, boxes marked "Christmas" were pulled from the attic. The children each helped with the decorations. This was a fun part of the holidays. When time would permit, we made candy and cookies as well. Tradition in our house consisted of giving a gift to each other. From the time that they were babies, I wanted them to learn that Christmas was a time for giving. They were as excited about giving to their brothers and sisters as they were about Christmas morning when Santa Claus had given to them. This year I helped each child with homemade gifts, giving them the experience of putting love and creativity into each one.

After Christmas Eve Mass, we went home to share the gifts that we had made for each other. Next, tradition had it that the children would gather, in their pajamas, in one of the bedrooms to hear the story, "The Night Before Christmas." All was quiet as I read. Then, out of nowhere, we suddenly heard the sounds of sleigh bells jingling outside the window. This startled the children, causing Jackie and Marty to look out the window. Leslie and Jonathan were a bit frightened. As long as I held them, they looked out cautiously. Charlie was absolutely terrified. He refused to look outside as did the others. He quickly pulled the covers over his head and insisted upon staying like that until morning. I noticed his heart palpitating rather fast. I hated to see him so scared, yet I enjoyed the fact that he still got so much out of Christmas. For some reason, Charles always missed hearing Santa Claus arrive. This year, he had gone out for firewood. By the time he came in, the bells had stopped. Marty was the first one to rush and tell him all about it. The others were equally excited, but Charlie remained partially hidden beneath the covers and didn't care to talk about it. He just wanted to hurry up and go to sleep before Santa came back.

With seven piles of toys and gifts crammed into a tiny living room, it was a veritable toy store on Christmas morning. The children were elated. Carols played. Stockings were filled with fruit. Great joy filled the house. It was another moment that brought tears of joy to me. Before the day was over, Charlie had time to evaluate his gifts. After a while, he'd realize that there was something that he had asked for that he didn't get. Now, this didn't disturb him because he was always delighted with whatever he got. However, he would come to me grinning because he knew exactly what he wanted for his birthday in March. I had to laugh because no matter what the occasion was, Charlie was always looking forward to the next special event.

The seasons changed and life went on. That spring Charlie brought me a ceramic Easter Bunny planter, which he had made for Mother's Day. It came with flower seeds and a gardening tool. He had made it at school. I thoroughly enjoyed receiving this gift made by his hands. Before long, he had made an item for everyone in the family, except for Leslie. Time had run out and the school year was over. He felt bad that he wasn't going to be able to make her something, too. So, we decided to buy her a ceramic item the next time the school had a function where they would be sold. It wasn't quite the same as having one made by Charlie, but she was pleased anyway.

As the school year was coming to an end, decisions needed to be made for the following year. There was still no transportation for him to school and this was costing too much. He missed the interaction with the more physically active children. There was so much to consider. Eventually, we decided to transfer him to a public school where he could be mainstreamed into regular classes when possible. After the decision was made, I was elected to the board at Ursuline-Pitt School. I accepted the position because I wanted to help this wonderful program regardless of whether Charlie was able to attend. I was then asked to be chairperson for the Ways and Means Committee. I accepted. An offer was made to allow Charlie to attend the following year free of tuition. This was very tempting. After careful consideration, I declined the offer based on the expense of transportation being $200.00 per month and the lack of opportunity for him to be among ordinary children without disabilities. I felt in my heart that he should change schools again.

Summer was a blessing each year. It was a time to enjoy our home life without the obligations of school. The demands of homework, school projects, and parent meetings disappeared, which took tremendous pressure off each of us.

This year, the family worked especially hard in having a successful yard sale. Our goal was to plan to take a vacation together. Until now, Charles' vacation time had been spent caring for the children when Charlie or I would be in the hospital. This year had thus far remained untouched by surgeries and new births.

Not having vacation in the budget meant the expense would need to come from extra resources. The yard sale paid off. I was able to purchase a used family-sized tent, which saved the cost of a hotel. Then Jackie offered to donate the $100.00 that she had saved from baby-sitting to make the trip possible. By gathering all our resources, we were able to spend five days camping at Mammoth Cave. The children greatly enjoyed the adventure and the serenity of nature. There was a handicapped cave tour offered that made it possible to take Charlie in his wheelchair. In addition to that, we also took him with us to another cave and took turns carrying him through. Meals were prepared at camp to cut the cost of food. The primitive accommodations were enjoyed by all except Jackie. After all, it was difficult for a teenage girl to fix her hair and makeup under these circumstances. Despite this adversity, we did have a relaxing and adventurous week.

That fall, Charlie was enrolled at Hawthorne Elementary where he had spent the first grade. Meetings were held to create achievable goals for him. He would be among both the disabled and those who were not. This arrangement would be best both academically and socially. Speech therapy was also arranged at the school.

In spite of the decision not to return to Ursuline-Pitt, I still remained on the board and planned their fund-raisers for the year. I found it both challenging and rewarding.

Not only was Charlie adjusting to his new school, but by October he received word that Jamie and Tony were moving to Florida. Their dad had taken a job near Orlando and plans were underway to leave at the end of the month. The boys took advantage of every opportunity to play, for they knew that time would quickly run out. They played football, kickball, or keep-away, depending on how many neighbors they could get to join. Moving day was a sad event. We drove downtown to the campus bookstore to buy a U of K football. Charlie and Marty gave it to Jamie and Tony as a going-away present. They wanted to make sure that they took some reminder of Kentucky with them to Florida. Despite the smiles on everyone's faces, we each wiped tears away as we watched the family car drive up into the moving van. It saddened us all to see them leave. My first thought was how different it would be to look out and see only half a football team playing. We tried talking them into staying for trick or treat, but their schedule wouldn't permit it. Holding back the tears, we waved them on knowing that life on Mosswood Lane would never be the same. Pam, their mother, was the spirited one on the street who brought families together. Another phase of our community life had just ended.

School was a helpful distraction from the loss of our good neighbors. Charlie was happy with the more natural environment that included all types of children. He enjoyed the challenge of school projects that initially appeared impossible. A major assignment on the history of Kentucky allowed him to overcome the fears of performing large tasks. At first glance, he was overwhelmed. With a little assurance, he discovered that it wasn't so hard. He learned to begin by taking one page at a time. Obtaining information from the encyclopedia, brochures and the library, he was able to write a good report and add many pictures that he cut and pasted. The end result was a fine booklet.

He failed to tell me that he was expected to show his teacher from time to time what he had been doing. Therefore, she did not believe him when he said he was working on it. She had assumed on the day before it was due that he hadn't started on the project. She sent a note home to that effect. However, she was both surprised and pleased when he handed in his final report. She praised him for what a fine job he had done. The positive reinforcement made him feel as good as the others in the class and he came home feeling very proud.

The year went smoothly. He had been able to take the school bus, which was a great help. The assistant on the bus often entertained him by singing, or teasing, or just being silly. He often felt nauseated from motion sickness and therefore would not feel up to the craziness, but if he were feeling good, he enjoyed it.

Christmas this year was a bit different than others, for on Christmas morning amid the excitement, I discovered that Leslie wasn't feeling up to par. Upon taking a closer look, I discovered that she had come down with chicken pox. This was a rather traumatic event because it meant that we could not take her to visit the relatives as we had planned. As a result, I stayed behind with her while Charles took the others to visit his family. Then, when he returned, I took them to visit my family. At first, I felt that we were cheated out of a special day. We would have to wait another year for the opportunity to return. It seemed unfair.

However, once everyone left, I found myself only concerned about Leslie's health. It didn't matter anymore that we were missing out. I cared for her and had her lie down for a nap.

Slowly making my way through the stacks of toys and gifts, I felt blessed that we were able to make Christmas so special for the children. I reflected on the birth of Jesus without distraction as I looked at the Holy Family in the nativity set under the tree. I said to Jesus, "This is a day that the family should be together. Why then, have you allowed us to be separated?" I didn't feel upset. I just wondered what His purpose was. It seemed to me that Christmas was the most important time of the year to be together with family. So, I wondered. How does God intend to use this for good? I did not understand.

The day was spent listening to Christmas carols and taking care of a sick child. Yet, it was peaceful and pleasant. I told Leslie that we would go visit her grandparents in a couple of weeks once she was over the illness. She was agreeable to the idea.

She remained ill through the beginning of the new year. We were anxiously making plans to visit her grandparents soon.

Then, one day, a disturbing phone call came. Charles was talking to a family member and I detected that something bad had happened. He hung up the phone and relayed the message that his mother was in a coma following surgery. He was greatly concerned. He was not aware that she was having surgery. She hadn't mentioned it at Christmas. He said that she apparently had an operation to open a blocked artery in her neck. She had been through the same operation on the other side just a few months ago. He recalled that she hadn't mentioned it then, either, until after it was over because she didn't want him to worry. She always felt that Charles had enough worries just dealing with Charlie's problems. He confirmed that she was very quiet when he last talked to her. He even asked her what was wrong, but she denied any problem. This is how she protected him. She hated to see any of us hurting and she especially didn't want to be the cause of it.

After days of praying and keeping a round-the-clock vigil between family members, his mother ended her life on earth on January 11, 1987. It was a devastating event for all of us. It was no secret how much she loved her children and grandchildren.

All I could think about was that I missed seeing her at Christmas. Leslie and I didn't even get to share that special time with her before she left. At the time, it seemed as though we experienced more pain by not being able to enjoy that last Christmas with her.

By the time of the funeral, I discovered my thoughts going in a different direction. I realized that Charlie now had a grandmother in heaven waiting for him. I saw that God was still working on the special family to greet Charlie some day. I remembered the scary thought. In a sense it was comforting to see that God was trying to make it easier for us. Yet, we were faced with this pain of death once again. The pain was getting closer and closer. I saw in my mind the family that He had gathered for Charlie so far: Betsy, his mother figure; the girl in his preschool, his sister figure; Carl, his brother figure; Paul Combs, his grandfather figure; and now his grandmother, all waiting for him. I wondered in what direction God was taking us. I had no idea nor did I even try to figure it out. The trust I had in God prevented my mind from considering the future. I could not have speculated what was to come, nor did I have the desire to.

As time passed, the pain of her death eased. It was in meditation one day that I realized why Leslie and I were not with the family during Christmas. God had protected us from those fresh memories to ease our pain now. Who knows how much more it would have hurt if we had memories from recent days? I recalled the excruciating pain that I felt when Betsy had died. That was because she was someone that I was spending time with every day. It was such a deep pain because I had just been with her. God had used Leslie's illness to protect me from that

219

deep pain once again. I loved my mother-in-law very much as we had many good memories together. Despite her passing, time marched on.

That spring, a contest was being held at Hawthorne. A collection of Cabbage Patch Dolls was displayed in the bookcase of the entrance hall. These dolls represented the different types of children in the school. The contest invited each student to pick a doll to name. Naturally, Charlie wanted to name the boy in a wheelchair. He was wearing a jogging suit with a towel draped around his neck. He gave you the impression that he had been racing. After seeing the movie, "Silver Bullet," Charlie was inspired to give the doll a name representing the speed of his wheelchair. I gave him some pointers on how to select a catchy name. First he thought of every word that meant fast. Then he put a boy's name with it that started with the same letter. He ended up with the name Rapid Wheels Roger. Out of all the entries, his was chosen. He came home quite excited when he won $10.00 for naming the doll.

As we neared the summer break, we had to look for another school. Although he was happy at Hawthorne and his self-image was improving, he would not be allowed to stay another year. This was due to the fact that the school only went through the fifth grade. It was now time for middle school, another dreaded step. How we both hated searching for a new school. The children in the special needs class were all going to Noe Middle School. This choice would mean a forty-five minute ride on the bus each way. I didn't believe it was a good choice, knowing that he was feeling some motion sickness even from the shorter ride to Hawthorne. We visited the school anyway in order to make a more informed decision based on what they had to offer. Our next option was to go to a nearby public school and place him in a class for slower learning children. I felt that with some guidance, he could manage this type of class. Charlie, of course, still missed his friends at St. Gabriel and wanted desperately to try the school again. I felt that it would be a great mistake, knowing that his class had advanced much faster than he had by now.

After much prayer, thought, and consideration, we decided upon Carrither's Middle School, which was nearby. This meant that he would not be able to ride the bus because the school was not designed for the handicapped. The only bus would be the regular one, which would stop three blocks away from the house. As he was not able to walk the distance, I planned to take him myself.

During much of this time I attended daily Mass sporadically. With the children's schedules, it was difficult to arrange my time to get there. Mostly, the mornings were very busy just getting them ready for school. This left no time to get myself ready before Mass would begin. At other times I would be so tired that I didn't push myself to go. Sometimes I didn't have a car. I realized that I made more of an effort on the days that the school children attended Mass. This was because I knew that Fr. Caster would have inspiring things to say during his homily to the children. His words gave me strength each day and the desire to come back. Once summer arrived, I found it easier to get to church more often. The children would still be asleep and Jackie was able to baby-sit during that time.

15

DREAMS DO COME TRUE

From time to time, as Charlie grew, he needed fitting for special orthopedic shoes. Because his growth had been stunted, he was the one child in the family for whom it was a pleasure to buy new shoes. It meant that he was growing. We went to the shoe store in the mall where we ordered a pair to fit him. His feet were extremely short and wide with a high instep as well. Sizing him was always a major ordeal because even the special ordered ones could never give him a good fit with his high instep. We settled on the best fit available and replaced the shoestrings with longer ones to allow more width in the shoes. These were brown leather high-tops that were not stylish for a young boy. He always wished he could wear shoes like Marty's. Charlie's dreams seemed simple enough sometimes that it hurt not to be able to provide them. Therefore, I bought him a pair of inexpensive athletic shoes and allowed him to wear them for short periods of time when his feet needed a rest from the binding leather and braces. This excited him so much. He felt like the other boys when he wore them. He often wore them to play football or when his orthopedic shoes were at the brace shop being transferred to new braces.

Returning by myself to pick up his shoes two weeks later, I discovered a table set up at the mall that was promoting "The Dream Factory." Having heard something about the organization in the past, I approached the table to inquire about it.

When I stepped up, a kind woman with a wide smile greeted me. I asked whom The Dream Factory benefited. She informed me that it was for chronically ill children. "Is it specific illnesses such as cancer?" I asked.

She replied that it was for any terminally ill child whatever reason. She said that they would grant the child one dream of his choice. It could be anything. "Many have chosen a trip to Disney World," she added. "Others have selected meeting stars or celebrities."

I told her that my son had congenital heart disease that was not correctable. "However," I added, "he's doing very well right now so I doubt that he would qualify." She encouraged me to take an application for him and stated that the diagnosis must meet certain criteria which included being life threatening. She pointed out that a section was to be filled out by his doctor. Then, the doctors on the board would determine if he qualified. She said that they are actually happier to see that the child is doing well when they obtain their dream because they will enjoy it more.

With that in mind, I felt pretty good about giving Charlie this wonderful opportunity. On my way home, I imagined what he might ask for. I felt confident that it would be a computer because he had talked about playing on Robby's before. Having often exerted himself too much playing football outside, he would come inside frequently to play at the table with his miniature teams. He would spend hours lining up the players and designing plays, keeping score on every game. Occasionally, he commented how much fun it would be to play football on a computer. I figured this would be his dream.

When I arrived home, I sat Charlie down to try on his shoes, making the adjustments as needed. We discussed going to the brace shop in the morning to be fitted for new braces. He quickly changed the subject to tell me how much he missed his friends at St. Gabriel. I asked him if he had talked to any of them lately. He confirmed that he had only talked to Jason. He believed that they had all forgotten about him. "They never call," he added. I told him that he shouldn't wait for them to call. I encouraged him to do the calling. "It's not that they forget you, it's just that they don't realize that you are missing them so much. They get busy and don't think about it, I'm sure." He was feeling like they didn't even want to be with him anymore. I assured him that wasn't the case at all. I devised a plan. I suggested that he might call all of his friends and invite them to the movies in the morning. "We could drop off your shoes at the brace shop and go on from there," I proposed.

"How many can I invite?" he asked with excitement.

"Ask as many as you want to," I answered. "The station wagon holds nine people." He quickly got on the phone. Before long he had four boys going plus Marty. I suggested that the six of them would be able to have a great time together.

Meanwhile, I pondered just how to approach The Dream Factory idea. I couldn't stand seeing him disappointed time and time again. There was a fear of giving him false hope. When Charles came home, I shared it with him. We both agreed that he would probably qualify based on his diagnosis. Recognizing my total dependence on the Holy Spirit to give me the right words to say, I was determined to be careful, for no promises were being made.

The following day I took a carload of six boys to the Kosair Brace Shop. They waited at the door while I took the shoes and braces in for the preliminary work to be done. From there we stopped at a convenience store so that the boys could get some candy for the movie. Then we proceeded to the cinema to see "Harry and The Hendersons." They laughed and carried on all the way there. The afternoon uplifted Charlie's spirit as nothing else could. They all came over for a game of football before they went home. Not only was Charlie the happiest child in the world to see that his friends still cared, I was made the happiest mom just by watching them.

The following day, after the excitement had died down, I started up a conversation with Charlie with the intent to address the possible dream. I began by asking him to think about this for a minute before answering. I began, "If you could have one wish to come true, what would you want it to be?"

"You mean anything in the whole wide world?" he said with surprise.

"Yes, if you could go anywhere, meet anyone, do anything, or have anything, what would you like it to be?"

As he was thinking, I added, "There is a group of people called The Dream Factory that *might* be able to grant you one wish. We don't know anything for sure yet, but they are going to try."

"You mean anything?" he said again in disbelief.

"Well, yes. You can ask for anything but, as I said, we don't know for sure if it will be granted." With the confirmation his mouth dropped and his lips began to quiver as he said, "I know what I really want I can't have."

"What's that?" I asked.

"What I really want is to run and play like Marty," he said with a sense of hopelessness.

"Oh, Charlie," I uttered as I placed my arm around him, giving him a consoling hug. What more could I say? I wasn't expecting that for an answer.

Then his frown turned to a smile and he added, "I want to meet Uncle Tommy."

"Meet Uncle Tommy?" I blurted astonished.

"Yes. I want to meet Uncle Tommy because I know all of my aunts and uncles except him."

Innocent as this may seem, Uncle Tommy lived in Germany. So, I said to him, "Charlie, do you realize how far away that is?"

His mouth dropped when he detected the improbability in my voice. Then he added, "But you said anything in the whole world."

"Well, yes I did, but maybe we need to talk about this a little bit." I went to the bedroom and brought back the globe. Placing it in front of him, I pointed out where Germany was in relation to Kentucky, showing him that it was halfway across the world. It didn't faze him. I could see that he had absolutely no concept of mileage.

He had been asking a lot of questions about his uncle for some time. Recent "Rambo" movies brought out more questions because he was aware that his uncle flew a helicopter in the army. The military fascinated Charlie.

In the past, I had shared childhood memories with the children about my family. He knew that Uncle Tommy had played football in grade school, went away to the seminary for a few years, then returned to graduate from Trinity High School. (This happened to be one of Charlie's favorite teams to watch.) When he asked me questions about Uncle Tommy's army experiences, I was unable to answer him. I didn't really know myself. He had written a few letters to his uncle, but the

226

responses did not fully satisfy his curiosity. Thus, he had a desire to meet him.

With further discussion, I explained to him that a trip like this would cost an awful lot of money. "They would have to send someone with you and then it would cost even more. Why don't we think of some more ideas before we decide for sure." I suggested Disney World as he had never been there and because his good friends Jamie and Tony had moved near there over a year ago. Seeing his friends would be great, but Disney World frightened him a bit on account of his fear of rides in an amusement park. Being uncertain myself as to what Disney World had to offer, I couldn't be very persuasive in recommending that destination. Because none of us had been there to describe it, I was afraid of encouraging something inappropriate for him.

I finally agreed to make his request to meet his uncle on the condition that he also write down an alternative choice in case they didn't have the money to grant it. He agreed to do that and then said that he would like to have a computer if he couldn't meet his uncle. He clearly did not understand about cost or distance. A sinking feeling came over me that I had just set him up for more disappointment. Reluctantly, I sent the application in and waited for a response.

Several weeks went by. Then the phone call came. I was feeling a little embarrassed about the unreasonable request that he had asked for. Mrs. Eubanks, the president of the organization, told me that the doctors on the board had reviewed his case and said that he had passed the health requirements by a landslide. They did not understand how he could be alive based on his diagnosis.

From there, the next step was to get approval from the board on his dream request. Mrs. Eubanks said that she would need to come out and talk to Charlie in person to determine that the dream was his own idea and to be certain that it was what he wanted. She assured me that it was normal procedure and to not take offense because they needed to verify it. I agreed that it would only be appropriate to confirm that the dream was truly his.

An appointment was made for her to come speak to Charlie. Much to my surprise, she came forty minutes early and I was not ready to greet her. As usual, the children had the first baths of the day and I had just stepped out from mine with wet hair. I introduced her to Charlie and left them alone while I made myself a bit more presentable. By the time I came back she said that she was finished with the interview. In just a few minutes, however, she was able to quickly determine that it was indeed his dream by the excitement in his voice. She said that she would be taking his request to the board and would be back in touch with me.

Before long, I received the shocking phone call. She told me that Charlie's dream would be granted. The board approved it unanimously without hesitation. She said that they would be getting reservations for seven. "*Seven?*" I exclaimed.

"Yes, there are seven of you, aren't there?"

"Well, yes," I responded.

She didn't indicate that the size of the family was an issue, as she made it clear that a child's dream always included the entire family. I was in awe when she pointed out that the reason for including the family was to provide a special memory for them later when the child would no longer be with them.

Wow, I thought to myself. How is it that they understand how much of an impact this special child is on the family? Our conversation ended with an agreement that she would get back with me on the details.

My heart was pounding as I hung up the phone. My eyes welled up with tears. My stomach turned with nervousness. I was in total disbelief. I paced the living room unable to calm down, saying repeatedly, "Thank you, God. Thank you for loving us so much. Thank you. Thank you. Thank you." I was in shock and alone at the time. Jonathan was taking a nap. The other children were still at school and Charles was at work. My mind was so preoccupied with this fantastic development that I was unable to function the rest of the day.

That afternoon, I was supposed to pick up the neighbor's child from preschool. Still in shock, my mind was whirling causing me to completely forget about the child.

When the children came home and heard the good news, they cheered in disbelief as well. Charles was the last one to hear. By then, Charlie was in ecstasy and exulting throughout the house. It was difficult for us to settle down.

That evening, my neighbor came home from work and rushed to my door with a deranged look on her face. She asked what had happened to me today, informing me that her son, Michael, had to go home with his teacher because I did not pick him up. All I could say was that I had forgotten and apologize profusely for my mistake. Strangely enough, I didn't even remember when I saw her at the door. How dare I tell her why I had made the mistake. I sensed that she would not understand. It was clear to me at that point that I had enough to keep up with that I should not attempt to keep up with the neighbor's children, too.

We continued our summer activities such as T-ball and baseball for Leslie and Marty. Yet, in the back of our minds was the constant anticipation of the upcoming trip. Numerous phone calls were made by The Dream Factory to start the process moving. Everything from passports to flights to hotel arrangements needed approval.

Every aspect was thrilling, including having our pictures taken for passports. Stepping up to the photographer meant that Germany would soon be a reality. It was more than my mind could handle. After all, the only vacation that we had ever taken was the past summer to Mammoth Cave. Somehow, it was hard to picture an airplane and a hotel for all seven of us, with a destination so far away.

Most of the preparations were falling into place except for the exact day of departure. This was becoming a bit unsettling due to the fact that Charles was limited as to when he could get off work. As time passed it became evident that the trip would not take place due to his obligations at work and the start of school being just two weeks away. The Dream Factory had not been able to confirm all the arrangements due to the numerous contacts that had to be made. Communication with the people to give approvals had become a continued game of phone tag. As time was running out, I dreaded the idea of having to tell Charlie

229

that we wouldn't be able to go. He had been looking forward to it all summer.

Watching the calendar closely, I put off telling him, still hanging on to a thread of hope. Then, at what seemed to be the last possible moment, I received the phone call from The Dream Factory. I was prepared to hear the worst. However, much to my surprise, the final details were secured, and I was told that departure would be in two days. Fortunately, although Charles had previously been told that he could not have time off in August, he was now granted the request due to the extraordinary nature of the trip.

I had been preparing things all summer for this time. Family and friends were on standby with luggage and clothing ready to lend. Last-minute essentials were put into place as I went down my "things to do" list. Our family car had just seen its last trip and was waiting for a tow to the junkyard. This factor made it more difficult to be prepared in a timely manner. Regardless, all details fell into place.

The following morning, I received a phone call from *The Courier-Journal* newspaper office. A reporter asked if he could come out the next morning for an interview before we left. I agreed to it with the understanding that it would be a brief meeting. Getting five children dressed and ready to go would take time. Charles and I would also need preparation time. Having one bathroom required a system to get everyone ready on time. A limousine would be picking us up and driving us to the airport at 9:30 A.M. I told the reporter that we would be quite rushed. As long as he didn't mind the chaos, then it would be all right. He said that he wanted to see the activity and busyness of getting ready. Therefore, I granted him the invitation.

The early morning alarm went off. Instantly, everyone was up and dressed in no time. Knowing that there wasn't time to wash dishes before leaving, I decided upon a quick take-out McDonald's breakfast. There would be nothing to clean up and the house would be in order when we left. Our neighbor Linda had offered to watch the house and water the plants. When I returned with breakfast, the reporter was there taking notes of all that was taking place.

The children were almost too excited to stop for breakfast. Charles and I were seeing that all bags were in order and nothing was being left behind. I gave the final rundown to Linda, pointing out the will, the plants, and the keys. The reporter spoke to each of us between activities and eating.

Then I heard a shout of anticipation from Charlie as he spotted the long black limousine pulling up into the drive. He was the first one to run out the door, dragging Leslie's carry-on bag alongside him. His shuffling gait didn't slow him down.

The limousine driver was very pleasant and seemed to be equally as excited for Charlie as anyone. He opened the shiny black door for the honorary recipient.

"WOW!" Charlie said with wonder. "This is totally awesome."

The driver smiled and said to us that he had driven every Dream Factory recipient so far. He was obviously proud of it and quite moved as he proceeded to load the luggage into the trunk. Charles helped with the wheelchair. The next thing I knew we were on our way to the airport in total disbelief that this day had actually come.

On arrival, more reporters and cameramen who were preparing a segment for the evening news greeted us. Charlie's face was glowing. When asked about his dream to visit Germany, he said he wanted to go meet his uncle. The whole concept of where he was going was not only misunderstood, but it was totally irrelevant to him. He had an image of what his uncle would look like and be like. Charlie couldn't wait to see if his uncle matched his image of him.

After a lengthy delay, Charlie boarded the plane and waved good-bye to the reporters. It was a long flight. The children tolerated it well and remained content throughout the trip. When we stopped in London, three-fourths of the plane emptied out. Upon realizing that we were almost there, Charlie jumped up in excitement and squealed, "Oh, I can't wait to meet him." He paced the aisles of the plane as we waited to resume our flight. His smile seemed broader than his little face. My soul was touched knowing how much it meant to him, not Germany, not the airplane, not the castles that we planned to see, but the unknown relative that tugged at his heart.

I wondered to myself if Tommy had any idea whatsoever how much this meant to Charlie. I contemplated what the meeting might be like. After all, Tommy didn't know my children. How could he be excited to meet them? They'll all be strangers to him. I figured that Charlie anticipated an uncle similar to the ones at home. He probably visualized wrestling and being great buddies. I decided it was best not to dwell on it because I feared that Charlie was expecting a hero, as well. Rather, I prayed that he would not be disappointed.

The children looked out the windows briefly while the plane rested on the ground. Suddenly, they realized that there were enough empty seats that they each could lie down. What a treat for tired children. Momentarily, the plane lifted off again.

Before long, the cabin attendant announced the plane was about to land. Charlie wasted no time departing from the plane. His wheelchair was in the cargo area, but he wasn't about to wait for it. His adrenaline was enough to take him where he was going. However, the considerate attendant was aware of the wheelchair and saw to it that it was brought out to him before the luggage was taken out. Tommy and his wife, Anita, quickly spotted us. We were the only group that consisted mostly of children. On sighting them, we rushed toward them. My worries were over. I didn't get the first hug from my brother; Charlie did. It was wonderful. Anita presented me with a beautiful bouquet of flowers while Tommy greeted and hugged all the children. He was equally as excited as they were. It was as though he had known them all of his life. How wonderful, I thought to myself. Charlie's dream had come true. Again, my heart was touched knowing that the most important thing in the world to Charlie was "family."

We stayed for ten days in a comfortable hotel. Tommy and Anita treated us royally, giving us a different grand tour each day. We visited castles, museums, cities, and the countryside. We toured many historical places, learning much about the history of the area from Tommy. He shared many interesting stories about the kings that once reigned there. Every part of the trip was beautiful. They went out of their way in providing hospitality. Anita focused on pleasing the children with specialty candies while Tommy focused on supplying the best beer. We met a few of their friends and shared a great time together.

Before the vacation ended, Marty and Charlie spent the night with Uncle Tommy and Aunt Anita. As it was a last-minute decision, they took a taxi from the hotel to Tommy's house. Naturally, this frightened me. Yet, Tommy insisted that it would be perfectly safe. It was their last chance because we were leaving the next day. How could I refuse to let them go? To Charlie, this would be the best part of the entire trip, spending time playing with his uncle.

The next day we heard about the pillow fight between them along with a story about a white rat named Matilda. According to Anita, Tommy was the instigator. As it turned out, Uncle Tommy qualified as another fun-loving uncle. He goofed off just like the rest of them.

Although the trip ended too soon, we were all exhausted and ready to go home. One thing that Charlie and the other children noticed was that German cooking was not like American. They realized that they missed having water fountains whenever they wanted a drink. As much as they loved the adventure, they came home with a different feeling for the United States. They had a sense of appreciation for being an American and they understood, "There's no place like home."

Grandparents, cousins, and video cameras greeted us at the airport. Everyone's excitement deeply moved us, including the limousine driver's. A few extra children (cousins) jumped into the limousine with us. The lights of the city at night were a joy to our eyes after flying among the clouds for so long.

The sight of home was refreshing. It seemed so long since we had been there. Upon entering the house I saw a stack of newspapers and mail on the table. The headlines read, *"Dream fulfilled: Seriously ill boy off to Germany to visit his uncle."* The picture on the front page showed Charlie excitedly walking toward the limousine with his dad. The family was in the background. I was eager to read it, but instead I visited with the family for a while and shared stories about the trip. Once everyone settled down, I helped the children to bed. Then, I picked up the paper and began reading. It was exciting at first, that is, until I reached a part that read, "The beefy, blond with buck teeth and blue eyes..." This appalled me. How dare this reporter come into my home, inconvenience us, and then write such a rude and insensitive statement. How could I allow Charlie to read it? These degrading remarks should never be directed toward another human being. I felt suddenly betrayed by the press.

I decided the only thing to do when Charlie woke up in the morning was to make up an excuse to read the article to him. That way he would not have to know about the callous remark. There was another distasteful comment about the family as well, which read that we were "wolfing down a late McDonald's breakfast." It was shameful to have an enjoyable human-interest story tainted with such words.

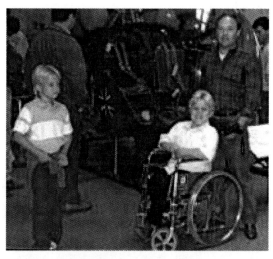

Charlie, age twelve, spending time with Uncle Tommy in Germany along with his brother Marty

Charles and I discussed our disappointment in the article. In the morning, I read it to Charlie and the other children, skipping over the coarse remarks. I silently and calmly ignored them in order to keep the children unaware of the offenses against their brother. They probably would have overlooked the remark about the family. However, they were always prepared to defend their brother's feelings.

I immediately wrote a letter to the editor to express my disappointment. Within a few days I received a letter of apology from the editor. I never heard from the writer.

Before long I discovered an editorial written by a woman whom I did not know. It read:

'Derogatory description'

"I must express my consternation concerning your July 24 article on Charlie Stopher, the youth chosen by the Louisville branch of The Dream Factory, to make an eagerly anticipated trip to Germany.

I wonder how (the reporter) would feel if he were a 12-year-old handicapped youth, bravely facing the challenge of daily living, to see himself described as a "beefy blond with buck teeth."

...I'm sure Charlie does not need to be reminded that his upper torso is well developed. Probably this is due to his necessary overuse of this area of his body. Anyone could tell from his picture that he is of short stature, well developed, and has teeth that protrude. The derogatory description was unnecessary...

Charlie may save this article for his memory book, but I'm sure he and his family were chagrined to see him described thusly.... Please, when you are writing about people, remember they deserve to be described in a dignified manner."

Written by a woman from Owensboro, Ky., the article touched me deeply. Her sense of understanding for the handicapped made me reflect on the compassion that some women in Jerusalem felt toward Jesus as he carried His cross. One woman, Veronica, was so moved that she offered her towel to Jesus. Many others in the crowd did nothing. Is that not how our society is? Some look the other way. Others are touched with compassion but don't step forward to offer consolation. Still, there is often one who will testify on behalf of a stranger. This woman from Owensboro was a perfect example. Although many editorials are written and never published, one is all it takes to know that someone cares. Oftentimes, the correlation between our present world and the times of Jesus's life would come to me while at morning Mass. Given this opportunity to listen to the Word of God is a blessing in itself, especially when understanding is granted me. Seeing that Charlie was exposed in a humiliating fashion for all of those in Louisville and its surrounding cities, brought to mind the exposure and humiliation of Jesus in front of a massive crowd. This verified Our Lord's complete understanding of those who are belittled. In turn, the comfort of Our Blessed Mother came to me again for I related to her pain as she did mine.

16
SITTING ON THE SIDELINES

The routine of life quickly resumed for our family. School would be starting in a few days and transportation needed to be worked out. We were forced to face the problems that we had left behind, such as finding a car to replace the one that died. Charlie would not have a way to Carrither's, nor did Jackie have a ride to the bus stop. Although the law required transportation for the handicapped, there were none attending this school. I agreed to take him this year with the stipulation that a bus would be provided the following year. I made this offer so that he could attend a school close to home.

We looked hard to find a suitable car. Financial hardship was a fact of life with five children and unusual medical expenses. The best we could plan for would be to put the current paycheck up for down payment and hope for a loan. It was necessary to keep in mind that space was needed for seven passengers and a wheelchair. Therefore, the description of such a car meant a station wagon. God blessed us with an affordable car without delay. The car dealer encouraged us to take the car on Friday and drive it over the weekend. We were told to bring it back on Monday after we had made our decision. We could process the loan at that time. Everything fell into place. Monday morning, I was able to take the children to school and then return to purchase the car.

Another immediate need was a refill on Charlie's medicine as his supply had diminished from the trip. Upon arrival at the local drug store, I was greeted with a smile from the pharmacist. He mentioned how inspired he was to see that Charlie had received such a fabulous gift from The Dream Factory. He had seen the article in the newspaper and was overcome with joy for all of us. He expressed how nice it was to read a good human-interest story. Then he added what a pleasure it was to discover that the good news was about someone he knew. He had been our pharmacist for several years and was accustomed to seeing us weekly. I was rarely in the store without several or all of my children with me.

It was comforting to hear that Charlie had positively influenced another person, especially in such an indirect manner. Of course by now the pharmacist had known Charlie for about six years and had been touched by him just by being familiar with his medical history, but this incident touched him in a different way. He witnessed the goodness of others toward this child that he knew and it moved him.

When school started, Jonathan and I began taking Charlie to Carrither's. Pulling out the wheelchair for the first time at this school made a number of heads turn. Although Charlie could walk, he could never have walked the distance of the hallway without taking an extremely long time and becoming short of breath along the way. He didn't like using the wheelchair because it made him self-conscious. I saw the need for a little pep talk after witnessing the taken aback response from the students. Instead of going along with his feelings, I approached it differently by telling him that the kids would probably think it was pretty neat. It was a novelty to them. I reminded him that once he got to the room and the kids saw that he could walk, everything would be okay. I encouraged him not to take it personally. I assured him that the only reason that they were all staring was because he had something that they weren't accustomed to seeing. I said, "When they start asking questions, just answer them. Once they find out why you need a wheelchair, they won't ask anymore. You'll see. They will all get used to it just as your friends have before."

It was a good thing that he couldn't see the knots in my stomach. I felt bad for him and the situation he was about to face. Starting over again in a new school was hard and being the only one in a wheelchair made it that much harder. God helped me portray an outward strength, which gave Charlie the strength that he needed each day. I was certain of only one thing. God would see him through this just as He had all other trials in his life.

It didn't take long for the family to get used to the routine of school. Jackie had just begun her first year of high school at

Sacred Heart Academy, which was on the other side of town. Marty was now in the fifth grade and Leslie was in the second grade at St. Gabriel.

The morning cycle began to fall into place. Jackie was driven to the main road at 6:30 A.M., where she caught the city bus. From there I returned home to wake up the rest of the children. Marty and Leslie were the next ones to leave and were fortunate to have a bus stop at the corner. Lastly, I took Charlie to school with Jonathan at my side. Throughout this time of getting the children out the door, I was concerned for Jackie. It was a bit frightening to have a young teenage girl out so early by herself. She had to transfer twice before getting to school. Periodically checking the time, I pictured her waiting at the two stops, praying that she would be safe. Aware that winter weather was ahead made it more difficult to bear. These were times that I wished I could be in two places at the same time. Yet, there were no other options. Charles' job was in the opposite direction, which meant that he would not be able to take her. I had to trust that God would protect her, realizing that this hardship would prepare her for future times when she would be alone. This growth would provide her with a strengthened independence.

After taking Charlie to school, Jonathan and I frequently attended morning Mass. On days that the school children participated I realized how much I missed seeing Charlie with his class. It didn't seem right that he wasn't there. It occasionally disturbed me that he was no longer a part of St. Gabriel School. Nevertheless, Jonathan was pleased to see Marty and Leslie with their classes. Fr. Caster's sermons were always a consolation when I struggled over Charlie's absence. His words continued to inspire me and fill me with a sense of great love from God. This daily ritual supplied me with the spiritual growth that I constantly needed.

While the children were in school, I worked in the lunchroom at Sacred Heart Academy. This not only supplemented the family income, it gave me an opportunity to make a regular connection with Jackie. Jonathan was able to go with me and seemed to enjoy eating lunch with the girls.

After school, the rule of "homework first" went into effect. As the children finished their assignments, they went outside to play. Before long, Jackie and Marty were bringing home rumors that were floating throughout the neighborhood. It greatly disturbed them when they heard that Charlie didn't deserve the trip to Germany. They heard that he wasn't even sick so he shouldn't have been given the trip. Another statement heard was based on the assumption that tax dollars were being used for such trips. Still another comment was made about taking some leftover money from The Dream Factory to buy a car. Naturally, it upset all of us to hear these remarks. Yet, I was not inclined to report to the neighbors about our finances or any other facts about the trip as the truth would not be believed anyway. Admittedly, the gossip did not make us feel very comfortable among a certain few. Believing it was best to ignore it, I instructed the children to play in their own yard. I relied on God to help me overlook the comments. Not feeling right about taking an action on this form of persecution, I chose to be silent and do nothing. Uncertainty was not from God. Revenge was not from God. This is how I knew to keep quiet. This prevented me from making the wrong decision and escalating the resentment. I understood that those who truly knew us were not the ones spreading rumors. The children were encouraged to concentrate on school. With the onset of winter, interaction in the neighborhood would lessen and time would heal the wounds.

The neighborhood had changed drastically since Jamie and Tony moved away, mostly because it was their mother who had brought people together. Friendships had become scarce, with few people really knowing each other well. In an effort to keep peace, we avoided opportunities for gossip.

As Charlie focused on his new school, he observed a new atmosphere within it. His thought patterns were equivalent to one and a half years less than his chronological age, due to the stroke that he had as a baby. There was a youthful innocence about him as well as a naive understanding of life. The middle school that he was now experiencing was different from any school he attended in the past. The parochial schools enforced discipline and expectations from the children. His public school experiences had been positive so far because he was in classes with other special needs children who were also innocent and well behaved. Now, at twelve-years-old, he was struggling with the behavior surrounding him at school. He came home, puzzled and upset because the kids were cussing and saying nasty things. I asked him if they were directing them to him and he replied negatively. Nevertheless, he couldn't tolerate being around it. With a fretful look on his face he said to me, "Why do I have to go to a public school? I'm not public. I'm Catholic." Oh how I wanted to laugh. Yet he was so serious. I could see how difficult it was for him to be in this atmosphere. I questioned him further about the children in his class and suggested how to handle them.

He found a new friend, Ricky. They talked regularly on the phone and occasionally spent time at each other's house. Before long, they had devised a way to play football over the telephone. Charlie would set up the miniature players on the table or the bed. With some imagination, he and Ricky proceeded with the plays and kept score. I never quite figured out how they were able to do this, but they enjoyed it immensely. Mostly it wasn't a problem for him to be on the phone too long because his chores and homework were completed. It kept him entertained at times when he felt abandoned. As Charlie grew, it became harder for him to keep up with Marty and his friends. Rather than holding Marty back, it was good for Charlie to find alternatives such as the phone conversations.

That Christmas Charles was able to find a used, inexpensive computer and printer. Very quickly, Charlie discovered that he could type in football plays by using the X key to make the players' location on the field. He was exacting in this and often spent hours making up plays. Once again, I saw that God had provided for his needs and had also allowed Marty to grow without the obligation of always being there for his brother. Although they spent the majority of their time together, each needed some time to himself as well.

The new challenge of teenage hormones stirred up new ways of thinking. Charlie had decided to take on a new identity at school. He began asking his teachers to call him Chuck. Perhaps he thought a different name would make him feel mature. Before long, phone calls were coming in for Chuck, making me stop and think who Chuck was.

Along with this new identity, he was granted his wish to have a flat-top haircut. He looked so different that we hardly recognized him. Although the style was not my choice, I could see how important it was to him. The quality of life at every age was what mattered to me. As a middle-school student, he wanted and needed to look the part.

Time passed quickly that year. Jason had moved to Tennessee and there were fewer boys in the neighborhood his age. His friend Scott had apparently found a girlfriend and tried explaining to Charlie that his interests were changing. Charlie had been calling him and asking him to play football for some time. Finally, Scott came to the house and the two of them sat on the front porch for a long time in deep discussion. Charlie came in puzzled, sharing with me much of what Scott had told him. He understood that the bottom line was that Scott would not be having as much time to play football with him as he had in the past. This was very disheartening. Charlie's mind could not understand how a girlfriend would make that much difference. I perceived that Scott had been sensitive to his buddy's feelings as he attempted to explain particular facts of life in a gentle manner to Charlie. Scott could see the age gap between them gradually expanding.

Charlie's social life was not what it used to be. It was becoming harder and harder for him to keep up with his friends, in most every aspect. They were all heading in various directions. The neighbors Jamie and Tony had moved to Florida, in the third grade. Jason had moved away, also. Now, Scott, who was a little older, was growing ahead of Charlie. His life faced many endings and new directions.

When football season began, Charlie wanted desperately to play for St. Gabriel. I was now forced to point out his inability to keep up with the exercises. That alone was enough for him to understand. It wasn't necessary for me to say those dreaded words; "You can't play." Instead, he would go watch Marty and his friends practice daily. He never tired of watching. Then one day, Charles asked the coach if Charlie could be the team manager. (We thought, with the help of Dr. Cottrill's idea, that he could sit on the bench with the players and be responsible for the boys' knowing about practice times. He could make phone calls to inform players of any significant changes.) However, the coach was not moved by his plea. Believing it was not feasible, the answer came back as "No," cutting off the conversation before given the opportunity to suggest that he could help with the phone calls. As a result, he spent the season watching, admiring, and dreaming of playing football.

In February, Charlie was sent to a new doctor to determine proper growth. As height became more of an issue, growth hormone testing was ordered. Charlie was now an average of 12 inches shorter than most of his friends. The testing consisted of a number of painful needle pricks every fifteen minutes for the duration of the test. Each time he was stuck, five vials of blood were drawn. Because his blood was so thick, it required extensive painful massaging of his fingers over and over. This continued for hours. Each finger on both hands was punctured. Charlie never cried but expressed the sense of pain through his eyes. As I watched the pain inflicted upon him again and again, I thought of the whips lashed against Jesus's body again and again. The pain Charlie suffered without screaming or crying out was a reminder of the scourging of Christ. He endured each stick with grace, knowing that another one would soon follow. He didn't fight back. He accepted all that was being done to him. When I was alone in meditation I began to understand a sense of reality of the scourging of Jesus.

Days later, the test results showed that his body was producing the correct amount of growth hormones. Therefore, treatment with more growth hormones would not be beneficial as he did not have a deficiency. The bone age, on the other hand, indicated that he was indeed two years behind his chronological age of nearly thirteen. The problem originated from other sources beyond our control. The spinal fusion was partly to blame because it had prevented a portion of his growth. Secondly, the cyanotic heart disease stunted his growth as well. Although never truly diagnosed, there were partial symptoms of short-gut syndrome indicated. His barrel-chested, compressed, stocky appearance was the result of an overworked heart muscle. Of course, coming from a short family didn't help matters, either. As he began to pick up weight during this potential growth spurt, his body was not stretching upward as it should have. This combination of factors was not in his favor. By now, it was disappointing to realize that nothing could be done to encourage a normal growth pattern. The emotional hardship of being significantly shorter than his friends would be another lifelong trial to endure. The thought of facing teenage years with this added burden was disheartening. Yet, I knew not to dwell on disappointments when good could always be found.

Charlie, age thirteen, shown with Louisville Redbirds just before the game

In the spring, Charlie received a special invitation from The Easter Seal Society to throw the ceremonial first pitch for the Louisville Redbirds baseball team. The University of Louisville football team had planned a simultaneous run from the baseball stadium to the university as a kickoff for spring conditioning, as well as a fundraiser for The Easter Seal Society. Naturally, Charlie came to mind as a representative due to his love for sports. He eagerly accepted the offer.

On April 21, 1988, Charlie enthusiastically met Mr. Miller and Mr. Jordan (from The Easter Seal Society), on the sidelines at Cardinal Stadium. It happened to be Jackie's 15th birthday as well. So, she brought her friend, Lisa, with her to make her day a little more special. The seven of us stood with Charlie and watched the warm-up of the ball game. Soon, reporters came with their huge cameras toward Charlie. They interviewed him, a football player and Mr. Miller regarding the run-related fundraiser.

As the baseball players completed their warm-ups and left the field, a second baseman ran up to Marty and asked him to hold his bat. Marty was taken aback and quite uncertain as to why he was asked to hold the bat. As it turned out, it had been cracked with the previous hit and this was the player's way of giving it to him. Charles and I were moved to see how this act of kindness toward Marty prevented him from feeling left out. Strangers were often drawn to Charlie and generally recognized the feelings of his brothers and sisters as well.

Within minutes, a football player wheeled Charlie out near the pitcher's mound. He proudly pulled himself up from the chair. Once given the ball and the signal to proceed, he hurled the ball with all of his might toward the Redbird's player. The crowd cheered with the first throw and the football players launched their run, simultaneously. Charlie grinned proudly as he was escorted off the field. The players took their places and the game began.

The spring rains made way for brighter days. Fresh air and sunshine enticed the children to get outside early on Saturdays. After breakfast and chores, the children wasted little time indoors. As I took my morning position at the kitchen sink, I found that washing dishes provided me with a peaceful time for reflecting on the homily from morning Mass. The scenic wooded view from my window gave me the opportunity to witness the miracles of God. I absorbed the beauty of the springtime buds on the trees as I noticed new growth each day. My soul was filled with an indescribable warmth as my eyes observed God's love all around me. Robins built a nest in the bedroom windowsill. I, along with the children, was drawn to check on the robins several times a day, watching as eggs were laid and hatched. In every direction I looked was evidence of God's love upon me.

Blessings were not limited within the family. They were manifested in nature as well.

The excitement of summer was soon in the air. The neighbors were drawn outside as usual. Charlie and Marty were gradually changing their yard games to include more baseball and soccer. An occasional football game would begin, but they mostly played sports of the season.

In watching the boys play, I was concerned over Charlie's inability to keep up with them. By now, most of the boys were riding bikes for fun. It was sad to watch Charlie sitting on the porch waiting for them to return. This summer he was not able to use his Tri-Kart because the battery would no longer hold a charge. I had called to inquire about its price and was informed that it would cost $150.00. I struggled to find a way to obtain the money. It was so important for his independence that I was determined to buy him one with the next paycheck. It didn't happen. The following week we had car repairs that could wait no longer. The next payday we were behind in other bills because of the car repair. The week after, shoes were a priority for the kids as they had outgrown them and were no longer fit to be worn. Then I had to go to the grocery because this, too, had been put off for too long. It was a vicious cycle. The Tri-Kart battery remained at the top of my priority list all summer. Yet, I could never manage to buy it even with the best of intentions. Charlie understood every dilemma that stood in the way.

He was so patient. He never expected me to rush out and buy one. When I told him it would be another week, he'd just say, "Okay, Mom." One day Marty helped him up the street in his wheelchair. He came home all excited after speaking to a man several streets away. This was someone who always spoke to the boys when they were out. He enthusiastically said, "Guess what, Mom. This man said that he knows where we can get a battery for just $100.00." The price did catch my attention because it was more affordable. I told Charlie that it had to be a specific kind in order to work. He confirmed that the man checked it out already and was certain that it was the same battery. With that in mind, I indicated that it would probably be attainable, which gave him a more hopeful outlook.

246

Meanwhile, Dr. Leatherman retired due to advanced age and declining health. Charlie was seen by a new orthopedic doctor, who brought about new changes. On examination, he measured Charlie's legs and saw that there was a difference of more than two inches. He confidently stated that it could be corrected by surgery. He suggested that Charlie have the operation to increase the growth in his right leg. The plan would be to break the tibia bone in his calf and attach a metal device used for stretching the leg. This would have a screw that would require gradual turning as the bone healed. Each turn would force the bone to fuse at a farther distance resulting in extra length over time.

Charles and I discussed the procedure with uneasy feelings about it. We both saw it as cosmetic. It was not a necessity as his other operations had been. In fact, surgery was very hard to justify considering all that he had been through already. We were both aware of the potential need to have future surgery on his heart. We felt that it was important to at least offer this to Charlie as it was his life and his future that was at hand. Knowing that he was not eager to undergo unnecessary pain, I doubted that he would even consider it. I described the surgery for Charlie. With very little thought, he decided that he was content with his unbalanced body.

By his June appointment, Charlie had gained weight as his body attempted to balance growth and teenage hormones. The spinal fusion prevented any noticeable growth upward, yet an older appearance was beginning to take place. The increase in weight affected all but his height. His feet were hurting most of the time now because the orthopedic shoes did not come in a greater width. Every adjustment possible was made on his shoes to no avail. The doctor suggested a new support for his feet. A prescription was given for ankle-foot orthosis (AFOs) to be worn inside regular athletic shoes. They were made from hard plastic, which was molded in conformity to his feet and calves. These would be made and fitted at the brace shop. Charlie was elated with the idea of wearing lightweight shoes. He gladly accepted the plastic inserts knowing that his shoes looked like those of other children. A prescription was given for a half-inch lift on his right shoe similar to the lift he had been wearing. This took up some of the slack in the length discrepancy.

As we were about to leave the office, a nurse stopped us to say that Dr. Leatherman was there for consultation with another doctor. She asked us to wait, knowing that he would want to see us. Moments later, Dr. Leatherman entered the hallway where we were waiting. He walked slowly with the use of a cane, which we had not seen him with before. His eyes glowed as they caught sight of us. An enormous smile was immediately followed with affectionate hugs. The joy of seeing each other was indescribable; each of us feeling elated that the other was doing well. He updated me on his recent health and recovery from heart surgery. In turn, he was delighted to see how well Charlie was progressing. Old memories surfaced as he looked over Charlie. The warmth of our meeting would carry us through the day. Yet, an underlying awareness was present that life was a fragile gift with the uncertainty of meeting again. We parted with high spirits and awareness of our love for each other.

That very day Charlie and I went shopping for new athletic shoes. It was, by far, the most exciting trip to the shoe store that he had ever had.

The AFOs were hot and more uncomfortable than the braces. Despite this added discomfort, he was willing to pay the price in order to look cool like other teenagers. He adjusted to it over time, although they were never comfortable to wear.

As summer slipped away, the money never became available for the Tri-Kart battery. In a matter of a few weeks, it was time for school registration. Tuition was due for grade school and high school. Although I had not lost sight of God, this particular need was not met. Food, shelter, and other basics were more of a necessity, which required them to come first. The disappointing factor was that Charlie's ticket to independence was taken from him when he couldn't use the Tri-Kart. Although he still had the wheelchair to get around in, he needed assistance. Without help, he could not go up hills or any significant distance. His forced dependence was a good thing for others to see. It gave his family and friends the opportunity to lend a helping hand and also appreciate their own health. I knew that God was answering my prayers although the response was not my ideal choice.

With the leaves beginning to fall, the scenery out my kitchen window was breathtaking. Standing in my favorite spot, washing dishes, I was able to reflect on why things happen as they do. It was difficult to understand why a $100.00 battery was impossible to obtain. I felt guilty because I couldn't do more for Charlie. I felt guilty because I was healthier than he was, and I could not trade that with him. As I enjoyed the beauty of the fall, my mind eventually forgot the guilt and turned to God.

My thoughts began with the daily homily as I recognized the gifts and graces that God had given me. Remembering that guilt was not from God, the focus of my deliberation changed. Blessings came to mind with a simple glance at the children outside. I could see how God was taking care of each of us. Watching Charlie struggle across the creek would bring tears to my eyes. These were not tears of pity. They were tears of the reality of God's love for me. He obviously loved me a great deal to give me such a special child. The observation of Marty's helping hand toward his brother brought more tears to the surface. My heart was deeply moved to see this special brother that God had given to Charlie. To even think that they were both given to me was almost more than my heart could bear. I meditated on the beautiful people that God put on our path to inspire or assist us. I thought of friends, family, strangers, doctors, nurses, priests, teachers, and many more. As my mind drifted, I watched the squirrels run up the trees preparing for winter, and the birds gather around the bread that we had thrown out for them. A sense of overwhelming love filled me. It was such a wonderful view for reflection that I would regret finishing the dishes. I laughed to myself when I discovered the blessing of not having a dishwasher.

I often thought of how magnificent it would be to someday have a grotto with Our Blessed Mother on the other side of the creek, facing the house. When I spoke to Our Lady, I pictured a grotto in her honor. As my thoughts moved from God to Our Blessed Mother, I found a great joy in talking to her. Moving from room to room cleaning house, I could easily empathize with her. I sometimes imagined what her day might be like with cleaning, cooking, washing clothes, sewing, etc. The one part that would always stump me was the mothering of one child. I wondered if it must have been very quiet in her house. I imagined that Jesus spent hours working with Joseph and learning the trade of carpentry. I couldn't fathom that sort of day for me. Children routinely surrounded my time. There would be some inside and some outside, some laughing and some crying. Activity was ever present. There was usually someone interested in being by my side and someone wanting to play alone. Boredom was an unknown factor in our home.

The children used their imaginations to create fun ways to play. When weather kept them indoors, they used furniture to make trains, or blankets to make tents, or boxes to make houses. They never ran out of things to do.

Witnessing this in my home made me wonder about the home of Jesus as a small child. How did He play? Whom did He play with? Did He have an active imagination as did my children? Did He help His mother clean? I would think of families with one child and assume they would understand this far better than I would. My mind was set in a different mode and I decided that I would probably never comprehend the household of Jesus, Mary, and Joseph.

Going about my chores, I would sometimes find myself relating my way of doing laundry, cooking, preparing bath water, and every other aspect of daily life to Mary's way. Although I had sewn many of the children's clothes in the past, I was also able to take advantage of good sales. What a difference it is to sew with a machine or walk into a store versus making everything by hand. The contrast made me appreciate my life exactly as it was. I was grateful for modern conveniences. No wonder I had five children. The gifts of our modern world have made it easy to raise five children.

As time passed, Charlie wanted to do more of the things that Marty got to do. Oftentimes, the boys would play in the woods and make their way into the next court. Charlie was aware that Marty would frequently walk or run around the block and come home a different way. One day Marty came home without him.

He said, "Charlie said to tell you that he is walking around the block."

I was flabbergasted. As simple as it may sound, I knew that his heart would never allow him to make it. His feet would also be in terrible pain. I became very frightened for him and began pumping Marty with questions. "Where is he now? How long ago did he leave? Is anyone with him?" My heart was pounding as I rushed to the car to begin my search for him. There were five courts he would have to pass before reaching our street. I spotted him on the main stretch between the courts. He could barely take another step. He was obviously short of breath. I knew it was important not to scold him. All he wanted was to be a kid like everyone else. I knew how important it was to him. An ill feeling came over me as I empathized with him for not being healthy enough to do such simple things. Pulling the car over, I stopped to help him in. He had a disappointed look on his face.

I asked him, "Why are you walking the long way home?"

He answered, "I just wanted to see if I could do it."

Being selective with my words, I pointed out that he should have someone with him in case he needed help. He was obviously glad that I had come to his rescue.

"How did you make it this far?" I inquired.

"I stopped and sat down three times. I can do it, Mom. All I have to do is stop and rest for a few minutes." Some excitement had entered his voice by now. He wanted desperately to be like Marty.

Informing him that it was different for Marty, I said, "He doesn't have a hard time breathing when he walks."

"It's not fair," he said sadly.

I responded, "You're right. It's not fair." Once again fairness was discussed.

Then he added, "**Yeah**, but Marty can do everything. He can play baseball. He **can play** football. He can run..."

I interrupted him **and** said, "You know, Charlie, life is not fair. We all are **given different** things in life at different times. You need to be **happy for** others and what they have. And, you need to make **the best of** what you have. Would it make you happy if Marty couldn't run?" He quickly responded with "No, I just want to do it, too."

"I understand that, but maybe the reason that you can't run is because God knows that it will kill you. Your heart would not be able to handle it. Perhaps that's why your feet are in such bad shape: to keep you from running so that you can live." (Dr. Cottrill had shared this idea with me in the past. I knew that it was appropriate to use it at this time.)

As we went into the house, Charlie went straight to his miniature football players without hesitation. He was satisfied playing indoors again and did not discuss the fairness issue any further.

An interest in wrestling had increased in recent years for the boys. Marty and Charlie would not limit their imaginations as the rounds began. Each identified himself with a role model figure of their choice. Wrestlemania had moved from the TV to the bedroom. They flexed their muscles as they took their designated places in the ring.

Excitement filled their voices. Before long, thumping and other strange noises arose. I'd walk in to find Charlie short of breath and Marty sweating from exertion. Both would be grinning and enjoying every minute of it. What could I say? No way would I stop their play for Charlie's health. He knew when he couldn't handle any more and would break frequently for a rest. I was always observant of his color when I opened the door to check on him. I just prayed that nothing serious would happen while he was playing with Marty. He was such an inspiration to Charlie that I did not feel justified in robbing Charlie of that grace. The love between them was as close as two brothers could possibly be.

Although Jonathan frequently wrestled with them as well, he spent most of his time with Leslie because they were closer in age. The two of them were far more laid back than the other three, probably due to their order of birth in the family.

Jackie always liked private time with Charlie. She mostly enjoyed talking and being creative with whatever came to mind. She would often interest Charlie into trying some experimental recipe. She felt a special closeness to him as his older sister. She never smothered him, but was always there for him, showing him the way.

Part III

17
FOURTH DOWN DECISION

Once school started again, it was a busy time for all of us. Marty had joined the football team and games became the family activity of the week. Charles made another attempt to give Charlie the feeling of belonging to a team. He asked the coach if Charlie could be the water boy. He offered to push Charlie out onto the field in his wheelchair where he could hand the boys their water bottles. Although it was agreeable to the coach, it didn't work out because it was too hard to push the wheelchair on the grass. Charlie saw the dilemma that the idea imposed and agreed that it was not practical to continue. As much as he desired to be with his friends on the field, he humbly returned to the bleachers. The intensity of the game, however, often drew him to park his wheelchair close to the fence for a precise view. He was making certain not to miss a single play. He was quite proud that his brother was playing for St. Gabriel.

The season ended with the thrilling accomplishment of winning the championship and the Toy Bowl. Marty brought home a large blue and gold trophy that stood out among all the other trophies on their shelf. Charlie was elated for him.

Life in the Stopher household was escalating with activities and responsibilities. Being a mother also meant being a volunteer in the schools, the church, and the community. Charles remained a full-time chemist by day and a most helpful husband and father by evening. His help was instrumental in allowing me to apply my abilities as a mother. This opportunity granted me success as Girl Scout leader for Leslie's troop and continued involvement in the interests of each child. His support for me also made it possible to maintain my recently acquired position as the director of a small craft company. The family worked well together at home keeping up with the housework, laundry, errands, and children's activities.

Making time for God through daily Mass and weekly prayer group quickly multiplied my time for all other responsibilities. I was gifted with an energy that I would not ordinarily have without God's presence. Being a mom meant juggling it all and hoping that everything fell into place. Day after day schedules clicked together. Aside from work and other responsibilities, I slipped away with Jackie for prom and teenage fashion shows while Charles stayed home with the others. Monthly Bunco (a dice game commonly played among women in Kentucky) with the girls and random time with friends over coffee or shopping provided invigorating breaks on a regular basis.

The establishment of lifelong friendships was important to me and I impressed this on my children as well. They were encouraged to always keep in touch with their friends. Moving out of town or from one school to another should never be the cause to end a relationship. Communication is the key and so easy to use.

Back at school Charlie struggled with social injustices. The daily surroundings took a toll on his typical cheerful attitude, causing it to deteriorate. Unable to exert himself as he once got away with, he chose to find an alternative form of entertainment during recess. He began taking a pocket football game to school, which he was allowed to play with after lunch. However, trouble started when a student began harassing him over it, making every attempt to take it from him. Eventually, the student stole the game from him when his back was turned. Charlie had left his backpack unguarded during gym class and discovered the game missing after school. There was no way to prove that the boy had taken it.

In time, another problem surfaced. His teacher was downgrading the entire class with insulting comments inconsistent with a teacher's respected role. These idiosyncrasies decreased Charlie's comfort level in the school. He came home asking to return to St. Gabriel. He didn't care how difficult it would be. He only knew that he could not tolerate the unchristian atmosphere that was surrounding him.

We discussed how much harder it would be for him to keep up with the class at St. Gabriel. He insisted that he could do the work. I knew otherwise. He began to plead with me. He was so unhappy. I found it disturbing to see the joy escape from his soul.

It touched my heart. He never wanted to leave the people at St. Gabriel to begin with. That was where his heart was and where it would stay.

I thought and prayed. I asked for guidance. With much prayer and reflection, I decided that the only way that it could work would be to arrange additional teaching at home. The teachers would be limited in their time and ability to give him the individual attention that he needed.

At this point I realized that it no longer mattered how much Charlie learned. Rather, I saw it important that he feel a sense of belonging somewhere. I was just beginning to see that his mission on earth was being fulfilled. I saw that he had probably already reached the people that he was meant to touch. No longer were new people on his path recognizing the example of strength and courage set before them. He was so "normalized" that his presence was much like those around him. I sensed then that it was only a matter of time before God would call him home. There had been a few fluctuations in his health, but not enough to cause this concern. It was all from a spiritual standpoint.

I made several proposals to Charlie. Plan one would be to ask permission that I sit in the back of the class each day in order to reinforce the material each night. Plan two would be that he go through the class as everyone else, but have the teacher require less homework from him without the other students' knowing. Charlie was still unable to work at the pace of the class. He was probably able to write at one-third the speed of the others. Plan three would be to give the regular amount of work, but allow me to write it for him, as he would give oral answers.

Charlie was so despondent that he was willing to try any of these options if it meant getting back into a school where he would feel good about learning. I made certain not to project any expectations whatsoever. I gave him every reason to see that it may not be able to work. At the same time, I offered to try. I told him of my plan to speak to the principal, Mr. Huelsman. This was enough to make him happy. He knew how fair a person that

Mr. Huelsman had always been and was therefore willing to accept his decision.

I approached Mr. Huelsman with the different game plans and a plea of understanding. He listened openly. I tried to relay the message to him that the grades were no longer an important issue. It's not the letter on the report card, it's the effort and sense of accomplishment that mattered. How could I say that it didn't appear, in my eyes, that Charlie would grow into adulthood? That would be like giving up on him. A lengthy discussion followed to determine the possibility of any of these options working. It was agreed upon that he would discuss the issue with Mrs. Dutton, who was the assistant principal, and with the seventh-grade teachers.

The response came back with concerns that it may become more frustrating in the long run if he were unable to keep up. Every issue that was mentioned was valid. Humiliation of having a mother in the classroom, inability to take tests along with the class and frustration with an overwhelming amount of homework, were a few. It would be difficult for the teachers as well, having a student whose assignments were different from the others.

I understood all that he said. Although it saddened me that Charlie would not be given a chance, I also knew in my heart that this was not where God intended for him to go. I felt good, on the other hand, that I had given it my best effort. As I had told Charlie, it doesn't hurt to ask. I said that we haven't lost a thing by trying. Now we would start all over again until we find the right school.

Charlie felt discouraged and rejected. Once again, I pointed out that the decision was made with his best interest in mind. "Mr. Huelsman would love to have you back," I said. "But, he doesn't want you to feel frustrated. He's not sure that St. Gabriel can offer you what you need."

I assured him that we had found the right school in the past and we would do it again. The next step was to check out Noe Middle School. We had avoided this school before because of the long bus ride being a potential for motion sickness. However, it was now necessary to face this fear and deal with it if it arose.

We could find that we were being concerned about something that wouldn't be a problem.

Charles took off of work to investigate the school with us. Before leaving home, Charlie had decided that he didn't like this school. "It's a dumb school," he said.

"How do you know?" I inquired. "Have you been there before?" He was aware that this was a school with classes for the disabled. I let him know very quickly that it would be very much like Hawthorne, which he was quite happy with. "It is not all for the handicapped," I informed him. There were many regular classes as well. I pointed out that his friends from Hawthorne were also attending Noe.

It was interesting to see that although he had many handicapped friends, he didn't see himself as being disabled. This was a classification that he wanted to avoid because of the limitations that it implied. He didn't believe that it bothered the other kids to be in a wheelchair. It only bothered him. He feared that making friends among those not confined to the handicapped classroom would be hard. His reluctance to be part of this class forced me to point out that his friends probably felt the same way. "Don't you think it disturbs them to be in that class, too?" I asked him.

He said that they were used to it and therefore it didn't upset them. "Think about it, Charlie. I bet it does bother them and they just haven't mentioned it. I bet they've all wished to be friends with kids in the other classes."

A view from the other side had never dawned on him before. The idea opened his eyes to a new perspective, leaving him more uncertain about his thoughts on the school. "Keep in mind that we're just looking. You won't go there unless it's right for you." He lowered his guard once he trusted in my promise, for he knew that I would not deceive him.

A tour of the school left him feeling a little better about it. Yet, he still had a sense of fear and uneasiness about adjusting his life and facing the unknown again. With encouragement, he agreed to give it a try. A pact was made to attend for one month before forming an opinion.

Just as he expected, he was placed in a classroom of handicapped children. His teacher was a very clever African-American man, Mr. Sims. He knew just how to make the fears of a new school disappear. Immediately picking up on Charlie's strong qualities, such as math, he soon had Charlie helping another student who was struggling. This made him feel better about himself and feel needed by others. The boost in self-esteem made him feel rather important.

Thanks to Mr. Sims, the transition was smooth. He always had encouraging words for Charlie. Charlie began coming home from school with a smile. It was wonderful. It was apparent that our trust in God had shown us the way.

As winter progressed, Charlie began having numerous headaches, much more often than he had ever had before. The headaches increased in intensity and frequently, lasting all day. He was taking a fair amount of aspirin each day, which allowed him a maintenance level of tolerance for the pain. Different medications were tried. Yet, no relief was found. He occasionally held his head in severe pain, saying that it felt like his heart was beating in his head. From his description, his head was obviously throbbing with each beat of his heart. Finally, after trying all advice from the pediatrician and cardiologist, I requested an appointment with a neurologist. It was tormenting me to witness his pain and be incapable of helping him. I searched desperately to understand what was going on with his health. My heart ached as I watched him suffer.

The neurologist could find no answer to explain the sudden increase in headaches. No changes were found on the CAT scan from the initial infarction at nineteen-months-old. An MRI was ordered next because this test would show the brain in segments and allow for more precise readings. After it was completed, he became violently ill with nausea and vomiting, thus causing more pressure on the brain and instigating another severe headache. After a complete evaluation, nothing was revealed to indicate the cause of his agony.

My only suggestion to him was for him not to get too excited and not to move too suddenly. These were difficult instructions for Charlie. He was always excited. He loved life and laughter.

Yet, his laughter was actually a factor in bringing about headaches. So, how was he supposed to enjoy life? He could no longer keep up physically and now I was encouraging him to slow down in expressing his emotions as well.

Sharing the update on his medical condition with Dr. Cottrill included a discussion on the possibility of his complaints stemming from the upheaval in changing schools. Sometimes it was difficult to determine the level of Charlie's discomfort due to the fluctuation with social acceptance, health, and the ability to always smile. An attempt was made to distract Charlie whenever he began complaining about not feeling up to par.

Having the school issue settle down before Christmas took a heavy burden off our minds. We were all able to enjoy the holidays more because of it. The teenager in Charlie was beginning to show in his desires for Christmas gifts. His greatest wish was to have a dual-cassette tape player. He anticipated having more music available by copying his favorite songs from his friends.

Just prior to celebrating Christmas, basketball season began. By January, the business of the season was well underway with Marty at practice or a game and Leslie equally occupied with cheerleading. Jackie, Charlie, and Jonathan teamed up with Charles and me to cheer them on at the games. It was wonderful family fun in spite of the demanding schedules. We anticipated spring and summer to be more rushed as all the children except Charlie would soon sign up for baseball, softball, or T-ball.

There were a number of other activities going on simultaneously. As Leslie's Girl Scout leader, I was planning special events and cookie sales. As mom, I took Marty to the doctor twice a week for allergy shots, handled the financial resources (or lack thereof), shopped for groceries, birthdays and necessities, and battled with the Social Security office for Charlie's disability. As a sister, I made wedding and birthday cakes, and tried always to lend an ear to those in my family.

I made sure to find time for myself, as well. I attended daily Mass as usual, enjoyed my weekly prayer group, and remained active in the Women's Club at church. It was not unusual to find numerous events on the calendar on the same day. I found it amazing how much God helped me with my schedule. Even when times overlapped, I knew that God would help me carry on in the most productive manner so as not to miss anything important. I don't recall ever turning down an invitation due to a packed calendar. Yet, it was generally full at all times.

I had been noticing that Charlie was struggling a bit more than usual this winter. His body had been attempting a growth spurt though with obstacles. Breathing had become more difficult with his short stature and weight increase. This change in size along with the trials of winter on his health, made January a miserable month.

It became more frequent that he would be short of breath. He began to use his wheelchair more than he walked. His legs and feet hurt more than usual. The laughter with which he had always filled our home was now causing him tremendous pain. Laughter was used as a form of medicine. A little joke would bring about a laugh so hearty that he would fall to the ground out of control. When he reached that point, Charles or I would stop our joking around. We loved to make him laugh because it was so genuine. It was his laughter that kept the joy in our home.

The excitement he felt when he planned to go outside for a football game would be the ultimate high for him. Now it was suddenly causing him severe chest pain. He would jump up with great anticipation and a huge smile. Then he would unexpectedly grab hold of his chest, his smile would drop, and he would fall onto the floor in great pain. Near tears, he would remark that he couldn't play football. I suggested that he rest a few minutes and then try again slowly. Although he had every right to feel discouraged, I encouraged him not to give in to it. He rested, he got back up, and he went outside to play. When I looked out the window, I saw how he took advantage of every tackle and rested a few minutes on the ground before getting back up. His brother and friends always waited patiently. Never did I hear anyone say to him to hurry up because he was holding up the game. It was remarkable to see how they catered to his needs. The boys played cautiously so that he could enjoy the game. It was more like a feigned aggressiveness to make him feel like all the rest. I watched as he threw a pass and then sat down on the ground. He struggled to get up for the next play. Then, he rested again. Occasionally, he would sit out completely. He'd watch them play from the porch. Yet, his spirits never seemed to falter. As I observed all of this, I prayed that he would not die while playing football with Marty. Knowing that it would be a happy way for him to die, it would devastate Marty.

In the following weeks, Charlie became more exhausted when he walked from the living room to the bedroom. He would sometimes crawl to the bathroom to save his energy.

I was troubled over this sudden decline in his health. Speaking with Dr. Cottrill several times a week, I kept her informed about recent changes. Charlie's next appointment was several weeks away, but my uneasiness over his suffering prompted a quicker checkup.

The current problem with headaches was getting worse. With the intensity as it was, he could scarcely do any activity without his head pounding. Often, I found him holding the left side of his head in excruciating pain. My recurring thought was the possibility of another stroke. I didn't feel that it was coincidental that his hand was always covering the very portion of his brain that had been affected earlier in life. This made me believe that it had something to do with the lack of oxygen to his brain. His cyanosis was becoming more noticeable as well. Still, no doctor was able to find answers to the problem.

Soon, new complaints arose about pain in his legs. He did not elaborate on this, but merely stated from time to time that his legs hurt.

The anxiety and helplessness that I felt were unimaginable. I began doubting my ability to be a good mother. Why couldn't I do something for him? Why couldn't I find a way to relieve his pain? What kind of mother would I be to be satisfied with no solution? Naturally, when I was at a loss regarding motherhood, I turned once again to Our Blessed Mother. She made me realize that, on occasion, we were all helpless as mothers. We can't always spare our children of the pain. She was unable to relieve her son's pain when He was inflicted with the crown of thorns. He, too, had to endure his pain without relief from his mother. She could do nothing for him.

Meditating on this thought, I pictured the thorns pressing deep into Jesus's scalp, causing a sharp, penetrating pain followed by intense throbbing. I pictured Mary during Christ's passion. I knew that she was not with her son, taking his pain away from him. I knew how her heart ached because my heart ached in the same way. Her understanding did not lessen my pain. Yet, I felt consoled by her. I understood the words that I despised so deeply years ago. I was "JUST A MOTHER." I had limitations. It was a painful lesson in humility. I didn't want limitations when it came to my children. I wanted always to be able to protect them from harm. I asked Mary to help me endure my heartache as she endured hers. Together we took one day at a time.

With immune defenses at a low, Charlie soon came down with a stomach virus. The vomiting caused his headaches to increase that much more. Before long, he contracted bronchitis, soon to be followed by strep throat. He was feeling worse every day now. On a visit to the pediatrician, it was discovered that his hemoglobin was twenty-three. Understanding that this was an extraordinary amount explained his misery in part. His blood was so thick that it was a wonder it even flowed.

Putting the whole picture together, it became clear that his heart was struggling to keep up with the demands of his body. He continued to smile and push himself in spite of it all.

Once he was over the illness, we continued our daily activities such as school. In the mornings, I woke Charlie up as always. I noticed a pattern developing that, once he sat up on the side of the bed, he would suddenly feel nauseated. I assumed this was due to the change in schools. He would tell me that he was too sick to go to school. Doubting him, I confidently told him that he would feel better once he got up and moved around. I assisted him to the bathroom and then in getting dressed. He had a sick look on his face the entire time. He always refused breakfast saying that it would only make him sick on the bus. Convincing him to eat some toast allowed me to hope that his stomach would settle down. As this became an everyday event, I looked at it a little closer. He not only got up feeling bad on school days, but on weekends as well. Several times he would insist that he couldn't make it all day. I reminded him that he usually felt better once the day got going. On Saturdays he would drag all morning as well.

Observing this, I began feeling guilty about pushing him to go to school when he felt so bad. On the other hand, I knew he enjoyed the interaction with the other children. Therefore, I made myself push him and then waited to see if he pushed me back. As time passed, I struggled more with the decision to push him or not. What was right? What was fair to him? Finally, I gave into my heart and suggested one morning that he just stay home. He looked worse to me that day. Much to my surprise, he said, "I don't feel like going to school, but I don't want to miss it." He knew that it would be boring to lie around the house. So, I agreed to let him go. Shortly after arriving at school, I received a phone call stating that Charlie didn't feel well and his chest was hurting. The teacher was convinced that it was real. Upon picking him up, he told me that while he was in class, something happened. He woke up and didn't know where he was. I asked him to explain what he meant. "Did you fall asleep or what?"

That wasn't it. He said that he was sitting in his desk with his eyes open. Then, all of a sudden everything stopped and he wasn't anywhere. He didn't understand it, but he was certain that he wasn't asleep. There was no explanation of time because he could not estimate whether it was short or long. He only knew that he suddenly woke up at his desk. Not knowing what to make of it, he was very uncomfortable with the whole episode.

I wondered if it was caused by the lack of oxygen to the brain and again contemplated the thought of an impending stroke. This was a very realistic fear that I dreaded thinking about.

Meanwhile, we had been to see Dr. Cottrill in Lexington. I knew that she would get the wrong impression when she saw him. After riding for an hour and a half in the car, he was well rested. Using the wheelchair in the clinic caused him no exertion, either. His smile and overall appearance looked as good as ever. He wasn't particularly more cyanotic than usual and acted as though nothing bothered him. Of course, the staff thought he looked great. I agreed with them that he looked and felt wonderful, as long as he wasn't doing anything. As long as he didn't walk, he was all right. Dr. Cottrill knew, without my saying, what the quality of life meant to me. Sitting still in order to exist was not the same as living.

We began with the usual testing. Once finished, we met again to discuss the findings. She had briefed Dr. Salley, the cardiac surgeon, on his history and recent changes. The question now was whether to have surgery at this time. How bad was he truly feeling? The determining factor would be a check on the pulse oximeter. With Charlie lying down and having rested the entire day, the oxygen tested at 80%. (A normal reading would register 97-100%.) Being fairly low, the true test would be to see if it changed much when he walked. Suzanne, Dr. Cottrill's nurse, proceeded to take Charlie down the hall. She told him that they would walk halfway and come back. Then she would see what the pulse oximeter read. However, that didn't happen. After a distance of about twelve feet, he was laboring with such exertion that she was forced to stop at that point. Suzanne returned to the room where I was waiting and informed me that upon checking his oxygen, the pulse oximeter registered at 50%. This took everyone in the office by surprise. They did not expect to see such a drastic difference. I was actually glad that the truth about him came out. Being with him daily, I was the only one who realized the pain he was in. As long as he stayed in his wheelchair and did not attempt to walk, he deceived all by his healthy appearance and pleasant attitude. I wanted Dr. Cottrill to see that this was a physical problem not a situation of teenage hormones or a need for attention. The real issue wasn't school, socialization, limitations, or frustrations. The bases of all his complaints were pain and misery. The headaches, chest pains, and leg pains were as intense as I had stated. This drastic decrease in oxygen shed a new light (or perhaps darkness) on the picture. His recent complaints were now clear and justified.

Having witnessed his suffering, I wasn't surprised by the findings. However, a strange sense overcame me the moment I heard 50%. I knew that this was the beginning of the end. He obviously couldn't live this way. I was certain that the time had come to face surgery again. God was telling me that the time was near for him to be called home. I was reminded of the little impact that he now had on those he met. I had the feeling that even those who had been so touched by him in the past were now seeing him as invincible. It was clear to me that the "time to be a child" was up. God had granted my plea after Charlie's heart surgery six years ago. Now, He's coming back for him. He allowed him to play, to have fun, to explore the world, to touch many (at St. Gabriel and elsewhere), and to feel normal.

Blending in so well with others, he was no longer bringing a multitude to Christ as he had in the past. Only an occasional person here or there could see God's gift within him. Just as people commonly blend together, they often do not recognize God's goodness in each other; that is, until tragedy strikes. Then, they suddenly see what God has set before them. This is why I noticed what God was doing. Only with tragedy could more people appreciate the child that God had sent them. His mission on earth was nearing completion.

My stomach was beginning to feel queasy at the thought of losing him. I sensed God leading the way. It's difficult to explain how clear this revelation was. There was no confusion whatsoever. There was no question about it. It was simply fact given to me. "This is the beginning of the end," a voice within me said. Despite the queasy gut feeling, there was also a sense of calmness and peace. I didn't feel angry, nor did I feel like screaming or crying. God planned to show me the way. I trusted that I would not be alone. He wasn't pointing and directing me to go on this path. Rather, the security that I felt was as though He gently placed His hand in mine and offered to take me down the rocky road. I accepted His guidance.

Before long, Dr. Salley came in to speak to me. Based on Charlie's history he had already decided that it would not be wise to do surgery now; until that is, he saw how little oxygen Charlie's body was working with. He explained that if his O2 was at 50%, then his PO2 was about 20-30%. "The fact is," he stated, "he can't live on this." I questioned him thoroughly about the anticipated surgery. Confronting the headache pain, I questioned the relationship between it and the lack of oxygen. Without hesitation, he elaborated on its cause being directly related to the fact that he had outgrown a previous shunt. With the shunt no longer effective, the heart was under enormous strain to pump the blood through the body. Knowing the minute amount of oxygen in the heart chambers led him to believe that surgery was undoubtedly necessary in order for Charlie to live. I spoke to Dr. Salley and then to Dr. Cottrill about the type of surgery required.

A heart catheterization was scheduled along with a meeting to discuss our options. The risks were disturbingly high. I was to return home and discuss it with Charles. At some point I was to explain to Charlie what we were facing.

As we left the hospital, we made our usual drive around the U of K football stadium. Next, we stopped for a hamburger at a drive through as we drove away from town. My mind was full of thoughts that I was not quite prepared to share with Charlie. Our conversation covered every subject except surgery. Then he asked me what Dr. Cottrill was going to do. Puzzled, I told him that we weren't sure. However, I did tell him that we would be back in two weeks for a heart catheterization so that the doctors could determine what to do. Not wanting to scare him, I didn't say too much. Charles and I needed to discuss the options together before projecting this frightening situation to Charlie.

I asked the Holy Spirit to guide me. I asked for the words to say, especially to Charlie. Then I thought of the other children, realizing that it would be just as difficult to explain to them. When I prayed, I did not attempt to plan how to tell them. I trusted that God would give me the words when the time came.

That evening, once the children were settled in bed, I began to explain to Charles what we had discovered at the clinic, explaining that the low oxygen level clarified the reason for the pain that Charlie had endured lately. We discussed the need for surgery and the risks involved. We talked about not doing the surgery as well. Many of the views we shared were the same as with previous heart surgeries. We could see that he wouldn't be able to live without it. Yet, the risks were going to be much greater than before. I shared with Charles all that Dr. Salley had described about the surgery. He would enter into the sternum as in past operations. That means there would be a great deal of scar tissue to be concerned about. The more scar tissue found, the more likely he would have excessive bleeding. "This would be his primary concern," I said.

Looking at the overall picture, we acknowledged how Charlie's age also added to our anxiety. The threat of death was difficult to face in the past, but now there was a stronger bond for each year that he had lived. Charles asked me what my thoughts were about the surgery. When I told him that I didn't feel good about it, he was so surprised. In the past, I spoke encouragingly about surgery. "Why not now?" he wondered. I pointed out that Charlie wasn't able to reach people the way he used to. "I believe his time on earth is over whether he has the surgery or not." He admitted that he didn't feel good about it, either. Maybe we should wait. Maybe we shouldn't go through with it, we both thought.

"On the other hand," I added, "I don't feel good about not doing surgery, either. It's killing me to watch him suffer. I can't bear seeing him in pain every time he moves. He can't spend the rest of his life on the couch. He can't even laugh without hurting."

We lay there in the bed sharing our concerns. Reminiscing over the past, we recalled the various people who were touched by Charlie. Charles talked about the time when Boss Hogg and Cooter from "The Dukes of Hazzard" TV show were in town. They had spent some time talking to Cooter's father-in-law, who was doing a promotion for the show. After a fun-filled conversation, Charles had turned the wheelchair away and walked on with the other children at his side. (It was not unusual for him to take the children alone to an event in town. Tickets were costly and we could save money if I stayed home.) A few moments later, Cooter's father-in-law ran toward them calling them to stop. He wanted to give Charlie a hat with The Dukes' emblem on it. After doing so, he decided to give all the children a hat, as well.

Hours passed as we recalled one memory after another with family, friends, and strangers. Our hearts tugged at the possibility of losing Charlie. Snuggling in each other's arms, we talked about how inspiring he had been to us. Charles was reminded of a time when he and Charlie had stopped into a White Castle for a bite to eat. An elderly man came walking in with a cane, shuffling his feet as he went along. Charlie was filled with such empathy for this man that his eyes filled up with tears. His smile disappeared from his face. His heart was so torn over this man's struggle to walk that he temporarily forgot his own problems.

We discussed telling Charlie about his need for surgery, knowing that it was my place to mention it. As heaviness filled our hearts and we both wiped away our tears, I promised Charles that I would find a gentle way to break the news.

The following week was harder than the week before. Charlie's spirits were decreasing. He wanted to do something fun. He never quit pushing himself, but he often became disheartened when the headaches persisted. He spent more time at the table setting up miniature football players and carrying out plays. A score pad was kept of game after game until he had two winners for a bowl game. His mind and hands were occupied with football even if his body wasn't able to play.

February was nearing an end. Aside from routine responsibilities, I was busy baking my sister's wedding cake. It being a Friday in Lent, and short on time, I set out to buy some fish for dinner from a drive-through restaurant window. To break the monotony of his day, I invited Charlie to go with me. As we drove down the street, he sadly said to me, "I'm tired of my dumb heart hurting. Every time I want to go outside, I can't. I wish Dr. Cottrill could do something."

This was my chance; so I said to him, "There is an operation that could help you feel better."

"Oh no." he exclaimed. "I'm not having any opteration," he added with his slurred speech.

"Why not?" I asked calmly, knowing full well that he was afraid.

"Because...(pause)...You know what can happen." he said with fear.

Not wanting to put more thoughts in his head, I continued in a manner that allowed him to express his concerns and fears.

"What can happen?" I inquired.

272

"You know...I could die," he blurted out.

"What makes you think that?" I questioned. "Do you know of anyone who died from heart surgery?"

"Nyeah," he added in his distinctive language. "Grandma."

I wasn't expecting that for an answer as that wasn't exactly how she died. Nevertheless, he got the picture. Serious surgery could lead to death. So, I encouraged his openness by asking, "What do you think about that?"

He quickly let me know, "Well, I don't *want* to die."

I continued, "What do you think about going to heaven?"

He answered, "I *want* to go to heaven but not right now. I want to grow up first and get married." A deeper sadness entered his voice. "But, I don't even have a girlfriend." I was aware that he had a crush on Christa, a girl from St. Gabriel, for years. However, his contact with her had become rare since leaving the school. His thoughts returned to age again as he commented, "I want to at least be eighteen."

Now, ordinarily it might seem funny that eighteen is a magical entry into adulthood. Yet, with time meaning everything, I could see how important it was to him to be grown up. Suddenly, a simple wish, that every child dreams of, seemed so far out of reach.

I felt a need to turn the conversation back toward heaven. "What about heaven, though?" I asked. "What do you think about it?"

He sadly responded, "I think that I'd miss you and everybody else."

I saw the need to calm his fears and said, "You know, Charlie, it seems like you would miss everybody, but you won't. I don't know how God does it because I've never been to heaven but I know that God promised us that we'd be happy when we get there. He won't let you be sad. He won't let you miss us because then you couldn't be happy. One thing about God is that when He makes a promise, you can be sure that He'll keep it. Do you think that God could break a promise?"

He agreed, "No."

"Do you remember my friend Kathy? Do you remember when I told you that God took her to heaven once? She said it was beautiful. She said that it was the most peaceful place that she had ever been. She also told me that she saw her parents and God didn't let her be sad for them. I suppose it's like we think of magic. We can't understand how it happens, but it happens."

"But, what if I die and I'm not ready? What if I'm scared anyway?"

These were very understandable fears that he mentioned. "I think it's like this," I began. "Right now, I'm not ready to die, either. But, if while driving down the road I happen to get in a terrible accident and I find myself dying, I might realize at that point that I AM ready to die. God will be with me. If I'm in a lot of pain and my body is weak, I might see that it's okay to die."

"But what if I'm still scared?" he insisted. I could see that what I said wasn't quite enough. So I added, "God does not want you to be scared. He only wants you to be happy. I think that if you are still scared when you die, then God will probably let you come back until you are ready." I had to stop there with my beliefs because I doubted that he would be scared once he entered heaven. I believed that his fears were strictly mortal.

I had to be strong and keep going. Thank goodness the line at the drive-through was long. (Many Catholics had set out for fish that night.)

"You know, Mom, all I really want in heaven is to play football." Now he was definitely putting me on the spot. I could never lie to my children so answering this one was tough. I responded with, "Charlie, you might be surprised. You might find that once you get to heaven you wouldn't even care about playing football. You might see that it doesn't matter any more."

In mere seconds, I could see that I had said the wrong thing. His heart was crushed at the thought of a remote possibility of no more football. His mouth dropped and let out an "Uh. You mean I can't play football?" Trying to retrieve my words quickly, I added, "Of course, I don't *know*. I'm sure that if God saw that you needed football to be happy, then He would find a way for you to play. Truthfully, I have no idea what He does when we die or how He does it. I only know that He promises to make us happy. Because it's your spirit that goes to heaven, maybe He will send your spirit to football games so that you can inspire the players. Maybe He'll let you play with any player that you want." This approach was certainly sounding better to him and he became more relaxed with the conversation.

There remained an uneasiness about the talk. Charlie had decided that he wasn't going to have the operation anyway, saying, "I'm still not gonna have the opteration." He didn't want to take any chances regardless of how bad he felt. So I told him that he needed to think about it. I asked him very slowly, "If you were drowning, would you want someone to jump in and *try* to save you?"

He agreed with, "Nyeah."

"If you were in a building that was on fire, would you want someone to rush in and *try* to save you?"

"Nyeah," he replied again.

I paused for a moment. "If you were running out of oxygen, would you want the doctor to *try* to save you?"

There was brief silence. The point was obvious. He said, "Nyeah, I guess so."

I elaborated a little bit, pointing out that this was what was happening. I reminded him that he couldn't live without oxygen. The picture was quite clear to him. Without surgery he was certain to die. Then he added, "But what about you? You're gonna miss me. And what about Marty and Jackie and Charles? What about Leslie and Jonathan and everybody else?"

His concern for us and for the grief we would bear pierced my soul. As my heart felt his words, I knew the importance of not breaking down. Assuring him I added, "God will take care of us somehow. You're right, Charlie. We would all miss you a great deal, but that's okay. We'll miss you because we love you. I don't know how we'd get through it, but I'm sure God would help us. I don't want you to worry about us."

We returned home with the fish for the family. I was relieved that we had crossed this hurdle. He had accepted the reality of his impending trial.

By now, it was more difficult for Charlie to complete a full day of school. He woke up wanting to go and wanting to stay home. I continued to encourage his attending school with the understanding that he could call home if needed. Over the next

275

few weeks he did not do well the full day. I was without a car on several occasions and therefore had made arrangements for a ride home in case of a problem. His grandpa picked him up one day when his teacher felt that he couldn't make it. By the time he got home, he was feeling rather well. However, within a few hours, he would be having chest pains and severe headaches again. I never knew if I was making the right decision about school. I'd feel bad if I pushed him too much and I'd feel bad if he missed school. All I could do was think optimistically and assume that he could keep going until he proved otherwise.

This encouragement was taken by Charlie that he could also play football when he wanted. He was beginning to see that it was almost impossible to do that, too. I watched him attempt it time and time again. By the time he got to the door or to the porch, he would turn around and come back in trying to hold back the tears. His mouth would be quivering and sunken. He'd say that he couldn't play. When I asked him why, he'd say, "Because my heart keeps hurting." I couldn't understand exactly what he meant as far as pain, but I knew it was real. Then I'd feel bad about sending him to school again. The funny thing about him was that even when he was hurting, he would manage to come back with a smile. His attitude was amazingly exemplary.

One dream that Charlie had in his heart for years was to go to the Pro Football Hall of Fame in Canton, Ohio. Charles and I had discussed the possibility of getting him there for his birthday in March. Our car was wearing out and we were both convinced that it wouldn't make the trip. The risks of being so far from home, should any medical emergency arise, caused added concern. His current health made it a frightening thought. Charles and I tossed the idea around but were not able to make it feasible. So, as an alternative we offered to take Charlie to the College Football Hall of Fame for his birthday and perhaps go to the Pro Hall in the summer. This would be better than not going anywhere. This birthday could not pass by without doing something really special. The strong suspicion in my heart reaffirmed that it could be his last. Charles and I discussed making it a family affair. However, I felt it should be just for the guys. That would make it all the more special. So, Charles, Charlie, Marty, Jonathan, and the boys' cousin Joseph planned the day to Cincinnati. It was to be an extraordinary day for Charlie, his dad and his brothers.

As Charlie had a heart catheterization scheduled for March 14, the day before his birthday, it was important to plan the trip for the weekend before. Noting that there was a risk of death with a catheterization, we could not take the chance of missing out on this trip. My feelings were that he would make it through the procedure fine. However, those feelings didn't alter the fact that the risk of death was very real.

Charlie graciously accepted the offer to go to Cincinnati. The group was prepared to leave early in the morning with coolers of food and drinks. Charlie was fired up. His all-time favorite college team was still Notre Dame. He went through all the statistics with me, informing me what players he expected to see in the Hall of Fame. We said our farewells and off they went.

As they pulled away in the family station wagon, I prayed that he would be able to enjoy it without suffering too much. I was delighted that Charles got to spend some personal time with just the boys. Although they wanted me to go with them, I knew that their day would be more special without me. I had been given many opportunities to enjoy special days alone with Charlie. I had the good fortune to attend many class field trips as well as the joy of taking him places with his friends. The best bonding took place when only one parent was around. Being a football fan myself, I had a desire to go. Yet, I saw how this small sacrifice on my part would enrich the relationship between Charlie and his dad. At times like this I was aware that it was God's will for me to forfeit my personal desires. Invariably, I was tempted to hoard all of Charlie's time. Knowing that his life would be short from the very beginning made me never want to share him with others. Recognizing that it would be unhealthful for all if I had been selfish with him, made me realize the importance of balancing his time with other family members. He would have been spoiled, without friends, and would never have gained true independence, otherwise. The family would have been unstable and I would have become more dependent on him than on God. In reflection, I understood the Holy Spirit's guidance throughout the years. Grateful emotions arose toward God for giving me the strength to make so many decisions against my own will. Charlie was a stronger and happier child because of it.

On March 14, 1989, his Dad and I took Charlie to the medical center for a heart catheterization. The meeting with the doctors was planned afterwards to discuss the findings and decide what was best to do.

The test went smoothly according to Suzanne, the nurse who stayed by his side and held his hand. It was comforting to hear her say that he found things to laugh about while undergoing the unpleasant procedure.

After seeing him through recovery, Charles and I met with Dr. Cottrill, Dr. Salley, and Suzanne. Another nurse stayed with Charlie during the meeting. All the cards were laid out on the table. The plan for surgery was to build a septal wall inside the heart to divide the two chambers into four chambers. The entire process was explained in detail. Charles and I asked every possible question. The risks were addressed. We discussed the types of pain that Charlie had endured. He was beginning to show mood swings that were distinct from just becoming a teenager. We all thought and pondered the situation for over two hours. Several times we fought back tears. I had told Dr. Cottrill already about my gut feeling that his time was up. She understood this to be from God, as well.

Weighing all the factors, it was obviously an even scale. Whichever side we put the decision on, the scale would sink and we'd reach the end. So, what do we do? Do we put him through the agonizing pain of an operation when he's going to die anyway? Do we sit back and do nothing and watch him suffer until he dies? What are we supposed to do? We were asked about Charlie's feelings over it. I explained his fears, his pains, and his uncertainties. Everyone in the room agreed that he could probably be persuaded either way, depending on our decision. He trusted us. He knew that we only wanted what was best.

The discussion did not lead to one direction over the other. Each of us remained unsure. I pictured the pain that I had been watching him endure and saw that I couldn't tolerate another day of observation. As a mother, I could see the pain even under his smile. He had no energy with which to enjoy life. I pumped the doctors some more begging for alternatives. I kept thinking if only there was a good medication that could relieve some of this horrible pain. Then we could avoid surgery and buy some time. In desperation, I cried out, "Isn't there some other way?"

No sooner had I gotten the words out, the Holy Spirit reminded me of the agony of Jesus Christ. In anguish, He asked His Father in heaven if there wasn't some other way. He pleaded that if it was possible to let the cup pass from Him. This shocking discovery silenced me. It hit me as though the cock had just crowed. (I thought of how instantly Peter was aware of his words the moment they fell from his lips.) Was I trying to interfere with God's will? I had to remember that God did not take this cross from Jesus. Jesus complied with Him by saying, "Not my will but Your will be done."

At that point I said, "Let me ask you one more question." Directing my interrogation to Dr. Salley, knowing how difficult it would be to answer, I began, "What would you do if it were your child?" I did not look at Dr. Cottrill for I knew what her response would be. I wanted the answer to come from the man whose hands would be responsible.

Dr. Salley was speechless. He knew the risks involved. He knew the skills of his hands. He knew that we were especially close to Dr. Cottrill. Finally, he said, "You really know how to back me up against a wall."

I said, "It's a fair question."

He agreed that indeed it was. The truth was that he was just as uncertain as we were about it. He admitted that he couldn't answer it. He clarified that it wasn't that he *wouldn't* answer it, but that he did not know the answer. There was nothing more for him to say. Being needed back in surgery, he was forced to leave. He gave us full support and would wait to hear from us. As he left the room, Dr. Cottrill let me know that if it were her child, she would take the chance on surgery. I knew that would be her response because she had already done that with her daughter. She took the chance and her daughter died during surgery. She knew me all too well. We were so much alike. She said that knowing me, she didn't think that I could live without every attempt at relieving his pain. The quality of life was most important.

With heavy hearts we all embraced as we departed. I was well aware that Dr. Cottrill knew my feelings. She said to me, "It looks like the final chapter."

"Yes, I believe it is," I replied. This was in reference to the prophecy. We had discussed prophecies in the past because she had been given this gift at times regarding various children. Other mothers had told her, as well, that they sensed a clear spiritual message that their child's life was near the end. We had previously agreed that the gift was to be used in preparation for God's plan. It was not a gift given to us so that we might change His plan. We both understood this to be true.

Charles and I were to go home and discuss it further. Then, after speaking to Charlie, I would call Dr. Cottrill back with a decision. We went down the hall to pick up Charlie where a nurse had been entertaining him. He was definitely ready to go after the extremely long wait.

18

FOURTH QUARTER

Decision pressures did not alter the activities of the day. Once home, we had a quick dinner before I left for school to the PTA meeting. In spite of my attempt to absorb the update on school matters, my mind pondered Charlie's future. So many memories flashed before me as I sat in St. Gabriel's cafeteria. I pictured the talent show and the Christmas program that he had participated in. I thought of the days when I worked in the cafeteria and served lunches to him and his friends. Everything from Boy Scouts to special speakers entered my mind. After the meeting, friends were quick to inquire about his health.

That night, as we lay in bed, Charles and I discussed at length the obstacles before us. Our conversation went in circles, once again. Our final conclusion was to proceed with the surgery. We were forced to give him a chance just as we had always done before. In the back of my mind I was hoping that I was wrong about Charlie's life being near the end. I wanted to be confused because I wanted to believe that I misunderstood what God had told me. In truth, I knew better, for the message was clear, never cloudy.

The next morning I helped the children off to school as usual. After going to church, I began baking Charlie's birthday cake for our typical family celebration. It was not a time to change plans to a larger get together. Regardless of my knowledge or gut feeling, I knew not to live as though he were dying. I knew that everything must remain normal. I believed that it was God's will to continue life and all its activities in a normal fashion.

Therefore, I made every attempt to resume my routine. Attending my weekly prayer group opened my mind to more reflection and provided a deeper understanding of the passion of Christ as we entered the Lenten season. God gave me strength to carry on. My success as director of Handmade Treasures (craft company) was made visible at the next meeting when the owners indicated that sales had doubled over the past year. A reward of inner peace was added with this accomplishment for I found great pleasure in helping others succeed. Social time at the Women's Club and Bunco furnished me with further support from friends. Each and every avenue of my life provided me with constant blessings.

Aside from my own interests, it was equally important to keep every member of the family in the same positive frame of mind and remain focused on individual needs. Besides school, Charlie continued his religious education classes once a week. Jackie was occupied with the teenage activities of telephone calls and dating. Leslie set out to sell Girl Scout cookies. Homework, playtime and basic routine remained unmodified. I found only one necessary adjustment to make in anticipation of the impending future. As Girl Scout leader, it was imperative to put a hold on plans for a camping trip. The uncertainty of the unfolding of events prevented me from making commitments beyond the present day.

Soon after Charlie's birthday passed, I talked to him about the surgery. Having already discussed much of it in general, I now had to verify his consent. We spoke again in simple terms about his running out of oxygen. He could not dispute how badly he felt. Wanting desperately to feel better, he finally agreed to have the surgery based on one stipulation. That contingent was to allow him to play football on a team. Discussing the team approach, I gently informed him that he could not compete with healthy boys because it would be too dangerous for him. He couldn't understand why the operation wouldn't make him as healthy as anyone else. I explained the anatomy of his heart and how differently it had to work. He was sorely disappointed to hear that his heart could never be completely normal. Seeing his despair, I suggested that we create a team for boys who had heart problems or other serious illnesses that required precautions. We could locate these children through the heart clinic or with the help of doctors. The idea became more appealing as we talked. Finally, I made the promise that he *would* play football. The dream seemed attainable with our determination. His hope and desire to play gave him the courage to face the surgery.

Our talk was good. Yet, a part of me felt as though I were deceiving him. When I spoke, I believed that I was projecting what God intended me to speak. At the same time I wondered why God would want me to present an unreachable dream. I had no doubts that we could start our own team. I had doubts that he would live to see it. When I addressed the concern with God, He reminded me to live for life. I should never take an action toward death. The words that God had me to speak to Charlie were intended to give him hope. They were to give him the strength and courage to face the fearful surgery.

Beginning to see the bigger picture, I understood that God wanted Charlie to have the surgery so that others may benefit from his courage and strength. Without the words, he would have neither one.

When I called Dr. Cottrill to tell her of Charlie's decision, she was not surprised. She asked if there were any important dates to avoid. Easter was the upcoming Sunday, which meant that most of the family would be together on that day. Spring break was the following week and Jackie's 16th birthday was two weeks after that. There were always special days in a large family. Two of his cousins were making their First Communions soon. Because events were ongoing, we opted that spring break would be the best time, knowing that he wouldn't hold out much longer.

Meanwhile, finances had finally caught up with us. In addition to the normal cost of raising five children, there were car and appliance breakdowns, continued medical bills, and student loans to pay off. All these added to the heavy financial burden. Barely staying afloat for months and having already tapped into community resources, the situation was worsening. Bill collectors were calling with their justified demands. It was not feasible to search for a new job under the circumstances. Foreseeing a tremendous expense ahead with the hospital stay was even more frightening. An undetermined amount of trips back and forth to Lexington would be costly. Resorting to fast food while away from home would add another expense.

Every situation compounded the other until we finally reached desperation and contacted a lawyer. Reluctantly, we arranged to file Chapter 13 under the bankruptcy law. Making it clear to the lawyer that we preferred to pay our debts rather than wipe them out, he wondered why. It was due to the fact that the bills of greatest concern were medical. I appreciated all the efforts of the doctors in making my son's life what it was. They had earned their money and I wanted to make sure they got it. A compromise was made that would stop the harassing collectors and would allow us more time to pay our debts. He was to inform us of a court date for the final step.

Holy Week was an extremely moving time as I reflected on what God had already shown me. He made me feel the pain that Jesus suffered through my connection with His Holy Mother. My heart ached tremendously when thinking of the suffering of Christ. Reading the Scriptures put me there in an instant. There was reality to the agony. "Is there no other way?" Every whip on his body, every thorn in his skull, every nail in his limbs was felt through the sword in my heart. His cross was heavy and full of splinters. It was not just a story. It was real. It was meant for me to understand. I had felt the splinters throughout my life. Now I was feeling the weight of the cross as well. I recognized Jesus's strength. He didn't stop when He fell. He continued on. That's what I must do. I must have strength and continue on. It was very hard to keep going, knowing that the crucifixion was close at hand.

Easter Sunday was spent enjoying time with both sides of the family after church. Charlie was somewhat distracted from his misery by Easter egg hunts at Granddad's and then again at Aunt Pam's.

The following week he made only one attempt to go to school. The headaches had become horrendous in spite of alternating pain medication every two hours. If he moved off the couch, his chest and legs would hurt. One day, as he found no relief whatsoever, he begged me to take him to the hospital immediately. He couldn't wait another week for surgery because the pain was unbearable. It amazed me that he didn't cry although his face showed his suffering. I called Dr. Cottrill again in desperation. "He *has* to get some relief," I said. I asked if I could give him some prescription medicine that I had in the cabinet. We discussed it and I was allowed to try it. Upon giving him one pill, he began vomiting almost immediately. It obviously didn't agree with him. He continued to be sick for the next six hours, which was even worse than before. All of this made his headache more painful than ever. Suddenly, next week seemed so far away.

As I cleaned house, I reflected on all that was happening. In prayer, I felt God tell me that I should go to the new pastor of St. Gabriel and prepare him for this funeral. I thought about it and told God that I didn't want to do that. Surely, Fr. Bill would think that I was strange or misled. I suggested Fr. Steve. As acting administrator since Fr. Caster's illness, he knew our family and was somewhat familiar with the situation. God refused to let me get by. It was the pastor who needed to know.

Feeling uncomfortable and shy about the situation, I tried to ignore my reflection on the matter. I couldn't just tell Fr. Bill that I expected Charlie to die without telling him the spiritual issues from the past. Until now, the only people with whom I had shared my intimate relationship with God were Dr. Cottrill and Bette Wheeler.

The next day was no different. Before I could gather my thoughts, The Holy Spirit was at it again. I had come to recognize The Holy Spirit by the clarity of His messages. He instructed me to call Fr. Bill and tell him about Charlie's impending death. It was out of respect for Fr. Bill as our new pastor. The Holy Spirit pointed out how difficult a child's funeral could be. It was only right that I tell him. Having my own free will, I knew that I could choose simply to ignore the request. However, I also knew (in a humorous sort of way) that I would never hear the end of it. It was only out of obedience that I found the courage to make an appointment with Fr. Bill on Saturday.

Meanwhile, many relatives and friends were not aware of the impending operation. Knowing they would be concerned, I sent letters to those special people to inform them of the surgery and to ask for their prayers. I did this so that Charlie's imminent death would not be a complete shock to them. Most people were not aware that his health had become so threatened.

On Thursday, while the other children were at school, Charlie sat at the table and played football with his miniature players. He smiled and kept score, content. After a short time, he needed to rest on the couch. He was in such pain that he fell on the way, which was a total distance of about twelve feet. He became very worried, not about the surgery but about playing with Marty. He said to me in a fretful voice, "How am I going to play football when Marty comes home?"

"Don't worry about Marty," I said. "Maybe you'll feel better tomorrow. Marty will understand."

My words were not consoling. He and Marty had made plans for the tournament games that they had been playing together. Sure enough, when Marty came home from school, Charlie got up only to experience the pain again. He held his chest and walked out the front door, determined at any cost. I thought to myself, This could be the day. I watched as they passed the ball. He sat on the ground between every play, smiling all the while. Watching him was heart wrenching. However, as I continued cleaning house, I also kept an eye on him out the window.

When Saturday, the first of April came, I kept my appointment with Fr. Bill. Although we had never had the opportunity to get acquainted, he probably knew me better than many parishioners. He saw me frequently at daily Mass and was aware of my involvement around the school. Not knowing how he would perceive me, I was nervous about sharing the information that I had obtained.

I began by telling him briefly about Charlie. He knew which child I was referring to as he had noticed him in church on Sundays. Although Fr. Bill did not mention it, I was aware that Charlie had a tendency to stand out by his shuffling gait. His slow pace often backed up the Communion line. Continuing as planned, I informed him that Charlie was facing open-heart surgery on April 6. Naturally, he was quite concerned. I summarized his previous eleven operations on his heart, spine and feet. Reluctantly, I believed I should be honest in sharing the fact that I didn't want to be there telling him this. I had only come because God urged me to make the situation known to him. Knowing that it would sound peculiar, I said that God had let me know that Charlie would not survive this operation. (In my mind, I figured that complications would mount after surgery just as they had always done before.) I did not clarify when I expected death to occur because I was not to know the hour or the day. Fr. Bill interpreted my words literally and assumed that I meant he would not live beyond the surgery itself. The misconception was not revealed at this time.

Fr. Bill made every attempt to comfort me with his wisdom and knowledge, adding reference to biblical stories. He suggested with empathy that I was probably anxious due to the seriousness of the surgery. An effort was made to explain to him that this was not the case. Remembering the surgeries of the past, God indicated at some point that Charlie would survive. This time He was letting me know that Charlie wouldn't. It was difficult to explain all that I had been through in a brief meeting. I assured him that I had never felt this before in spite of facing equally serious operations. The threat of death had always been present, but the knowledge of it had never been exposed to me before. Once there was nothing further to add, Fr. Bill offered to give Charlie the Sacrament of the Anointing of the Sick. Pleased with the offer, I invited him to dinner on Tuesday, the day before leaving for the hospital. Fr. Bill was concerned about putting me out too much just prior to leaving. He rightfully assumed that I would have many things to do. I quickly let him know that I planned to prepare a special dinner that night anyway. It would be our last dinner together as a family and I had every intention of going all out for it. With this understanding, he graciously accepted the invitation and said that he would administer the sacrament after dinner. This was fine with me.

I left with a sense that Fr. Bill didn't grasp what I was saying. I said to God, "I told him but I don't think he believes me." A peacefulness enveloped me with a clear sense that God was okay with this. Regardless of how Fr. Bill perceived it, my visit to him would be a preparation for what was to come.

Charles and I had been invited to an annual party that night with a group of friends from St. Gabriel. Knowing how awful Charlie felt, I didn't want to leave him. Yet, I felt a need to go as well. These were friends who were always there for us, always concerned about us and eager to help us when there was a need. We decided to attend the party for a short time, instructing the children to call without hesitation if there were any problems with Charlie.

Sure enough, about forty-five minutes into the party, Marty called stating that Charlie's head was killing him. Unable to get my mind off him anyway, I told Marty that we'd be right home. I knew that my presence would not change things a bit. However, I felt better about being there with him due to the preciousness of time.

The next morning, the family separated with Charles and I attending different Masses in order for someone to remain home with Charlie. The distraught, agonizing look that remained on his face that morning haunted me. The dreadful thought of watching him suffer another day was foremost on my mind. It was difficult to decide the best way to spend the day. Any movement caused more pain. Yet, staying on the couch sounded too boring and I feared that he would remain focused on his pain. I prayed to make the right decision when I got home.

As a minister of Communion, I was allowed to bring the Eucharist home to Charlie. The reassurance that Jesus was with him gave him hope. In trying to decipher how to get the most of this day, I suggested that we visit my brother, Bruce. Charles and I agreed, along with Charlie, that he wouldn't feel up to it. Yet, we hoped that it would be a way of distracting him from his pain, even if only for a short while. He had not seen this uncle on Easter and I believed that it was important to see him one last time. Charlie admired Uncle Bruce and often talked about the time that he brought his impressive motorcycle over to the house.

As usual, Bruce and his family greeted us with open arms. Obviously moved by Charlie's condition, Bruce offered to take him outside to see his horse. He thought that perhaps it would cheer him up. However, Charlie could not muster a smile over the idea because he was too weak to get up. Bruce offered to carry him next, but Charlie declined. This was not the same boy that Bruce had been accustomed to seeing. Bruce's wife, Betty, then suggested that he lie down in the bedroom so that he could be more comfortable and Charlie graciously accepted the invitation. There, his cousins gathered on the bed to talk to him and keep him entertained. Charlie smiled a dull smile but was not being himself as he restrained from laughter, knowing the increase in pain that it would bring about.

Charlie expressed several times that he wasn't feeling well. Therefore, we left shortly after dinner. Attempting to use up the hours in the day did not lessen any pain. I anguished with every minute that he suffered. Time could not pass fast enough to surpass the suffering. Yet, knowing that the end of suffering also meant the end of life on earth made me understand that I was in no hurry for the next two days to pass.

As we drove home on the freeway, I wondered how much more I could bear to witness. Coming upon the I-64 intersection, I heard Charlie call out from the back seat, "Turn here, Mom."

"What?" I responded without understanding. Turning would not take us in the direction of our home.

He repeated, "Turn here, Mom. I want to go to Lexington *now* for my opteration. I can't wait two more days."

My heart immediately sank, weighed down with guilt for not turning *now*, with fear of facing the ordeal, with greed for wanting to have two more days with him and with sorrow. An overwhelming amount of sorrow was tugging on my heart, pulling me once again into that space of complete helplessness. My instant connection with Our Blessed Mother gave me consolation. When her son knew that it was time to face the ultimate will of God, she was helpless in changing it as well. She was not to stop Him from riding into Jerusalem. Her submission was due to her trust in God, for she knew that He would be with her son. In the same way I, too, knew that God would be with Charlie. It was that trust in God that gave me the strength to obey.

By the time that I realized what was being said by Charlie, I had passed the I-64 intersection. I told him that I would call Dr. Cottrill when we got home and see what she had to say about it.

I struggled to think of something to do that would help Charlie get through the rest of the evening. I offered to let him invite Robby over to spend the night, believing that this would lift his spirits. When Robby accepted, I suddenly felt ill, wondering if it may be traumatic for him later to have seen Charlie like this. He was used to Charlie's laughter and positive attitude, but Charlie had not been showing much of either lately. In the past, they were rowdy when spending the night together, playing basketball in the living room or just finding things to laugh about.

When Robby came, every attempt was made to maintain a normal evening. We tried humor that night, but it seemed a bit stale. Charlie fell asleep unusually early, which made the evening even stranger. I was certain they would at least talk till midnight. If Robby noticed his behavior being any different, he did not let on. Yet, it was quite obvious to me. A great concern entered my mind, wondering if Robby may experience nightmares later after spending this time with Charlie just before surgery. The uneasiness caused me to worry if I had done the right thing.

When morning came, Robby went home appreciative of the invitation. It was the beginning of spring break and all the children were home. Our lawyer had arranged for us to meet him that day to finalize the bankruptcy claim. This was the last thing that I wanted to deal with at this time. Charles and I left the children and drove downtown to take care of business. I had a sick feeling in my stomach, but it was not because of the finances. Walking in the brisk cold wind toward the lawyer's office, my mind and heart focused on home. That's where I wanted to be spending these precious hours, not in a lawyer's office. As we walked into the room, our lawyer immediately picked up on my sour look. Instantly, he reminded me that things were not that bad. "Remember, I'm on *your* side." With that remark, I had an obligation to explain that it was not the finances that disturbed me. It was that our son was to be admitted the next day for open-heart surgery. With great sincerity, he shared his condolences. He informed us that a court date had been arranged for the next day as well, but insisted that we not worry about it. He would take care of it. We thanked him and upon finishing the details, went on our way.

Tuesday, our last day, was spent getting bags packed not only for the hospital but also for the children staying behind. During this preparation time my heart was being torn, as I didn't want to leave any of the children behind. I knew that I had to devote all of my energy to Charlie. Yet, I was distraught over the idea of not being with the other children during such a difficult time. Who would answer their questions the way that I would? Who would hold them and comfort them as they worried about their brother? I was not able to withstand the thought of our separation. How desperately I longed to be in two places at one time. The pain of motherhood was greatly intensifying as my desire to hold them and talk to them individually increased. Throughout the day I restrained from crying to avoid the communication of fear. It was imperative to wait for their need as well as to be cautious of the words I spoke. Complete dependence on God allowed me to remain calm and open to His guidance.

That evening Fr. Bill came as planned. We enjoyed getting better acquainted with him. We sat down to a delicious dinner and invited Fr. Bill to begin the blessing. As we passed the food, the thought of Jesus's sharing His last meal with the disciples entered my mind. I wondered how Charlie felt. Looking at the children, I thought of the disciples, not realizing what was about to take place. Jesus had tried to prepare them, but they couldn't fully understand. None of us could possibly picture what was about to unfold at this time, either. Yet, there was a sense of sadness among the family. In spite of the fact that Jesus told his friends that He would be taken away, they still hoped that it wasn't true. The children at the table had hope, too. God had been preparing us for fourteen years and we still couldn't imagine that the reality of death would ever come. The evening remained strangely somber yet pleasant.

After dinner we socialized a bit more. Then Fr. Bill took Charlie into the bedroom by himself to hear his confession. Next, the family gathered together for the anointing. We bid Fr. Bill a farewell and began getting the children ready for bed. The house was strangely quiet, unlike it had ever been before. I suspected that everyone had some uneasy feelings about the days to come.

I went to my room to pull myself together before any of the children would see me. Even Jonathan at six-years-old noticed that the atmosphere was abnormal. He came to me and asked, "Could Charlie die tomorrow?"

Thank God that the Holy Spirit was there with me to give me the words to say. "You mean from the surgery on Thursday?" I clarified.

"Yeah. Is he going to die?"

I began by sitting him on my lap as I sat down on the side of the bed. "Well, Jonathan, any time there is a serious operation, there is a chance that the person might die," I said. I couldn't very well say yes or no.

With that thought he added, "I don't want Charlie to die."

I agreed that none of us wanted Charlie to die and told him that this is why he had to have the surgery. "Charlie is running out of oxygen," I explained, "and he will die if we don't do something about it." We talked about Charlie's breathing so heavily all the time. He had seen that Charlie was constantly short of breath as if he had been running. We talked about how exhausting it would be to keep on running. He understood the difficulty that one undergoes after this exercise. The example helped clarify for him how Charlie felt all the time and what it was like to run out of oxygen.

"So," I continued, "Although he might die from surgery, we have to *try* to help him breathe."

"Is that why Fr. Bill came over? — Because he might die?" he inquired.

I refused to present the fear of death to him. I said, "Fr. Bill came over to pray for Charlie so that God would help him through the operation." He listened with nothing further to add but seemed so sad as he hugged me. I promised him that Charlie had good doctors and that they would do all that they could.

Just as the atmosphere had settled in this peculiar solemn state, the phone rang. It was Jamie calling from Florida. When Charlie answered the phone, a joy came over me that made me want to burst into tears, for I had already been holding back an immense amount of emotion. I was so thrilled that one of his friends was thinking of him on this terrible night, knowing how alone he had been feeling. He often felt abandoned by his friends and commented from time to time that his friends didn't think of him anymore. I supposed that Jesus must have felt even more alone in The Garden of Gethsemane. He knew His friends were near and that they loved Him but how many went out of their way to go comfort Him? Charlie's friends were no different than any of us or any of the disciples. Most of us would do anything for our friends. Yet, unless asked, we often don't. Jesus, knowing Charlie's anguish, must have inspired Jamie to call.

To know that distance did not break the bond between them was all that Charlie needed. The spirit of their friendship was as close as the house that Jamie once lived in. Jamie may never know the joy that he gave to Charlie that night as they reminisced on the phone, but it served as an end to his loneliness. After talking to Jamie and his brother Tony for over an hour, Charlie came away with a smile that I hadn't seen for a long time. His spirit was filled because he now saw how much his friends cared about him.

As I put the children to bed, I couldn't help thinking about the last everything. It would be the last time that I tucked Charlie into his bed, the last time the boys would spend the night together, the last night that our family would be complete in our home. These thoughts were most uncomfortable. I looked around his room at the U of K paraphernalia. My eyes caught a glimpse of the autographed basketballs, the Wildcat statue and the posters. The toy shelves were filled with footballs, miniature players, wrestlers, and games. None of this would ever be the same on our return. Picturing one empty bed, I kissed the boys goodnight and encouraged them to say their prayers.

Next, I went to the girls' room to tell them goodnight. Although their room would not be changed by Charlie's absence, their hearts and lives would forever be changed. Upon leaving their room, I reflected on how different life would be from this day forward.

Jackie was prepared to go with us in the morning. Charles and I agreed that she was old enough to come along. Although I wanted to protect her from this trial, I knew that I would be unable to do so. She needed to be allowed to support her brother

293

even at the cost of her pain. In part, it was also good for me because it made one less separation to deal with at the time.

Leslie kept me puzzled, as she was always quiet with her thoughts. It was difficult to know how much she understood. She appeared a child of great faith and trusted that all would be well.

The next morning Marty attended Mass with me to pray for his brother. Absorbing God's presence, my heart was questioning again if I was doing the right thing. Knowing that Charlie was going to die, I wondered why I was allowing him to endure the pain of surgery. Watching him suffer at home was not acceptable, either. Leaving the children behind as I took Charlie away made me momentarily feel like Judas. I somehow felt that I was betraying the whole family by making this decision. At the same time I felt that it was what God wanted me to do. I struggled greatly over these thoughts. Knowing the conflict within my heart, Jesus consoled me. In the midst of my despair, I suddenly heard Jesus (in an interior voice) say to me, "It's time to leave your children and follow me." Upon hearing this, I sobbed deeply. Then I heard repeatedly throughout the rest of the Mass, "Leave your children and follow me." These words caused tremendous anguish because I didn't want to walk this path. Yet, they were also consoling by the affirmation that I was indeed doing God's will. The pain was unbearable. By the grace of God, I was given the strength to adjust the cross on my shoulders and accept it knowing the crucifixion was near. Upon my return home after Mass, I gathered my emotions and tucked them away.

19

OVERTIME

Arrangements had been made for the children to stay with friends and relatives. In an effort to keep their spirits up, I made sure that the children were staying with someone their own age. That way they would be preoccupied enough to lessen their worry while we were gone. Leslie and Jonathan kissed everyone good-bye and went joyfully with Uncle Bob to their cousins' house to play. Charles took Marty to his friend's house. Each child was fairly content and prepared for the separation when they left. Being off for spring break took daily pressures away. Soon after the children had gone, Charles, Charlie, Jackie, and I climbed into the car for the long drive to Lexington. Charlie didn't appear nervous. He was smiling and actually looking forward to some relief. Wearing a new 49ers hat and holding a new baseball card book in his arm, he peered out the window as we pulled out of the driveway and coasted away from home.

Our neighbor Linda stood at her front door to wave good-bye, her heart strings being pulled as she spotted the 49ers hat and baseball card book that she had just given Charlie days before.

There was only light conversation in the car as we each had our thoughts on the anticipated surgery and days ahead.

An hour and a half later, we pulled into the parking garage of the U of K Medical Center. Charles unloaded the wheelchair. Gathering all necessities, we made our way toward the ramp leading to the hospital. Charlie clung to his baseball book as we entered the front door. The atmosphere was unlike what we had always remembered. Renovation had taken the nostalgia away and made me suddenly feel like a foreigner in my own home. Stopping at the admitting office, we were instructed to take Charlie to the lab for blood work. Even the lab had been renovated and gave a sense of being somewhere else. However, the uneasiness disappeared when Charlie and I spotted a familiar face. This was what mattered. The traumatic needle pricks were yet to come. Being that Charlie was too big to sit on my lap, I knelt next to him in consolation, holding his arm down once again. It was strange to be thinking that I would actually find myself missing this procedure. Not wanting to think about it, I rubbed his back to ease the tension.

From there, we went upstairs to the hospital room that had been prepared for him. With an electronic football game in his possession, Charlie immediately began to focus on the playoff games that he had prepared on his clipboard. He went into great detail on each game, player, and play. Although I wasn't certain just how he was playing this on paper, he knew exactly what he was doing.

Making ourselves at home, we quickly eased any tension with off-the-wall joking and teasing. Laughter was the best medicine and sometimes our only resort. Although it did not remove the anxiety from within, it enabled us to enjoy the moment. That precious moment would soon pass with the hands of the clock. I valued the gift of time more than anything else. A top priority was to make this day the best, not allowing it to be destroyed with sadness.

Eventually, a nurse came in to assess Charlie. She glanced through the room almost as though she didn't see him sitting on the bed. "Are you Charlie?" she asked in a bewildered voice.

"Nyeah," he responded.

With a friendly mannerism about her, she welcomed him, took his blood pressure, and asked him questions. Then she turned to me and added that after reviewing his chart, she was expecting to find a frail child with a sickly appearance. She was stunned to find such a jubilant and healthy looking boy before her. His outward appearance had deceived her just as it had many others. A sense of relief came over her face, making it clear that she would enjoy having him as a patient.

Old friends from Lexington and vicinity were informed about the impending operation. Faithful friends Rob and Judy paid Charlie a visit that evening. They had not seen him for some time and wondered if he would even remember them. Meanwhile, I was down the hall speaking with Dr. Cottrill and her nurse, Suzanne, not knowing that visitors had come by.

Coincidentally, Charles and Jackie had just stepped out of the room as well. As a result, Rob and Judy had the opportunity to see Charlie privately. After spending some time together, Judy came to the conclusion that he probably didn't remember them very well. They anticipated looking for me, but they were fearful about leaving Charlie alone. Much to their surprise, they noticed that it didn't faze Charlie to be by himself. At fourteen-years-old, he was fairly independent as far as being alone in his room and he also felt quite at home in the hospital. Being left alone in a room for a while was no different than playing alone in his bedroom at home. Therefore, when it came time for Rob and Judy to leave, he simply said, "Bye," in his typical innocent way, not indicating that it mattered if they left.

When I met Rob and Judy in the hallway, they laughed at his behavior, amazed that he was in such good spirits. They understood his simple "Bye" as "Don't let the door kick you in the butt." Fortunately, they were not offended. Rather, they thought his nonchalant attitude was funny as well as consoling to them. They were pleased to see that he was not upset over the surgery.

Feeling their compassion for us made my own evening complete. I sensed their hearts pouring out to us at this difficult time. Once again, my spirits were lifted by the love of friends. It was wonderful to see that God always sent people my way for support.

As the evening closed in on us, Charles and I were once again faced with a challenging decision. Only one parent would be allowed to stay with Charlie overnight. Sleeping arrangements were made for us at the Hospitality House and we had also been put on a waiting list for the Ronald McDonald House. Out of his love for me, Charles immediately offered to let me stay with Charlie. However, I knew in my heart that it shouldn't be this way. I had had so many opportunities to be with Charlie through the years when he was hospitalized, whereas Charles had not, due to work. It was clear to me that the night should belong to them. I proposed that it would probably work out better because Jackie and I could stay together. Rooms at the Hospitality House were designed for women to sleep on one floor and men on the other. The most difficult part of the arrangement was a 10:00 P.M. curfew set for all guests. Once the doors were locked, there was no getting in.

Although it was hard to give up this time with Charlie, it also made me feel good to see the two of them together. They were best buddies. I'm certain that their hearts ached equally for each other. Charlie idolized his dad and he greatly admired his son.

Kissing Charlie and her dad goodnight, Jackie and I headed out, taking Charlie's wheelchair with us as he would not be needing it any more in the hospital. Upon exiting the main door of the hospital, an eeriness came over me, realizing as I looked down at the empty wheelchair, that he would never ride in it again. The knots tightened in my stomach as I fought back the tears. I mustn't reveal my fears to Jackie, knowing she would not understand. I must be strong for her, I thought.

When we arrived at the Hospitality House, we were given a tour of the time-honored, rustic home with high cathedral ceilings. We were made to feel right at home and were offered food that volunteers had brought. A living room with antique furniture gave a warmth and instant comfort to those who came in. We were directed to our room up the hardwood staircase. A warm feeling came over me as I entered the large bedroom sparsely decorated with antiques, reminding me of an old family farmhouse that I used to visit as a child. Even the walls seemed to let out a distinct welcome.

Knowing that the morning would come too soon, Jackie and I decided it best to go straight to bed. Two elderly women shared the bed next to us. They discussed the surgery that their brother and husband respectively, was having in the morning. As I overheard them making arrangements to call for a cab, I offered to take them with us. They were overcome with gladness at this simple offer and accepted with great appreciation. Plans were made to leave by 5:00 A.M.

Being overcome with exhaustion, I sank back into the conforming mattress. So many thoughts of God's revelations to me filled my head. Being so overwhelmed by these blessings, I found His love for me to be more than I could bear. It was more than I ever deserved. By now, my gut had worked its way into my throat. "Who am I that You would give me so much? Who am I that You would answer my prayers, my questions, my uncertainties? Who am I that You would choose to go against medical science and allow my baby to live for all this time? How did You see me worthy to grant me such favors? I am not worthy. I am a sinner. Yet, You have overlooked this and blessed me anyway." Tears were now flowing down, trickling into my ears. I felt numb with disbelief of all that had come to pass.

Jackie, after completing her shower, joined me in bed. She began reminiscing on funny things of the past. One thing led to another as we attempted to lighten the emotional load. She talked about the time that she and Marty were fighting and Charlie locked them out of the house. He was so afraid that he would be in trouble when Mom and Dad came home and spotted the two of them climbing in the window. He couldn't stand fighting and would do whatever he could to stop it. After a short conversation, I suggested that we go to sleep, for we would need to be getting up by 4:00 A.M.

When the ladies went to bed, one of them asked about my son's surgery. She asked very positively, "Does he have pretty good odds that everything will be okay?" assuming that he did.

I replied, "No, not really."

"Will they be able to correct his problem?" she added.

"No, actually it can't be corrected. We can only hope that it will make things better." Realizing that I had been rather vague, I didn't want them to think that I was being pessimistic and without faith. So, I proceeded to emphasize that he had come a long way since birth and that we had been abundantly blessed. They both offered to pray for him. With that we all decided that we desperately needed some sleep in order to face the morning four hours later.

Before daybreak, the alarm sounded. Normally, I would get right out of bed. This day, I did not want to for fear of facing at the day ahead. I sure didn't want to miss seeing Charlie before the operation. Yet, I didn't want to face him, either. Nevertheless, I knew I should move fast. Rolling out of the bed, I made my way to the bathroom to freshen up. A quick face wash was all I wanted to spend time on. I could come back and shower while he would be in surgery. I was familiar with the extensive amount of time that he would be in surgery. Expecting him to be a minimum of eight hours behind the doors, I would have plenty of time to get cleaned up later. This hour should be spent with him in preparing for the operation.

By the time we reached Charlie's room, he was just waking up. A nurse came in to give him a shot that would help him relax before the operation. The routine order of starting an IV was waived due to the difficult history of finding his veins. It had been decided that they would start the IV once downstairs in surgery. Dr. Cottrill agreed to spare him what pain she could.

After inquiring about their night, Charles told me that Charlie wanted to have pizza before his 12:00 A.M. cut-off of food and drink. I asked if he was able to get it and was told no. As I had the car, he had no way of going out to pick it up. Instead, he went to the cafeteria and bought him a hamburger. He said that Charlie was fine with that, but it was pizza that he really wanted. I was instantly trapped in the guilt syndrome. If only I had known, I would have gladly gone out after pizza even if it meant I had no place to sleep. If only I had thought of it myself, I could have searched for a delivery service. If only, if only...I could have made his night just a little bit better. What a simple last wish. I felt that he would never eat again. This bothered me for a while until I realized that it was okay if he didn't get the pizza. After all, he wasn't distraught over it. Why should I be? Again, I needed to let go of the fear of death that overwhelmed me at that very moment.

Soon, the orderly came to take Charlie to surgery. Charles, Jackie, and I followed alongside the stretcher. As we approached the doors of the holding area, we were told that only one of us could go in with him as he waited for surgery. Torn again, Charles insisted that I be the one to go with him because he had the honor of spending the night with him. Jackie and Charles kissed him good-bye as we proceeded through the door. My heart was sinking and my stomach was rising as I observed their saddened faces being left behind. Charles assured me that they would be all right.

300

Charlie was taken to a spot in the room where a curtain separated him from other patients. The area was barely large enough for me to stand next to him. As we waited we talked. I held his hand and stroked his soft skin. After fourteen years he still had the skin of a newborn baby. I never quite understood how his skin never aged despite the many other physical changes in his body.

I asked him how his night was with his dad. He said, "Dad was crying last night." He said that his dad was worried about the operation. I could see that he was very touched by his dad's emotions. I told him that none of us wanted him to have to go through this operation. We wished that it wasn't necessary. It was difficult to talk with a straight, brave face, but I had no choice. There was a pause. As he looked calmly into my eyes he spoke with a surrendering voice, "Mom? All I wanted was to play football." My heart broke as the words fell on my ears. (What he was really saying to me was that he had devoted his whole life to this goal. Now, he was willing to risk death in order to obtain it. He came across as being apologetic for wanting it so badly.)

Then, looking straight into those baby blue eyes, I said to him, "Charlie, you *will* play football. One way or another, you *will* play football." My thoughts were such that it would not happen in this world, but in the next. I was certain that it was the correct thing to say. Yet, at the same time, I never imagined football to be an activity in heaven. Regardless, it was what God intended me to say. A gleam came across his face. I added, "If it means that I have to coach the team myself, you *will* play football." He was elated with the promise. He trusted me because I had never broken a promise to him.

Suddenly, his smile disappeared and a worried look engulfed his innocent face. He recognized his limitations and questioned, "What about cleats?" acknowledging the difficulty in finding shoes to fit his malformed feet. "How am I going to wear cleats?"

My heart fluttered with a touch of laughter. "Oh Charlie. I'll find you some cleats. Don't you worry about that." This brought smiles to both of us.

301

As for me, it would be something to deal with later. It would all depend on God's will. I told God that I hoped that I misunderstood the message which He revealed to me. I would not mind being wrong about the prophecy foretelling that his time was soon to be completed. Although it remained clear to me, I had hope that I was wrong. I was willing to do whatever it would take to help him play football if he should live. This was a minor challenge compared to what I was about to face.

Before long, there was interaction with the anesthesiologist. She had the choice of putting him to sleep by way of a mask or an IV. Charlie had become very frightened of masks over the years. She was quite patient with him, however. We discussed it until he agreed that the mask would be best. She offered to go slowly by holding it away from his face a little at first. He would be taken from the holding area into surgery where the process would begin. The orderly led us toward the door where we had to part. I kissed him on the forehead. He held my hand tightly as we stopped at the door. Pulling my hand up to his lips, he kissed it softly. "I love you, Mom," he said.

"I love you too, Charlie," I responded with a choking sensation. "I'll be waiting for you with your dad and Jackie," I promised. The doors to surgery opened. My heart sank deeper than before, as I was unable to imagine how this trial would unfold.

Walking through the double doors toward the waiting room I quickly spotted Charles and Jackie. We all embraced. We could barely speak. Quietly, we proceeded to walk hand in hand toward the elevator, agreeing to stop at Suzanne's office to let her know that surgery had begun.

She prepared us for a long day and invited us to use her office any time throughout the day. Should a doctor need to locate us, we could be found easily and quickly by keeping contact with Suzanne. Not expecting any early problems, I informed her that we would be going to the Hospitality House to get cleaned up and to eat. She encouraged me to take my time because the wait would be endless once we returned. She suggested that I soak in the tub for a while to help me get through the day. It sounded like a good suggestion, especially

302

due to the fact that it would take a while before the surgeon would become deeply involved with the operation.

Slowly we dragged ourselves outside toward the parking garage. The air was cold with a brisk wind for an April day. I experienced an uneasy feeling about leaving the hospital in spite of the fact that I would be close by. At the same time, I convinced myself that it would be the best thing to do, believing that it would be hours before any progress would be made. It was important that I get myself prepared for the events that would follow the operation. Recalling past ordeals, I was certain that it would be a minimum of half a day before anything could go wrong.

The Hospitality House was only a few short blocks away. Yet, it was too far for comfort. Having complete trust in Suzanne, I knew she would call if anything went wrong. We could get back in a flash if necessary.

Not wanting to waste time eating, I started the bath water in the old, claw-footed bathtub. I was feeling exhausted already after having four hours of restless sleep. My body was tired and my mind was dull. Sinking into the tub, I found myself numb, not wanting to move much less wash. My mind was spinning with thoughts of what Charlie was going through and anticipating what God's plan might be. Admittedly, I had no idea. My only thought on the matter was the presumption that he would not die until after the surgery. The doctor was well aware of anticipated problems with bleeding due to the extensive amount of scar tissue he expected to find. Every complication possible was prepared for. Thus, my knowledge of the medical expertise convinced me that the operation would be well under control and problems would start sometime after surgery was over. I forced myself to relax and take my time in order to make it through the day.

Once dressed and with our bags in the car, we drove back to the hospital. We had been gone for about an hour and a half. Going straight to Suzanne's office, we informed her that we were back. She looked upset as she stated that there had been a problem. She would have called, but by the time she found out, the problem was resolved. There was nothing to do about it so

303

she decided to wait for our return. I believe it was the longest wait that she had ever encountered. Just seconds before we walked in, she had made the decision to call us anyway because she could no longer withstand the pressure of not sharing the incident with us. She invited us to sit down. Suzanne began to tell us that when Dr. Salley opened the sternum (the chest bone) blood gushed out profusely. Unknown to him, the aorta was stuck to the sternum due to the Massive amount of scar tissue. Therefore, when the sternum was pulled apart, the aorta tore. With every beat of the heart, his blood gushed out. Moving quickly, his head was packed in ice to prevent brain damage as Dr. Salley applied pressure and immediately hooked him up to the heart bypass machine by way of the groin. Charlie was literally gone from us for about five minutes before the doctor was able to revive him. This was long enough for renal shutdown, which was now the beginning of numerous other problems. It was a miracle that he was able to bring Charlie back, according to medical professionals. The incident took place shortly after we had walked out of the hospital.

We were stunned to hear this news. I could understand Suzanne's predicament --- to call or not to call. The trauma was over, yet she feared more serious trouble before we would return. Dr. Salley believed that he should continue with the surgery as planned because there would be no benefit to canceling at this point. The chest was already open. Despite the level of difficulty, it was more certain than ever that Charlie could not live without the surgery.

After hugs and consolation, we went to the waiting room to pass time. I quickly sank into a chair and became dazed. I knew that Charles and Jackie were in the room with me, but I was not aware of their thoughts or activity. My eyes focused on a spot on the carpet. I froze in that position for hours, beginning to reflect on what had happened. It bothered me to think that Charlie watched us walk out of the hospital. I was certain that he could see us while his spirit left his body temporarily.

I spoke to God. "I had no idea that You would take him so quickly. I expected this to be like all the rest of his surgeries. So, why did You bring him back? What are Your plans now?" My

304

stomach was in knots. My throat was being choked quietly. I was aware that I could not have opened my mouth to speak to anyone. I stared out and waited for an explanation from God. In my state of numbness, I soon realized that it was Charlie's will that brought him back. I was reminded of our conversation about his not being ready to die. I had told him my belief that God would allow him to come back if he truly were not ready to die. Knowing Charlie and the goodness of heaven that had probably just been shown to him, he more than likely wanted to come back to tell me that it was okay. I could picture him talking to God with concerns about his family. He probably offered to endure suffering for the opportunity to console his family. I was not certain of these things. They were merely thoughts that passed through my head.

Despite the horrendous pain in my heart, there was an obvious sense of peace and calmness about me. I knew this entire ordeal to be part of God's plan. My eyes never shifted from the spot on the carpet. My hands remained clinched together as I sat slumped in the chair.

Soon, I went to Mary with my thoughts. I said to her, " What did you do when they took your son away from you? You could not be with Him when He was scourged. Although not a scourging, the doctors are in there manipulating Charlie's body. Their hands are in his chest in full control of his outcome. My hands are tied. I cannot be at his side just as you could not be with your son. What did you do? Were you numb like this? Could you pray?" I didn't cry. I didn't shed a tear. I just sat. I pondered. I said to Mary, "What was the crucifixion like? How did you bear it? What am I supposed to do when Charlie dies? I remember that Jesus gave you the whole world to mother when He died. He can't do that to me. What am I supposed to do? How did you live without Him? I don't see how I will be able to live without Charlie."

I continued to throw out many questions to her without allowing her to answer. I finally said, "I know how you did it. You were assumed into heaven to be with your son. That's not going to happen to me." I was sure of that. "So, Mary, is this where we part? Is this the time when you will never have any more answers for me?" I finally began to cry. I was losing my son and I couldn't even talk to Mary any more about it because her outcome would be so different from mine. My eyes filled suddenly with tears although I never made a sound, nor did I move an inch from my frozen position. Admittedly, I was feeling envious of Mary. She was taken to heaven and her pain was over, I thought. I was not expecting to go to heaven any time soon. I began feeling sorry for myself. Time was a treasure of the past. Now, it was a gift that I did not care to have.

Finally, I said to Mary, "I don't know what else to say. There is no more. You've helped me all that you can and this is the end." Upon discovering there was nothing further to say, I decided to recite the rosary for the first time in about twenty years. I did this because I wanted to talk to Mary but knew not what else to say.

I remained stiff in the chair. Beginning very slowly, and with deep concentration on every word, I recited: I believe in God, The Father Almighty, creator of heaven and earth... (I thought of the magnificence of His glory)... and in Jesus Christ, His only son, Our Lord, Who was conceived by he Holy Spirit (I saw in my mind St. Gabriel, speaking to Mary. I imagined the Holy Spirit engulfing her entire being), born of the Virgin Mary... (I pictured that Holy Night in Bethlehem)... suffered under Pontius Pilate (remembering Charlie's first Christmas when I reflected on the nativity only to recognize that the precious gift given to Mary would so soon be taken away.)... was crucified, died, and was buried...(This is what we are still facing, I thought.).... He descended into hell and on the third day rose again from the dead. (I pictured the glory of Easter.... how coincidental. It was The Easter Seal Society that gave Charlie so much life and so much joy. He was afforded so many golden opportunities to meet many special people and do many special things that most people only dream about. I could see that his soul was brought to the fullness of life by means of The Easter Seal Society. On second thought it was not coincidental at all. It was all part of God's plan.) He ascended into heaven and is seated at the right hand of the Father (I felt happy for Jesus to be able finally to enjoy the glory of heaven after so much suffering.... Charlie deserves such happiness, too.) He will come again in glory to judge the living and the dead, (This seemed so far away at the moment.) I believe in the Holy Spirit (thinking of the time that the Holy Spirit revealed to me that Charlie would live)...the holy Catholic Church (how blessed I felt to be a part of it)...the communion of saints (my mind showed me clouds filled with saints)...the forgiveness of sins (again feeling good that God had blessed me so much in spite of all my sins)...the resurrection of the body, and life everlasting, Amen (knowing that we will meet again).

Continuing with Our Father, who art in heaven, hallowed be Thy name, (A sense of honor and glory befell me)...Thy kingdom come, Thy will be done...(I paused for an extended amount of time and reflected on God's will, knowing what He had already told me. Although I didn't fully understand what Charlie could do in heaven to fulfill God's will, I was still without question about the fulfillment of God's will for Charlie on earth. I said to God, "I trust in You and I accept Your will.")...on earth as it is in heaven. (I understood that there was a connection between God's will in heaven and His will on earth. I did not understand what the connection was.) Give us this day our daily bread, (He nourishes us with food for the body and the soul. I felt so grateful for the opportunity to receive His nourishment every time I went to Holy Communion. I depended on Him for strength to endure the weight of my crosses)...and forgive us our trespasses...(I felt forgiven already.)...as we forgive those who trespass against us...(I could think of no one who had done wrong to me, but many who had done wrong to Charlie, both children and adults. I thought of the suffering that he endured over the years, which was a direct result of doctors' mistakes. I had forgiven them for their human imperfection and prayed that they may learn from it, so as not to cause the same burden to others.)...and lead us not into temptation... (I asked for help that I not ask for my will over God's will...It was tempting to ask God to spare his life once again. After all, He had saved him many times before. I believed in miracles, too. Yet, this time I knew not to ask due to the clarity in God's message. I understood that I could still have hope and that God could still grant a miracle if He so desired. Yet, I saw the importance of accepting God's will with complete trust in Him)...But deliver us from evil…(I prayed that I not be tempted to expect God to change His will for my selfishness)...Amen.

As I began the Hail Mary, I finally understood what the words were saying. Now I could relate to them. Hail Mary, full of grace (pondering her infinite graces that she has to offer us)...the Lord is with thee, (Yes, the Lord is with you in heaven, but not only because you are both in heaven but also because you are His mother. You are inseparable in spirit. You are one. I can feel it already with Charlie. We are one and distance cannot keep our hearts apart. The strength of the physical bond does not compare to the strength of the spiritual bond. The physical can be separated just as he is in the operating room and I sit in the waiting room, but the spirit cannot be separated.)...blessed art thou among women (I know that you are greatly blessed, for I have been given so much myself. God has blessed me with His presence in my life. He has shown His immense love for me through my children. Feeling so overwhelmed at what He has done for one as inferior as I, my imagination cannot allow me to fathom the blessings He has given you, the mother of His son.)...and blessed is the fruit of Thy womb, Jesus. (Reaching the point of tears again at the thought of these words, I thought of the child that I once carried in my womb. Having given birth to a child so extremely blessed in disguise, was a treasure of which I was certain others would not understand. You, Mary, would understand. You know how blessed you and your son were in spite of the suffering you both endured. I was beginning to receive some consolation. Someone understood what I was going through. I paused for a while and thought of how I could always depend on Mary to know my sorrow. Once I stopped my thoughts and listened, she explained to me that she did not experience assumption into heaven shortly after her son died. It was many years later before she was able to join Him. She, too, had to suffer the loss of her son and endure the pain in her heart. She promised me that she would still be here for me and would guide me through the difficult times ahead.) I continued with: Holy Mary, mother of God, pray for us sinners (my unworthiness

308

overwhelmed my soul)...now and at the hour of our death.... (I knew that she would remain with me until the hour of my death. I no longer felt abandoned.)... Amen.

Budging not an inch, I continued the rosary meditating on the Sorrowful Mysteries. My reflections continued with each Our Father and Hail Mary as well as with the other prayers of the rosary. Not having a rosary with me, I gently pressed one finger at a time against my folded hands to keep track of the ten beads per decade. I prayed for over an hour, meditating on each mystery. The correlation between Jesus's suffering and Charlie's suffering was again striking. The agony in the garden was just recently felt at our last dinner together. The scourging at the pillar brought thoughts of the years of needle pricks and invasive acts on Charlie's body. The crowning of thorns was intensified by the throbbing headaches that he endured. The carrying of the cross was a constant for fourteen years. The crucifixion he now faced remained incomprehensible, yet very real. When I finished the rosary I found no need to ask God any more questions. He had made it clear about the end of the journey.

I recall thinking that I should move. My eyes still fixed on the carpet, I concentrated on moving, yet found that I couldn't. I really didn't want to move. Time was standing still for me while in this trance. I felt that I could live this way forever. This numb state protected me from the pain of the world. If I didn't move, I would not have to face anyone around me. However, the mother and wife in me made me think differently. Aware that Charles and Jackie were sitting nearby, I felt a desire to comfort them, but I could find no comfort to give. It was not within me. Forcing my eyes to turn slightly toward my foot, I willed it to move. Energy was not available. My willpower was weak. I thought hard about it, but felt paralyzed. Charles may have asked me if I wanted to get something to eat. With great mental effort, I managed to shift my feet slightly and scoot myself up in the chair. My body was stiff, as I had sat there for several hours. I did not feel like eating, but I knew that I must move. Standing slowly, I attempted to walk within the room to relieve some stiffness in my joints.

Just then the phone rang in the waiting room. Someone called out for Stopher. I went to the phone to hear the nurse speak from the operating room. She said that the doctor was having a very difficult time finding and identifying the various arteries and veins in the heart. Everything was twisted and mangled and covered with scar tissue. There was so much scar tissue to remove that the procedure itself had not even begun yet. She kept repeating how difficult things were. There was a tremendous amount of bleeding. His body was extremely edematous now because his kidneys were not functioning. It was clear that she was trying to prepare me for the worst. She agreed to keep us posted but did not anticipate significant changes any time soon.

Assuming that it would be a while before hearing from her again, the three of us went to see Suzanne. We talked briefly. We informed her of the latest news from the operating room and added our intention to go to the chapel and the cafeteria. The waiting had only begun. Slowly, we shuffled through the hallways of the hospital. Reaching the chapel, I sat down and thought of nothing at all. I merely rested with God and felt comfort knowing that He was with me. Eventually we went to the cafeteria to discover how difficult it was to put food in our mouths. It was an action that we forced upon ourselves. Even our senses were too numb to taste the food. Soon we found ourselves back in the waiting room.

Dr. Cottrill approached before long with more bad news. Results of Charlie's blood work did not become available until after surgery began. A liver study indicated that his liver enzymes were extremely high. She was uncertain as to why and could not predict the exact effect that it may have on the outcome of surgery. It was clear that there was another major organ to be concerned about. The picture became more disheartening.

As the hours passed, I found myself back in the chair in that familiar paralyzed state. My mind was empty of all thoughts. The only sense that I was aware of was that God was with me. My soul was at peace despite the tension within my gut. Hours later, the nurse called out again to say that the situation was much the same but worse. Much of the scar tissue had been removed, which meant more bleeding was taking place. His kidneys were still not functioning, causing more serious edema. These two factors made it that much more difficult to locate with preciseness the particular arteries and veins, keeping in mind that the anatomy of his heart was abnormal, anyway. We waited. We visited the chapel. We stopped to visit Suzanne from time to time.

When evening fell, a new update came in. The nurse called to say that Dr. Salley had located and identified the parts of the heart and was now attempting to proceed according to his original plan. Again, she stressed that it was extremely difficult. Each time she called I sensed a lack of hope. This came across to me as confirmation of the prophecy.

Fifteen hours after entering into surgery, Dr. Salley and Dr. Cottrill came out to report the findings. The time now was about 10:00 P.M. Dr. Cottrill started with a hug. Serious faces looked upon us, as we stood eager to hear. Dr. Salley began to explain the events of the day. He was able to build the septum, which is the wall separating the right and left chambers. Feeling confident that the surgery was successful, he was not so confident that the recovery would be. He explained that due to the extreme amount of swelling, he was unable to close Charlie's chest. Each time that he attempted to do so, Charlie's blood pressure would drop to the point that they were losing him. He was forced to keep his chest open after failing in three attempts to close it. Although a dressing would be placed over his heart, he emphasized that Charlie would be extremely susceptible to infection. His immune system was low and major problems had surfaced. I looked at Dr. Cottrill and said with despair, "And he doesn't have a spleen." She could only laugh, surprised that I would even think of it at this time, as there were far more serious things to be concerned about. Yet, in my mind, it was one less weapon. (Once considered a vestigial organ, it is known today that the spleen helps fight infection.)

Along with the open chest, there was kidney failure to contend with, which they hoped would end with renewed renal function. We discussed the fact that he had lost life for about five

311

minutes. There was concern about serious brain damage. The entire picture was frightening. The uncertainty of proper liver function was another serious concern. It was still a mystery why his liver enzyme levels were so high. We were told that we could go in to see him once he was transferred to the Pediatric Intensive Care Unit.

Audrey, a nurse in the unit, had been following the case all day in anticipation of getting a new patient. When Charlie got settled in, she called us in the waiting room to say that we could come back. Meeting us halfway down the hall, she asked Charles if he was Charlie's father. Getting a positive response, she then inquired as to where his mother was. I informed her that I was his mother. Taken aback, she apologized for thinking that I was his sister. I expected her to be looking for someone older so this did not surprise me.

We were led into the unit and directed to the side of his bed. The sight of him astounded me. With his head doubled in size, he looked like a monster about to explode from within his skin. The swelling was such that the skin of his face was taut and appeared as though it could actually tear open. Not even fertile imagination could have prepared me for this moment. Even a nightmare could not compare. What have I done to my baby? His face is so ugly. His head is so huge. Why did it have to come to this? I thought. I was speechless. I was helpless. I was responsible.

Charles and I were offered a chair as Jackie stood beside us. Before we could sit down, Charles felt strongly inclined to pull back Charlie's blanket and look at the condition he was in. He asked me if he should look. I could only shrug my shoulders, not certain how I felt about it. Then, without further hesitation, he pulled the covers down. We spotted the clear dressing covering his heart, watching every beat in disbelief. My thoughts were drawn to infection as well as great concern about something falling on his chest. In my state of shock, I finally forced myself into the chair.

Fr. Dan, a priest friend of Dr. Cottrill's, arrived almost immediately. Carol (Dr. Cottrill) stood behind me with her hand on my shoulder. She began to rub my back as I sat locked and

312

frozen. I was aware that Fr. Dan was behind us, but I could not speak. My eyes were glued to Charlie in disbelief. My thoughts were to God. "You told me," I said. "You told me that this was it, but I had no idea." I held Charlie's hand gently. Its skin, too, was stretched as tight as it would go. I wondered what would be the purpose for Charlie to be allowed to return after such a simple death was offered to him that morning. There was little conversation going on around me. I could do nothing except stare at his chest and tell God that I had accepted His will.

Knowing that Fr. Dan was behind me, I felt that everyone was waiting for a proper moment to administer the last rights. I wanted to thank him for being there, for he added great comfort, but I was unable once again to speak or move. I hoped that he would not think that I was cold or ungrateful. I'll have to explain to him later, I thought. I was glad that he was present and wanted him to stay, but I could not convey this to him in any way. The room was relatively quiet and still. No one spoke except for some murmuring between the doctors and nurses. Dr. Cottrill remained solemn. Continuing to rub my back, I sensed her love for me. Words were unnecessary.

The staff monitored Charlie's every fluctuation with intensity. As unstable as he was, there were periodic moments of stability keeping everyone in suspense. After what seemed to be hours, we were encouraged to get some rest. When Fr. Dan started to leave, I wondered what he thought about my not asking him to administer the last rights for Charlie. The moment remains blurred to this day, as I am uncertain about whether he administered the sacrament.

Eventually, I dragged myself from the chair and stood by Charlie's side once again. Only when the staff convinced me that he would be closely watched every moment, could I agree to leave. A doctor would remain at his side the rest of the night. They promised to call me if any changes occurred.

Totally exhausted, Charles and I left with Jackie to get some rest. Arriving at the Ronald McDonald House sometime between 1:00 A.M. and 2:00 A.M., we were instructed by the housemother that she would awaken us if she received a call from the hospital. The policy was that the hospital staff would call her and she would be prepared as to how to inform us of the call. This prevented unnecessary panic as well as support in the event of a more serious call.

With heavy hearts, we fell asleep rather quickly from complete mental exhaustion. Wrapped in the arms of my husband, tears flowed quietly down my face. My heart went out to Jackie in the other bed by herself. This was not a time to be alone. I could only hope that she would be able to sleep.

Rising early, I rushed to the hallway pay phone to call the hospital. The update on Charlie's condition was that no changes had occurred. Quickly, I showered and hastened over to be with him, allowing Charles and Jackie to sleep. I left a note for Charles instructing him to call me for a ride once they were awake. A kidney specialist, Dr. Jenkins, had been called in to determine treatment for Charlie's kidney failure. There was an obvious need for dialysis to begin immediately. A portable machine, which was new at the time, was suggested for continuous use in the bed. The kidney tube was only about twelve inches long. This would be less vigorous and stressful for him than the regular form of hemodialysis. Although it was a trial portable kidney, it did appear to be the appropriate way to proceed in order to reduce trauma on an already weakened body. I was highly anxious to see some of the body fluid removed. It was extremely difficult and heartbreaking to observe him like this. Each doctor and nurse willingly shared information with me. By now, I had established a reputation for wanting to hear the whole truth, in spite of how bad things could be.

Dr. Cottrill came in that morning hoping to get some response from Charlie. Loudly, she called out his name. Again, she called out in a louder voice, "Charlie? Can you hear me?"

With eyes tightly closed, he nodded, affirmatively.

She shouted, "Your operation is over and you're okay."

He replied by nodding his head, negatively.

"You're not okay?" she questioned. Then she pushed him a little further and challenged him to open his eyes by adding, "Open your eyes and look at me."

He shook his head, no.

314

Continuing, she added, "Can't you look at me? What's the matter? Am I too ugly for you to look at?"

With that he nodded yes, which was the best response because it indicated to me that he still maintained his sense of humor, therefore implying minimal brain damage. One thing that Charlie would never do would be to intentionally hurt anyone. Having such a close relationship with Dr. Cottrill over the years, he knew that she could handle the joke. What was most comforting about this conversation was the fact that it indicated to me that there could not have been too much brain damage from his time without oxygen. Being satisfied with his responses, we allowed him to sleep.

Later that morning, as I stood next to him and spoke to him, he opened his eyes. Looking deep into my eyes, he became very anxious and vigorously attempted to speak. Having the respirator down his throat, this was impossible to do. He began to squirm in the bed. His eyes were bulging with great desperation to speak. Despite the respirator, his lips moved with fury in an attempt to get a message to me. Not knowing what was so important to tell me, I consoled him and suggested that he try to rest and calm down.

I said, "Charlie, you can't talk with that in your mouth. Do you think that you could wait a few days and then tell me? I'll be right here with you. As soon as they get this out of your mouth, you can tell me. Okay?"

With that his big blue eyes surrendered sadly. I observed that there was something drastically important on his mind. He suppressed his emotions not by choice but out of defeat. As he took in his surroundings, his eyes shifted up and down examining the IVs and monitors. His nurse, Audrey, came over to the side of his bed and gave him words of encouragement. She smiled at me and let me know that Charlie was special to her. She said that they had bonded in a special way. Not only did she love his blond hair and blue eyes, there was more to it than that. She had a specific indication of joy in her eyes when she spoke to him or about him. There was an awareness that she had been sent by God, but I did not know what spiritual activity was ongoing at the time.

As the dialysis began, the swelling slowly decreased. Dr. Salley watched for the opportunity to return him safely to surgery to close his chest. Being extremely concerned about infection, time could not have passed any slower. Antibiotics were given in hopes of preventing complications. Eventually, after three days of dialysis, he saw his chance. The swelling had gone down a fair amount but not completely. Charlie was taken to surgery where Dr. Salley was able to close his chest. However, due to the time lapse from the original operation, the skin could not be closed. Rather, it was necessary to heal from the inside out. Therefore, the incision, about seven or eight inches in length, was packed with a dressing and changed several times a day. A chest tube remained in place.

During these few days of trauma, it was no secret to those in the unit's waiting area that we were sunken in grief. Although, we were mostly at Charlie's side, there were occasions when we were asked to remain in the waiting room while special attention was given to a child in the unit. Sitting there among the people, it was easy to spot the various parents within the room. There was a solemnity about them and complete lack of interest in the world around them. Yet, those who appeared to be suffering the most could easily spot the others in the same position. As Charles, Jackie and I waited for visiting hours to begin, there was another couple in the hall near us. They were also eager to visit a patient in the unit. Having worked up the strength to talk, a saddened father, Scotty, asked about our son's condition. His wife, Wilma, was at his side. A brief description informed them that the circumstances were life threatening. Scotty commented that he knew it was critical by the long faces that we carried when Charlie was first brought to the unit. He and his wife had already discussed it. After spending several weeks there, they could spot the critical cases right away. As we inquired about their reason for being there, they replied that their two-year-old, Shane, had drowned. The horrifying experience was relayed to us. Recognizing their pain as they empathized with ours brought a sense of support for each other. They had a teenage son who was also with them, waiting.

Before long, we were able to go back into the PICU. When Charlie woke up from surgery, he checked out all the apparatus around him. Then, he slowly took his left hand and moved it up and down his chest patting the incision. His eyes indicated curiosity about the dressing that he felt. I explained why he had returned to surgery as well as the particulars about his current condition. Any time that he was awake I spoke to him. There was never a lack for conversation. Once the health issue was addressed, I talked about sports, family, friends, or anything that came to mind.

With the situation remaining critical, Charles or I stayed continuously. We would take turns going out of the unit when visitors came. Neither of us had a desire to eat, but we were soon informed that a fruit basket had arrived for us and was in Dr. Cottrill's office. The strange emptiness that I felt wasn't the same as an emptiness from hunger. Frankly, I couldn't care if I ever ate again. Nevertheless, my feet led me down the hall to her office to see who had sent the fruit. When I saw that it was from a group of my high school friends, it brought the first trace of a smile to my face. These were friends who knew me well. They knew that I would not want to leave Charlie in order to eat. Therefore, they were determined to do what they could to provide me with strength. Their thoughtfulness and generosity moved me. When I realized that it was almost dinnertime, I forced myself to open the basket and pull out some grapes.

Dr. Cottrill came in and I offered her some fruit, as well. Busy as she had been, I knew that she had not eaten all day either. Her comments on how good it tasted were beyond my comprehension for I could not taste it. My throat had maintained a constant sense of being choked since before the surgery. I forced down a banana simply because the clock said that I was supposed to be hungry. Again, the flavor was undetected by my numbed senses. As I went through the motions, I thought of how wonderful all of my friends had been toward us and appreciated the comfort those thoughts brought me.

Wound cultures soon indicated positive for a fungal infection called Candida Albicans. Charlie's body became covered with a red rash along with generalized itching. Another

317

doctor was called in who specialized in internal medicine. Speaking to him in the hallway, he quickly realized my search for explanations. He described the drug, Amphotericin, which was needed to fight this sort of infection. My interrogation prompted him to be up front with me about its adverse effects on the kidneys. Certain to cause kidney failure, it was not recommended for use on a patient with renal distress. On the other hand, it was the only drug to use to fight the deadly fungal infection. Backed constantly into corners, we had to forfeit any hope of normal kidney function in order to offer some comfort by destroying the potentially fatal infection. Charlie could not be left to suffer without treatment.

Returning to the unit, I stayed and monitored every intensifying moment. Charles and Jackie stayed in town for several more days until stabilization occurred. Once things settled down slightly, they were forced to return to Louisville and continue life at school, work and home.

Being at Charlie's bedside day and night, I found myself on a roller coaster ride of emotions to coincide with the events of the day. I learned about every monitor: IV, respirator, NG tube, dialysis, chest tube drainage, etc. I recognized what was normal and what was not, offering my assistance to the nurse regularly.

In just a few days, Charlie began a twitching of his body that was uncontrollable. First thinking that this was seizure activity, I held down his leg to test for movement. I found that when I would pat, stroke, or hold him down that he would stop. The twitching immediately returned the moment I lifted my hand from him. My observation of this ruled out seizures and implied that it was muscle spasms. Remembering the first seizure he had following heart surgery as an infant, I recalled how to determine a true seizure. Different medications were tried without success. Keeping my perspective the same as always, I saw that it was still important to make each day of his life the best possible. So, I stayed in the unit without taking breaks for the entire day, holding his leg down to prevent him from twitching. I believed that this uncontrollable movement must be bothersome to him. After hours of keeping him still, I attempted to release my hand, but he began the spasms again. Later that evening Dr. Cottrill came in and noticed me in the same position as when she had last seen me early in the morning. Confirming this with the nurse, she suggested that I take a break, but I could not leave. My continued questions concerning medications, side effects, and game plan to calm him kept her mind searching for answers. Eventually, the drug Lorazepam was used to stop the spasms and proved effective. Meanwhile, my consolation to him was comforting. Therefore, time did not matter. Time, in fact, was standing still for me. There was no difference between the days or the hours. I sat at his bedside and held his hand, stroked his arm or ran my fingers through his silky blond hair, until forced to leave at night due to exhaustion. I told Charlie that I was going to bed across the street by the football stadium and promised that I would return early in the morning. Each night I reminded the nurse to call if any problems arose. The Ronald McDonald House was about a five-minute walk away. I had come to trust his night nurse, Bess, fairly well, which enabled me to leave for a while.

As days passed, new problems set in. Not only did Charlie have an open chest wound to heal, he also had an enormous open wound in his left groin. The heart bypass machine had been connected to the artery in that groin. Not healing well, it too needed to be packed with fresh dressings several times a day, as it would heal from the inside. The depth and look of this wound concerned me. It looked painful and did not appear to be healing at all.

With each step forward, there followed several backward. Before long, cultures from the wounds indicated that he had contracted a strep infection. More antibiotics were ordered. More problems surfaced. Renal failure remained obvious. Addressing each doctor with multiple questions, the answers I received were not promising. With goals to correct one problem, came causes for further trauma in other areas. Medications were damaging to the kidneys and liver. Electrolyte imbalance caused continued acidosis. The inability to wean Charlie from the respirator caused further complications.

My request for a tracheotomy was not a possibility because Charlie's incision was too high up on his chest. He had a short

319

chest and little neck. Therefore, there was no room for a tracheotomy. It greatly disturbed me to imagine how sore his throat must feel over such a long period on the respirator.

It had still not been determined why his liver enzymes were high at the time of surgery. With medication not being detoxified properly, the massive doses required to do the job would remain in his body for long periods of time. The risks remained high with any choice we made. In a catch twenty-two situation, unwanted choices were made according to the lesser of two evils. Charlie was sleeping most of the time and was considered semi-comatose. I strongly believed it was due to the drugs in his system. Although he was not taking much that would cause this at the time, I was aware that every drug he took would linger on because of the sluggish liver. Often, he would open his eyes to look at me. Because it was for such brief periods, others mostly did not see this take place.

Considering Charlie's deteriorating health, his dad was anxious to return and be with us. The children wanted to see their brother as well. Midway through the week, Charles picked them up after school and drove them to Lexington. It was wonderful having the family together even for just a few hours. The unity lifted our spirits in spite of Charlie's deteriorating health. The children had many questions. Speaking the truth without creating fear required great assistance from the Holy Spirit. With calmness, I prepared each of them prior to seeing their brother. Special permission was granted for the little ones to come into the unit. Although it would be disturbing, I was certain that they should see their brother, as I had never hidden the truth from them before. This would serve as preparation and gradual adjustment for whatever we faced. I spoke with hope so as to eliminate their fears. Although it was not pleasant, they were thrilled to see their brother. After visiting Charlie, I took them to the cafeteria for dinner while Charles spent some private time with him.

My time with the children was too short. At nearly 10:00 P.M., I walked them out to the car and prepared beds for them by rolling out sleeping bags over the back of the station wagon. After a kiss and hug from each of them, I tucked them in and

320

arranged everyone to have ample room. Charles and I embraced with torn emotions. Waving them on, I turned to go back to Charlie's room.

Daily reports from the unit were becoming harder to bear. Day by day the situation worsened. Before long, a staph infection was added to the rest. As a rule, I stayed at Charlie's side from about 7:00 A.M. until after 12:00 P.M. or 1:00 A.M. each night. Once in a while I would leave briefly during the day to have lunch with friends. One day I looked up to see Fr. Bill along with some friends from St. Gabriel. It lifted my spirits tremendously to see them. The support that I received from the people at St. Gabriel was inspiring to me. I found myself wanting to cry from unworthiness. Mostly, I was stunned to see that Fr. Bill had taken time away from being a busy pastor to come visit me an hour and a half away from home. His genuine concern touched me deeply. Only a few people could lure me away from the hospital for lunch or dinner and this group did. I felt complete trust in Charlie's two primary nurses, Audrey and Bess. This trust enabled me to break away briefly when visitors came.

As I observed all that had taken place and the pendulum of emotions, I said to God again, "I wouldn't mind if You were to tell me that I misunderstood You." I continued to hope that I was wrong about Charlie's impending death. Yet, any opportunity to sit and listen to God only reinforced what I already knew. Frequently I would go to the hospital chapel and sit without intentional thought. Although my heart remained heavy, my mind was empty and open to God. He continued to grant me peace even through the worst days. Weeks passed by with numerous changes taking place. One day was up; one day was down. The balance of those days kept me puzzled, not knowing the direction in which we were being led. Often, I thought he might survive because he was such a fighter. However, in my time alone with God, I sensed again that he would not. I wondered if the fluctuation was taking place to remind me that only God would know the day or the hour.

God sent many good people to watch over me. Friends and family were sending care packages, cards, and flowers to keep my spirits up and to let me know that they were thinking of my family and me. I discovered that people were praying all over the world because of this one brave boy. My brothers and sisters all kept each other posted on his latest condition. They were praying in Tennessee, California, and Germany, as well as several cities in Kentucky. Family members and friends found themselves telling others about Charlie. Then their friends began to pray. Prayers had spread to Wisconsin, St. Louis, and Washington, D.C. I began receiving cards from people I didn't know. I was deeply moved in witnessing the power of prayer brought about because of one blue baby that was born fourteen years ago. It made me realize how each one of us affects so many other people. The total picture was more than my mind could handle.

Friday after Charles got off work, he brought the children back to Lexington. This time I knew that things needed to be different. I knew that I needed to be a mom to each one of them and not just to Charlie. Trying to maintain some stability within their uprooted lives, I believed I could do this best by spending time with them at home. The struggle with the idea came at the thought of leaving Charlie, not knowing how much time he had. I pondered and prayed about what to do. Charles had been taking care of them all week and needed time with Charlie. My heart remained torn, no matter what I did. Understanding that this would not change, I focused on the five children. Taking each one of them into my soul, I contemplated their individual needs. As I faced these facts, I could see and feel my heart break as I was forced to choose between my children. They all needed me. Yet, I had only given the quality time to Charlie.

"I should stay with him," I said to myself. "He has very little time left whereas the other children will most likely outlive him. I would have time for them after this is all over." Very strong thoughts that I should stay with him controlled my mind.

Following this thought it came to me that Jackie, Marty, Leslie, and Jonathan needed their mom now more than at any other time in their lives. Talking by phone just wasn't enough. Visiting me in a strange location could not provide the security that they desperately needed. They were in the process of losing a brother, and I was sure they sensed it. Along with that they were losing the family unit at home and the daily routine that they were accustomed to. They had lost their mom because she left them behind to go be with their brother. They had a lot of adjustments to deal with as well.

I wanted his dad to have time alone with Charlie, but I didn't want to give up my time with him. I was feeling a strong desire and temptation to be selfish about being with Charlie. Time was too precious to give away to someone else. I discovered that every time I walked out of the unit, my heart felt anchored to the floor. Whether it was for five minutes or hours, the feeling didn't fluctuate. Even when I was enjoying a meal with someone, I was hating it at the same time. I was hating the awareness that time was slipping away. As long as I was with him, I could see that I might have another minute. On the contrary, when I was not at his side, I had no knowledge that I would ever have another minute with him. This is precisely why it was so difficult. Despite the unlikeliness, I was also aware that this may be the case with any of my children. Who was to say that no accident would befall them and take one of them away as well?

Making a decision, I based it on what I believed to be right not what I believed to be best. My mind could not comprehend what *best* meant at this time. Nor was my choice based on what I wanted to do. As I indicated, any choice was an enormous sacrifice for me. Finally, the plan was to have the children stay at The Ronald McDonald House with Charles and me on Friday night. I would get up early to go visit Charlie. Then, Charles would bring the children over for a brief visit with their brother. After a short stay, I would take the children back home to Louisville and spend Saturday night with them. We'd go to church on Sunday at 12:00 P.M. to reestablish our lifelong routine. This could be enough to remind the children that life was still stable. Charles would spend the weekend with Charlie until I returned to switch places with his father. This arrangement would require a lot of riding for everyone, but I believed it would be worth every sacrifice.

The following day, Saturday, we began what would be our weekend ritual. When it came time for the plan to unfold, I experienced the most difficult suffering of my life thus far.

Driving away from the hospital that Saturday was like stretching my body in a torture chamber. The farther away I drove, the worse it got. I had never experienced anything comparable to it. I pleaded with God not to take him while I was away. I believed that He would honor my request although He did not indicate that He would.

Driving home under these circumstances was a strange experience. Pulling into the subdivision meant that I would have to face neighbors. I would be obligated to share with those who had been so concerned. Oh how I dreaded to share such bad news. Upon entering my home, I sensed an abnormal atmosphere about it. The house had been kept clean with the help of friends, which made coming home refreshing. Yet, at the same time, the emptiness of the house made it feel as though it weren't even my home. Four children and a mom didn't make this house a home. It was the family unity that was missing. I understood that this feeling must be the same for the children while I was gone. The familiar décor and smell of the house weren't enough to make it comfortable. How did Charles and the children endure this emptiness all week long? My gut felt like it was still in Lexington. Having no solution for my emotions, I decided it best to do what I had come to do. I was to be a mom for the other children. Keeping motherhood my focus, I began cooking dinner. We spent time talking about school, Girl Scouts, Charlie, or whatever topic came up. They having various school needs, I took them shopping to get supplies that they anticipated needing.

With Jackie's sixteenth birthday approaching the following week, a neighbor offered to give her a surprise party as I would be out of town. Being not particularly close to this neighbor, I declined the offer. I was surprised that she wanted to do it. Reflecting on this, I found it rather puzzling because our relationship had never been close. Then it occurred to me what was beginning to happen. It was through Charlie's suffering that others could have the opportunity to do good deeds. Perhaps I should have allowed her to plan a party, but I feared it would be awkward for Jackie. The neighbor could have been granted graces for her kindness. Unknowingly, I had robbed her of this possibility. Although I'm certain that she was given graces for her offering, she could have received greater by carrying through with it. After realizing this, I vowed to accept future offers from others whenever possible, knowing that it would take special effort in cases of more distant relationships.

As the day ended, I tucked them in bed and realized how precious the time was. It would be another week before I could be "Mom for a Day" again. This day was gone. The morning would be too short. Slipping into my own bed, I spoke to God about the happenings of the day, wondering what it was all about. Why are things going as they are? Why am I here while Charlie is there? What will tomorrow bring? I sensed that my many questions were all right with God, for He knew what an inquisitive person I was. I was well aware that I did not understand His plan. Yet, I also knew that as time would unfold the future, it also opened the explanation for the past. So often I would ask questions of God, knowing that He would answer me at a later time. Answers were often made clear when I would least expect it. As I prayed, I was in awe over the peace that I felt. Even at my lowest points, I was at peace. It amazed me that God would grant this tremendous gift to me. How could a stomach so full of knots and a heart so torn in pieces coincide with an overall peace? Only God could make this possible.

When morning came, I looked forward to going to St. Gabriel for Mass. Upon entering the church filled with familiar faces, I suddenly felt as though I had never left. After church, people were eager to hear how Charlie was progressing. They all wanted to hear that the situation was improving. To the contrary, I could not reveal a false interpretation of the setbacks of the week. Acknowledging their concerns, support, and prayers with appreciation, I gave them the update and then moved on.

After lunch, the children and I drove back to Lexington. Having not heard from Charles, I was comfortable assuming that there had been no changes for the worse. My heart still fluttered thinking of the possibility that I may get back too late. This intensity remained with me until I stepped foot in the pediatric unit on our return.

Now, Charlie was specifically concerned about missing Jackie's birthday. I had promised him that we would celebrate at the hospital if he were still there. As for Jackie, my heart went out to her for the memories that she would forever have of turning "Sweet Sixteen." It should be special. Yet, with her brother near death, she could never have fond memories of this birthday. Aware of my necessary absence, I called on my faithful friends from St. Gabriel. They were pleased to go by the house and put up a "Happy Birthday" sign so that Jackie would know that I was thinking of her. She understood that I could not be there for her. Charles would be bringing the children back to Lexington that day, but it would be late. As it turned out, my friends decorated with more detail than I had requested. They spruced up the living room with colorful signs and balloons to make it as special as they could. Jackie was quite surprised when she came home from school to see that Mom had pulled this off from Lexington. She never expected it, assuming that her birthday would be overlooked with all of our minds on Charlie.

That evening, Charles came with the family and presents. We gathered around Charlie's bed and sang "Happy Birthday" to Jackie. I had promised him that weak or not, he wouldn't miss it. We celebrated together.

Over the weeks, visitors continued to appear to brighten our days. Friends and relatives came. It was interesting when those whom I least expected to see, would come. Several people whom I hadn't seen in years were there to support us. Then there was the local priest, Fr. Dan from the Newman Center, who took us under his wing by dropping in regularly to check on us. Fr. Bill stunned me when he came back for a second visit as well.

Two close friends and co-workers, Theresa and Anne Marie, drove in to visit one day. They were the owners of the craft company for which I worked. I worried about the company going under without its having an active director. We had made such tremendous strides in the last year and I did not want them to lose it because of me. I begged them to replace me with someone else, but they wouldn't hear of it. Their loyalty to me was more than to their company. It disturbed me that I was incapable of helping them. Yet, they both understood that I was powerless to function in any role other than mother at the time.

326

As friends had always been so willing to lend a hand, even old friends from Lexington came to our needs. Butch and Kathy insisted that I take their Volvo to drive so that I could easily get to and from the Ronald McDonald House. They were uncomfortable knowing that I walked late at night by myself. As we had been having car problems that required money we lacked for repairs, I did not have a car with me. These friends were adamant about helping. Reminded of my recent vow to allow the grace of God to be bestowed on His helpful servants, I accepted their offer. It was very difficult for me to drive away in their car with the instructions to keep it until Charlie left the hospital. I was told to drive it when I went to Louisville, also. That way, Charles would not be stranded, either. This was a good lesson in humility for me as well. The love that was being poured out for us day after day was overwhelming me. This continual giving from people made Charlie's suffering understandable from a spiritual outlook. I could see how God was using Charlie to bring the goodness out of all those who knew us.

20

THE FINAL PLAY

Despite the apparent stillness of time, the days passed. The weeks blended together, yet events marked their differences. The upcoming weekend Jackie was to attend her boyfriend's senior prom. It was imperative that the event not be slighted because of the emotional trauma that surrounded us. Preparation and planning had been worked out weeks before so that all would go smoothly when the special night arrived. The possibility of not being with her had rightfully entered my mind. However, Charlie's temporary stability allowed me to devote this day to Jackie.

Most of my usual responsibilities had been delegated to others. Before long, Charles signed the children up for summer ball teams. My co-leader continued to hold the weekly Brownie meetings for Leslie's troop. Every part of our life seemed under control by God's provision of good people to take care of our needs. The peace and smoothness of family activity around me rested my mind from the typical problems of parenting. Where people saw a need, they offered to help us.

At the hospital, relationships between some of the parents grew. Wilma and Scotty often talked about our children leaving the hospital together. A part of me was bothered about this because she was referring to Shane's going home with them. My thoughts were that when Charlie left, he would be going to his home in heaven. My belief was that God could change this, but I doubted that He would. This gut feeling surfaced because I did not believe that God would have revealed His intention of taking Charlie to heaven now if He intended to do otherwise. Nevertheless, I went along with Wilma's suggestion as a means of hope for her. I sensed that our children would be leaving together. Yet, I could not tell her the fullness of my thoughts.

Another woman, who was a single parent, also had a baby in the hospital. Although her baby was not in the unit, she, too, had a serious case to deal with. It was obvious that her little girl was slowly slipping away. The sad thing that I noticed about her in conversation was her desperate need for God in her life. She had a tendency to blame God and she felt angry with Him. I tried pointing out more positive approaches to the situation, but she could not fully understand. She had missed out on a solid Christian upbringing. My heart went out to her for her misfortune and lack of faith. Whenever we talked about our children dying, she always commented in the negative. This gave me the opportunity to share some of my beliefs on heaven. She would be touched for the moment. Then, the following day she would be completely down again. Knowing the terrible suffering that her baby was undergoing, her actions and statements were perfectly understandable. Yet, she didn't realize that her sadness stemmed from her lack of dependency on God.

One rainy day she commented, "I know that it will be raining on the day that my baby dies." I didn't say a word. Rather, I thought to myself, I know the sun will be shining on the day that my son dies. Despite my encouragement of her to talk to God about her baby, I understood that she probably didn't know how. The woman had a ten-year-old son with her as well. He was her only support system. Observing the two of them in their hardship, I believed that their suffering would probably enhance their future life together. I prayed that she would someday come to know God better through this trial.

As Charlie continued his ups and downs and traumatic moments in the unit, I developed a closer relationship with his nurse, Audrey. We discovered, in amazement, many interesting facts about each other. She informed me that when Charlie first came to the unit, she was moved to inspire him to live. She had whispered into his ear something that caused his vital signs to suddenly stabilize. The doctors were closely monitoring the screens at the desk anticipating drastic problems as the situation indicated. They were stunned when heart rate and blood pressure returned to normal the moment that she spoke to him. The synchronization of timing was such that the doctor wanted to know what she had said to him to make him react this way. It was actually very simple. She encouraged him by telling him that he was going to make it. Convincing him of his strength, she told him to fight hard. She spoke to him with strong conviction that God wanted him to live. She was sincere in her belief that he could live despite all the odds against him. That's why he stabilized. He believed her and she gave him willpower.

As we shared stories, I told her about Charlie's having been the Easter Seal Society Poster Child in 1980. She smiled and shared that she, too, had been a poster child for The Easter Seal Society when she was young. Her story was fascinating. Having spent years in an iron lung, she should never have survived according to medical technology. Yet, God chose to save her. We immediately began sharing innumerable spiritual events of our lives. The bond that we made was clearly brought on by the Holy Spirit. Again, I found myself in awe that God was taking such good care of me. There were no strangers in my life. They were all put on my path to be a part of my journey.

The weeks passed only to witness more and more goodness. Charlie's condition never stabilized for any significant amount of time. When one factor improved, several more worsened. Numerous problems occurred. In discovering a horrible bedsore on the back of his head, I requested a special air flotation bed, by suggestion of my sister, Nancy. This was a luxury item that was unheard of at this hospital and was not possible to obtain. After persevering with more assertiveness and persistence, my request was finally approved and a bed was ordered from an outside location. My goal for him was comfort. Money, doctors, nurses, and rules never intimidated me when it came to doing what was best for him.

With his health deteriorating, people were beginning to recognize that he might not be invincible after all. I noticed that when I visited St. Gabriel one Sunday, those who had been giving so much encouragement and hope seemed to respond finally with acceptance that all was not well. When week after week the picture dimmed, reality was finally being considered. Now, the words that were offered were those suggesting that miracles do happen. My inmost thoughts as my friends would suggest this were that God had given us far more than a fair share of miracles. How could I dare ask for more? The

331

understanding of God's will that was revealed to me kept me subdued in asking for a miracle.

When my mother visited one day, she said to me, "There's always a miracle." She indicated that she understood how very close to the end we were. She wanted to give me hope, knowing that the ultimate decision was God's. Having already pondered every aspect of the matter, both spiritual and physical, I quickly responded as she barely finished the sentence, "It would take more than a miracle." My heart was heavy with grief at the thought of losing him. She was stunned at my response that implied a sacrilegious thought of a higher power than God. I could not tell her that God had indicated His will to me prior to Charlie's admission. The thoughts that I had were that I should not ask God to grant my will, but "Thy will be done." I was feeling submissive to God's will but could not indicate this to her. So I said, "It would take a grand miracle." I realized how stupid that must have sounded, but I was at a loss for words. By *grand miracle*, I meant a change of God's will. I could not relate to God (the Father) thinking in our human terms. Therefore, I couldn't fathom God's changing His mind as man would. I had to let it go. I couldn't explain myself and I didn't feel like talking anyway.

I was finding it harder and harder to be a good mother to all of my children during these long weeks of separation. Although they continued to come to the hospital on Wednesdays and I went home with them on Saturdays, I still found that time and distance created an inability to mother the way that I knew they needed.

Jackie frequently came with her boyfriend, John, and spent many hours at Charlie's bedside. I saw that she was leaning on John more for support than on me. He was very good to her and was a tremendous source of strength for her emotional needs. Yet, I knew that she was also in need of her mother. She was at the most fragile age to console. It was not feasible to speak to her as a child, for she was beyond that stage. At the same time, however, I could not share my adult views for she had not grown in experience to fully understand them. I struggled with not being available for her when she returned home.

My sister, Nancy, noticed Jackie's need for her mother as well. Knowing that I was unable to guide her appropriately from a distance, she offered her support and spent some time with her. It was choking me inside not to be there for her. It was providence again. No matter the need, God provided. Swallowing my pride, I was forced to see that I could not be the mother that I always believed I could be. I needed others to help me and was fortunate to have such a caring family.

One weekend when I came home with the children, I discovered a package had come in the mail. It was addressed to Charlie from his friend Jason, who had moved to Tennessee. Eager to open it, I knew how much it was going to mean to Charlie to get something from Jason. In the package I found an audiotape. Immediately, I knew that I had better listen to it before taking it to Charlie. Not being sure how much Jason knew about Charlie's condition, I couldn't take a chance on Charlie's hearing something that may be too difficult to bear. When I had the opportunity to listen to it privately, I did. For some reason I found myself in Charlie's room using his tape player to listen to Jason. I lay back on top of the blue football bedspread which draped over Charlie's bed. It was daylight and I don't recall how it came to be that I was alone in the house. Nevertheless, I was aware that I had about an hour before the children would be coming home.

With hesitation and anxiousness I pressed the play button and rolled back onto the bed, facing the ceiling. Jason's words began: "Hey, Charlie --- It's me. How have you been? I heard about your heart, and your kidney, and whatever. Wish I could come down, but I don't have time. You know with school and everything. But I hope you get better --- uum --- and I pray for you every night." With that my heart cracked as I broke into tears wondering how in the world these children would be able to make it through the death of their friend. "(pause) Well what's been going on? Nothing much here. I resorted to a tape (shy laugh) because I know you can't read or write right now."

Wow, I thought to myself. How thoughtful for a twelve-year-old boy.

"Send me a tape back. I don't care. If you want to or not, but it's your decision."   (His voice was beginning to sound sad.) "Well the house is pretty good. I'm sitting up here in the attic. I don't want anybody to hear me. And uh, I've been up here for (laugh) ten minutes. I've been okay. Still got some girlfriends? Well, if you're in the hospital listening to this --- well --- Your parents are probably there so --- not much to say, but I hope you get better. And maybe they'll let you play this in the hospital. Maybe, if I get the chance, I'll come see you. Next time I'm down, I'll come and see you though. I'll make sure. It'll be my first stop. It'll be the first place I check into. It'll be your house. And we'll play football. It's a deal, bud. Play some football (his voice beginning to choke)."

By now my face was drenched with tears, knowing that this would never happen. I felt the sorrow in Jason's voice, sorrow for not being here with Charlie. It was the love of a grade school friend stranded so far away. Helpless, I asked God, "How will these children bear it?"

"Are you still going to your school? I can't even think of the name of it, Ursuline-Pitt? I don't know. But, the last time I was in I think that was where you were going. I'm doing okay in school. We got our report cards today. Yeah, I got a 60 in math. How's your neighborhood? How's your mom, dad, Jackie, Marty, Leslie and Jonathan? I remember all them. Well (laugh), I can't think of anything to say. Hold on. uuh --- I really miss you. uuh --- I wish I could be there so we can play some football. I really like playing football with you. You can really play. Man, remember when we did that 'Born In The USA' thing? I remember that. I had to be black. Painted me up black. You played the guitar. Remember that day when we went to see 'Harry and The Henderson's'? That was pretty cool. That was funny. We were sittin' up there and we started slidin' down on that carpet. Yeah. I wish I could come and see you. I really miss you." (By now this desperate child's voice had really gotten to me. I wanted to put him on a plane myself. Yet, at the same time I didn't want him to see his friend in this condition either. My heart went out to him as the bedspread beneath my head became saturated with tears.) "Cause you know I've been busy and everything. I got an autographed Cubs ball. You know the baseball team? Just thought maybe you wanted to know. Kurt sent it to me. He and Craig are okay. Craig's mom told me that you were in the hospital. So I just wanted to make sure you were okay. I'll be there if anything bad happens, real bad." (This told me that he did understand the seriousness of his friend's condition. My heart sank deeper into the mattress as I listened to him.) "Don't worry. I think of you every night, man. --- But I know that nothing's going to happen. You're going to come out and be fine. 'Cause you've done it before. You're strong. They said that you were going to die when you were about three-years-old. You haven't died yet. So you're gonna live. Charlie Stopher don't die. He's tough. The guy I knew was tough. And I hope he still is. So I miss you, little buddy. And I'm gonna come see you some day. Whenever I get the time this summer, I'm gonna come see ya'. Uh-huh. First thing I'll do. I'll get there and I'll *jump* out on my bike and I'll ride right to your house. And we'll do somethin'. Play some football or some basketball. Maybe go down in the creek. (deep breath) Do you still have your braces? On your feet? I don't know if you do or not but when I come, (there was an interruption of thought). I came down to Louisville for a day or two a couple of weeks ago. And I thought you were in the hospital. So I didn't know where you were. I called your house and nobody was home. I shouldn't have waited so long. I was gonna call you, but then Craig's mom called and told me that you were in the hospital. And I said that we got our report cards back today. School's okay. I'm almost done. We're goin' to Hilton Head Island in South Carolina this summer. And there's this soccer team. It's a Junior Olympic team and I might be makin' it. I'm gonna try out next weekend. I'm goin' to a party Saturday. And I told all of my friends about you, man. They feel sorry for you, you know? I told 'em you were a real cool dude. They said they want to meet you, man. Maybe you can come down sometime. And I guess I want to say that you are one of my best friends. And that I love you. And nothin's gonna happen to you 'cause you're strong. So, if you want to send me a tape back there's a lot on here and on the other side probably. I don't know if I'm done yet or not. But, if you want to, there's probably gonna be some tape on the back that you can use and send it to me. Or, something like that. Maybe next time I'll send you a videotape with my picture on it. That would be pretty cool. We can talk to each other. I'll be sittin' in front of the TV and say 'Hi, Charlie.' My friend Kurt, yeah, I saw him and I saw Krista, when I went to Louisville. And I didn't know if you were home so, I wish I could have seen you. So I just heard about you. And I pray for you every night. Uh-huh.

I'm makin' my Confirmation this year. You know. You know what Confirmation is. 'Cause at our church we only have it every other year. Pretty stupid. I gotta go to Confirmation class tonight which is the fourth, no, April 19, 1989. (Attempting to be humorous, he stressed in a silly way) --- Very important day in my life. Nah (slight laughter). Yeah, I got a couple --- I like this girl. Her name is Laura. She's pretty. I don't know if she likes me though. But, I still remember when we all used to play football. Me, you and Jamie, and Marty and Tony. Remember your little scooter we use to ride on? When we used to have races in your wheelchairs? The best time though was probably when we came over for your birthday party. I remember that. The same year as my sister's...my little sister's. My little sister, Ashley." (He was bringing to surface many memories for me. Charlie was worried that Jason might miss his party due to his mother about to give birth. But that didn't stop Jason. He wouldn't have missed Charlie's party for anything. We all felt excitement for Jason when we heard that his sister was born on Charlie's birthday.) "I got a basketball goal set up down here. I gotta big yard, a riding lawn mower, a whole bunch of stuff. I wish I could come see you though. It's not the same here without you. Well, I guess I don't have much else to say. I'll come see you soon. I know you're gonna pull through. 'Cause you're tough. See ya later, little buddy. I love you --- Bye."

So moved by his words, I sobbed with deep emotions. I spoke to God about my concern for the children. I dreaded their grief. My own grief was great. Yet, I had been given so much to help me through it. I had been given time, age, wisdom, and insight from God in preparation for this. Still, it was unbearable.

What about these children in their innocent, trusting state? How would they take it? Would they not trust from now on because they prayed and God still took their friend? How does a child cope with such a loss? Immediately, I recalled my earliest awareness of death in my own life. Fr. Foltz, who was the pastor of my grade school, came to mind. I was ten-years-old. This man was my connection to Jesus. I remembered the details as if it were yesterday. The fall Kiddie Karnival was postponed. With hearts still sunken with grief, we could not enjoy it even when it was held. I pictured the exact location in the church where I stood in the pew with my family when I heard the news. I remembered how deeply I cried, hoping that no one around me would notice. It was difficult for me to control my tears. My thoughts were of how loving this man was. He treated us children with love and respect. I remember the warmth. I could not recall his face, but the spirit was as clear as a bright summer day. My thoughts drifted. Going back to that young, vulnerable age, recalling the loss, the pain, and the memories, I knew that Charlie's friends would surely remember him forever, too. But, it was not the memories that I felt concerned about. I was afraid of the pain that they would feel. I imagined my best friends from grade school. How could I relate to their loss of a friend when someone this close to me had not died when I was their age? Charlie was like the "Joe Cool" on campus. He was loved by many and known by many. His absence would be obvious in many circles of people. I found myself grieving for all the people that I knew would be affected by his death. Believing that the adults would not have their faith shaken by this, my thoughts returned once again to the children. I grieved for my own children, with separate concerns for each one of them. I grieved for all of Charlie's cousins, and all of his friends. I considered the many children who knew him. Having gone to several schools meant the involvement of numerous children. I was more concerned that I would not have the opportunity to talk to them. I could explain the goodness of God to my own children, but how could I prevent the anger and disappointment in God that other children would be feeling? I couldn't bear the thought of Charlie's death causing childhood faith to be diminished. My soul experienced tremendous pain over this. Pulling myself up from the bed, I went over to the tape player and felt a need to hear Jason's tape again. I played it over and over until I could not cry any more. The tape was a beautiful testimony of friendship. Jason spoke with such sincerity, love, and even a sense of guilt for not being there with Charlie. I was enthused about letting Charlie hear it because I knew that it would mean more to him than anything. Knowing that I must have the ability to contain my emotions when I played it for him, I was compelled to release my feelings beforehand.

As I listened over and over again, I knew what I had to do. I had to find someone that knew Charlie to give a eulogy. I had to find someone who knew God. I had to find someone who could explain to the children how much God loved Charlie. The children needed to see how good God was to Charlie. It was important that they not misunderstand the purpose of Charlie's death. Various priests came to mind. Fr. Bill had been so supportive. But, he did not know Charlie's past. Even if I was to tell him, I knew that it would not be the same. Fr. Castor knew him well. But, he was in a nursing home and would not be available. Fr. Bruce was someone who knew. But, he, too, was unavailable. I was stuck. The person that my mind was searching for had to have witnessed God in Charlie's life. This person needed to recall Charlie's smile even in his suffering in order to be convincing to the children who witnessed this as well. I was unable to come up with a candidate at that time. Once my tears dried, I stopped playing the tape. Releasing the heaviness in my heart, I placed the tape back into the case and put it with my belongings that were to return to the hospital with me.

Aware of the closeness of the imminent death, I acknowledged the fact that I should prepare Charlie's clothes for the funeral. There was only one picture that came to mind. A football uniform. That would be the only appropriate attire for this occasion. I promised him that he would play football. Going to his drawer, I pulled out his new white football pants that he had just gotten for Christmas. He had several football jerseys to choose from. There was no question as to the one to use. Although he had some with team names or player numbers, it would be important to select the one that represented where his heart lived for most of his life. It had to be the royal blue jersey that would represent his love for U of K and his love for St. Gabriel. There was no name or number on the jersey. It was perfect. Although he loved the Irish of Notre Dame, the Pittsburgh Steelers, the San Francisco 49ers, the Trinity Shamrocks, and a few others, his true love existed mostly with the University of Kentucky Wildcats and the St. Gabriel Leopards. This had to have been because of his connection with the people at both places. There was a spiritual tie between them as well as his love for the sport. I carefully inspected the clothes to ensure that there were no stains on them. Then, I neatly folded them and rested them on top of the other clothes in the drawer so that they would be ready.

As the following week unfolded, I watched for a good opportunity to play the tape to Charlie. It would be one afternoon after the doctors had visited and when I did not anticipate any interruptions. Charlie kept his eyes closed in that semicoma state most of the time. Generally, I could get his attention for brief interactions. In an attempt to wake him, I mentioned that I had a tape from Jason. He barely opened his eyes in response. Believing that he could hear me, I told him that I would play it for him. No sooner did the tape begin with, "Hey Charlie. It's me," his eyes popped open and began to look in the direction of the tape player. Smiling at him, I said, "It's Jason. He sent you a letter on tape because he knew you couldn't read right now." His eyes remained wide open as he listened. Happiness was all over his face. I was so delighted that I had heard it previously, making it much easier to smile and add positive comments about what Jason was saying. It didn't disturb me at all to hear it this time because Charlie was enjoying it so much. The reminiscing was a tremendous joy. The love he felt for his friend Jason was expressed in his blue eyes. The only drawback was that the tape was over too soon. When I offered to play it again, he gave me a look of affirmation. So, I did. And it was good. What struck me was the response I got from Charlie. So often, when I would coax him into opening his eyes, he would either not open them or he would barely open them for a short time. Not this time, however. It was obvious that hearing from a friend had the most effective healing power. In spite of his weakened body and inability to speak, his eyes conveyed the message of joy. It was similar to the night that Jamie called. It was apparent that Jason gave him strength to live on.

The first week of May, Derby Week, was not quite the same as it had always been for us. Our festive traditions were not the priority. Nevertheless, it was important to maintain what traditions we could. Charles brought the children to Lexington a day early that weekend because school was out on Friday. They stayed with us a little longer interchanging our time between the hospital and the Ronald McDonald House.

Taking them home on Saturday as usual, I ended up at my parents' house to watch the Kentucky Derby. The children all put their quarters in the jackpot and picked out a horse for the race. The oddity about it all was the lack of spirit among us. Always inspired in the past by the spirit of jockeys and horse owners, as well as the beauty of the horses, I felt strange not experiencing this now. There were always good stories to hear about the people involved with the Derby. So often, perseverance and determination comprised the underlying message brought to the surface through the prestigious race. Each and every year of my life I felt a burst of excitement within me over the activities of Derby Week; it was plain to see that my heart was in another area now. There was no room left for anything else. I merely went through the motions of routine for the Derby.

When we returned on Sunday, I discovered that Charles had included Charlie in the Derby activities in the unit. Audrey offered them an opportunity to participate in the jackpot. It turned out that Charlie won. They had made a big deal out of it, making sure that Charlie enjoyed it, too. Actually, it was just a matter of tradition. It gave Charlie the opportunity to include normal activity amid the trauma in his life.

For the most part, Charlie had slipped back into sleeping most of the time. One day, when all factors indicated that we were losing ground, Dr. Jenkins came in with a feeling of conviction that it was time to stop treatment. Reviewing the charts, he had pretty well made up his mind. He walked over and stood beside Charlie's bed. As he began to examine him, Charlie looked straight into his eyes. He must have reached the doctor's soul with his piercing look. Immediately, Dr. Jenkins returned to the nurse's station and said, "I was ready to give up, but he's telling me not to." With that thought, he ordered the continuation of treatment.

Soon afterward, an evening came much like any other evening. It was after midnight when I told Charlie goodnight. I wished Bess, his nurse, a pleasant evening with the routine comment to please call if there were any changes. With her giving me her absolute assurance, I was able to leave without reservations. Arriving at the Ronald McDonald House late, I was ready for a quick night's sleep. As I freshened up and looked into the mirror, I decided that I could not go on another day with my hair looking so horrifyingly bad. It had become annoying and distracting to me throughout the day. Something had to be done with it without further delay, for it was important to be well groomed. At the same time, I despised having to spend so much time each morning trying to accomplish this. As tired as I was, I thought it best to go on and cut it before going to bed. After doing so, I decided to set my alarm an hour earlier so that I could give myself a perm. This would not only make me feel better, I knew that time was running out. I needed to be prepared at all times for what was to come. Knowing that I would not have time later to deal with uncooperative hair, my only choice was to fix it now.

As with every night, I prayed as my head hit the pillow. I lay there talking to God and reflecting on all that He had shown me. With my ears half opened for the voice of the housemother, my sleep was never in a deep state. All the parents were aware that the sound of a telephone meant trouble at the hospital. There was only one phone for incoming calls. It was in the housemother's room for a very good reason. She was also a counselor. If a child was critical or if death occurred, she would be prepared, as our cushion, to handle the family in their shock. Each night I listened. Once the phone rang, I waited and followed the sound of her quiet footsteps until she knocked at the door of the family

341

who received the call. My heart would flutter until I determined that she was not at my door. Judging her location according to sound, my empathy-filled soul throbbed for those parents as I prayed for God to be with them. The sincerity and support from the housemother were much appreciated by the parents, as she was always there to listen to those in need.

Morning came too soon. When the alarm went off at 5:00 A.M., my first thought was the same as every morning. Good. No phone calls. This meant that all was okay. I was tempted to call the hospital on the pay phone in the hallway. I even walked out to do so. Then, I decided against it. I hated to bother them, knowing how busy they were. I knew that they would call if there were a problem. So, I decided to go back into my room and just hurry in order to get over there as soon as possible. I dreaded having to give myself a perm. I really wanted to go on. But, I convinced myself that I should do so anyway. I had brought everything with me in case I ever got around to it. So, that's what I did. The entire time I worked on it, I thought of Charlie, frequently checking my time. No matter how many times I had given myself perms before, it was still not an easy task for me.

When the time came for the perm to set, I anxiously found myself in the hallway again with plans to call the unit to check on Charlie. As I picked up the phone I realized that it was nearly 7:00 A.M. It was time for shift change between the nurses. Realizing that it was an inconvenient time for them, I hung up the phone and decided I should just wait. Assuming all must be well, I tried to calm down and get ready to leave as soon as possible. Back in my room, I quickly cleaned up and finished doing my hair.

Just as I was walking out the door, a phone call came in from the hospital. I was taken aback to see the housemother at my door. She said not to worry but that Dr. Cottrill was on the phone. Dr. Cottrill began by saying that things were okay now, but Charlie had had a difficult night. They expected that I would have been there early because I normally was, and this is why she had not called me sooner. When she saw how late it was getting, she knew that she'd better call anyway. Dr. Cottrill went on to say that Charlie had kicked his right leg causing the

342

dialysis shunt in the femoral artery to fall out. When this happened, he lost a tremendous amount of blood. It being a major artery meant that blood gushed out with every beat of the heart. (He could have died within minutes.) She suggested that I come quickly to the hospital.

I was out the door immediately. When I arrived, Bess was still there. The day shift nurses were trying to explain to me what had happened, pointing out how awful Bess felt about my not getting the message. Several nurses were off to the side consoling her. I went over to Charlie's bed immediately to find him very agitated. I sensed a fear about him. After giving him reassurance and calming him down, I stepped to the side to speak with Bess. She was so apologetic. She said that she had given instructions for the charge nurse to call me and assumed that she had done so. She was somewhat composed, but her words indicated a feeling of betrayal toward me. She began to explain the course of events. She had just spent some time with Charlie and then turned and walked away. Within a couple of minutes, the respiratory therapist came in to check the respirator. As she straightened out his blanket, she pulled it back to spot a huge puddle of blood about the sheets. In shock, she hollered for help. Bess related that she rushed over and quickly applied pressure to the site. Fear aside, she took every appropriate step to save his life. She issued orders for others to get blood immediately. The crisis was intense as all were pitching in to help. Two units of fresh frozen-packed cells were administered immediately, followed by a third pint of blood.

As the tension began to break, Bess instructed the charge nurse in the unit to call me at the Ronald McDonald House. Bess was not about to leave his side for a second. Her being caught up in the moment, a great deal of time passed before she realized that I still had not arrived. Knowing my priorities, this surprised her. She inquired of the charge nurse if I was on my way. It wasn't until then that she discovered that I had never been called. The charge nurse told her that she decided not to call me because she figured that I needed my sleep. She saw that there was nothing that I could have done. This greatly upset Bess because she rationalized that the trust I had in her had now been broken.

There was much commotion going on in the unit now between working on Charlie's stabilization and the next shift change. Dr. Cottrill had come in as well to check on the crisis. This is when she discovered the course of events did not include a phone call to me. She immediately called me at that time.

Once Charlie had stabilized, Bess broke down and cried. Knowing the closeness that families and nurses feel at these times, her counterparts consoled her.

As I listened to the explanation of events, I was in disbelief over the nurse's decision not to call me. How could anyone assume that a mother who had been at her child's side for his whole life would rather sleep at a time when her child's life was so threatened? I let Bess know that I did not hold her responsible.

I had called Charles and told him about the event. He left work early that day so that he could get there sooner. The children were picked up early from school so they could all come and see him.

I knew that it was imperative for me to talk to the charge nurse who made the decision not to call me. I inquired as to who she was and where she was. She had already left for the day and would not be back until the 11:00 P.M. shift that night. The reason that I did not recognize her name was because she had been pulled into the unit from the neonatal intensive care unit. She did not normally work in that area, but staffing was short, which made it necessary. I informed the nurses that I wanted to talk to her. This should never have happened and I did not want another parent to ever have to go through something like this again.

They could probably see that I was terribly upset. I felt angry and nervous. I did not believe that I could handle not being with him when he died. I was in total disbelief that an outsider (so to speak) had made a decision about a life-or-death matter. Audrey was concerned about my reaction. Although she could understand it, she had never seen me upset before. She said to me, "I hope you're not too hard on her." She could see my stand but was worried about a potential conflict. I could only assure her that I would definitely speak to the girl and I would handle it

344

in a rational and justifiable manner. I knew that she could see my heartache, disappointment, and anger as the steam surfaced on my face.

Standing at Charlie's side, I saw that he remained frightened. Giving him assurance that he would be all right and that I'd be with him didn't help. I read cards and letters to him. I talked to him all day long. Hours later his eyes were getting heavy, yet he was determined to stay awake. It disturbed me to see him so scared. He probably didn't trust anyone at that point. I tried to talk him into closing his eyes to rest. I told him that his dad would be there soon and I would wake him up when he arrived. That didn't work either. His eyes remained wide open, taking in all of his surroundings. He stayed awake until Charles arrived. I was so happy for him to see his dad. Their special bond was obvious with the excited look on his face when Charles walked in the door. Charlie appeared more relaxed now. Still, he would not close his eyes for the rest of the day.

Dr. Jenkins made the decision at that point to start the regular form of hemodialysis, due to the complications at hand. This was something we all wished we could avoid. It required a huge machine, which made the treatment far more harsh on his system. Plainly, this trauma caused him more suffering.

That evening, Audrey brought in a recliner chair and invited me to stay the night in the unit. All the nurses went out of their way to make me comfortable. We stayed late but I felt that as things had settled down and stabilized that I should continue staying at the Ronald McDonald House. The primary reason for this was so that I would be more rested and committed to Charlie during the day.

That night, the charge nurse reluctantly came in to apologize to me for taking the situation into her own hands and not following the orders of Charlie's primary nurse. I looked into her eyes (although she could hardly look into mine for very long), and I said to her, "I have one question for you. Do you have any children?"

"No," was her reply.

Then I added, "I didn't think so. Perhaps this is not a good area for you to work in. I have five children. Do you have *any* idea how many times I've gotten up at night for a sick child? Do you know that I get up when they throw up? --- when they cry? --- when they fall out of bed? --- when they can't stop coughing? --- when they struggle to breathe?

She made a comment implying admiration for me.

Quickly, I said, "No, that is nothing to be admired. I've not done anything that any other mother would not do for her child. That's why I knew that you could not have any children. Someday you will understand when you have children of your own. Do you know that it doesn't bother me to get up for my children? Do you know that I *want* to be there for them? Do you think that a mother who gets up ten times a night for a child who is vomiting would not want to get up *once* for a child who is dying? Think about it. Didn't your mother get up for you when you were sick?"

She had little to say. She tried to explain her position and her decision. I told her that it was not her place to make the decision. She did not know me. Bess knew me and knew that I would want to know. She said that she did not ordinarily work in this unit.

I quickly came back with "all the more reason to listen to the primary nurse who knew the family better."

She promised that it would not happen again. I said to her, "I know that it won't happen again to me. Everyone will see to it, I'm sure. But, I'm more concerned about other parents. It should never happen to anyone ever again. If you call a parent and they decide not to come, then the consequences are for them to deal with. I doubt that any parent would not come. Just promise me that you'll think about this." I thanked her for coming in to listen to me. As bad as I felt for her, I knew it had to be said.

I was angry that this had happened. I could not allow it to be simplified in her mind. It was important to take a stand for other parents.

When the children were in town visiting the following day, I requested a VCR so that they could watch a movie with Charlie. This helped to pass some time with them. I was impressed that the nursing staff realized the importance of family unity. For them to allow four small children in the unit along with two parents was asking a lot. Yet, they never suggested that any of them leave. It helped that they were disciplined. When they did take a break away from the room, I put Charlie's favorite tape into the VCR. It was a Notre Dame football game that he had taped the previous season. Charlie enjoyed having it on while some doctors were taken by surprise to see Notre Dame playing football on a sunny spring day. Discovering that it was an old tape made them laugh. They were forever surprised to see what extremes we would go to, to have a good day.

When stabilization finally occurred again, Charles took the children back home. We did all that we could to prevent any unnecessary loss of school for any of them. Knowing that concentration was hard, it was important that they be at school every day. I instructed Charles on these unusual occasions when they would get home extremely late, to allow them to sleep in the morning. He could take them a couple of hours late rather than miss an entire day. He was equally exhausted. People were understandable about their being late for school or work. All were supportive.

When I had last spoken to Bette, Robby's mom, she asked what she could do to help. I suggested that she ask the seventh grade class from St. Gabriel to send Charlie some cards. His heart had always remained with the children in that class although he had been away now for four years. I told her that nothing would please him more than to hear from them. So, that's what she had them do. Bette brought an envelope full of letters from the class. When I was alone with Charlie, I began to read some of the letters. He lay there looking calmly into my eyes as I read. As he tired, his eyes began to close. After a few moments I stopped reading, assuming that he was asleep. Right away, however, he opened his eyes again and stared into mine. He was letting me know that I should continue reading. With that, I chuckled at him for getting the message to me to go on. I suggested that he could hardly hold his eyes open. I said, "Tell you what, Charlie. You close your eyes and rest and I'll keep reading until I've finished the last one." Hesitant at first, he kept his eyes open. It was only with a repeated promise that he closed his eyes. I read letter after letter from all his friends. It was one of the most consoling things that I could have done for him. He found great comfort hearing from the people that he loved best. Those friends that he was sure had forgotten about him were the ones that gave him strength. Oftentimes I would go back and reread cards and letters. It was clear that he enjoyed hearing them more than once.

When the certainty of death became closer, Fr. Dan came to visit. He offered to give Charlie the last rights. He also inquired about Confirmation. I established that Charlie had not made this sacrament just yet, adding that he would have made it the following year. Without hesitation, he offered to do it now. I was quite surprised, as I was not prepared for it. We had not discussed a saint's name to use, according to tradition. Fr. Dan stated that Charlie's real name would be fine and I was not to be concerned about it. He saw this additional grace as being a source of strength for Charlie.

So pleased that he offered, I graciously accepted, having never witnessed this sacrament individually before. It was a beautiful and uplifting experience although Charlie remained in his semicomatose state. There was never a time that I questioned if Charlie was aware of the activity around him. I knew that he understood. The prayers said over him gave me comfort and allowed him to maintain a sense of peace.

Once the formal prayers were completed, Fr. Dan offered his consolation. As we talked and shared, he pointed out to me that Charlie was not alone. I knew that and never questioned it. Yet, as we stood over his bed, looking down on him, I listened openly. Fr. Dan added, "Jesus is with Charlie as he suffers. He is lying there with him, not next to him, but within him. He is one with Charlie as he suffers. Jesus always suffers with us. He would never ask us to go through anything alone."

I contemplated his words after he left, knowing how right he was. I looked at Charlie and thought of how Jesus was with him so often in Holy Communion. I recalled my own very first experience of Communion when I could literally feel Jesus within my heart. Recognizing the joy that lived in Charlie's heart, I could easily picture Jesus being with him always. Now with the sacrament of Confirmation given Charlie as well, I felt even more secure. I had been asked to speak for him during the ceremony just as I had when he was baptized. I felt so blessed to have been given this opportunity especially because Charlie had revealed to me his concerns about his fear of death. The peace he displayed confirmed that Jesus was with him and his fears had dissipated. I found great comfort in Fr. Dan's reinforcement on this matter, which freed me from ever questioning the issue of his fear. There was never a temptation to assume that God had ever left either one of us. His presence was felt at all times.

Audrey and I had been drawn more frequently to share stories of our pasts with each other. Often, we discovered miracles of God occurring in our stories. Each of us was in awe over the other's experiences. The activity of the Holy Spirit was plainly visible between us. As weeks passed, we became closer. It was a beautiful experience every time we shared. I was a bit concerned once again about provoking an unethical relationship between a patient's family and staff. Nevertheless, our spiritual bond ruled every time. One day, in our excitement, Audrey invited me to go out to dinner with her. She was convinced that it would do me good to get out of the hospital for an evening. We discussed planning this for the following Wednesday when Charles would be coming back in town. I agreed that he could watch Charlie while we were out, providing Charlie didn't have any drastic setbacks.

When Wednesday rolled around, his health remained steady. I changed out of my jeans into something dressier and informed Charlie that I would not be gone long. Audrey came to the unit dressed sharply as well. Out of her scrubs, she had a different appearance than what I had been used to. It was funny how just the clothes that we wore lifted our spirits. She came over to speak to Charlie before we left. This departure from him was strangely uplifting. Whereas, any other time that I left the unit, it was heart wrenching. We both sensed the power of God between us.

Arriving at the restaurant, we were seated and began a relaxing conversation. Shortly thereafter, our thoughts became spiritual again. She said to me, "There's something very different going on in Charlie's room. I don't know if you've sensed it or not, but I can feel a presence every time I go in there.

It doesn't matter if I'm going to be in there for a long time or just to hang a bag of fluids. I can feel a supernatural presence every time I enter his room. It's almost eerie. It's so profound. I just had to tell you that."

"Wow! That's really something." I said.

She went on to say that it didn't matter who else was in the room. The presence was always there. I was taken aback by the words she spoke. I felt her sincerity and conviction. I knew that Jesus was with Charlie. I could feel His presence with me, too. But for her to recognize His Spirit in Charlie's room was a beautiful testimony. She finally said, "I can feel God in his room. In all of my years of nursing I have never felt anything like this before."

I was so touched that God was using Charlie in this capacity. I felt honored to be able to offer my child's suffering for the sake of bringing others closer to Him. Meanings began to unravel. I could see God using Charlie now just as He used Charlie at St. Gabriel, and just as He used Charlie to touch people at his other schools and everywhere else that he went.

We discussed the decision to have the surgery. I told Audrey that God revealed to me that this would be the end, whether he had surgery or not. Several events and memories were shared with her. I knew that Charlie would not be leaving the hospital. I disclosed my feelings of betrayal as a mother in that I should have kept him at home to die. She assured me that it would have been much worse to watch him struggling to breathe, knowing that I could have given him a chance. Oddly enough, in spite of the whole event, and in spite of struggling with guilt, I remained steadfast in the decision that it was right. I was reminded of the words that I heard while in church: "It's time to leave your children and follow me."

The rest of the evening we discussed every topic relating to children and family. She said to me how good it was for the nurses to see the unity in my family. The love, support, and happiness within us impressed her. She watched us when the trials were hard and when things ran relatively smoothly. She actually looked forward to seeing the children come in.

I don't know why on that particular night, I felt peace and protection. There was a sense of security having Audrey's beeper with us for quick contact from the hospital, but there was more to it than that. There was a serenity about the evening that gave me confidence that all was well.

The next afternoon, Bess came by the hospital to pick up her paycheck. Upon stopping in to check on Charlie, we began to talk. As our conversation quickly became intensely personal, she invited me to go out with her for a drink. As Audrey was on duty with Charlie, I agreed. We walked to a nearby club and sat down to share more over a beer. Although I wasn't particularly fond of beer, the intimacy of our conversation made it taste suddenly good. Our souls seemed to connect as we were drawn to talk about God in our lives. Not long into our discussion, she openly said to me that she felt something supernatural in Charlie's room. She added that she felt it every time she tended to him.

This instantly brought a smile to my face as I asked her "Have you been talking to Audrey?" Assuming that she had to have been discussing it, I was quite taken aback when she denied it saying, "No. Why?"

"Because she just told me the very same thing yesterday," I exclaimed. My statement surprised both of us. Yet, neither found the content surprising. God was working through Charlie in a powerful way.

Walking back to the hospital, we shared much about our families and the times that God was there for us. She admitted having lost touch with God at times and commented that she had not been to church in about twenty years. There was a longing in her voice that indicated her awareness of missing her relationship with God. I then shared with her how God had helped me through so many trials and assured her that it was only by the grace of God that I could find strength to get through this one.

By the time we returned to the unit, we had established a deeper bond; one that was united with God. Together, we were made to feel more prepared to face the remainder of this trial.

The following Friday night, Shane, Wilma and Scotty's son, died. It was a horrifying experience for the family and all of us

351

who had grown close to them. It was reality that we couldn't grasp. We knew. We saw. We understood it to be real. Yet, our minds could not analyze the reality. Our minds were numb. Our hearts were sunken. Our bodies merely existed.

He was to be laid out on Sunday at a funeral home in a nearby town. This Sunday happened to be Mother's Day. I would be staying in Lexington this weekend with all the children so that the family could be together on that day. Each mother at the Ronald McDonald House was presented with a flower and small balloon from the manager of the house. It being Sunday, Charles and I attended different Masses so that one of us could stay with Charlie. Afterward, the children all gave me their special gifts. Ironically, Charlie woke up to the fullest degree that day. He remained awake longer than ever before. He smiled his biggest smile and made my day complete. He remained alert for most of the day. I told him that his smile was the best Mother's Day gift that he could give me. My heart was filled with indescribable joy as I kissed his marshmallow cheek and stroked his fine hair. He remained awake long enough for everyone to get a chance to visit with him. His cousin was allowed in for a few minutes and shared a poster with him. Charlie moved his eyes up and down scanning all around him. He continued to smile as his eyes caught a glimpse of everyone in the room. I didn't want this time to pass. Yet, I knew that I needed to go to the funeral home for Shane's family, in particularly for his mother. I couldn't imagine a harder day of the year to be there than on Mother's Day. With great hesitation, I left Charlie and told him I'd be back shortly. The young woman whose baby was also in the hospital had asked to go with me. She didn't have a car and I would be her only way of getting to the funeral home. Together, we went to visit, talking about God and the certainty of our children going to heaven. I felt a little guilty that my son was doing so well that day and other children were not. When we arrived at the funeral home, Wilma asked about Charlie with sincere hope for good news. I told her of the wonderful day that we were having. She was truly happy for me, as she did not express any sign of jealousy or envy toward me. Although she had lost her son, she was able to maintain her love

352

for God and her neighbors. Astounded at her strength, yet not surprised, I hugged her and supported her in her grief. Before we parted, she wished me well with Charlie. I commented on how blessed I felt for having this special day with him. Then, I expressed that it was the calm before the storm. Although I hoped that the outlook would change, I believed that God allowed us this special time because it was Mother's Day. I imagined it was like that for Mary when her eyes met with Jesus on His way to Calvary. Through the locking of eyes they must have experienced the joy of their meeting as they suffered the awareness of each other's pain. Only through the power of God could I experience these emotions at the same time. This same power allowed Wilma to feel joy for me as she grieved over the loss of her son. I sensed blessings poured out in abundance over all of us.

Within a week the other woman's baby died as well. Speaking to her at the Ronald McDonald House, she commented, "I knew it would be raining on the day that she died." She was right. The day was as dark as they come. The rain was heavy. We both peered out the window with little to say. I wasn't surprised. The darkness seemed to indicate the state of her soul. I do not mean to imply sin. Rather, it was the unawareness of God in her life. I empathized with her more for the loss of God than for the loss of her daughter. Picturing the separation from her precious child was enough to tear my heart in many pieces. Not understanding God's purpose at the time was even harder. I feared that this woman would never know God in her despair.

Time crept onward. One day when Audrey came in to work, I noticed her usual smile of compassion turn brighter as the joy from within her soul escaped to cover her entire face. She proudly brought out a gift for Charlie. It was a stoneware dove on a simple ribbon necklace.

She then shared an intimate experience that she had with God on the day before. Having the day off, she went to a quiet, special place on top of a mountain not too far away. She lay back and enjoyed the serenity of the eagles that flew ever so gently over her head. While there, she made a vow to God pertaining to

353

Charlie. (Oh how touched I was to feel our souls meet with God's love.) After descending from the mountain, she stopped in a gift shop and bought the dove necklace for Charlie. We embraced in tears as I thanked her for sharing so much of herself with us. I then wrapped the necklace around Charlie's wrist where it could be easily seen. The respirator, tubes, and IV prevented me from placing it around his neck. This simple dove served as a constant reminder of God's presence and the spiritual union among God, Charlie, Audrey, and me.

As Charlie's health worsened, I noticed that there was a strange distance growing between Dr. Cottrill and myself. I felt her choosing not to say much to me. A grief counselor came in one day to offer support in dealing with Charlie's illness. She suggested that I join a support group that met regularly in the hospital. Not feeling a need for this, I declined. She informed me that Dr. Cottrill was very concerned about me. I told her that what I grieved for at this point was not Charlie. Rather it was the distance that seemed to suddenly exist between Dr. Cottrill and me. I didn't want to hurt her for anything. Yet, I felt that I had already done so by being friends with her. Now she would have to undergo Charlie's death not only as a doctor but also as a friend of mine. "I never intended to hurt her like this," I said.

I was being selfish by becoming her friend and putting her in this awkward position. I told the counselor that I believed that she had certain knowledge about Charlie and was hesitant to share it with me for fear of hurting me. I was crushed. The woman tried to console me, but it was difficult to express to her just how much Dr. Cottrill meant to me. She offered to speak with her for me. This suggestion made me feel rather strange. I never needed anyone to speak for me before. I wasn't afraid to speak to her myself, but she just didn't seem to give me the opportunity. It was as though she were avoiding me. Then I said, "I believe that Dr. Cottrill knows that Charlie is dying, but she can't tell me."

Again, the counselor offered to speak to her. Finally, I agreed. However, I also asked her to let Dr. Cottrill know that I wanted to speak to her, as well. This distance disturbed me more

354

than the events of the day because I could not bear dealing with the end without her at my side.

Once the counselor spoke to Dr. Cottrill, the truth came to surface. Dr. Cottrill came to assure me that she wasn't keeping any specific knowledge from me. Rather, she expressed her concern about me, wondering if I was accepting the reality of what was taking place. I asked her if she was feeling hesitant to share Charlie's condition with me. I asked if God had told her anything that I should know. Her answer was, "No." She had been thinking of what I shared with her before the operation about Charlie's time being complete here on earth. From a medical standpoint, things were not getting better. She feared that I was living on false hope.

I told her that although I believed what God revealed to me was true, I still had hope that I was wrong about it. I could see the roller coaster that we were on. "I know that the complications are serious. I also know that they have been serious in the past. I know that Charlie has surprised the doctors before and I could not be certain that it would not happen again. With all due respect, I'm waiting for God to tell me when it's over." She was concerned that we might be causing him unnecessary suffering by prolonging his life with treatment. I told her that until God tells me otherwise, we must continue to treat him. It was a day-to-day, hour-to-hour watch. "One day he looks like he's going to live and the next day it looks like he's going to die." I could see that from a medical standpoint that he was dying. However, I felt that it wasn't right to make decisions solely on that. God had always indicated to me the right moves to make in the past. I knew in my heart that He would guide me this time, too.

With the observance of Charlie's continued semicomatose state, Dr. Cottrill suggested that a CAT scan be ordered on his brain and a neurologist called in to verify brain activity. This would assist in decision making. I agreed, knowing that she felt that he had a significant amount of brain damage. Personally, I believed that he was very much aware of what was going on around him. I had seen him respond when no one else did. By being at his side constantly, I was given these treasured moments. Understandably though, most other people seldom

355

witnessed any responses, whatsoever. He would often fall back to sleep before anyone had this opportunity.

The scan was done and the neurologist reported that there was very little brain damage. She said that he had scattered spots throughout the brain, but nothing to indicate serious damage. This was a relief to me, for I had prayed that he would not become vegetative. I supposed that it was only making it harder for Dr. Cottrill, though. It was clear that no decision could be made based on brain damage as it was minimal.

With every passing day, I found it more frightening when I had to leave the hospital. The next weekend was the annual Mother-Daughter breakfast at church. As with every other Saturday afternoon, I dreaded leaving for Louisville. Yet, again I was reminded of the importance of being a mother to all of my children. I had always looked forward to this event at St. Gabriel and knew that this year, in particular, was even more important. It was not the speaker that made the difference. Rather, it was important to show my girls how special they were to me.

I was apprehensive that my children would question that I loved Charlie more than any of them. They needed to know that they were equally special. I feared that they would misunderstand why I needed to spend so much time with their brother. In spite of all my attempts to spend time with each of the children, I knew that they felt abandoned by me. Our time together was mostly at the hospital with the exception of the one day a week. From Saturday to Sunday afternoon, the other children had me to themselves. To me, it was a joyful time filled with intense heartache due to the separation from Charlie. The separation was painfully long and the visit was painfully short. Six days passed between my visits with them at home. As much as I wanted to be with them, I could not allow them more time.

As the days passed, one problem after another occurred. Charlie began to have esophageal bleeding, which required immediate irrigation. The nurses were in constant watch over him. On occasion I offered to assist in the routine treatments, as I had learned how things were done. It gave me something to do and the opportunity to be a mother.

356

Gradually, the intensity of matters worsened. Dr. Cottrill was still very much concerned if we were doing the right thing by keeping him alive. He was now getting blood on a regular basis without improvement in his condition. She suggested that a meeting should be called among all the doctors involved in the case. They needed to address their own area of expertise and see how each treatment of a particular body part was coinciding with the other. There were so many doctors involved by now that a joint decision on the overall potential of improvement needed to be made. It was imperative for the group to collaborate on the issue. I agreed that this was necessary. I told Dr. Cottrill that I did not want to see him suffer, but if I was supposed to keep fighting for him, I also didn't want to give up. She understood where I was coming from.

That night when I went to bed, I pleaded with God. I said to Him, "What am I supposed to do? I can see that medically speaking things are going downhill. I also sense that Charlie is still being strong and holding on to life. I need for You to tell me what to do. I cannot stop the aggressive treatment without You telling me to do so. I wouldn't feel right taking his life into my hands. You must understand that I can't go strictly by the doctors. You've got to show me. Please, Dear Lord, please tell me what to do. My heart aches for Dr. Cottrill. She thinks that I don't see. She thinks that I am denying the truth. She feels responsible for all this pain and suffering that Charlie is going through. She believes that it's over and we are putting him through unnecessary treatment. She may be right. But how am I to be sure? Just when I'm convinced that he's dying, he takes me by surprise with a turn in the opposite direction. So many times he should not have lived, but did. You've always directed me during those times. Please show me. Please tell me. Please, Dear Lord, please. I'm waiting for You to tell me that his time is up." My heart throbbed. The pain was as sharp as a grinding sword. The pillow was soaked. I turned it over. After exhausting all tears, I reached for the other pillow, as my bed was empty. I thought of the family at home. I thought of Charles trying to sleep in his empty bed as well. I thought of the children having to face school in the morning with torn hearts. Surrendering my mind and body to God, I finally drifted off to sleep.

In the morning, I moved quickly to get to the hospital, never knowing quite what to expect when I got there. Walking into Charlie's room, I noticed something about him that told me instantly that the time had come. I don't know if it was the grayish color or the look on his face. All I knew was the clarity of the message: "It's over. The end has come." It took me aback because I did not go into the room looking for or expecting to find an answer to my prayer. The only thing I had on my mind was the same thought that I always had each time I returned. That thought was the hope that he was still alive. I feared whenever I left the Ronald McDonald House in the morning that he might not be alive by the time I reached his room. My thoughts and prayers in traveling were always the same: "Please let him be alive." I wanted to be with him when the time came for him to leave.

I was pleased to get a message from God this morning. It was the answer that I had been waiting for. It was not the substance of the answer that I was waiting for. Rather, it was clarity from God in accordance to His will. That's what I needed to hear. I could not see interfering with His plan even if it meant more suffering for Charlie. This is why I could not say, "Turn the respirator off or stop the dialysis." God had never specified the time with me and therefore I felt an obligation to provide Charlie with the fullness of life every minute that he was alive. There was a stubbornness in me that prohibited giving up with even the smallest of gifts. Although I did not know the extent of God's reasoning for the prolonged suffering, I knew that it was His will to have Charlie live for this extended amount of time.

The group meeting was to be held that afternoon. However, at this point I no longer saw a need for it. God had just made it clear to me what His intentions were. After spending a short time with Charlie, I went out to call home. I told Charles that he needed to take the children out of school and bring them all to Lexington. I told him that the time was very near.

"Are you sure?" he questioned. "What happened?"

"Nothing specific. I can just tell by looking at him," I responded. "Pack enough clothes for a few days and plan to stay here until it's over."

"What do I tell them at work? How long do you think I'll be there? Are you sure?" he repeated. I could understand his questioning because for almost two months Charlie had been going back and forth between progress and regression.

"Yes, I'm sure. You need to come and you need to stay. You'll have to tell them that at work."

He was concerned that they would not understand, that they might not like him taking off like that. I said to him, "Right now, work doesn't matter. If you lose your job, it doesn't matter. What matters is the little time you have left with your son. You need to be here. You will regret it later if you're not." It puzzled him that I was suddenly so certain that death was near. Just yesterday, I was more encouraging about Charlie's life. Nevertheless, he trusted what I said and began to get the children's clothes packed.

I called Jackie's school, Sacred Heart Academy, and spoke to the counselor. I told her that Jackie's brother would be going to heaven soon. Her dad would be picking her up and she would be staying until it was over. I couldn't be certain that she would return for the end of the school year. Although exams were scheduled for the following week, I knew that her mind would be in no condition to take them. I was told not to be concerned about it. It would be taken care of later.

I had the day to myself with Charlie. I found that I just wanted to be close to him. Leaning over the right side of his bed, I began to stroke his hair and talk to him. My heart began to speak: "Oh Charlie, I didn't want it to be like this. I never wanted you to suffer this way." My throat was tight, my heart was heavy, and my stomach was jittery. "I love you, Charlie. I love you so much. I'm so sorry. I'm sorry that you had to suffer. I would give anything to take your place."

He opened his eyes and looked at me. His beautiful baby-blue eyes gazed into mine. I said, "Charlie? I believe that Jesus is going to take you to heaven pretty soon." He stared calmly. He didn't appear scared. He looked at me as though he already knew. As I thought back on the moment that his surgery began, I imagined what it was like when his heart had stopped for five minutes. I knew in my heart that he must have had a supernatural experience at that time.

Then I said to him, "I believe that Jesus has shown you a little bit of heaven already." Instantly, his eyes widened. He began to squirm and his eyes got even larger. He was telling me "Yes, I've been there." His eyes pierced my soul with affirmation. It occurred to me at that moment that this must have been the message that he so desperately was trying to tell me when he first woke up from surgery. It was no wonder that he shook his head no when Dr. Cottrill told him that he was going to be okay. He knew otherwise. He knew it all along. I added, "He did show you heaven, didn't He?" He started to calm down. I continued saying, "Oh Charlie, I know you'll be happy because God promised you that. But you were right. We are going to miss you terribly. I don't want you to worry about that though because I know that God will take care of us. We'll be okay. I want you to know, Charlie, that I will always be with you. And you will always be with me. Nothing will ever separate us. Remember that, Charlie. We will always be together because you will always be in my heart. By now, we were both crying. Fat teardrops rolled down the side of his face. My eyes seeped although I did not cry aloud. Our hearts were locked, sharing our ultimate love and pain. I continued to speak, feeling it was important to cover many areas, about which I figured he would have questions, interests, or concerns. "You know, Charlie, there are a lot of people in heaven waiting for you. You're going to be so happy. Betsy will be there. And Grandma. I know Grandma can't wait to see you. And Paul Combs. And Carl. And you'll get to meet Dr. Cottrill's little girl, Crissie. She'll be happy to meet you, knowing that her mother has taken care of you. Do you know that it is because of Crissie that Dr. Cottrill was here for you? She became a doctor because of her little girl." I elaborated some on her story and how it was that she became his doctor. "And there's another special person waiting to meet you, your uncle John. Do you remember how you couldn't wait to meet Uncle Tommy so that you would know all of your aunts and

360

uncles? Well there's one more for you to meet, my younger brother, John. Do you remember me telling you about him?" He died as a baby and I never saw him. I went on telling him about saints, relatives, and ancestors that he would meet. By now, I had lain my head on his pillow with him. My legs were locked and I no longer felt the weight of my body on them. I continued to stroke his hair and occasionally kissed his soft cheek.

Then I had to address the touchiest subject of all --- football. I began by saying, "I know that I promised you that you would play football. I'm sure that God will take care of that for you." I really didn't like talking about this topic. I was so afraid that I would say the wrong thing. I had to find the spiritual part of football and go with that because no matter how I thought about it, I could not picture material things in heaven. So I said to him, "When you get to heaven you will be able to pick any football game that you want to go to and join any player you want to play with. Your spirit will be able to play with them. I will be watching for you in all the games." Still feeling a bit confused over this, I felt an obligation to mention it. It was what he always dreamt of. It was his life. It was his personality. I myself could not picture Charlie without football. So, how could God separate this part of his soul? His love for football was the largest part of his spirit. The more I thought about it, I couldn't imagine God's taking this away from him. So, I told Charlie, "I'm sure that God will let you play football." Immediately, I said privately to God, "I sure hope you have some spiritual way for him to play the game." For the entire rest of the day, I talked to him, lifting my head only when medical personnel came to do whatever treatment. I addressed each sibling in my conversation and cited memories for Charlie to recall. He listened, sometimes with eyes opened and sometimes with eyes closed. I knew that he could hear me, so I continued talking, only stopping when interrupted by someone's entering the room.

That evening, Charles came with the children. The meeting was being held among the doctors. While they were in discussion, I took the opportunity to speak to the children. As his dad, Jackie, and Marty visited with Charlie, I walked Leslie and Jonathan down the hall. Beyond the waiting area, there was a long row of windows. I liked being in that spot because I could enjoy the sunlight. I sat down on the ledge above the registers with my arms around my little ones. The sun warmed my back. After hearing about their week, I proceeded to tell them that Charlie would be going to heaven pretty soon. When they asked why, I told them that all the medicine and treatments weren't helping him to get any better.

Then Jonathan, in his youthful innocence asked me, "Why can't Jesus save Charlie?"

Putting him on my lap, I told him why. I began, saying, "Jesus *did* save Charlie. Jesus saved Charlie lots of times. The last time He saved him was when you were a baby. You were six-months-old and we had just moved into our new house. Charlie was real sick and needed a heart operation. I asked Jesus to let him live so that you could get to know him. I asked Him to give Charlie some time to play with you. All of Charlie's friends went to church and asked Jesus to save him, too. And so, that's what He did. Jesus saved Charlie so that you could be happy and know your brother. Now it's Charlie's turn to be happy. He's been sick for a long time and he's not very happy. He's been in a lot of pain. He's had that respirator in his mouth for weeks and he's really uncomfortable. So, you see, Jesus is going to take Charlie to heaven so that he can be happy, now."

There was a somber acceptance of what I said. With my right arm around Leslie, I noticed that she had nothing to say. I held them both in my arms and clung tightly to the knot in my throat, hoping that I would be able to control my emotions. How could I convince them that Charlie would be happy if I were crying? We sat there for a while sharing our thoughts. I was pleased that the Holy Spirit had given me the strength and the words to say that comforted them.

Next, I went back to the unit and told Jackie and Marty. They were both quiet in their thoughts. Jackie had a definite anger expressed on her face. Marty maintained a serious look, taking everything in.

In due time, the group meeting among the doctors came to an end. The consensus was that all aggressive treatment should be stopped. In reviewing his progress and course of events since his admission, it was clear that in spite of more aggressiveness, his body was deteriorating. There was no dispute over this. All the records proved it. Not only that, I knew it was time to stop as well. My concern at this time was for Charlie. What would be the best and least painful way of proceeding? I was determined to make it the best it could be. Piece by piece, I picked apart our options. Starting with the dialysis, it could be turned off. This was not a good choice I maintained, explaining that I didn't want to see him blown up as he was before. This was bound to make him more miserable, so I could not agree with it. I also didn't want him to die and look down upon the body that I had seen weeks before. I couldn't bear seeing him like that again, nor did I think that Charlie would want to see himself like that. I agreed to cut back on the dialysis so that he would not have to take the force against his weak body as often. Next, there were blood transfusions and antibiotics to consider. It was recommended that we stop both. I would not agree to stop the antibiotics. My reasoning for this was because infection causes misery. Comfort was my goal and I could not allow infection to take him over.

Dr. Cottrill explained the course of events that would take place if the transfusions were stopped. She explained that we could expect him to bleed out from his esophagus and from all orifices. It could not be determined how long it would be before this would happen, but usually within a few days. I was concerned about the bleeding from all orifices. It sounded like a horrendous sight. I was told that because of the outpouring of blood becoming so great, it generally clots in the tubing, thus forcing it out another way.

"What about pain?" I asked.

"Actually, this is the least painful. It just looks horrible," Dr. Cottrill explained.

"Then that's what we'll do," I said. She added that those who go in this manner are very calm and not agitated.

The respirator was not an option because he continued to have adequate brain activity. This was a blessing in itself because I did not want to deal with deliberate suffocation. Pain medicine would continue to be given and I requested that the Lorazipam also be made available for agitation.

Although my discussion with Dr. Cottrill was private, the children had grasped what was taking place. I briefly explained to them what we had discussed and emphasized that it was not fair to make him suffer any longer. I noticed the expression on Jackie's face. She refused to say much except that she couldn't believe that I would let them give up. I knew that she was feeling betrayed and would not have anything to do with me. The room was filled with crying eyes. Not only was the family crying, so were doctors and nurses. Everyone hugged and supported one another. Leslie, whose faith was strong at eight-years-old, walked across the room to retrieve a box of Kleenex. She was the only one in the room that wasn't crying. Going from person to person, she handed out Kleenex to everyone. When she came to me she said, "Here Mommy. You're gonna need this. It's going to be okay, Mom. You know Charlie's going to be happy in heaven. Besides, I want you to come home. I want all of this to be over." I wrapped my arm around her and sat her on my lap with Jonathan at my side.

Leslie had already accepted the ending, knowing that God would take Charlie to heaven. It had been a year since her First Communion and I sensed that it was because of the Eucharist that she was so open to Jesus.

After the initial shock among us, Dr. Cottrill went up to Charlie and told him that he would be going to heaven. She spoke to him a while and concluded, "Now you can be quarterback for Notre Dame." She never forgot his first true love, Notre Dame football. It was a moving moment.

Over the next few days, I notified various people to inform them of the expectation of Charlie's death. Wanting to spend every moment with Charlie, I agreed to let others help me. The word was passed on to all those who had been following the trial. Relatives helped in every way that they could. One called funeral homes to ask the questions that I was concerned about, thus saving me many phone calls. I was able to let go of responsibilities around me and concentrate on Charlie and the family.

I kept vigil at his bedside from that moment on. I found myself speaking softly into Charlie's ear for endless hours. This time was a treasure. I had the opportunity to speak to him from the heart about all the things that mattered. I spoke about his friends and cousins. I spoke of how it hurt me to be so helpless. I spoke about all the good people that God had put in his life, including those from The Easter Seal Society, celebrities, teachers, doctors, nurses, relatives, friends, and acquaintances. There was no topic untouched. After all, we were given time to share all that we could.

Other times when I found myself exhausted at night, I slept sitting in the chair next to his bed. I held his hand as I slept with my head on the heart-shaped pillow on his bed. This pillow was a gift from the hospital, which was used for autographs from those who visited. I frequently read the signatures and contemplated how Charlie's death may affect their lives. It crushed me to think of all the broken hearts. I sobbed endlessly at times with my head hugging the pillow, not realizing that my tears were causing the names to run. I never let go of his hand even when I slept. This way I could detect if he became agitated or sense if he should wake up.

By Friday, his condition had not changed significantly. Jackie and her boyfriend, John, were also keeping a close vigil. There came a time when I took Jackie downstairs to the coffee shop so that we would have the opportunity to talk. She was in a tough spot. John would celebrate his high school graduation on Sunday. She didn't know whether she should go to the graduation in Louisville or stay with Charlie. She desperately wanted to go and felt that she should go because she anticipated a future life with this young man. I could see that it was very important to her. As we sat in the coffee shop and talked, she said to me that she wanted to be here for Charlie, too. I could see how torn she was. "How long do you think it will be? Could this go on for days? If so, maybe I should go. I just don't want Charlie wondering why I wouldn't be here for him. Do you think that I would have time to go and come back before he dies?"

I assured her that Charlie was aware that she had been here for most of the last seven weeks. "He knows that you've been here for him and he knows that you love him. One thing that we can't know is exactly when someone will die. He could very

365

easily die while we are sitting down here for these few minutes. We have no way of knowing." I could certainly understand her dilemma. I was torn every time I left the room, too. "I believe that if Charlie could talk, he would want you to go to John's graduation. But, most importantly, the decision has to be yours. It has to be one you can live with. Could you live with it if he were to die while you were gone? Could you live with it if you stayed and missed the graduation and he didn't die until after it was over? It's going to be hard to decide, but I can't tell you what to do. The decision has to be yours. Only you know what choice you can live with. When is John leaving?"

"He has to go on back tonight," she replied.

"What if we find someone to take you late on Saturday? You could spend the night at Granddad's, go to the graduation in the morning and then come back on Sunday evening." This sounded like the decision she wanted to hear. I asked her again, "Are you sure that's what you want to do?"

I did not want to encourage her in any way because I was afraid that I might force a decision that she could not live with. Again, I questioned if she could handle it if he died while she was gone. In the attempt to help her be certain, I insisted that she look closely at how her choice would affect her. She could make her final decision the following day.

Dr. Cottrill and her husband, Tom, watched the other children and allowed them to spend several nights at their house. This was a tremendous relief as there was hardly room for them all in the unit. Nor would it have been appropriate for them to stay endlessly. By going with Dr. Cottrill, the children could have time to play and relax rather than spending endless hours at the hospital.

After a very agitated evening on Friday, I insisted that he be given more medication for comfort. The nurse was concerned that he was already getting far more than the recommended dosage for an adult and she didn't want to be responsible for his death. I was upset seeing him suffer and squirm for hours after a visitor had come in. My own sleep deprivation added to my sensitivity as well. Regardless, it was heartbreaking to see him suffer the way that he did. Knowing what we were facing, I could see no point in depriving him of comfort. No one should have to suffer this way on his deathbed. After debating with the nurse for some time, I could no longer be tormented watching Charlie's restlessness. Around 2:00 A.M. I finally went down the hall and called Dr. Cottrill, dreading to wake her from her sleep. Yet, because the nurse was not responding to my plea, I had no choice. I could not allow him to suffer for several more hours by waiting for the next shift to make a decision. The nurse blamed the late visitor for getting him stirred up because until that time he had been resting well. But, I saw that the time was now. None of us could undo the visit. We could, however, address the agitation. Whether it was the visitor or not, I still didn't feel right allowing this agitation.

Finally, a doctor came in to monitor him. Standing at the door with the nurse, I could see that he was apprehensive about doing anything more. I suggested Lorazipam rather than more morphine. I didn't want to deliberately kill him either. I just wanted him comfortable. He agreed to give Charlie a small dose, which did ease his agitation.

His dad slept on a cot at the foot of Charlie's bed. The nurse wanted me to sleep and have his dad get up with Charlie. But, I didn't want to. I had already tried to sleep in the recliner but couldn't. It was not because of comfort but because I couldn't reach Charlie's hand while I slept. I was adamant about holding his hand so that I would know when he reached the hour of his death. I was petrified of lying on the cot and chancing his passing without me. So, I sat on the edge of a recliner and lay my head on Charlie's bed to sleep, holding his hand all the while.

Saturday morning, I finally agreed to nap on the cot trusting that Charles would wake me if there were any changes. I could no longer trust that the nurses would wake me. Both Bess and Audrey were off that weekend. Not having bonded the same way with the other nurses, I sensed that they would not understand the importance of holding him when he died. Having been deceived before by well-intentioned nurses, I could not take the chance this time.

The attitude of the night-shift nurse proved her lack of understanding. She mistook Charles' sleeping on the cot as selfishness on his part. Had she known us, she would have seen that I wanted him to sleep as well as he could. I had absolutely *no* desire to lie down, as the three-foot separation from Charlie's bed would have caused a pain in my heart far more intense than what was already present. I knew that his dad could trust me to wake him up if Charlie's condition worsened. I also knew that if Charles slept through the night, then I could trust him to do the same for me when I rested during the day.

I later called Fr. Bill to inform him that Charlie was about to go to heaven. Although he could not be with us in person, I was aware that he was with us in spirit. He, along with the parishioners of St. Gabriel, would be praying for Charlie at the Sunday Masses. When I spoke to him it hit me that he did not understand what I had tried to prepare him for a couple of months earlier. In a resigning voice, filled with sincere empathy, he spoke to me with hopeful words. He said, "You thought that he would die in surgery, but he didn't." I knew that he had heard me, but he was still trying to console me with hope to the very end. It was also evident that when I had first told him that Charlie would not live through this surgery, he took it literally. His mind understood my words to mean the surgical procedure itself, rather than the surgical event and it's aftermath. As kind and well meaning as he was, his words of hope did not speak to my heart. I knew what I knew.

Saturday came and went with Jackie having decided to go to Louisville. That night Charles stayed at the hospital, too, rather than at the Ronald McDonald House. The more time that passed, the more obvious it became that the end was near. Charlie had last opened his eyes late Friday night, but this day he never opened his eyes.

Saturday night I stayed at his side again, resting my head against the side of his bed as I held his hand. My thoughts strayed in disbelief that the time was at hand. I could not imagine my life without Charlie. My mind could not envision the reality.

Sunday morning, the blood began to flow through the nasal gastric tubing. I notified the nurse immediately so that we could monitor the flow. When it became sluggish, the only hope to eliminate profuse bleeding from all areas would be to change the nasal gastric tube when it began to clog. The bleeding started slowly. As it became thicker, the nurse came over with a new NG tube. It was the largest one to offer, making it the least likely to clog. However, because of its size, it would also be the hardest to insert. I prayed as I watched her change the NG tube. She was quick and efficient. She had told me previously how scared she was that it could not be done. A sense of relief came over her when she accomplished the task. I watched for changes in vital signs on the monitor and then woke up Charles when the end seemed apparent. Dr. Cottrill was notified and she came right away with the children. Immediately I thought I should call Jackie in Louisville and let her know. She would probably want to return now. I called Granddad's house to find that she had just left for church. From there, she was going straight to the graduation and then to John's party. I suddenly felt as though I had misled her. Knowing that I had no way now of reaching her, I had to let go of it and trust in God's will.

I asked the nurses to call Audrey and Bess. Neither one of them could be reached. It concerned me that there was no answer at their homes. The nurses on duty agreed to keep trying to reach them, knowing that they wanted to be called when the time came.

When Dr. Cottrill arrived with the children, I told them that Charlie would be going to heaven real soon. I could not imagine being their young ages and losing a brother. Although I vividly recalled the loss of my baby brother a few hours after his birth, I was well aware that this separation would be far different for my children. I had not experienced the loss of an established relationship at their ages. I asked Marty what he preferred. Did he want to stay in the room with us when Charlie left for heaven? Or did he choose to go with Dr. Cottrill and Tom? He adamantly stated that he wanted to stay with us. I informed him of how difficult it would be to watch Charlie literally bleed to death. I suggested that he might not want to witness this. Without hesitation, he convinced me that he wanted to be there, no matter what. This is what I needed to hear. I needed to be certain about how he felt at eleven-years-old about seeing his brother die. The thought of how dreadful the rest of his life

369

would be, should I insist that he leave the room, was an image I could not accept. He would always wonder. He would always blame me for robbing him of that last minute with his brother. I had to respect that. I received a renewed understanding of how sensitive children can be. If I were a child, I would want the same respect for my feelings.

I considered the issue of sharing Charlie's death with the children many times in my heart. My conclusion was this. Whenever I brought a baby home from the hospital, the baby became part of the family. The baby did not belong to Charles and me solely. We all shared the joy as we were all one. We were not one as a couple, but one as a family. The children had been through a lot together. It would not be fair of me to prohibit that family unity now. My respect for their thoughts at their ages was an important issue to me.

After speaking to Marty, I went into the hallway to see Leslie and Jonathan, telling them that the time was near. Being a bit more apprehensive, I was afraid for them to witness this frightening scene at their tender ages. Yet, if they convinced me that they wanted to be with him, then I knew that God would help me through it. I asked them, "Do you want to come in and stay with Charlie when he goes to heaven? Or, would you like to come in and kiss him good-bye and then go with Tom to Dr. Cottrill's office? Without hesitation they both agreed that they only wanted to tell Charlie good-bye. They did not want to stay in the room. This didn't surprise me because they were well aware of the long hours that we normally spent there. Tom was being playful with them and they saw it to be the better choice. A relief came over me after giving them the choice. This would be one heartache that I could prevent. I could not deal with the responsibility of making this decision for them. I knew that not only would Leslie and Jonathan have to live with this forever, but so would I.

I then brought them into the room and held each of them up to Charlie to give him a kiss and to say their good-byes. They appeared to be satisfied after a brief visit, then I took them out to Tom. Standing with them momentarily for our own good-byes, I felt confident that they had made the right decision. My thoughts drifted back to Jackie several times. I had not prepared myself for being unable to reach her. Yet, I also thought that it could have happened this way so that she could steer her thoughts away from pain momentarily. Her boyfriend's graduation would bring an element of joy into her life that she had not been able to experience for some time.

As Tom and the children turned to walk away, I went back to be with Charlie, his dad and Marty.

The three of us had little to say, as our hearts were so heavy. We stood together beside Charlie. We looked at Charlie with crushed hearts. We each held his hand or stroked his arm or hair. The nurse came over to us to inform us that she had reached Audrey and that she was on her way. Bess was still not home. I couldn't imagine where she might be on a Sunday morning.

As the hours passed slowly, I saw that it was shortly after 12:00 P.M. Thanking God for this time on Sunday was a foremost thought. I felt so grateful that God had allowed all of St. Gabriel the opportunity to pray for Charlie on this final day. The last Mass began at noon and I was aware that the petitions were being announced at that very moment.

Before long, Audrey came rushing in, with her waist-length blond hair still wet from her shower. She was dressed in a beautiful long skirt. With a painful smile, she came over to hug me. She said she came as soon as she had gotten the message. She was in the process of getting ready for church. "For some reason, I just felt like I wanted to go to church today," she said. "I don't know why, but I just felt really strong about it. Oh well, I can go next week. I think it's more important that I be here with you today."

My heart melted when I heard of her plans, knowing that it had been many years since she had been to church. I saw that God had used Charlie to help bring her back to Him. I cried knowing this.

The clock soon passed 1:00 P.M. This is good, I thought. Now everyone has had the opportunity to pray for Charlie at church today. There was a predominant sense of comfort in the timing, for I recognized the number of prayers that were said on that day alone.

By now the bleeding had increased, flowing faster and continuously. I realized that death was only moments away. I prayed that Bess could know to be there.

Just then, the nurse informed me that she had reached Bess. She said that Bess had just walked in from church and was on her way to the hospital now. I was stunned. Bess, too, had just recently told me that it had been about twenty years since she had been to church. Now, all of a sudden, on the day of Charlie's death, she had gone back to church. Again, I cried as I saw what God had done.

Moving closer to Charlie, I walked to the left side of the bed, looking at him in amazement over God's continued use of him. Marty struggled to be closer to him. Observing this, I lifted him and sat him on the edge of the bed. All was quiet and somber with the exceptions of tears and somewhat controlled sobbing. Charles remained on the right side of the bed. Each of us frequently reached over to console the other and to wrap our arms around each other.

It was obvious that we were all engrossed in our own thoughts of Charlie. Yet, when my eyes met with his dad's, my heart was filled with empathy for him in the loss of his son. I sensed the same feeling from him toward me. We hurt for each other as well as for ourselves.

As I looked at Charlie, I understood that Jesus was indeed lying there suffering with him. Recalling the words from Fr. Dan, I could feel Jesus's presence inside Charlie. I felt the presence of God over all of us in the room. The power of the Holy Spirit was as strong as I've ever felt as He pulled all of us into the room that day.

Looking at Charlie's body, recognizing the suffering that he had endured not only now but throughout the years, I pictured Jesus transposed on the cross, in the bed. Through Jesus, I saw Charlie's newborn hands tightened at the wrists due to muscle spasms. I saw the pain when I stretched out his small hand to place in the splint as he cried. This reminded me of the pain from the nails in Jesus's hands or wrists. He experienced pain throughout his arms as well. All the past infliction on Charlie's body came to surface in my thoughts. Each reminded me of the infliction upon Jesus. Then I saw new parallels in their suffering and humiliation. The gash in his chest that remained from surgery corresponded with the gash in Jesus's side. The hospital gown that barely covered him would have embarrassed any teenager. Jesus had been stripped down to a loincloth. Charlie's parched lips remained thirsty for seven and one-half weeks as he was not allowed anything by mouth. Jesus, too, died thirsty. I recalled offering him a mint-flavored sponge toothette just the day before, but he made a terrible face implying that it was nasty. So closely did this simulate the gall offered to Jesus on a sponge. The resemblance of all was a profound example of Jesus's suffering and crucifixion.

Upon visualizing this, Jesus spoke to my heart, saying, "This is my body which shall be given up for you." Upon hearing this, I was startled and deeply moved. These words explained why Charlie was asked to suffer again and again. It was through his suffering that others might be saved. I had heard of two people on this very morning whose lives had been turned back to God because of Charlie's suffering.

Next, my eyes were drawn to the canister on the wall, which was filled with blood. Tracing the blood-filled tubing leading to Charlie, I then heard the words, "This is the cup of my blood (there was a pause)." I looked back at the canister on the wall. Then the message continued, " the blood of the new and everlasting covenant, which shall be given up for you, so that sins may be forgiven. Do this in remembrance of me." Immediately, the Holy Spirit made clear to me the meaning of this message. Charlie was an instrument in God's plan for salvation. It was necessary for him to give up his body and his blood, just as Jesus did, in order to awaken those who might have fallen asleep spiritually. I understood that the term *you* was plural. He was referring to all that knew Charlie and all that were touched by him. I saw how God used Charlie to bring people closer to Jesus Christ. Suffering united with Christ allows us to see the power of God through our human weaknesses. I witnessed Charlie's suffering being used for the purpose of reparation. Although our human weakness takes us away from God, our physical weakness brings us back. Suffering makes us dependent on God. God used Charlie's suffering to bring many people close to Him in prayer. Suffering was used to give us the opportunity to reach for God, thus allowing forgiveness for our sins. My unworthiness overwhelmed me as I recalled how Jesus gave up His life for me. The words, "Do this in remembrance of me," indicated that Charlie's death should remind all of Jesus's death. When God said, "Do this," I understood "this" to mean die. Die in remembrance of me, also meaning in union with me. God knew the pain that I felt watching my son. He revealed His words to me so that I would recognize that same pain from the death of His son. A vivid realization of the event on Calvary was suddenly so clear to me. It was as though I had witnessed the crucifixion myself.

As friends and family had become comfortable with Charlie's normalcy, they no longer recognized the power of God in his life. Many came to believe that he was invincible. He could beat all odds. But God was saying no. Life was not to be taken for granted. Life was not dependent on good doctors alone. It was only by the grace of God that Charlie had ever lived. When He shared those words, "Do this in remembrance of me," I was aware that although suffering is a consequence of original sin, when united with Christ it served as a means in His great plan of salvation. The connection between Charlie and Jesus allowed me to understand how much God loved my family, my friends, and me. I witnessed this so that I might be saved. An absolute certainty surfaced that I must share this with others so that they, too, might be saved.

I was overcome with pain. As a mother, I understood the sword that pierced Our Blessed Mother's heart. I felt that Jesus had taken me to Calvary that day as I stood watching my son die. He showed me His crucifixion transposed over Charlie so that I might make the connection and understand how very much He loved me. The gift of this revelation filled me with comfort beyond the expression of words, yet did not lessen my anguish.

The recognition of God's great love for me brought forth a painful cry. My heart was overwhelmed with the reality of Charlie's death before me and the magnitude of God's love being shown to me at this exact time. I could hardly bear the emotional contrast.

Looking at Marty as he watched his brother was by far the most painful part of all. He couldn't seem to get close enough to his brother. I picked him up and told him to go on and hug him if he wanted to. Marty was afraid that a hug might be painful to Charlie, as the dressing extended the full length of his chest. I assured him that Charlie would not be able to feel any pain at this time and told him to go ahead. "You can even lay your head on his chest if you want to," I said. With this, I lifted him closer and he indeed did lay his head on his brother's chest and cried out with love. His dad and I leaned over Charlie. With my arm wrapped around Marty, I attempted to comfort him. My eyes glanced frequently at the monitors, observing for changes that would mark the moment of death. His heart rate dropped quickly until the line went flat. At that moment, I had a sudden impulse to disconnect the respirator. I couldn't undergo the thought of Charlie's spirit looking down upon his lifeless body and seeing air blown into his lungs. I, myself, did not want to see his lungs filled once his spirit had left. Therefore, as the monitor read no heartbeat, I pulled the respirator from his mouth. The time was 1:30 P.M. The room was filled with tears.

I saw that Bess had made it just in time. Dr. Cottrill, Dr. Salley and Fr. Dan were there also. Love and pain filled the room. Marty wailed. Devastation was clearly visible with every outcry that poured forth. The pain was excruciating. Charles, Marty, and I hugged for a long while. Then I continued to hug Marty and console him, but the cries and wailing became magnified. He could be heard throughout the hospital. After a long while, I asked him if he'd like to go out in the hall with me, hoping that this would assist in the settling of his emotions. His response was, "I *can't* leave my brother. No. I just *can't* leave my brother." I knew what he was saying. The greatest part of my emotions felt the same way. I had no desire to leave although the pain was unbearable.

Once Marty had settled down, Leslie and Jonathan came in to be with us. Dr. Salley had left, but I asked for him to come back so that I might be able to talk to him. God had made it clear to me that Dr. Salley was to learn from Charlie and I needed to tell him this. The nurse feared that I would be upset with him and would accuse him of causing Charlie's death. She attempted to tell me that there was nothing that he could have done differently. I thought to myself how sad it was to think that the fear of a lawsuit was first on their minds. However, this was not God's purpose for allowing Charlie to die this way. A lawsuit would not change anything. I knew that the doctors and nurses were only human before I ever agreed to the surgery. Therefore, I did not find it surprising to see them make mistakes. So, I simply said to her, "I am not calling for him so that I may question him, I just need to tell him something. It's very important and I'd appreciate it if you would ask him to come back. She was hesitant still and implied that she may not be able to reach him. I sensed that the staff had been waiting for me to lose control and she figured the time had come. In spite of this, she respected my appeal and called for Dr. Salley.

When he returned, he apologized for Charlie's death. My mother was nearby waiting to hear my questions and to find out what Dr. Salley had to say about the event. I explained to her that this was personal and requested a moment alone with him. As she and others left the room, I stood close to him and looked him in the eyes. I said to him, "Thank you for doing what you could for Charlie. I know that his was an extremely difficult case. I didn't call you to question you." He looked relieved.

"I need to tell you something," I continued. "Before we ever decided on surgery, God made it clear to me that Charlie's time was up. I knew that he would not live through this operation. I knew that he would not live without it, either, but we chose the surgery because I felt directed to do so. I believe that there was a reason that God wanted you to be his surgeon. I believe that He wanted you to learn something from Charlie." (My thoughts passed quickly from the beginning of his involvement to the present. With keen eyes and ears, I recognized what I believed God intended for him, but I did not feel that God wanted me to point this out.) "I want to ask you a favor," I continued. "I want you to think about all that has happened and promise me that you will learn from it. I want you to know that I don't blame you for his death. It was all part of the plan. And you were part of the plan." Again, I thanked him. He gave me a caring, empathetic hug and thanked me for speaking to him.

The nurses opened up an adjacent room for the family to grieve in. This allowed each of us to move about freely, spending time with Charlie and time with each other. All of us were together except for Jackie. There was a strange feeling about her not being there. I watched the clock closely for the anticipated hour that she would arrive at her boyfriend's house for the party. The more time passed, the harder it was to anticipate telling her. I dreaded having to speak to her on the phone, rather than being there to hug her. I was comforted by the thought that she was with someone that loved her. I knew that John would console her as much as possible.

Glancing at my watch, I saw that John and his family had probably just gotten in from the graduation. Then, I couldn't pick up the phone easily for two reasons. I knew that this news was going to curtail John's celebration and I knew that someone needed to be aware of the news to understand whatever Jackie's reaction might be over the phone. I decided to wait another half-hour so that John's guests would have some time with him before I broke the news to Jackie. I was certain that she would be totally dependent on him once she heard.

Fortunately, when I finally called, John's mother answered the phone. I told her that Charlie had gone to heaven. I apologized for having to put a damper on her celebration, but I had to tell Jackie. She was very understanding and supportive. To be expected to console someone else's daughter was not a comfortable position to be in at this time. Yet, she needed to be prepared for Jackie's reaction when she heard the news. After a very brief talk, Jackie came to the phone. Her response was far more subdued than I expected. She didn't seem especially surprised. She calmly stated that she figured it would turn out that way if she decided to go to the graduation. She controlled her emotions. Yet, it broke my heart all over again, not being there for her. I asked if she wanted to have someone bring her back to Lexington, but she saw no point in it. She believed that she would be all right staying in Louisville until we returned on Monday.

Returning to the unit after the phone call, I saw that Marty was still having a frightful time. He couldn't take his eyes off his brother's body. Neither words nor hugs could console him. Until now, he had been sitting on my lap since the death occurred. I suggested that he sit with me again. However, all the love I offered could not touch the pain in his heart. The wailing had stopped, but the sobbing and jerks of quivering breaths continued. Time was passing. Yet, no one forced us to leave. Stepping out into the hallway to speak to my parents, I discovered that some relatives had come to visit, not knowing of his death. They arrived smiling and glad to see me. Immediately, I felt concerned for their feelings as my mother shared the news with them. The smiles disappeared from their faces. They had come a long way to show their support and offer their hope, only to discover that it was over. I was so glad to see them and to know that they thought enough of me to drive the distance from Lebanon, Kentucky. After a few words, I returned to the unit to be with the family.

Eventually, Marty needed to go to the rest room. He resisted the idea of walking out of the room and leaving his brother. He felt supportive of Charlie by staying in the room with him and he did not want to walk out the door. It was only with much encouragement that I was able to walk him down the hall to the bathroom. He was embarrassed for crying and didn't want anyone to see him. I assured him that his crying wouldn't disturb people. "It's all right to cry. Crying is a good thing. It shows how much you loved Charlie." With my arm around his shoulder, I gently guided him down the hall. I understood that feeling of walking away. It was tantamount to abandonment for us. My stomach was in knots over the pain experienced by my children. After stopping at the bathroom, we returned to Charlie's room where the atmosphere was more tolerable. Family and nurses still consoled one another. Audrey and Bess were like family, by now. They grieved along with us.

Feeling Charles' pain was a tremendous heart-wrenching experience. Football would never be the same. It was their game.

It was their life together. How could he ever go to another game without pushing that wheelchair through the crowd? How could he cheer on the team with much of his spirit taken to heaven? I witnessed in that room that day how each of us would lose a large portion of his/her spirit, as it was being taken to heaven with Charlie. I could not foresee how life could go on in a normal fashion.

21 VIEW OF THE SCOREBOARD

Eventually the tears were controlled, yet the pain remained intense in our souls. Departure was difficult. Knowing that it was over and life outside the unit did exist, made it that much harder. Marty was as much aware as the rest of us that once we left Charlie, we would not be with him again until we met in heaven. There was no sense of his existence there within his body, but there was a sensation of his presence in the room. Leaving him meant abandoning him. None of us could bear leaving him alone. The idea of covering him up, placing him in a bag, and sending his body to the morgue turned my stomach all the more. If we stayed, this didn't have to happen. Finally, we pulled each other to the point of facing the separation. More relatives came to be with us. Some assisted in removing the Get-Well cards from the walls and gathering up all Charlie's belongings.

I didn't feel compelled to kiss him good-bye because I didn't feel his presence within his body. His body was strangely no longer important. As I looked at his soft skin and his silky blond hair, I felt very appreciative of the precious gift that God had given me. I thought of the bear hugs that Charlie gave that were so full of love. His hugs were hearty and different than any others. Perhaps it was the solidity of his barrel chest. Perhaps it was the power of love that he released. Whatever it was, I could see that the physical hug would be greatly missed. I touched his hand and felt the coldness. There remained an absence of any feeling toward his body. Audrey offered to let me give him his last bath, but I felt no desire to do so because he would not feel it. I saw no purpose in it. The body was as lifeless as the bed he lay on. I recognized it as a mere shell.

Removing the stoneware dove from Charlie's wrist, I turned to ask Audrey if I could keep it. She not only allowed me to, but insisted that I take it. As I put on the necklace, I experienced a close connection with the Holy Spirit. I sensed that God was pleased with me about cooperating with His plan of bringing

Charlie into the hospital for surgery. I thought of the talks that Audrey and I had shared. Seeing how God used Charlie to rekindle Audrey's awareness of Him, made me understand why God directed me to take Charlie to the hospital rather than allow him to die at home. This way God continued to use Charlie for the sake of bringing people back to Christ. Looking down at the dove, I pictured Audrey in complete serenity with God as she sat on the mountaintop absorbing His Holy Spirit. The dove was a symbol of God's Spirit bringing all of us together for the enhancement of our love for God.

Jonathan and Leslie joined us prior to leaving. It was 7:30 P.M. before we were able to walk away from the unit. The staff and relatives offered help and consolation. Slowly, we walked toward the elevator discussing our immediate plans. By now hunger had set in, as we had not eaten all day. Although I didn't expect the food to settle over the knots in our stomachs, I knew it was necessary. The children unanimously suggested having pizza. Instantly, it registered as the perfect idea because that's what Charlie would have wanted as well. As he was unable to get pizza the night before surgery, he could join us in a pizza party now. So, that's what we set out to do.

Leaving the hospital was difficult. Yet, the moment we stepped outside my heart was lifted as I noticed the beauty and warmth of the sunny day. Looking into the clouds, I said privately to God, "I knew that the sun would be shining on the day that Charlie went to heaven." In a way it felt like Easter. This was not too surprising as the Resurrection was sure to come after the suffering and death. It was a new life for Charlie, I thought, a life of complete happiness just as God had promised for those who believe in Him. Oh, it wasn't necessary to have a sunny day to know that Charlie was experiencing the glory of heaven. I just wasn't surprised that God granted me this added gift. It didn't take away any pain, nor did it release the anchor which weighed greatly on my stomach. It did, however, allow me spiritual comfort.

After having pizza and raising our drinks in a toast to Charlie, we went back to the Ronald McDonald House for the night. We were completely exhausted. Lying down to rest, everyone fell asleep except for Marty and me. As my heart sank further into numbness, Marty informed me that he couldn't sleep. I suggested that we go out into the hallway to talk.

While sitting on the couch together, I placed my arm around him to console him. My heart cracked frequently with sharp pains. We sat quietly at first. Then Marty asked, "Can I call Aaron?" I knew that he needed to do this. It was imperative to share this tragedy with someone special; someone his own age, a friend who had been there for him, a friend who understood how much he loved his brother.

I responded, "Yes. Talk as long as you want." It being a long-distance call, he did not expect to be given this privilege, much less without limitation.

Upon hearing him tell Aaron that his brother had died, my heart was crushed again. I felt the pain in his voice. I pictured Aaron on the other end hearing this news about his friend. Again, there was a stabbing in my heart. Now that Marty's pain was divided by this sharing, Aaron now faced going to sleep feeling the pain of a friend. Impassioned empathy and appreciation for Aaron escaped from me. My mind, my heart, my soul, and my gut were overwhelmed with emotions. My personal loss created emptiness in my heart. Yet, my soul was filled with compassion and pain for all those who were affected by Charlie's passing.

When Marty finished his conversation, we sat lingering in disbelief. We thought about going out but had no place to go. We could not leave our pain. We needed to share our pain, but didn't know who would understand it. Then, I suggested that I call Audrey and visit her. Marty had become very comfortable with her and agreed that this was a good idea. By now it was late. One thing that I felt certain about was that Audrey was probably having trouble sleeping, too. When I called and asked if we could visit, she was pleased to offer the invitation.

We went to visit and found ourselves entertained by a parrot. We talked about things other than Charlie and the visit was good. We didn't need to talk about him. We all felt the pain and the loss and we understood each other. We simply needed to be comforted by each other's presence.

The next day a limited autopsy was performed. I reluctantly agreed to it in order to benefit other children. Adding understanding of the total picture could serve as education to the doctors. Actually, I didn't want it or see a need for it in order to answer our questions. Although I knew that Charles had some questions, I was satisfied understanding that everything came about according to God's plan. From a human standpoint, there were legitimate concerns. Perhaps better technique for infection control could have been used. Perhaps there was a way to prevent the rent in the aorta. Perhaps -- Perhaps -- Nevertheless, these issues would not change the course of events. The life would not be returned and I did not want Charlie to be aware of having to have one more "operation" per se.

I discovered something that morning as we prepared to leave the Ronald McDonald House. I saw that I didn't want to face a single person. I didn't want to hear those inaccurate words, "Good morning." I hoped not to see anyone. They might ask about my son and I'd be forced to say that he had died. No desire was present to open my mouth for any reason. I asked God to keep people away from me. As I sat in the dining room for coffee, I made sure that I parked close to the window facing out. That way I could ignore whatever might take place around me. Of course, this didn't work completely. A young mother with a toddler came downstairs and took her child outside to play right in front of me. I acknowledged her with a nod and a somber smile. Watching the toddler caused me to reflect on my children when they were younger. I remembered the joy I felt watching them play and making them laugh. My thoughts were filled with blessings.

Having no desire to move my body, I had to force myself to get up and pack for the trip home to Louisville. During this time, talking was by far the most difficult task that I had to face. I had no strength to force a breath across my vocal cords. Thank goodness Charles was able to talk. He found the strength to explain the circumstances to a concerned woman at the house. We had shared our updates before, but I could not attempt to do it now.

He also spoke to the housemother. I had to say very little. We finished our business and left.

Our first stop in Louisville was at my father-in-law's house. Jackie had stayed with him and I was eager to put my arms around her first. I had mixed emotions when I saw her. After some consolation, Charles and I left to make funeral arrangements.

Once these were completed, we returned for the children and ate at their granddad's. Then we hesitantly set out as a new family toward home. Having six people now in the car instead of seven was a scene that we were going to have to get used to. I thought of how it had been so long since we had all been together in our home as a family. The last time was nearly two months ago when we sat down for that last meal together. My mind was not able to comprehend this family of six coming home.

On our arrival, much to my surprise, we were greeted in the driveway by relatives. The house was full of more relatives waiting for our arrival. They had prepared food for dinner assuming that we would not have eaten. In my state of mental exhaustion I remained unprepared to face anyone. I was speechless. My mind had been anticipating how it would be to take our new family of six into our empty home. Instead I was caught off-guard with their generous hospitality. They were both concerned and curious about our arrival. One person stated that they had been waiting for hours for our return. A shock came over me, making it difficult to settle my pain and attempt to socialize.

Immediately, I was approached with an issue that someone from the local newspaper had phoned to inquire about the obituary. Because I was not home, the journalist told my sister-in-law who had answered the phone that a charitable organization must be listed for memorial gifts. Being put on the spot, she responded with The Dream Factory, recalling the fabulous trip that was granted Charlie. Then she was instructed that if I preferred someone different, I would have to call back before the 6:00 P.M. deadline. Otherwise, that's how they would print it.

Now, I found this upsetting because the journalist had asked someone other than I and intended to do this without my consent. As it turned out, I had exactly two minutes until the deadline for calling in a change. Unprepared and unable to think clearly at this time, I had no choice but to call them quickly. I informed the man who answered that we did not have life insurance for Charlie and I preferred not to have memorial gifts sent to charity for this reason. I had already explained this to the funeral director. I also did not appreciate his plans to change it without my permission. Ignoring this dilemma, he insisted that I give him an organization to list. He said that there would be too many flowers if I didn't do so, strongly stressing the amount of space that they would take up as well as the money put into them. With Charlie being fairly well known in the community as well as being a child, a lot of people would be donating gifts. With the pressure on, I then agreed to have The Easter Seal Society and the Dream Factory as beneficiaries. The minute I hung up the phone, I felt trapped. As much as I loved these organizations, I feared the expenses of the funeral. I felt an obligation to the funeral home first and didn't feel right in using resources for charity. It was too late and the paper was on its way to the press.

Once the issue was finally settled over the phone, the relatives left, granting us time alone.

Certain preparations had been made for the funeral long before now. I went to Charlie's drawer and removed the football uniform that I had placed there. Realizing he needed a belt, I called on my friend Bette. I also wanted a U of K football to place in the coffin with him. She went out promptly and located both. The athletic director of St. Gabriel donated socks and a blue belt to complete the uniform. Remembering how important it was to Charlie to look just right for playing sports, I understood that these things were necessary. The socks brought me a smile that quickly turned into a burst of tears as I recalled the words he said just before surgery. "What about cleats? How am I going to wear cleats?" I sobbed deeply with the belt and socks clutched in my hands against my chest. My immediate thought now was that he would not need the cleats in heaven and

I was certain that he understood this also. Besides, no one would see the feet in the coffin.

The night before visitation, we met with Fr. Bill to arrange the music. It had to be fitting. It had to be beautiful. It had to express to those in attendance that Charlie was in a happy, glorified place. One song in particular that I requested was a song written by a mother of another Easter Seal Poster Child. It told of the dream of heaven and of being able to do all the things that he could not do on earth. The song was very moving and would bring anyone to tears. Fr. Bill suggested that it might be too upsetting. However, I saw it differently now. It was a sad song for a child who longed to ride ponies or play ball. Yet, it wasn't sorrowful for the child now in heaven. Charlie no longer had to dream of those things. Now, he could do all that he ever dreamt of doing. There would be no disabilities in heaven. To me it was a glorious thought to be able to say, "Yes, in heaven, you can do them all." With the twist in meaning, he saw what I meant and agreed to play the song. Two members of the folk group took time to learn it overnight. Again I experienced the comfort from caring friends.

As I prepared the children for bed, Marty called me into his room for a private consultation. He held his large blue and gold football trophy in his hand. (This was the trophy that he had won the previous year when St. Gabriel won the Toy Bowl.) Looking at the trophy, he asked me, "Can I give this to Charlie? Besides, he deserves it more than I do." We were both being strong on the outside as our hearts were breaking on the inside.

I said, "You deserved that trophy. You earned it and played hard for it." I did not want him to ever think that Charlie was better than he was.

Then he said, "Yeah, but I only played because of Charlie."

"Well," I answered. "Do you realize that once the coffin is closed, you'll never be able to get it back?"

"I know," he responded. "I don't want it. I want him to have it. He deserves it."

I hugged him and said, "If that's what you want to do, you can. I know that Charlie would love it." I could hardly suppress my emotions. Feeling his pain within me multiplied my own pain a hundredfold.

The other children had heard part of the discussion. Immediately, Jonathan went to the shelf and pulled down his T-ball trophy. He said, "I want to give this to Charlie. Then, every time I get up to bat, I'll know that Charlie is swinging the bat with me. He had recalled this from an earlier conversation we had together about Charlie's helping him from heaven. I was more concerned now about Jonathan's request because of his young age. I feared that he would surely regret it later. When I suggested that he may not want to do this due to the fact that he could never go back and get it, he reminded me that he had another trophy and would not miss it. Reluctantly, I allowed him to go along with the plan. Getting them into bed, I next went to settle the girls in their beds. Jackie said that she didn't know what she should give Charlie. I stopped her before we got on the wrong path with the idea. I said that Charlie did not expect everyone to give him gifts. It was not necessary. I pointed out that the reason for Marty's giving the trophy was because of Charlie's great love for football. I did not want to take away from Marty's gift by adding others for different reasons. I consoled the girls and suggested that they not be looking for things to give. It was late and the next day was going to be plenty long at the funeral home.

Numerous friends came to offer their condolences. God lifted my pain during their visitation. Knowing that so many people cared for us was the greatest comfort that we could have had.

The second day, I looked up to see Jason come in. He was with a friend as his parents weren't able to come. I went over and put my arm around him, knowing the condition of his heart. He cried heavily. The words from his tape flashed through my mind. His promise to be here for him "if anything bad happened" surfaced quickly. I was crushed knowing how much he wanted to see Charlie before all of this happened. Yet, I felt that God had sent him away to protect him from a portion of the pain. I thought the same about Jamie and Tony. They were all too close and the pain would be unbearable for them unless he were taken

388

away gradually. They would all be going through the kind of pain that Marty was experiencing if none of them had ever moved away. Jason was almost speechless. I let him know that Charlie would always be with him, helping him through his life. "Just pray to him and he'll be right there," I told him. I was quick to tell him that the gift of his voice on tape was by far the most uplifting experience of Charlie's stay in the hospital. I told him how much it meant to him and what a wonderful idea it was. I then walked him up to see his buddy. I wasn't sure that I was going to make it now. His heart was broken. He could hardly bear it, but he was determined not to let his buddy down. Jason was one of those children about whom I was worried. He was a child so close to Charlie that his loss would be overwhelming. He was a child who was likely to think like a child and blame God for what happened. He was a child who was praying and didn't hear an answer to his prayers. This child loved Charlie and was the perfect example of a friend. He loved him enough that he found a way from Nashville to Louisville when his parents weren't able to make the trip. He was a twelve-year-old boy whose future faith could depend on his understanding or acceptance of this loss of a friend. I prayed that he would not be angry with God.

One of the most important parts of the funeral to me was to give understanding to all the children who were hurting over his loss. Weeks earlier, I spoke to Dr. Cottrill about my concerns. One day as we talked, I told her that my greatest fear was how this death would affect all the children. Seeing how difficult it was for adults to accept and understand God's will, how could children possibly understand it? I had witnessed many good things. I was aware that others had not been given the same revelations as I. I told her that God had used Charlie to show how much He loved us. I saw the correlation between Charlie and Jesus Christ. The children need to be told that God was good to Charlie. I did not want them to be angry with God over this due to their lack of understanding. I did not want them to lose their faith over this. They were bound to wonder why God did not save Charlie after all their prayers. My concern in this particular area was more for the friends and cousins than for my own children. I knew that I would have many opportunities to explain to my children the good that God had given us, but I would never have that opportunity to explain it to the other children. In my mind I searched for a priest who knew Charlie for a long time. I needed someone who had watched him undergo surgeries and had witnessed at least some of the miracles that I had witnessed. It had to be someone filled with faith to give this eulogy. Earlier I had considered that Fr. Caster was the most informed, but his illness kept him from being a candidate. Fr. Bruce followed a fair part of Charlie's life, but he, too, was no longer available. Fr. Bill witnessed the end of the road and understood that much, but he didn't have the chance to know Charlie throughout the years. I didn't know where to turn. Then Dr. Cottrill suggested her husband, Tom. He had known Charlie since he was nineteen-months-old. Dr. Cottrill had kept him updated on all the trials and we frequently visited together. He knew his laughter, his character, his suffering, and his passion for life. He was a spiritual man and would therefore have the guidance of the Holy Spirit in his talk. Yes, he would be perfect for the job. I asked Dr. Cottrill if Tom would mind coming to Louisville to do this for me. She assured me that he would be most happy to. Once I received approval from Fr. Bill to have him speak, my fear was relinquished. I knew that it would not matter what he said because he was knowledgeable of both scripture and Charlie's life.

After getting home late from two days at the funeral home, I had little trouble falling to sleep. My mind still could not comprehend what we had been through or what we were facing. When my head hit the pillow, the tears poured out. Once my eyes ran dry, I began to doze. Naturally, my thoughts were with Charlie. I heard a voice in my mind calling, "Mom? Goodnight, Mom." Quickly, I opened my eyes because I sensed Charlie standing at my bedroom door. Of course, there was no one there, but the memories of him coming to my door on nights that I went to bed first were as clear as the present. I thought to myself, How will I ever sleep again? My mind will always be filled with memories. Surprisingly, I did manage to fall asleep rather quickly anyway.

I slept soundly but not for very long. Once I had rested a few hours, I began to toss and turn, my mind spinning with events. Mostly, I kept seeing the many blessings that God had shared with me through Charlie. I was wishing that others could know what I had been through, not physically but spiritually. No one will ever know or understand the gifts that I've been given, I thought. So, I decided that I should get up and write a prayer to God and thank Him for these gifts. This needed to be included in the funeral Mass in the morning. It was 5:00 A.M. when I sat down at the kitchen table. I began:

Dear Lord,
    After allowing us fourteen long, happy years to prepare for our bodily separation from Charlie, You somehow knew that none of us was ready to let go. I would like to thank you, Dear Lord, for giving us the extra seven and a half weeks with Charlie, to better prepare everyone for this moment. I know that You've heard many prayers for Charlie and the family. And again, You have asked him to endure once more for the sake of those around him. You sure picked a tough little guy to help spread your word. Thank you for choosing us as parents. We have been more blessed than anyone could ever know. Keep him by Your side and send his spirit to every football team across the nation. I promised him You would.

                                                                Mom

Now I felt ready to face the day. I planned to ask Tom to read it for me after he gave his eulogy, knowing that he could do it.

This final tribute to Charlie was intended to be special. By the morning of the funeral, both my mind and my body were drained of energy. I had been planning this occasion in my mind for a number of years, bit by bit. As time closed in, I could foresee that I was going to miss its effects. I feared that due to my emotional state I would not absorb the spiritual impact of this tribute to Charlie. Suddenly I had an idea on how to preserve it.

391

It dawned on me that people had offered to help. Now, I saw a need.

I called on some friends from St. Gabriel to ask a favor. I knew I could count on Larry and Kathy to respond to my difficult request. As I spoke to Kathy on the phone, I told her of my desire to have the funeral on videotape. I knew it would sound strange, but I boldly asked anyway, "Do you think that Larry could tape the funeral for me?" She couldn't be sure that Larry would be able to tape it due to the emotions involved. Their son Adam was a special friend of Charlie's and they each had fond memories of him. She had such care and empathy in her voice, and she offered to try. I thanked her abundantly for making the effort, knowing that Fr. Bill may not permit it and Larry may not be able to handle it. Hoping against hope that it would work out, I hung up the phone and asked for God's help as I left with the family for the funeral.

Yes, the morning was difficult. Arriving at the funeral home, there was a brief time when we in the immediate family were allowed to say our last good-byes to Charlie. The boys placed the trophies in the casket. The U of K football had already been in place on the backside of the casket. Most importantly, however, was the string of beads draped in his hands. It was his First Communion rosary signifying his unity with Christ.

After saying our final good-byes, the director escorted us to the limousine. It was a strange ride, recognizing that our last ride and only ride together in a limousine was under far different circumstances. It was our ride to the airport for the fulfillment of Charlie's dream to meet his uncle.

Not a word was spoken as we could each feel the emotion in our hearts and stomachs. Upon arriving at St. Gabriel's Church, my thoughts were with Charlie's thoughts. I knew that this was his home in his heart. The school, the church, the people all reflected the most enjoyable moments of his life. This was where he always wanted to be and he was here for a final tribute. A number of school children stood in the doorway of the school lobby adjacent to the church. All eyes were on us. All showed their grief by expression or tears. As the procession began, Fr. Steve led out in radiant song, which moved me deeply. It was as though the power of his voice lifted Charlie among the angels of heaven. From there, every word of every prayer was uplifting and moving.

After reading from the Scriptures, Fr. Bill gave a homily relating to many areas. He spoke of Charlie's childlike trust, encouraging us to trust God in the same way. He encouraged us to take our hurt, pain, loss, frustration, memories, and dreams, and offer them all back to God. That would be childlike trust.

He recognized the grieving family and many friends in the pews. He spoke words of comfort. He pointed out Jesus's understanding of our pain as He, too, suffered the loss of Joseph, John the Baptist, and others. His sermon was understanding and empathetic. He recognized Charlie's qualities of innocence and determination that we were being called to imitate. He pointed out the limitations that Charlie had faced but not allowed to conquer him. "His laughter, his questions, his hopes and dreams would inspire those lucky enough to know him. Any setback simply became another challenge to be conquered." He added that more people of this world should share his love for life and his childlike trust in God. "His youth and his spirit were some of his greatest assets. Charlie was one who could invite others to a greater appreciation of their own talents and gifts and who lived as an invitation to serve and care for others.

"It has been one of my reflections from knowing Charlie for such a short time, but observing him at church, visiting him at home and the hospital, there is much as the apostle Paul suggests that we could learn from Charlie's bravery under trials, his thoroughgoing service. Clearly we can rejoice, even as Paul did in writing to Timothy, that we knew someone who fought the good fight, who indeed won the race, even one so young as Charlie.

In referring to the question, "Why," he addressed Jesus's rejecting the "disciples' logic that the blindness was the result of the blind man's sin or anyone else's sin. It was no one's fault." He continued to explain that God did not cause it. Rather, the blindness was used as an opportunity for God's work to show forth in him.

He went on to explain Jesus's concern for grieving families. Jesus left his survivors a special gift, the gift of Holy Communion. This gift of His Body and Blood joins us with Him and with the living and the dead because we believe in the One Bread and One Cup of Eternal Salvation.

I saw that Fr. Bill had come to learn a fair amount about Charlie in the short time that he knew him. I was impressed by his observation during such limited circumstances.

Next, Dr. Cottrill read the intercessory prayers. I had arranged for her to come up with these as she saw fit. However, I also had a few that I wanted included. She combined them appropriately. She was articulate and clear as she spoke. However, when she was forced to include the petition concerning herself and other medical staff, her voice quivered momentarily. Then, she resumed in a strong finish that expressed her love for Charlie and her desire for his happiness in heaven. The prayers covered concerns for political leaders, discriminations, the Catholic Church, and justice issues. Others were as follows all ending with, "We pray to the Lord."

—For the family of St. Gabriel, that they continue the wonderful display of support and love for the Stophers; for our parish...

—For the medical professionals, that Charlie's endurance will help them with other children...

—For teenagers, that they may have Charlie's strong will to live during difficult times...

—For Mary Jo and Charlie, that they realize that the ultimate task of parenting is to return to God that which He gave them earlier...

—For Jackie, Marty, Leslie, and Jonathan, whose brother will always be with them, helping them, watching them, praying with them; for the brothers and sisters...

—For grandparents, uncles, aunts, cousins, and friends who were touched in a special way by this special boy...

—And for Charlie, may you quarterback to your heart's content on the best team ever, God's team...

I smiled upon hearing this last prayer. She and I both knew whose team Charlie would be playing on. The courage that it took to share this was available due to her closeness with him and with The Lord. Although she gladly and proudly agreed to read the petitions, I knew the emotional burden that it was. I stood up to hug her and thank her as she stepped down from the altar.

The Mass progressed in beautiful continuity. A sudden burst of tears came forth from Leslie upon hearing, "He will raise you up on eagles' wings," in song. My heart sank, too. The song was now secondary to my baby girl's heartache, which I heard. I was almost in disbelief over hearing her cry. It was the first sign of tears from her since his death. In a way, I felt relief that it had finally hit her. I was afraid that she might have been ignoring the pain so well that she may never deal with it. I was happy to console her in spite of my pain.

After Communion, Tom was invited to share a few words. I was looking forward to hearing how he was going to explain God's great love for Charlie. He began slowly:

Charles Anthony Stopher –– born March 15, 1975 – – died May 28, 1989 –– and lives happily ever after. When we talk about someone's life, we usually tell all the accomplishments –– all the big things that he's done. Mostly, we don't know the inside story, just the outward appearance of the accomplishments. When Charlie was a baby, he needed a heart operation. His parents prayed. His doctors worked. And God delivered Charlie through the operation just as He saved Noah and the animals from the great flood. When Charlie was a bit older, he needed some operations on his spine. His parents prayed. His doctors worked. And God got Charlie through the operation just as certainly as He helped David in his fight with Goliath the giant. Later, Charlie had a stroke. But, he fought back just as bravely as the Israelites journeyed back to their chosen land. As Charlie grew, his body needed more oxygen. And God helped Charlie again, just as He helped the brothers from the fiery furnace not to be burned. Charlie had foot surgery. Then, another heart operation. Again, Charlie came smiling through, with God's help. In April of this year Charlie had his last operation. He was sick for a long time in the Intensive Care Unit. God was telling Charlie that this time he would be saved in a different way. God was telling Charlie, just as He told Jesus on the cross, that there really was no other way. That this time, Charlie would have to die, in order to *live*. As I wondered what it was like for Charlie, I decided that it was sort of like when your mom's calling you from behind the screen door, to come in for supper. You know your mom's a good cook, and that she's prepared a special meal, that you really want to come inside, but you are having so much fun outside that you just don't want to leave your friends to come in. Charlie decided on May 28, to come in, to come into God's kingdom. And he now is enjoying that meal which has been prepared for him. So you see, when we think about Charlie's story, it really parallels with the stories in history. That is, Charlie's life reflects all the good things that God had done throughout history for His people He loved. That is why we know that Charlie lives ––– happily ever after."

Immediately, I felt blessed for God's sending Tom to explain this to the people, especially to the children. I was amazed at the reflections he had and the correlation between the stories in the Bible. His thoughts were totally different than mine with the one exception of God's telling Jesus that there really was no other way. Yet, although our thoughts were on different paths, it was remarkable how fitting his eulogy was. The explanation made sense. It was clear enough that no one should have left the church feeling as though God had abandoned Charlie or neglected the prayers that had been said for him. His words of reflection pleased me greatly.

Following this, Tom moved right into the prayer that I had written that morning. I was nervous as he began, knowing that it may upset some people, but it was important that everyone know that I was not angry. I was blessed in spite of the anguish I was experiencing. The church was silent as he read. An occasional sniff or sob was heard. By now, the emotions had reached a peak. Then Fr. Bill called for the Easter Seal representative who was going to present a memorial from the Jefferson County Judge/Executive, Harvey Sloane, MD. Tim Jordan came forward with a lump in his throat after hearing the reflection and prayer that had just moved the church. I could tell that the timing was less than ideal for him. Taking a deep breath, he began (attempting to block out his emotions):

"This is a memorial from the Jefferson County Judge/Executive."
He slowly proceeded,

WHEREAS,	Charles Anthony Stopher, during his fourteen short years, exhibited extraordinary courage and determination; and
WHEREAS,	Charlie approached each person in his life with a bright smile and sunny disposition; and
WHEREAS,	Charlie's enthusiasm and vigor have served as an outstanding example for others to follow; and
WHEREAS,	Charlie as the Kentucky Easter Seal Poster Child promoted and improved services for the disabled community, his own disabilities notwithstanding; and
WHEREAS,	Charlie has been an inspiration to all the citizens of Jefferson County;

NOW, THEREFORE, I, Harvey I. Sloane, Jefferson County Judge/Executive, wish to honor the memory of Charlie Stopher and extend my deepest sympathy to his family and many friends.

Done in the County of Jefferson,
The Commonwealth of Kentucky, this
First Day of June, in the year
Nineteen Hundred and Eighty-Nine.

Harvey I. Sloane, M.D.
County Judge / Executive

After reading this in full, he came down from the pulpit and presented it to Charles and me. We embraced. Not only was I touched by Dr. Sloane's wishes, but also by Tim for having read it.

The two-member folk group began to sing the song that they had rehearsed for me. It was a revised version of the song written by a mother to her child. By now, there wasn't a dry eye in the church. I realized that the tears shed that day were but a small portion of all the love that filled the church. The sadness only existed because of the love that everyone had for Charlie and for us.

At the conclusion of Mass, the congregation followed the funeral procession out of the church. The drive to the cemetery was like a foggy dream. I thought to myself that I was merely going through the motions. I was denying the reality of what I knew to be real. Part of me wanted it to be over so that I could stop long enough to absorb it. The driver moved on toward the cemetery. Once there, Fr. Bill presented a brief graveside service. Then we were quickly directed toward the limousine. We weren't allowed the time to absorb it the way we were in the hospital. They were directing us so that we knew it was over. It was too fast, I recall.

Jackie's boyfriend, as one of the pallbearers, was directed into another car. My heart went out to them both as I felt that they should be together. There was no opportunity to discuss this or even think about it. As we pulled out onto the road, Marty began to get sick. Charles made every attempt to get the driver's attention to pull over, while I finally grabbed a box of Kleenex to use for the emergency. This poor child, I thought. His life will never be the same. Finally, the driver heard Marty gagging and understood the need to pull off to the side of the road. Marty was as white as a ghost. He stepped out of the car with Charles until his stomach was no longer upset. He'll never survive, I thought to myself. The pain was excruciating for all of us, but for Marty, I was certain that it was multiplied even more. My personal pain was so horrendous that I couldn't imagine hurting any more than this. A fear overcame me that Marty may never fully understand Charlie's life and death. An awareness of his extra burden lay heavy on my heart.

Family and friends coming to the house after the funeral lifted my spirits. It gave me a chance to share good memories and smile. The support I felt was enough to get me through the day.

Once everyone left, I lay back on the couch in disbelief. I suppose we were all in our own world at that moment, for I cannot recall what the others were doing. Kathy and Larry were able to present a tape of the funeral to me. It turned out that he was allowed to tape it from the choir loft where he would not be a distraction to anyone. I had a longing to watch it because I wanted to absorb the beauty of the prayers and songs as an observer rather than as a grieving mother. Yet, that's what I was, a grieving mother. Nevertheless, I needed to reflect on the tribute. It was a way of healing and facing what had just taken place. The element of time took me through the entire event in such a way that I could not assimilate how the day came to pass. I didn't want to bypass any of it, although it was painful. I needed to cry. I needed to relive it over and over until the reality soaked in.

Physical and emotional exhaustion reached its climax. Within a few days I had a longing to drive off in the distance and spend time reflecting on God's plan. I wanted to understand, "Thy will be done." Too many distractions took me away from meditating. The children all needed me. My husband needed me. But, I was too drained to guide them through their pain. How could I have been of help to them if I could not understand it myself? I longed to spend time alone with God.

Knowing that our cars were not reliable, I hesitated to drive any great distance. As I pondered a way to escape, Carol, my friend from St. Gabriel, called to offer some assistance. I had no need for food, as so many people had brought it that the covered dishes would last us for weeks. I could think of nothing that she could do for me. I thanked her and told her that what I really needed no one could help me with. I needed some time alone to reflect. I wished that I could spend the day driving because this was the most peaceful way for me to reflect on the will of God. It would allow me to absorb nature and God's love in all things. This was what I needed, a day alone.

She wondered if I was mentally okay to drive, fearing that I might be so depressed that I would hurt myself. I assured her that this was not the case. My pain was excruciating but my goal was not to eliminate it. My desire to get away stemmed from the longing to understand. I needed desperately to cry. Yet, I needed to remain strong for the others while at home. My heart was like a water balloon about to burst. I just wanted to be alone without a curfew. I wanted to drive. I wanted to be as close to God as I could possibly get. I wanted to hear God in the music by listening to the songs from the funeral. I knew that the only way I could ever get through this ordeal was to face it and live it again until I made my way through it. It was impossible to turn it off and allow it to be over so easily.

It was a mountain blocking the road of my life. As I once heard from a motivational speaker, I could struggle many years by climbing it. Or, I could take the long way around it, hoping to eventually make it to the other side. Or, I could go straight through it by way of a tunnel. It may be dark and scary at times, but it would still be the fastest way. Before long, if I persisted without turning back, I would soon be able to spot the light at the end of the tunnel. This was my perception. This was my established way of dealing with all of life's problems. Now would be no different. I knew the light was there. I just needed to face the darkness in order to find it sooner.

Carol knew my faith. She understood my need to be alone. She knew that I would be better if I was allowed this time. So, she offered me her car. She said that it was reliable and I could drive as far away as I wanted. Although I was reluctant at first, it didn't take much for her to persuade me to accept her offer. The next morning I prepared a picnic lunch and set out in Carol's car, promising to be back sometime that night, probably before midnight. Still being concerned about my well-being, she gave me the keys with a slight sense of uncertainty about my independence.

My plan was to drive south on I-65 without a destination in mind. So, this is what I did. I had several tapes with me. Mostly, I wanted to play the funeral tape, explaining to God how grateful I was that He had done so much for us. I reflected on the words of every song, praying and crying as I drove. I listened carefully again to the words from Fr. Bill and Tom. They were powerful and so full of meaning. Again, I was pleased to have been able to save this. I listened to Fr. Steve singing and lifting Charlie into heaven with the angels. The beauty of the ceremony made me cry often. The tears were filled with love and pain. They were filled with thoughts of God's grace. They were filled with humility, still in disbelief that God would love me so much as to show me so many glorious understandings of His magnificent power.

After several hours, I stopped briefly and pondered where I was going. My reflections were at a peak and I could not see turning back just yet. So, I traveled on, playing the tape over and over again, attaining more understanding each time I listened to it. Finally, I found myself near Bowling Green and feeling hungry. I pulled off the expressway and drove through the town looking for a good private place to stop. Soon, I spotted a football goal post in the distance. I was drawn to it like a magnet. It turned out to be a football field behind a high school. There was a long drive alongside the field. There was no one around. A row of small houses outlined the outer edge of the drive with

401

their back yards facing the drive. I saw that I would not be disturbing anyone, nor would anyone be disturbing me in this spot. I turned off the engine and proceeded to take out my picnic lunch that I had prepared. By now, I had finally finished crying.

I sat on the grass and reflected on the memories of Charlie's love for football. I pictured him and his dad at the U of K football field kicking field goals when he was three-years-old. I contemplated our many conversations about his love for football and his dream of playing. I recalled the promise that I made him as the words of my prayer were repeated over and over again in my mind: "Keep him by your side and send his spirit to every football team across the nation. I promised him you would." I pictured young boys playing on the field and saw that if they needed a spirit such as Charlie's, God would send Charlie to them to inspire them in some way. He could teach them determination and perseverance. Not knowing the opportunities of heaven, my imagination allowed me to accept that these things could be possible. I kept thinking of my explanation to Charlie. Although I could not picture the need for football in heaven, if that were really what Charlie wanted after he got there, then God would find a way. Looking up over the goalpost, I said to Charlie, "Do you still feel a need to play football?" In seeing that it was such a part of his personality and spirit, I did find it difficult to picture him any other way. I decided that God would know exactly what to do with him. He would find a spiritual way for him to play football.

In one sense, I felt that I had let him down. I didn't protect him and save him the way that a mother should. I made him a promise from God that I probably had no right to do. Many thoughts questioning my decisions and actions entered my mind. As my thoughts raced in circles of doubts and misunderstandings, I began to cry again. Before long, God comforted me in the belief that Charlie would be happy just as he was promised. That was all that mattered. I was consoled in the arms of Mary that I had been a good mother, doing all that I could to make Charlie strong while promoting his independence. I gathered that she was pleased that I had prepared him for heaven.

"Did I do enough for him?" I questioned. "Was there more that I should have done or said? Should I have kissed him once more before leaving for surgery?" My guilt began to return over several issues. He had been without a battery for his Tri-Kart for over a year. Why didn't I get him a battery and pay another bill late? I promised him that I would get him a new U of K trash can after his brother accidentally fell on it and dented it. I never got it because I never had the money. Why didn't I do these things? The time had passed and I couldn't fix it now.

Soon, I came to the realization that Charlie wasn't concerned about these things any more. He obviously dealt with it on earth because he rarely reminded me of them and never complained about not having them. He was always understanding of the money situation's being the reason that he didn't have things.

Despite my legs and feet falling asleep, I did not have the urge to get up and leave. I had found a certain peace and closeness with heaven in the spot that I had chosen. I merely shuffled my position from time to time and sat longer. I stayed until my thoughts grew numb. I sat and simply enjoyed the presence of God and the comfort of Mary, knowing that Charlie was being well cared for.

When the sun went down and the skies darkened, I forced myself to get up. Slowly placing my small cooler back into the car, I turned to look at the field one last time. It was difficult to leave. Starting the engine, I managed to put the car in reverse and back slowly out of the drive. A final stop at a gas station was made before facing the road back. I realized then that I had gone a fair distance from home. Yet, the drive back did not appear to be a lengthy, tiring trip. Rather, the hours ahead were seen as an opportunity to hear and understand God that much more. I began to listen to some music on a different tape, but my mind was still with the songs, the words and the prayers of the funeral Mass. I discovered that I didn't want to listen to anything else. The desire remained to reflect again and meditate on the way home as well. By the end of the day, my questions and doubts had been resolved. I saw that my life ahead was difficult, but I would be carried through it. Entrusting my life to God, I arrived home with a sense of comfort and strength to face the next day.

403

22

TOUCHDOWN

For days, great comfort arrived in my mailbox. Sympathy cards were my new focus. Now that it's over, does life return to normal? Does anyone understand or care? The answer was a constant yes. From simple cards with few words to more lengthy verse, each had the message of love and compassion enclosed. I knew that we had not been forgotten. It amazed me to open cards from people I didn't even know. They were thinking of us because they had heard about us through family and friends. People who had seen us in church but never got acquainted with us also were thoughtful enough to share in our grief. The ripple effect seemed nonstop. Wow, I thought. The Holy Spirit was visible all around me. The pain and sadness remained deep in my heart and did not lessen by reading the cards. Yet, I could not wait to open the next one for I knew it would be filled with comfort.

A couple of days after the funeral, I received a strange phone call. Jackie had answered it and quickly handed the phone over to me saying that I would have to take care of this one. As I said "Hello," the voice of a young boy answered in a slow, slightly impaired form of speech. He said, "Is Charlie there?" My heart sank as if falling to the floor. My first thought was that this was a school friend who surely must know what had happened. I knew that it was important to choose my words carefully so that he might handle what I had to say. I asked him if he went to school with Charlie and he replied, "Yes."

From that I added, "Did you know that Charlie has been real sick in the hospital for a long time?"

Again he replied, "Yes."

I wondered, did they not tell these children that Charlie had died? Surely, they did. He just doesn't want to believe it and that's why he's calling.

Thoughts flashed through my mind quickly. Maybe the school didn't tell them. Maybe they were trying to protect the children. With this group of handicapped children, they may very likely fear their own death if they were to hear such news. I was trapped. I knew that I had to speak the truth but very carefully.

So, I said to him, "Charlie has gone to heaven. You know that he was very, very sick. So, God took him to heaven so that he would feel better."

He replied, "Oh."

Suddenly I thought to myself: What have I done? Should I have said this to him? Of course. I had to tell him. I could not pretend that Charlie would return home. The boy would call back for him. I felt horrible. I felt responsible for taking his friend away from him. I asked him if his mother was home. I thought that I needed to explain to her about our conversation, but he replied that she was not there. Then, I asked him if he was okay. He said that he was. I thanked him for calling and as I hung up the phone, twisted knots settled in my stomach. Looking at Jackie, I didn't know what to say. I could see that the conversation had upset her.

Several days later, I received another upsetting phone call. A woman from the TARC transportation system called to inform me that Charlie now had a spot on the handicap bus. I would simply need to call and let them know the times that he needed a ride. Caught completely off guard by this due to the fact that I had applied for it almost four years earlier, I responded, "It's too late now. He died last week." These words just fell from my lips without even thinking. The woman was stunned and apologetic. She was almost in tears and felt very ashamed and embarrassed over calling. Instantly, I found myself trying to console her by acknowledging her innocent mistake.

I said to her, "It's all right. You would have no way of knowing that he had died."

My words did not relieve her emotional distress. I added that it was a shame that it had taken so long to get him a ride in the first place. I explained that he had to leave Ursuline-Pitt Academy due to the cost of transportation. Because it was across town from our house, it was necessary to have him attend a school that was closer. I added that it would be helpful if the handicapped had better access to transportation. She agreed.

Being in a state of paralyzed senses, it was difficult to enjoy any part of life. The emptiness within me absorbed my whole being. While the rest of the family watched TV to distract their pain, I could find no entertainment in it. The once favorite comedies were no longer funny. There was an obvious void in my existence. There was no one in the family who needed braces and shoes put on in the morning. No one needed a hand to get up or down. No one needed their bath water run for them. What was I supposed to do with myself? The children had been taught independence from the start and were accustomed to doing basic self-care.

I quickly recognized that not only had I lost my son, I had lost a huge part of myself as well. My identity as a mother was related to the extra requirements of Charlie. Then, I found myself wondering why in the world I ever thought I wanted to be a mother. Why was I so naive to believe that being a mother was so terrific? Why did I only see the rewards of being a mother and never notice the pain that it would entail? Was I so blind that I did not see the pain and suffering that I had caused my own mother? It was becoming more and more apparent that children do cause heartache. Although it was not deliberate infliction on me, mistakes and mishaps that my children had undergone in the past caused pain. Then as I looked at Charlie, I felt the ultimate pain that a child can cause a parent. This pain was of no fault of his. Yet, it was by far the worst I had ever encountered in my life. I began to foresee that eventually all of my children would cause me great pain in some fashion. Some would be due to their mistakes, some to their suffering. Whatever their life brought them, I was going to undergo their sufferings with them. I wished at that point that I had never been a mother, knowing that I could never deal with this type of pain again. I'll never make it, I thought to myself.

I went on through the motions of preparing dinner and contemplating the need that the children had for a mother. Despite their independence, they each needed someone to talk to and someone to listen to them. I could not let them down. Before

407

long, I saw that it was the children who spared me from the temptation of depression. The fact that they needed rides to their ball games and parents supporting them in the crowd kept me going. I frequently said to myself, "I don't feel up to this."

Summer did not bring the ordinary desire to go outside this year. On the contrary, I didn't care to ever go outside again. I did not want to see anyone. I especially did not want to hear that typical question, "How are you doing?" How could I answer "Fine"? Even going to the grocery store was difficult. The first trip brought out thoughts that had never occurred to me. I found myself looking at strangers differently. My mind was filled with thoughts of my emptiness as well as my awareness that no one around me knew what I had been through. As I placed items in the cart just as normally as the next person, I thought to myself how I looked no different than any other shopper. Yet, I felt different. Looking at their ordinary movements, I pondered, wondering what trials they might be carrying with them. I wondered if some of those whom I passed in the aisle had ever lost a child through death, miscarriage or abortion. Some of these people had surely experienced pain similar to mine. Who was to know? We all looked the same as we shopped.

A reality hit me that awakened me to the pain of others. Although I felt somewhat separated from the world around me, I was aware that I was not the only person in this community with those feelings. Who was to say that the lady behind me in line didn't have a tragedy of her own? As I drove home, I wondered about the people traveling around me. What tragedies might they be going through? Life went on even if I didn't feel like accepting it. I knew that I, too, must go on. I must get my family through this. I did what I had to do only for the sake of the children. If it had not been for them, I would have done nothing at all. I had lost all desire to enjoy life. I couldn't smile, nor did I feel any desire for joy. I was convinced that I could never be truly happy again. Even if I could smile, it wouldn't come from within.

With these feelings, I knew that I was incapable of energizing the representatives of the craft company that I directed. Again, I pleaded with the owners to find someone else before the company took a turn for the worse. Again, they refused to do so and were determined to wait for me no matter how long it took.

After several weeks I began to force myself to go outdoors. It took great effort when the neighbors held a block party and expressed their hopes of seeing me there. Yet, I knew that it was important for the sake of the family to regain my strength and avoid the temptation of depression. I was unable to speak much, but I ate and sat with them anyway. The children and Charles also worked up the strength to join the group. After a short, agonizing visit, we returned home recognizing once again that life was different now.

One morning, after dragging myself from bed, I passed slowly through the hallway, gazing upon the family pictures that adorned the wall. My eyes were drawn to the left where a picture of the Sacred Heart of Jesus hung. Looking into His eyes, my soul was filled with awe over how much He had given me. Moving back toward the smiling faces of the children, I reminisced over the people in our lives during the various stages of their growth. Focusing then on Charlie, a number of people came to mind. People who were touched by his presence, people who were amazed by his miracles of health, people who gave their time, talents, and hard-earned cash to The Easter Seal Society, people who brought out their long-hidden smiles, all came to mind. Reflecting on the good that he drew from people brought warmth to my soul. Looking back at the Sacred Heart picture brought about a twisted smile to my face. It was then that I recognized how God had used Charlie's heart disease to bring us closer to His Sacred Heart. How ironic, I thought, with the realization that to God it was not ironic at all.

Meanwhile, I had been making attempts in the morning to resume going to daily Mass. I wanted desperately to be there. What was making it difficult was the reality of my pain combined with the experience of recognizing the suffering and death of Jesus on Calvary. I found that each Sunday when I attended Mass, I would be moved to tears. Feeling empty and brokenhearted was only the start. During the consecration of the Mass, I heard those words again: "This is my body, which shall be given up for you." This is when I would break down. With eyes of faith, I could see the body of Christ in the Eucharist and feel the reality of the pain that His mother experienced as she watched Him die. The pain was real and fresh. My empathy for her was immense. Visualizing Charlie's blood flowing into the canister brought reality to the blood that flowed from Jesus's pierced side. "This is my blood..." The thought of Jesus's having given His life so that we may be saved was what triggered the emotions. Why couldn't we all just obey the Ten Commandments? I thought to myself. God tried to make life simple for us, but we had to go against Him with sin and make life so difficult. Charlie was used as an instrument to help me see that. I was blessed through Charlie's suffering. Yet, the pain of this blessing was unbearable. I saw the glory of God manifested through Charlie's suffering and realized that all who suffer are being given the same opportunity. God uses innocent people to reveal what Jesus endured for all. Now the suffering made sense. Those who suffer and those who witness suffering understand pain. Those with open hearts also understand the reality of our salvation because of it.

In an attempt at closure, Charles and I discussed our plans for Charlie's headstone. Two images surfaced without hesitation. A cross would signify the union that Charlie had with Christ through suffering. An Easter Seal Lily would show the beautiful life he was granted through the assistance of The Easter Seal Society. We both acknowledged that had he never attended Cardinal Hill Preschool, his opportunities would never have flourished the way that they did. Significantly symbolized, the Easter lily also expresses the new life that he now experiences in heaven. With these thoughts, we made our way to the monument company.

After expressing our preferences, we were shown several images of crosses and Easter lilies to choose from. However, after careful consideration, we saw that an ordinary Easter lily would not tell the whole story. It would reflect his new life in heaven, but not the life he was offered on earth. Therefore, we presented our own image of the Easter Seal emblem, making it more appropriate. To our satisfaction the stone was ordered. We left with a good feeling that those who knew Charlie would understand our selection.

After weeks of avoiding the weekday Mass, I finally summoned the courage to attend. Fr. Bill was pleased to see that I had returned to join them. I prayed that I could hold back my tears. My throat became tight as the bread and wine were consecrated. I loved being close to Jesus although now the pain was excruciating. Fr. Bill offered me the opportunity to assist in serving Communion as I had so often done in the past. I was touched by his simple gesture. Suppressing my emotions, I managed to control them until I had returned to my seat from serving Communion. Then, I broke down quietly. The sword was piercing my heart as I felt Jesus's love for me, a sinner.

I continued to have a burning desire to attend Mass. However, it would take several days before I could muster the strength to face the pain again. Over a period of time, I was able to attend more frequently although I was still unable to get through the Mass without crying. Each morning was a struggle. If I could make it two or three times a week, I felt that I was doing well. I hoped that it would become easier to tolerate. However, I could not avoid the experience during the consecration and therefore was moved to tears each and every time.

At home it seemed as though every member of the family would plod through the expectations of daily life. The house had been peculiarly quiet since Charlie's death. There was no more laughter and no more excitement. There were no more fun conversations. The absence of Charlie was so visible it was as though we were in someone else's home. When relatives would visit, they, too, recognized the silence in the house as his absence was felt by all.

August was the beginning of school and football. Marty had begun playing football on a team in the community, but his heart was not in it. A teammate, who was unaware of Charlie's death, asked Marty where his brother was. He had remembered how Charlie always watched them practice in the past. It was not easy for Marty to explain that Charlie had died. When it came time for the first game, he simply could not bring himself to play. He was aware that his spirit for football had always come from sharing with Charlie. Emotionally drained, he did not have the strength to call on Charlie's spirit at this time.

Later, as the fall days were passing, Marty picked up his football and slowly walked outside. He stood in the front yard where he had played football with Charlie for many years. He held the ball loosely in his arms, seemingly lost. My heart ached as I watched him slowly toss the football into the air. He had no one to play with. I imagined the thoughts that went through his mind causing the sword to grind at my heart once again.

That evening after Charles came home, I suggested to Marty that we go out for a while and talk. I drove up to St. Gabriel's where we would have space and privacy. Placing my arm around his shoulder, we slowly began to walk around the school building and church. I said to him, "Marty, I know that this is really hard for you. Everyone in the family has lost someone special. You kids have lost a brother and Dad and I have lost a son. We are all hurting. But, I know that it is different for you. You have not only lost a brother, you've also lost a best friend."

He seemed surprised that I recognized this part of his pain. He said, "Yeah, Charlie was my best friend, Mom. Nobody understands. The teachers don't understand and none of my friends understand."

He expressed how mad it made him to hear a teacher say that she understood when he didn't believe it was possible. I acknowledged his anger over this. Then I agreed with him that he was right.

"No one really understands what you are going through. That's because they probably didn't lose a brother when they were eleven-years- old. Even I can't fully understand what you are going through. I have lost a son, not a brother. It's different. But, I've thought about what it must be like. You know, my brother Jude and I were very close. Although he was a year older than I was, we were in the same class together growing up. We did everything together. We had the same friends. We were in the talent show together just like you and Charlie. We laughed and talked and shared our secrets together. I can only imagine how awful I would have felt if he had died when I was eleven-

412

years-old. That is as close to understanding as I can get because he did not die. You know, Marty, no matter how much someone wants to understand it won't be possible but they still mean well. They know that you are hurting. So don't be mad at them because they can't fully understand. You don't understand my pain, either, but that's not your fault. You're not a mother. So, what you need to keep in mind when a teacher says that she understands, is that she is trying to make you feel better. Most adults have lost someone in their life. So, they do understand some of it, just not as an eleven-year-old."

I went on to tell him about The Compassionate Friends group for bereaved parents. Charles and I had gone to a couple of meetings and found that everyone in the room understood us because they had all lost children. There was a sibling group that offered the same thing. Although those attending would be adults, they had all lost a brother or a sister. I suggested to Marty that it may do him some good to go, believing that this was what he needed. It was important to find someone who had been there. I promised to make arrangements for him and the other children to attend the group. It took a little persuasion to help him see that these people would understand. After sharing many thoughts, and numerous trips around the buildings, we returned home.

Meanwhile, I had discovered in my reflection that if I did not make use of the many things that I had learned from Charlie, then his spirit would no longer be a part of me. If I merely accepted that this part of my life was over, then it would indeed be over. His life and his death would be in vain. However, if I used it, then life with his spirit could continue. I had learned much about heart disease and every part of the body. I had also learned many spiritual lessons about life. I gathered that it was important to use all that I had learned. It was clear that I should share these experiences with others.

Then I recalled the encouragement that I had received from Bess (Charlie's nurse). She believed that I should become a nurse, pointing out that I had been nursing Charlie for fourteen years. Suzanne, (another nurse) also acknowledged that I had seen just about everything there was to see. She, too, encouraged me to take up nursing. Funny thing, however, it had never been my desire. Therefore, I had not considered it. Understanding that they were right, I decided to pursue the possibility. I thought that if I took one college course in the fall, I would quickly discover whether I would be capable of concentrating on school. Not feeling at all certain about my capability, with the mixed emotions that still filled my heart, I decided to give it a try.

The weather soon changed as football season crept in. I could not bring myself to go to a game. The big game between Trinity and St. X was being talked about. I didn't care to go this year because I feared the pain it would bring me. But, when the day came, I saw that it couldn't be allowed to pass without my being there. If Charlie's spirit would ever be at a game, he would be at this one. The game was intense. St. X led early on. As the quarters passed, I felt worse and worse watching Trinity lose. I said to Charlie, "I guess you didn't need to play football in heaven after all. If you were playing, something would surely be done about this game." I thought of the boys on both teams, knowing that many of them knew Charlie. I wondered if any of them was feeling inspired by him during the game. Just then Trinity scored the winning touchdown with only three minutes to go. I couldn't believe my eyes. My heart was thumping and my eyes were filled with tears.

After the game Charles and I, along with the children, walked down to see the players as they returned to the buses. Our neighbor Todd, whom Charlie had played football with many times, was heading for the bus. Charles congratulated him for the win.

Todd said to him, "Did you see that charge at kickoff? Before I took off I said, "This one's for you, Charlie. Then I plowed the guy with all of my might."

Grinning and feeling so proud, Todd proceeded toward the bus. Charles' eyes were filled with emotion. The pain felt so good because he saw that Charlie truly was an inspiration.

As the football season was coming to an end, we noticed that most of Charlie's favorite teams on every level were number one. St. Gabriel had just won the Toy Bowl, Trinity was State Champs, Notre Dame was number one and The San Francisco 49ers were headed for the Super Bowl. Who could ask for more?

But there was more. I received a call from Ron Bierley, the athletic director from St. Gabriel. He invited Charles and I to attend the annual football banquet at the school because Charlie had been such an inspiration to the players. I graciously accepted the invitation.

On the evening of the banquet, many thoughts raced through my mind. I had a strong sense that St. Gabriel would win this year because it was Charlie's eighth-grade class playing. Fr. Bill presented Charles and me with a plaque that honored Charlie's memory and expressed how he inspired the players. We were greatly touched. Charles offered thanks to everyone there as he accepted the plaque from Fr. Bill.

Then, I was moved to share some memories of Charlie's love for football. I told the players that I knew that they would be champs this year. It was a certainty in my mind. I shared with them that Marty had given his trophy to Charlie at the funeral home. I pictured Charlie holding the Toy Bowl trophy from Marty, and I knew without doubt that he would be helping them win. "Now I know that Charlie is playing football in heaven." The crowd was moved as all could surely feel his presence.

By the end of December, I earned a "B" from my college course as well as a vote of confidence. Now able to handle school, I enrolled in a nursing program the next semester.

One of the most difficult times to face was yet to come: Christmas. I knew the importance of making it the best it could be. It would be different than any in the past, but there would be a way to include Charlie in our Christmas. First, the family selected a live Christmas tree and planted it in Charlie's memory. It was planted in the front yard where Charlie spent most of his time playing football. Making it a special occasion, we made hot chocolate and took it outside for a toast to Charlie. Standing around the freshly planted tree, we raised and clicked our cups saying, "To Charlie. Merry Christmas." As we stood there, sipping on our hot chocolate, Jonathan discovered that something was missing. He said in his six-year-old youthfulness, "Mom. We forgot the toast." He didn't grasp that toast had another meaning besides a piece of bread. We all chuckled, as he stood puzzled. Then I explained to him the other meaning of toast. It was good to laugh as a family again, even in such a childish way. Charlie would have been rolling on the floor, as he loved to hear the cute things that his baby brother would say.

Over the next few days, I went around to gum machines through town searching for miniature football helmets. They being a fairly popular item, it wasn't too difficult to find. The children enjoyed putting quarters in the machines and hoping for a helmet that we hadn't already collected. One thing certain was that I could not stop without finding a 49ers helmet as this had been his most recent favorite team. Eventually we had enough. I gathered heavy string and glue and set up a place on the table for the children to help transform the helmets into ornaments for Charlie's tree. Everyone enjoyed the project.

When we pulled out the other decorations from their boxes, we came upon the family stockings. There were seven, each with a different name on it. As the box was opened a fear of uncertainty came over me. I recalled a frequent vision from the past of hanging stockings someday when he would not be with us. Through the years, when I would think of this, I was never able to imagine one less stocking. Just then Jonathan asked, "Mom, what are we going to do with Charlie's stocking?"

Not knowing myself, I replied, "I don't know. What do you think we should do with it?"

Without hesitation, the children responded in unison, "Hang it up."

I was relieved that they had made it so easy for me. Of course we should hang it up. He would always be part of the family and part of our Christmas. I concluded with, "Then, we'll hang it up."

There were other parts of Christmas that were difficult as well, but I knew that we would get through them because there was no choice in the matter. We were here and Charlie wasn't. We would have to depend on God's guidance to get us through every step. I was certain that He would.

In February, I began an LPN program, which would last for a full year. It would be a total commitment of time and energy, leaving very little left for the family. Charles supported my decision. With Jonathan now in the first grade, the timing was good as the children were all in school for the full day.

The following year I was graduated and I set out to help others with the knowledge that I had obtained. I began in pediatrics due to my sensitivity toward children. During this time of healing, I remained active in the other aspects of my life. I continued to be wife and mother. I continued my social life with friends at monthly Bunco and at weekly prayer group. Special occasions would take me back to decorating cakes and time restrictions generally limited my simple home-improvement projects.

One aspect of healing remained a struggle. This was my increased sensitivity at Mass. Still attending daily Mass on a regular basis, I did not see any relief in my anguish. Then one day, at my prayer group, I listened to a tape that a friend had brought. The tape was from a talk given by Daniel Mohn, who was said to be a visionary of Our Blessed Mother. The talk had been given at a Marian Conference at Notre Dame. I was first impressed by the introduction given to him by his spiritual director. The priest was convincing and believed in his supernatural experiences. Due to the support of the priest, I was open to what he had to say. As I listened to this eighteen-year-old speak, the words fell on my ears and the inspiration made an impression in my heart. He spoke with conviction despite his youthfulness. Ordinary life would generally prohibit the opportunity to learn about the issues of which he spoke. I had a very strong sense that this was real. With discernment, I believed that the experiences which he shared about heaven, hell, and purgatory, could only have been presented in this way by a heavenly power. I was moved by the Spirit to follow up on this apparition.

In my excitement over hearing his talk, I promptly borrowed the tape so that I could share it with Charles and the kids. We all had many questions about eternal life. There was a struggle in our ability to fully understand where Charlie actually was and what it was like for him. What was he doing? Oh, we believed him to be in heaven. Yet, any sort of confirmation on our thoughts would be comforting. I found this comfort in the tape.

The family listened to Daniel with great interest concerning his knowledge of eternal life. Being moved as we were, I suggested to Charles that we go to Canfield, Ohio, where Daniel had experienced his apparition of Our Blessed Mother. I said to Charles, "We've always wanted to go to Medjagore. This would be the next best thing." Charles asked me what I expected to see or to happen. My response to him and to the children was that I truly didn't expect to see anything. Nevertheless, I thought it would be wonderful to be in a place where Mary had appeared on earth. I simply felt that I would be touched in some way. I said to them, "I believe that she did appear to him. I believe that Our Lady can appear in our country as easily as she can in any other country. She appeared in Lourdes and at Fatima. She can appear here."

I had no doubt that it was possible. Charles was concerned that the Church had not approved the apparition. This did not matter to me. As I told him, by the time an apparition is approved, it's over. If it's real, it will take many years to be approved. I didn't believe that it would do any harm in going. After little discussion, we agreed to go to Canfield and look for the chapel where she visited Daniel.

"What if we don't see anything or if nothing happens?" he asked. "Are you going to be disappointed?"

Again, I assured him that I didn't anticipate anything happening. My own personal mission here was to step foot in the chapel where she had been. I wanted to feel closer to Mary. I believed that I could accomplish this just by being where she had been.

Now we did not know exactly how to find this chapel. Yet, with faith in God's direction, we set out toward the town of Canfield. I had a discussion with the children so that they would not expect to see Mary. However, it was important to share my faith with them that Our Blessed Mother could appear to anyone, anywhere. Therefore, they were to understand that if Mary wanted any of us to see her, she could show herself to us here, in our home, in our church or wherever she chose to do so. They were not to think that just because we were going there, she would naturally present herself to us. I stressed that this would be an opportunity to be close to her. We could go into the chapel and pray for as long as we wanted. We could ask her anything about Charlie or any other issue. I promised them that she would listen to them.

It seemed that everyone understood our reason for traveling. There was a sense of hope among them. Upon locating the city of Canfield on the map, we noticed that it was a rather small town. The only clue that was given on the cassette tape as to where the chapel was, was the fact that this chapel was in honor of St. Anthony of Padua. Daniel said that he spotted it on the side of the road one evening as he was driving with a friend. I determined that the small town couldn't have too many roads passing through it and should, therefore, not be a problem to find.

Driving was something I greatly enjoyed. Having discovered it to be the perfect opportunity to meditate since the death of Charlie's teacher in 1980, I looked forward to driving every chance I got. Being surrounded by blue skies enabled me to keep my eyes on the road and my heart on heaven. I contemplated what I wanted to ask of Mary. There remained a sense of losing connection with her. Desperately wanting our relationship as it was, I recalled how abandoned I felt since Charlie's death. At the death of her son, she was to become John's mother. She was to be mother of the world. That would never be my job. So, what was I to do after Charlie died? I already had four other children to nurture and care for. Not understanding my role at that point, I was aware that the answer lay in the missing link. Was I asked to mother the world as she was? No. Nor did I expect to be called to this task. Therefore, our connection was broken. I still longed to discover God's plan for me as well as how to relate to Mary at this stage of my life.

Continually being drawn to pain through the witnessing of the crucifixion each day at Mass, I decided that this is what I needed Mary's help with. I wanted so seriously to be as close to Jesus as I always was, but without this suffering. Comfort and consolation were what I needed. I decided to ask for relief from this horrendous feeling that persisted in my heart. I anticipated asking for removal of the sword which pierced my heart each time I engrossed my thoughts in the consecration. I wanted to be close to Him with joy. I wanted to feel peace and love without more pain. I wanted to look at the consecrated host without tears falling down my face. These are the requests that I had of her.

Nine hours later, we entered Canfield. It was late at night and the sky was dark. The children were tired from riding so long. We came upon a small hotel and requested a room for the night. The night manager kindly gave us a special rate as he acknowledged how expensive it was to take a family of our size on a trip. Before going to our room, I inquired if he was aware of a chapel in Canfield that was dedicated to St. Anthony of Padua. He hesitated momentarily. He pondered the chapels and shrines in the area that he was familiar with. Hesitantly, he began to direct us to Our Lady of Lebanon Shrine. Then, he reneged and said, "Oh no. That's a shrine for Mary." Bewildered, he finally gave up, saying that he knew of no such chapel for St. Anthony. Each place that he thought of was in honor of Our Blessed Mother. He said, "I just can't think of any in honor of St. Anthony, but there's a little chapel about a mile down the road if you want to visit that one. It's a shrine where Mary has been appearing to people." Stunned to hear this confirmation, I established, "That's it. That's the one that I'm looking for."

"You mean you came all the way here from Louisville just to see that chapel?" he said with amazement, admitting that he had never made it down there for a visit. "Yes, that's why we're here," I acknowledged. He was impressed that it meant so much to us. "Maybe, I'll get down there soon," he added.

After settling into the hotel, we took the children out for dinner. The topic of discussion was the chapel. We would visit after dinner and be respectful of the amount of time that each of us wanted to spend there. The children were instructed to go quietly outside or to the car whenever they were ready. However, they were instructed not to interrupt our prayers when they were finished.

With satisfied appetites, we drove down to the shrine. From the street we could see that the chapel was well lit with candles. Upon entering we saw three statues, which were spaced apart with many lit candles in front of each. St. Anthony of Padua was in the center; St. Joseph was to the right and Mary to the left. Behind the statues was a large stained-glass window. I focused on the statue of Mary as I pondered the beautiful gift of the apparition that had taken place there.

Knowing that she had been there was enough for me. As I spoke to her about my concerns, I felt comforted. This is great, I thought. I was filled with peace. Nothing spectacular happened. I merely sensed that she heard my plea. I prayed that the kids would not feel disappointed. They had their own particular questions about Charlie. I prayed that they would have their prayers answered in a way that they would understand.

The time was approaching midnight. We returned to the hotel to get some sleep. Feeling quite exhausted myself, I didn't foresee any trouble falling to sleep. As I lay my head on my pillow, I experienced a satisfaction about being there. On the other hand, I needed some time alone in the chapel. I decided to rise early to visit the chapel again. It was around 6:30 A.M. when I slipped quietly out of the room to venture out on my own. Arriving at the chapel, I could now see the beautiful colors of the stained-glass window on display. It was by far the most gorgeous sight that I had ever seen. The morning sun had risen brightly, its exuberant rays stretching out to the ends of the earth. The setting was perfect for meditation. My soul was lifted to a new horizon as I knelt to pray. At first I reflected on the scene in the stained glass. It appeared to be that of St. Anthony in the midst of people. Those that surrounded him gave the impression that they were listening to his teachings. The significance of St. Anthony was not revealed to me although Anthony is Charlie's middle name. Continuing my prayers to Our Lady, I poured my heart out to her, addressing the trials of my life and thanking her for her guidance. I thanked her son, Jesus, for sharing His mother with me. Just as I intended, I addressed the issue of the consecration, asking for consolation from the pain.

Believing that I was alone, I was soon distracted by the sound of footsteps at a distance outside. The door to the shrine opened. A priest entered to replace the burnt candles with new ones. Upon noticing the license plate on my car, he inquired if I was on vacation. An interesting conversation ensued covering

421

my reason for coming. He informed me that had he known that we were here the night before, he would have directed us to Daniel Mohn's home where we could have attended a prayer meeting. He offered new information and verified that Our Blessed Mother had visited Daniel on several occasions both in the shrine and in the monastery on the grounds. He stated that Our Lady said that she would return on the thirteenth of the following three months as well. He invited me to return for it and gave me directions to Daniel's farm. He shared many insightful stories and also took my address to write me about someone else from Louisville that he had met. He spoke of how inspiring she was and suggested that I look her up when I returned home. I thanked him for his generous time and information, as he was leaving the shrine to prepare for Mass in the church. Having a few minutes prior to Mass, I knelt back down to thank God for this wonderful gift that the priest had shared with me.

After Mass I returned to the others at the hotel to share the exciting news about future apparitions. Once everyone was up and moving, we went out to visit the shrine as a family once again and then on to another great shrine in the area, Our Lady of Lebanon. I was excited about all that had taken place. I sensed that heaven was coming to us in the United States. Known and approved apparitions in the past had all been in other countries, mostly in Europe. This did not shake my faith for I was convinced that this was real.

The next Mass that I attended at home was a weekday Mass. It was not until after the consecration that I realized I had not cried. Still feeling just as close to Jesus, my heart was without pain. Instead I felt the blessing that He had shared with me. Two weeks later, I concluded that this was to be ongoing. Mary did, in fact, intercede for me as she took my heartache to her son, Jesus. He had left a lasting impression on me and allowed me to appreciate it now without the pain. My heart was gradually being filled with some happiness and peace.

On May 13, 1992, the family returned to Canfield and located the farm on which Daniel lived. It was in a nearby town. A great spiritual sense was present in seeing the number of people who had gathered from various locations. Stories were being shared among them. I was still in awe myself over the instant relief of pain that I had received just for the asking. I knew that Mary would hear my prayer, and I sensed the appreciation from her over the extremes that I went to. Although there was no apparition at the shrine when I was there, I still felt closer to her because I was able to be where she had been. The excitement was now building. Prayers began. A total peace came over the people during the apparition. Petitions had been placed in a box. The spirit moved everyone in various ways. Leslie noticed a strong smell of roses while we all witnessed a sudden gust of wind that came and left mysteriously. Other than for this brief period of wind, the weather was completely calm without the slightest breeze. Afterward, the priest blessed holy items. Daniel stayed to greet people. I went up to shake his hand, but was surprised when he reached out to hug me. He was a stocky young man, a bit taller than I was. He gave me a bear hug similar to only one person's hugs that I had ever felt. That person was Charlie. It was warm and full of powerful love as though I truly mattered to him. It was as if Charlie sent this hug to me. I was truly impressed. Then it occurred to me that Daniel was close to Charlie's age. It's amazing how God provides connection between our physical and spiritual worlds. I had been touched by the experience generally, leaving with much to discern. There were messages from Mary shared, but also there was great concern about the outbreak of war in Bosnia. Fr. Yozo had sent a letter pleading for our prayers. Suggestions had been made to contact senators for help. A personal message that I felt was to pray more for the unborn and an end to abortion. There was so much to absorb and reflect upon that my mind could not rest without prayer.

The next day we returned home. The long drive again gave me opportunity to reflect. Being very concerned about the outbreak of war and the tension building in Bosnia, I was inspired to do what little I could on their behalf. I could make copies of the handouts and messages, and take them to those in my prayer group and to relatives. The dilemma was knowing that I had to work early in the morning and would not be off for several more days. The plea from Fr. Yozo indicated that a few days could be too late. Realizing that I was only one person with little influence, I determined that I could not do much. Then, I understood why people came from so many different cities to the apparition. If each of us took the information home and shared it with a handful of people, then word of the problem and prayers would spread greatly. It had to start somewhere, so why not with me?

Of course for every answer, came a new problem to prevent me from participating. As I was scheduled to work in the morning, I would not have an opportunity to make copies and pass them out. It would be days before I could do anything. So, I continued to pray, thinking of how I could help, wishing if only I didn't have to work in the morning. Then I resigned myself to the fact that God would understand my desire.

The following morning, as I prepared for work, I prayed. Just as I finished curling my hair, the phone rang. It was about 6:15 A.M. and I was scheduled to be at work at 7:00 A.M. It was a nurse calling. I couldn't imagine why she'd be calling me as they had never done so before when I was due to come in. An apologetic voice was on the phone. She told me that they had mistakenly scheduled me to work the wrong day. I was supposed to be off today.

"That's quite all right." I assured her. Then she apologized for my having to get up so early and get ready before knowing that I didn't have to come in. Again, I assured her that it was perfectly all right.

"I have other things that I'd love to do today anyway," I exclaimed. Excitedly, I hung up the phone, threw my fist in the air and said in a loud whisper, "Yes!" This is just great, I thought. Now I can go to Mass, get copies made, and take them to my friends' homes this morning. I was so excited. I could not believe how things were turning out.

Arriving at church a little early, it didn't surprise me that no one was there yet. However, after a long wait, only one other woman came into the church. Finally, after we both determined that there was not going to be a Mass, we walked out of the church together. We were naturally drawn to speak to each other as we made an effort to determine why there was no Mass this morning. She questioned me about the stack of papers in my hand. I had brought them into church to share with someone else whom I expected to see there.

I knew that I was on fire and sensed the glow from within me. The conversation led to the apparitions which, in turn, led to my explanation of why I went in the first place. I made it clear that I did not expect to see Mary, but I went in order to feel closer to her. I went originally to ask for comfort. Now this wouldn't make much sense unless she knew the rest of the story. Finding myself backtracking to Charlie's life and death, I shared bits and pieces of his story. She was fascinated upon hearing it and continued to ask many questions of me. She said that her son, Jimmy, had played with Charlie many times in the woods. He would come home talking about Charlie. I was touched to see that my son had affected this woman, whom I knew only through her son. The more we talked, the more astounded she became. Eventually, as time was getting away from us, I suggested that we best be going about our day. She thanked me for sharing Charlie's story and told me the reason why she decided to come to Mass this morning. She said that she had not gone to weekday Mass before, but was looking for some sort of inspiration in her life. She thanked me again and again because Charlie's story had inspired her. I was elated and so was she. The mutual feeling was the obvious power of the Holy Spirit.

As I drove toward home, I enjoyed the fresh spring flowers and landscaping in the yards. Contrary to my typical rushed mode, I drove the speed limit of twenty-five miles per hour, absorbing all that had just taken place. Once past the curves in the road, I glided down the tree-lined street, my eyes being drawn to the beauty of the bright blue sky. God is so magnificent, I thought. He does so much for each of us. He puts us in precarious situations that help each of us draw closer to Him. I was so pleased to be able to share Charlie's story and show how Our Blessed Mother was there to help me.

With my eyes focused on the sky, I noticed a most beautiful cloud in the shape of a cross right before me. It was a large cross with oval curves bringing the four ends to a slight point. It was absolutely splendid. I slowed down even more, so as to enjoy this scenery to its fullest extent. Oh how I wished I could package it up and save it. I had never seen anything so beautiful in the sky before. As I was thanking God for showing me this, I noticed another cloud coming in from the right. It seemed as though it would probably run right into this cross and ruin its appearance. Admittedly, I had never talked aloud to myself before that moment. However, I couldn't resist. It was as though I had some power over the cloud.

I said with tension in my voice, "Oh. Don't mess it up."

I watched closely as I scooted to the edge of my seat waiting for the clouds to crash. Then it happened. The cloud moved in right behind the cross. Just as it did, the cross was instantly transformed into the most beautiful Easter Seal lily that I ever saw. The arms of the cross dropped, with the points becoming the tips of the petals. The top and bottom rounded off with such perfection. It was distinctly shaped like the Easter Seal emblem. I was breathless. My heart was full of joy and, without hesitation, my right hand left the steering wheel to give a great big thumbs-up toward heaven. With this gesture and a broad smile, I said, "All right, Charlie. TOUCHDOWN!"

There were no cars around. I stopped and stared in total awe. I felt that Charlie had passed me the ball when I shared his story, and together we made a touchdown for heaven. It was for God's team, just as Dr. Cottrill said he would be playing.

Yes, Charlie. I knew that God would find a way for you to play football in heaven. Now every time that someone reads or hears your story, the game is being played. When they are touched by your story, you can chalk up six points. When they pass it on to someone else, consider it a field goal or a two-point conversion. For in the end, all will see that God's team will win.

Part IV

23
REFLECTIONS AND MEMORIES

In gathering stories from friends and relatives, I found it interesting how familiar their thoughts were. Some shared stories that I never knew, yet could picture so easily when considering Charlie's personality. Because people knew him from different situations, their stories were portrayed as such. Not only did Charlie's life affect others, but they, too, had an effect on him. Without the love from family, friends, doctors, teachers, coaches, priests, neighbors, and strangers, his life would not have been so blessed. The following comments come from those who knew him well.

Although my dear friend Carol knew his story best, she felt inspired to share the bottom line about Charlie. That is, she understood the spiritual connection between Charlie's story and his mother's heart. Although her focus is on me, it must be understood that my strength came solely from God.

I remember Charlie's mother. Of course, I remember Charlie, too, but mostly I remember Mary Jo. The first time I saw them in 1975, Mary Jo was sitting on an orange leather couch with Charlie in her arms and Jackie standing beside them. I can visualize it as if it happened yesterday, the bright September sun coming through the trees casting its lacy effect on the wall behind them. They had been referred to me by Barbara Carter, who was at that time working for the Commission for Handicapped Children. I dutifully assumed the role of the physician -- pediatric cardiologist, and took a history, finding out that Mary Jo was a little older than appearance, that of a teenager. She was married to a UK student and the two towheads were her only children. I found her an articulate and intelligent individual. After examining Charlie and obtaining a chest x-ray and EKG, I hesitated before going back into the room for the consultation part of the visit. I knew that Charlie had devastating heart disease. I also knew that this was a perceptive and loving mother. I must choose my words carefully. I prayed to the Holy Spirit for guidance, and taking a deep breath, went into the room and sat down (marveling that God had the sun shining so brightly when I was to be the bringer of such bad news) to talk. I said, "From what I can tell by examining Charlie and looking at the tests, I think his heart is such that there is no one big operation we can do to fix it up." Mary Jo very openly and evenly established eye contact and said, "I've known that since he was born." I was struck deeply by the image before me of this terribly vulnerable mother hanging on to and nurturing her baby boy, when she really needed nurturing herself, and an urge to somehow protect her from what I had experienced with my daughter's death welled up. She went on to tell that he'd been whisked away at birth to be taken to another hospital, leaving her and elder Charlie to worry until their worst fears were confirmed. I sensed her interaction with Charlie's early caregivers had not been very positive, and knew I must do better. I must not only give medical care to this family, I must also love them.

Then began an over twenty-year relationship with a remarkable woman. Throughout all of Charlie's heart, back, and feet surgeries, she was the dominating force in his recovery. An early challenge was his admission to the hospital for a "shunt" operation to palliate the situation by giving more blood to Charlie's lungs.

Following Charlie over time led to the discovery that he wasn't moving his legs properly and had lost some of his earlier abilities to function neurologically. I referred him to Dr. Kenton Leatherman at Norton's, to assess his suitability for an operation on his spine, which had a malformed vertebra, which was pressing on his spinal cord. If left alone, Charlie would eventually have become paralyzed. After much urging by me, Dr. Leatherman agreed to do the operation, even though

430

Charlie's heart was not optimal. After the operation, Charlie had a stroke, which left him unable to use his legs and left arm, and he lost his speech abilities. The first time I saw him after the operation, Mary Jo was pulling him in a little red wagon on a big pillow. I felt very responsible that I had pushed for the operation that left him worse off than he'd been before. Mary Jo, however, was undaunted, enrolling him in Cardinal Hill's program, taking him here and there, pushing him to become the best person he could be.

After working all my life with parents and children, I have come to the conclusion that the best parents are those who recognize their children's' gifts and enable the children to take advantage of what gifts they have. Mary Jo personifies this "best parent" concept. Whether making special birthday cakes, or driving many miles, or getting just the right football shirt, she does it all for her children.

How could Charlie not respond to this kind of mother? Of course he improved, began to be able to use his arm and legs again, learned to talk again. Attention needed to be given to his feet, so he had surgery on both feet, and eventually began to walk with the help of a walker. I first saw Charlie walk alone when he was six-years-old, and he walked down my front sidewalk. With increasing physical activity came increasing demands upon Charlie's heart and he again had heart surgery. During all this, Mary Jo was able to keep Charlie's attitude (and her own) very positive. His education was varied; a mix of parochial and public schools that fit Charlie best. He had his share of the limelight, too, being the Poster Child for Cardinal Hill and going to Germany with his family to visit his uncle via the Dream Factory. He knew he was special.

With all the involvement with Charlie and his family came questions for me. How close should one get to a patient? Over time, I came to the realization that if a doctor shares life and death with a family, why not

431

participate in other family events? I found great strength, love and acceptance from this family without detracting from my role as Charlie's doctor.

The decision for a final operation for Charlie was not easy. Only when he demonstrated to us that his oxygen saturation was dangerously low during attempts at physical exertion did we opt for an operation that would make him "pink" forever. With a good attitude ... the night before surgery, Charlie began his last journey. His ventilator was stopped on May 28 of his 14th year, ending 14 years of good times and bad, health and sickness, and love — lots of love. He died with his family, the surgeon — Dr. Robert Salley, the local priest — Fr. Dan Noll, and me. He moved from the arms of his mother to the arms of his Heavenly Father in peace.

But that isn't the end of the story -- it's only the beginning. Charlie's influence is far-reaching and felt by many. I no longer have questions about how "close" I should become to patients and their families. It is a privilege to be involved in loving them. Mary Jo is collecting other stories about Charlie and his journey through life. It is really her story -- a story of personal and spiritual growth all made possible by a little blue baby boy that I met on that sunny September day. I cared for him and am pleased that he now lives happily ever after.

Carol Cottrill, M.D.
(Pediatric Cardiologist)

THE CONTAGIOUS SMILE

One memory that is synonymous with everyone who knew Charlie was his smile. Naturally, to put a face to a name would bring his personal characteristics to mind. The blond hair, marshmallow skin, short, stocky build does not represent the entire picture. To see his face would be to see a smile. His smile was nearly always present. Yet, in those few instances when he was not in the best of spirits, all it would take would be a greeting or remark and a smile would instantly appear.

One of my earliest memories of Charlie is when I was looking for a nominee for the state poster child for the Kentucky Easter Seal Society. I contacted the staff in the preschool program at Cardinal Hill Hospital for their input on likely candidates. Unanimously, it was Charlie. When I went to the preschool to observe, I soon realized why. I remember seeing a cute little blond boy who, despite his physical limitations, was active, playful and in good spirits. I could see what the preschool staff had seen and, in turn, nominated him to Mr. Combs, who was the public relations director for the society at the time. I remember being delighted that Charlie, my nominee, who was selected from among all the Easter Seal Centers, would be the statewide Easter Seal Poster Child.

Mr. Tim Jordan
(Public Relations Director
The Kentucky Easter Seal Society)

As Charlie's music teacher, I remember the sparkling eyes every time we passed each other in the hall. Charlie was very good in music and you could tell he loved it, hence the talent show year of their "band" and "Born In The U.S.A."

Mrs. Jean Kern
(Music teacher)

I was always struck first by what a beautiful child Charlie was. Charlie's cherubic face, bright eyes and blond hair were always a visual magnet and a mirror of the inner beauty in such a small child.

Miss Kyran Daugherty
(Pediatric nurse)

Charlie's smile. I can still hear his giggle as a first grader and see that crooked smile. His eyes always had a smile, too.

Mrs. Sharon Dutton
(First grade teacher)

When I think of Charlie, I remember his smile the most. I also remember his determination to do as much as he could. He loved being around people, and people loved being around him.

Mrs. Kathy Stivers
(Second grade teacher)

Charlie was always a positive, loving person. He always had a smile on his face. He was friendly and easy to talk to.

Mr. Alan Huelsman
(Principal of St. Gabriel)

Charlie had a gift to give everyone he met—the gift of love. He displayed his gift with his smile. Charlie was always making new friends. Anyone he met became his friend.

Mrs. Linda Koontz
(Neighbor)

MEMORIES

Life is a volume of memories. Those created today will become our strength or weakness when facing tomorrow. It is so important to be involved in life so that we may create those memories for others. God so often used Charlie to bring out the kindness and generosity of those around him. We do make a difference in the lives of others. Yet, we generally don't recognize the blessings until much later. Reflecting on another's life can bring inspiration as well as a peace in knowing our role in creating their happiness. There were times when Charlie's presence alone enticed others to do for him. People saw that his handicap prevented him from participating in many forms of childhood fun. Their empathy for him often moved them to go out of their way in order for him to experience a moment of happiness.

When I remember Charlie, I remember a little tow-headed boy standing on my front stoop wearing a football helmet and holding a football. He would ask for Trevor or Todd to come out and play and he didn't care which one. He liked them equally, I believe. He enjoyed the time they could give to him, sometimes tossing the ball around, but lots of times just 'hanging out' with the big boys. He had an infectious laugh and a smile that could melt my heart.

Mrs. Joyce O'Neil
(Neighbor)

One day, when Charlie was spending an afternoon at Mom's (Charlie's maternal grandmother) house, he became very excited when I pulled up on my motorcycle. He wanted so badly to take a ride so, I let him get on with me.

We rode down the street then stopped to turn around. He was having so much fun. Then, as I attempted to turn the bike around, it fell over and Charlie fell off. I was pretty shook up about it and I asked him if he was okay as I helped him up. Laughing, he said, "Yeah. That was fun. Let's do it again."

Charlie was so filled with spirit. It was hard to watch him play football and see that he really couldn't play.

Uncle Bruce Clark

I remember Charlie had a great love for sports. Whether he was watching them or playing them, he really enjoyed sports. I remember when we were just little kids; we played a lot of football together. Although Charlie was handicapped, he never wanted to be given any advantages in the game, such as being considered tackled if we tagged him. If we happened to be playing tackle football, Charlie wanted to be tackled like everyone else. Or, if we were playing baseball, he wanted to run the bases himself. He didn't want people running the bases for him.

Charlie was always a happy kid. He never once complained about being handicapped. He always seemed to be smiling. I can remember always making him laugh so hard. One time we were sitting together at Donna and Perry's (neighbors) wedding. During the wedding we both started laughing. I didn't think we would ever stop.

Jamie Combs
(Friend, classmate, neighbor)

One of my memories of Charlie was that he always wore his favorite shorts which were blue with white trim. He would ride his orange and black electric cart (which he called his go-cart) to my house and ask my dad if I could come out and play. We used to go all over the neighborhood on that cart. I remember always playing kickball in front of his house with all the neighborhood kids. He was one who never backed down from anyone, he was always right there with everyone else ready to play whatever games they wanted to play.

Dana Guenthner
(Friend, classmate)

Charlie always talked about football and U of K. Charlie, Jamie Combs, and I hung out then. One night we all stayed at my house and we watched 'Rambo' twice and we played games. I still have that little picture Mrs. Stopher gave me of Charlie after he died, in my room. He inspired me to live every day for what it is and always try to have a smile on my face.

Chad Hennesey
(Friend, classmate)

The first time that Charlie and I met was when I got his lunch box down off the shelf in 1st grade. I got it for him because he couldn't reach it and I wanted to help him. This is what started our friendship. I helped him everyday and went to lunch with him. Another memory is playing T-ball with Charlie. I used to run the bases for him when he wasn't feeling good, which was most of the time, but that didn't stop him. He wanted to be right there with the rest of us playing T-ball. Again I wanted to help a friend, a best friend in need. I didn't think too much of it at the time. I just wanted to help a friend.

Robby Wheeler
(Friend, classmate)

My most favorite memory of little Charlie was having the privilege of being at one of his T-ball games when he was six or seven-years-old. He had his leg braces on as I watched him go to bat. He swung and had a good hit that went past the pitcher. He ran as fast as his legs and braces would allow, to first base. All the way, he had the biggest, brightest smile that covered his whole face. He was playing baseball. Just watching that little boy having so much fun with all his friends and being a participant instead of a spectator, stole my heart away.

Aunt Trudy Taylor

Whenever I think of Charlie, I always think of his BIG smile. It was so contagious. He would brighten up any place, just by smiling. I will never forget the smile on his face when he was playing T-Ball. He was so thrilled to be on the team with his friends. I know there were times when he didn't feel well, but his determination kept him going. It was truly a very special time for us all. I feel especially blessed to have shared a part of his life.

Mrs. Bette Wheeler
(Friend, Robby's mother)

GRATITUDE

I remember the first time I saw him, and if my memory serves me right, it must have been in the summer of 1978 when Anita, Susy, and I were in the States. He must have only been a couple of years old then. Susy was eleven at the time. She and Anita were taking him into Charles's pool with all the braces on, etc. and he wouldn't get out even though his lips were dark blue to purple.

He used to try to "run" (on his knees) after Touché' (the dog). I remember that he had just gotten over the stroke and went from a right-hander to a southpaw. The thing I remember the most at that time was that he was a happy child in spite of the problems he had, and was ever grateful every time Anita took him into the pool.

Later, when the family was here, I still can see the smile on Charlie's face when he showed up in Munich.

Uncle Tommy &Aunt Anita Clark

My favorite memory I shared with Charlie was when we were left alone. Every time the whole family would leave and only the two of us were left at home, we would make lots of special desserts and 'pig out' on every junk food item in the house. We never told anyone because it was something that was just for us and we didn't want anyone else to have a part in it.

Jackie Oeswein
(Sister)

Jonathan, being the youngest in the family, was forever getting hugs and kisses from the others, and especially from Charlie. By the time he was four and five-years-old, he had become quite tired of all the attention. He had decided that he was too big for this. He didn't want to hurt Charlie's feelings, but no longer wanted to be treated like a baby. It took a while for Charlie to get the message, but he finally did.

I remember one time that my brother and I were playing football in my room. (I never did like to give hugs or kisses.) But, I tackled him and gave him a hug and a kiss. And he said, "Oh my God. He kissed the quarterback. "

Jonathan Stopher

Later, when Jonathan was almost seven-years-old, he began playing flag football on a team. Mostly, he played center. Before long he was going out for passes and catching them. We watched his confidence build. On one occasion the coach sent him out for the kickoff. He became very worried and explained to me that he didn't know how to kick well. I told him to go out there and kick it for Charlie. He felt so inspired that he kicked the ball the entire length of the field. The coaches and players were all in disbelief. They figured that we had been keeping this special talent a secret. Charles and I were just as stumped as they were. In fact, Jonathan himself couldn't believe what he had done. He told me that he asked Charlie to help him. It was all I could do to hold back the tears. Yes, I knew that Charlie was playing football.

During basketball season Charlie and I would get along great because we would both cheer for Kentucky. Although, when football season came, we would rag on each other when our teams won. Charlie would cheer for the 49ers and Trinity and I would cheer for the Bengals and St. X.

So we were complete opposites. All in all Charlie and I were best of friends. One thing that I have always felt good about was the way Charlie looked up to me. If you didn't know us you would think I was 'Big Brother' and Charlie was "Little Brother." I always felt real close to Charlie.

John Oeswein
(Jackie's husband)

Aside from sports, Charlie did have other interests such as family, girls, school and just plain having fun.

Mom (paternal grandmother) and Charlie had such special bonding due to their walkers and illnesses. They would have races. Boy, Charlie really worked up a sweat. Of course he won.

I remember how many girlfriends he seemed to have, even me. He would beat me every time in video games. I swore he was cheating. Of course, he only laughed at me. And he laughed all the time.

Aunt Mary Ann James

I remember pulling him in his red wagon down the school hall and he sat there like a 'king.' (This was for a parade.) We all loved him so much and I always felt he loved us back so much. He loved to play. Charlie always tried so hard to be like the other students and I could see my first graders admire him back. He was so special. I'm sure he is making people happy in heaven, too. I miss him and think of him often. I bet he is playing football right now.

Mrs. Sharon Dutton
(First Grade Teacher)

I remember when I taught Charlie in second grade. He was not able to sit in his desk for part of that year (due to bilateral leg casts after surgery). We set him up in his own 'private office' in our classroom. He had a table and a carpeted area of the room.

What always inspired me about Charlie was the way he approached life. He always gave his best effort and always with a smile on his face.

Mrs. Kathy Stivers
(Second Grade Teacher)

In second grade Charlie was in (double legged) casts. He was so dependent on others for his needs. He never complained. I think about Charlie often especially when things don't go your way. My wife pictures the time I carried him to the grotto for the May Procession. He had those heavy casts on.

Mr. Alan Huelsman
(Principal)

He will never know what he meant to me. That determined, strong-willed third grader, who was constantly struggling for life, taught me more than any teacher ever could. I feel privileged to say that Charlie always brings a smile to my face, and he will always have a place in my heart.

Christa Birchler
(Friend, classmate)

STRUGGLE WITH SPEECH

Charlie would often get tickled at hearing himself speak. He tried so hard to enunciate his words but often fell short due to the damage left by the stroke. When he was very young, he enjoyed teaching the baby how to talk. Leslie was just over a year old

441

when Charlie began to teach the simple phrase, "I Love You." He began, "Leslie? Say I." She responded, "I." He added, "Love." She repeated, "Love." And he ended with, "Lou." Not realizing when he said it that it came out incorrectly, he began to roar with laughter when Leslie repeated, "Lou." He saw instantly what had happened. I was pleased that he was able to laugh at himself instead of becoming angry or embarrassed over his mistake. He made it easy to laugh with him, as he was well aware that he was not being laughed at. Throughout his life he struggled with pronouncing words correctly. Yet, he never let his mistakes get the best of him.

I taught Charlie in CCD class (religious education for those in public schools). Once when he was interrupting the class, I sat him at the teacher's desk. I don't recall exactly what happened, but somehow found out the interruption wasn't his fault. I felt so bad about having chastised him that I called him at home and apologized.

Mr. Bill Mouser
(Religious education teacher)

I can hear him so clearly saying... "Zamie, Zamie," when he wanted Jamie.

Mrs. Pam Combs
(Neighbor)

He struggled balancing himself from side to side as he came to join his reading group. For Charlie everything was cause to giggle. I can remember trying so hard to get him to find a root word, decipher a word, spell a word; whatever the lesson, he giggled. Only after talking with you (Mary Jo) later did I realize how he struggled at home in tears over his schoolwork.

Mrs. Karen White
(Teacher)

Charlie and I were friends from the start. I can clearly remember the first day that Charlie called me. I returned home from an intense neighborhood game of jailbreak when Mom informed me that Sally had called. The bizarre thing was that I knew no one by the name of Sally. A puzzled look came across my face and Mom realized that she didn't know the mysterious "Sally" either.

I tried for a long time to figure out who this Sally was but there was no success, until the phone rang later that night. I lunged at the phone and picked up the receiver before it had completed the first ring. From the other end of the phone came the voice of the mysterious "Sally." Only this voice was not mysterious at all. It was the unmistakable voice of Charlie, the boy in my class. As I struggled to understand Charlie over the phone I could see how Mom thought he was saying, "This is Sally." When I realized this, I quickly explained why I hadn't returned his call. The unforgettable laugh sounded from the other end of the phone. Charlie laughed uncontrollably for an extremely long time. Because he thought it was so amusing I decided to start calling him Sally.

Charlie called me everyday following the first time that we talked. He would constantly beg me to be his girlfriend; however, I didn't have that in mind. When Valentine's Day rolled around I opened the letter and scanned what it said.

"Dear Christa,

> Roses are red, violets are blue.
> Whenever I see you, I feel like kissing you."

There was no name signed to this letter but there was no doubt in my mind that Charlie was once again trying to win my affection. At times I would get irritated by

443

these attempts, but I really enjoyed having Charlie as a friend.

Christa Birchler
(Friend, classmate)

Charlie and I shared the same interests in girls. I remember he would talk to me every day about the apple of his eye, Christa Birchler. Now let it be known that Charlie and I both had a crush on Christa, but for Charlie it was more. She was a pretty girl who treated Charlie as a regular guy. No different than other guys, but quite a sweet talker Charlie was and Christa loved to talk to him. How could you not like the guy? He had never harmed a soul and was your friend till the end. I recall the countless hours we spent talking about girls and all the great topics in a young boy's life.

Jason O'Coin
(Friend, classmate)

LAUGHTER PRODUCES STRENGTH

Although not specific, my general impression of Charlie was his good sense of humor. Charlie was seldom in a state of feeling "well", as I know it so it was amazing to see and hear him laugh so much. The corniest of jokes or silly remarks would set him off with belly laughs, which often in itself would give him physical pain. The night before his final surgery we shared some fast wheelchair rides down the hospital corridor and my weak attempt at humor set him howling.

Uncle Jude Clark

For someone his age to go through the life he did, Charlie was a strong and happy child who laughed all the time and carried a positive attitude. He was always

444

determined to do what everyone else did, no matter what it took.

Dana Guenthner
(Friend, classmate)

I could never forget the times that we attended the dinners and events that Little Charlie was at the center with The Easter Seal Society. He traveled with Harvey Sloane to different parts of the state in a private plane to be the representative of the Easter Seal campaign. He would approach the mike and come out with "Hello, my name is Charlie." You can imagine the applause that he received.

Another memory of course is the trip to Munich, Germany that was awarded to him by the "Dream Factory." It was not only for him but also, for his entire family. It was an award that he surely deserved.

On a more personal note, I remember a talk I gave in a public speaking class at the University of Louisville. I touched on the highlights of Little Charlie. I had all the props I could find; shoes with braces, pictures of celebrities — Harvey Sloane, Nancy Reagan, U of K Basketball Players and Governor John Y. Brown. It was quite a rendition, I might say and I could see by the look on the face of each student that it was a success. When it was over I was immediately asked how I knew all about this boy named Charlie. My answer was, "I know this to be true, because he was my GRANDSON."

Grandpa
(Mr. Thomas W. Clark, Sr.)

FAMILY STRENGTH — A GIFT FROM GOD

Charlie stood out as the focal point of the family, as if it was his job to keep everyone laughing. He could make a joke out of everything when there was nothing to joke about. He was the one his brothers and sisters looked to — to show them the way. His sense of humor was definitely a God given talent and the thing we miss most about him. I believe God gave him that gift as a comfort for his family. He was more concerned for them than he was for himself.

Grandma
(Mrs. Jo Clark)

In my memory I cannot separate Charlie from memories of the Stopher family. I remember all of you as a wonderfully cohesive family that made Charlie and his disabilities a family rallying point and positive life factor, rather than a cause for sadness or pity. Charlie had a wonderful smile that would light up a room or all outdoors when he was at camp. He was full of life and lived his life to the fullest.

Mary Jo, you and your family made Charlie's life a happy and productive one. In his few short years he contributed more to the lives of the people with whom he came in contact than anyone else I can think of.

Mr. Guion Miller
(President / CEO,
Kentucky Easter Seal Society)

Although his pain was great so much of the time, physically and emotionally, Charlie never let it consume him. He did what he could to minimize the pain and accepted what he couldn't. He found ways to enjoy the good parts of his life, particularly his loving family. He had an incredible trust that all would be O.K. As a nurse I admired such incredible seemingly unlimited faith exhibited.

Kyran Daugherty
(Nurse)

446

THE PAIN AND TREASURE OF FRIENDSHIP

I woke up this morning having a clear vision of that smiling blond-headed boy, my friend Charlie Stopher. It was a face I think of often and I wish were here with us today. But, God had a greater mission for Charlie. He was no regular boy, but one I will never forget in the many years I have ahead. It seems so long ago; but then again just yesterday that Charlie, Marty, and I had our front yard football battle, Charlie being the legendary quarterback Terry Bradshaw. Rolling out for a pass with his classic smile, living and loving every minute of a life he was told he wouldn't have. But, in classic Charlie Stopher style, he became a wonder of God's creation; one that no one has explanation. A guy that I can gladly say that I was one of Charlie's favorite friends, and that means the world to me. I will always remember the lifelong lessons I learned from him, the struggles he went through and how strong that little guy was.

Jason O'Coin
(Friend, classmate)

My very first memories of anything to do with Charlie had to do with my first day at St. Gabriel. I had just been hired as the third grade teacher, and Mr. Huelsman had given me a class list. Another teacher, wanting to be helpful, looked over my list to tell me about my students. She told me about Charlie's medical problems and what it would require of me physically to be his teacher. I heard I may have to literally carry him during emergencies or wait as long as it takes for him to walk down the halls, across the playground, or to use the bathroom. This person made it sound as if Charlie would require much attention and patience. Although she made Charlie sound like he could be a burden I knew I could make Charlie's year a good one if I kept a positive attitude. I must admit I was a bit apprehensive.

As soon as I met Charlie and you, Mary Jo, I knew that the year would be a rewarding challenge. My heart overflows with memories of a little pudgy blond hair, sweaty boy with a smile that reached from ear to ear.

Reflecting back, I've often wondered if Charlie knew he had a few short years to pack a lifetime in. He lived more in fourteen years than most 'old' people ever do. He taught me many lessons about living with pain and fear. He taught me to face each day with hope and a smile. He taught me that even when life isn't the best of times that I can reach out to others and my joy would be multiplied. Above all he taught me that the most important gifts I have received, those of faith and love, are the greatest. Charlie's love for his family and friends, and his great faith in God's promise of heaven sustained not only him in his darkest hours but those of us that had to say goodbye.

Mrs. Karen White
(Third grade teacher)

INSPIRATION

Charlie made me glad to be alive. Not because he was a sickly person with heart problems (and I was healthy) but because he brought such happiness and joy by his presence. His great attitude made even the dreariest day seem sunny. He was a little saint on earth and I know a 'sure-thing' in heaven. I'm glad Charlie was my student; he was an inspiration and a gift.

Mrs. Sharon Dutton
(First grade teacher)

I have been and was inspired by Charlie both before his death and also after his death. I feel I know him as well now as I did when he was in class. For, I remember and recall frequently all those children I taught and loved, and prayed for them that God would protect them from the many vicissitudes in life, their joys and sorrows that might not jeopardize their eternal happiness.

Mr. Bill Mouser
(Religious Education Teacher)

He always took time for the little children, to talk and play with them. And if he ever felt bad you didn't know it. Watching Charlie was an inspiration. He made you feel like you could do anything, by his actions. He seemed to never tire playing with his football. He just kept going. In this way you hated to complain of anything bothering you.

Mrs. Barbara Dix
(Neighbor)

In his life Charlie inspired me by his determination to keep trying in whatever he did. In sports he kept on trying and was so proud of any small accomplishment. This determination has inspired me to have faith and keep trying — no matter what.

Mrs. Linda Koontz
(Neighbor)

Charlie was absolutely one of the most inspirational children I have ever met. His love for life was so sincere and displayed daily by the 'huge' smile he always managed to have, although some days he was too weak to express his feelings in other ways. He loved to be competitive, and although he could not always be a 'winner' in the game, he was a 'winner' in everyone's hearts.

Mrs. Pam Combs
(Neighbor)

I don't really think I thought of this at the time we were friends, but realize it now that I'm older, that is Charlie's courage and determination. When I look back now I think how hard it must have been for him to keep playing with us even after he was tired. But he never let his medical condition stop him from doing what he wanted to do. He had the drive and nothing was going to stop him. No matter what people told him, he was going to do it. I also remember that he hated to be treated differently. He just wanted to be treated normally and be a normal kid. That's what he did and that's what inspired me to believe that I can do anything I want to do if I want to. Nothing will stop me except my own self. Charlie didn't let him stop himself.

Robby Wheeler
(Friend, classmate)

In my eyes, Charlie is a saint. When I picture him I see a sweet, happy, loving boy who never complained but wanted to be like everyone else and always had a smile on his face. He made me realize that people with special needs are no different than anyone else. He did everything his friends could do and he wouldn't stop until he won or accomplished what he was attempting to do.

One way that Charlie has inspired me is when I think I've had it bad or something goes wrong, I look back on all that he went through and realize that it's not that bad, and everything will work out the way God wants it to.

Dana Guenthner
(Friend, classmate)

Charlie had so many fine qualities — courage, determination, and patience. I learned so much from him. He taught me bravery by the way he faced the many obstacles (surgeries) in his life. I am a pretty determined person, but Charlie showed me that you can do anything when you really want to. Patience is something I have always needed more of — and again Charlie showed me time after time the true meaning of patience. I have learned some of the most important things in life from Charlie. A part of him will be with me always, showing me the way.

Mrs. Bette Wheeler
(Robby's mother)

One of the things that I remember and find inspiring was Charlie's smile. His smile captured the hearts of many people; national and statewide leaders of the Easter Seal Society, governors, mayors and other political leaders, military leaders, volunteer leaders and ordinary citizens. They were motivated and inspired to donate their support, both personally and materially, because of his smile and captivating nature. I remember working with photographers across the state at various campaign functions and seeing them capture his smile on film.

Charlie's smile seemed ever-present. Even when he did not feel well or was otherwise out-of-sorts, it always seemed to me that he could be coaxed into a smile without too much difficulty. His joy and zest for life serves as an inspiration to us all.

Mr. Tim Jordan
(Kentucky Easter Seal Society)

A FAMILY TOUCHED

Loving Charlie gave me a special appreciation for all challenged people. I have always wanted to adopt special needs children and am quite sure I will as soon as the time is right.

When I was pregnant with Becca, I talked to Charlie every night. I wanted to make sure she would be a healthy baby. When she was born she looked just like her Uncle Charlie and I knew then that he was watching over her. Becca talks about her Guardian Angel all the time and will grow up having Uncle Charlie as part of her life.

Mrs. Jackie Oeswein

Charlie never sold himself short. No goal was impossible to reach. No dream was too ridiculous, because he would always prove you wrong, starting at birth. No one imagined Charlie would live as long as he did. No one thought he'd ever be able to play sports, but he did. No one thought he'd be able to visit his Uncle Tommy in Germany, but he did. Nothing was unattainable to Charlie.

Mr. John Oeswein

My memories of him are always of a bright boy who smiled at everyone. His hopes and dreams for the future helped me realize how stagnant and dissatisfied I was at NPC (my workplace). Transferring back downtown was my first step in accomplishing a satisfying career. Each time I visit Charlie's grave, I promise him I will pursue my dream of making others happy through drawing cartoons.

I still cry every time I think of him.

Aunt Angela Stopher

Remembering Charlie's walk is inspirational — all the harness he had to wear, one leg shorter than the other, back brace, leg braces, heavy shoes — he persevered with every step.

Aunt Mary Ann James

I have been very much inspired with his courage. In my days of naval combat I have never seen the courage that has been displayed by Little Charlie.

It was a few days before Charlie was to enter the hospital, which was to be his final operation. He was visiting Grandma and Grandpa and there were several other grandkids around. The swimming pool had been drained for cleaning. The kids were playing in the empty pool going up and down the steep incline. Little Charlie, who could never swim in the deep end, now saw his chance. With the self-determination that he had, he went down into the deep end. With that same stubbornness he came up and out of the pool. Out of breath, he laughed and said, "I hope I don't die before the operation." I have never seen this courage before or since. This is an inspiration for all of Charlie's cousins, brothers, sisters, parents, and grandparents as we all continue on this road of life. I truly believe this is why God allowed us to have "Little Charlie" for fourteen years on earth and surely forever in Heaven.

Grandpa
(Mr. Thomas W. Clark, Sr.)

Charlie inspired us with his patience and the suffering he endured so courageously. In my 50 years as a registered nurse I never witnessed such suffering with such patience that Charlie underwent. He was an inspiration for all who knew him. It is a joy to look at the happy picture we have of Charlie and know that he is truly and forever happy in the Kingdom of God and will never suffer again. Now we can pray to Charlie and know that he will answer our prayers.

Grandma
(Mrs. Jo Clark)

Without being overly analytical, Charlie's death has changed my view of death in that I do not fear it as I might have before sharing his passing. My perspective toward living was changed in that I'm less petty and concerned with trivialities. Materialness has a lower priority and I am living more intently and focused and simultaneously less seriously. My involvement in the Hospice volunteer program is a direct result of Charlie's influence. Friends ask if volunteering with the terminally ill patients is depressing and it isn't. Spending time with those ill is rewarding and comforting to me as well as the patient.

Uncle Jude Clark

A LETTER TO CHARLIE

Dear Charlie,

Oh how I miss you. I really miss your beautiful face. You will never know the hero you are to me. You are my picture of courage. You remind me to look inside a person to find their beauty and to discard prejudices based on outward appearances. Oh how I miss playing tackle. It was always more tackle than football. As long as we had fun, it was all that mattered. When we were neighbors, I looked forward to coming home and seeing you busting out of your house and tackling me. You must have seen the "big sucker" stamped on my forehead when it came to you.

I write this letter to thank you. Thank you for your inspiration and courage. Thank you for the gift of love, love without question, love that gives without counting the costs.

With love, affection, and gratitude,
Uncle Ray Stopher

I'm sorry to say I don't remember much about Charlie. We didn't spend much time together, mostly because he was always playing football. I can honestly say he has helped me out a lot in my life. I feel his presence in everything I do and know he is behind me pushing me along. I feel he is the only one I can talk to about problems and know he will make it better. Although I can't recall certain memories, I see his smile everyday and that tells me everything will be okay.

Leslie Stopher

FOREVER LEARNING

When I bring my thoughts, memories, and questions to God, I discover that He is forever teaching me new understandings. As I had completed my writings about Charlie's life, I found myself at the foot of a statue of the Sacred Heart of Jesus. It was the feast day of the Sacred Heart that drew me to meditate in front of this statue in St. Bartholomew Church. Mass was over and the people had cleared the church. I was moved to thank Jesus once again for all the blessings bestowed upon me. After sincere thanks and joyful adoration, I sensed a desire to remain at His feet. A feeling of amazement still overwhelmed me when I summarized all the revelations that I had received through the years. My reflections from the past quickly surfaced as I gazed upon His Heart and thought of the comfort that He had given me after Charlie died. My thoughts were taken to the hallway of my home where family pictures told the story. Remembering that day that God revealed to me that it was Charlie's heart that brought me to His Sacred Heart, I realized that my face had to be glowing with appreciation, as my heart could not possibly contain the feeling inside of me. After a period of time passed, I began reflecting on particular happenings and the correlation between Charlie's suffering and the passion of Our Lord. In doing so, I noticed that I had never made the connection of Charlie's spinal surgery. I was certain that God had not given Charlie any more suffering than He did His son, Jesus. So, I asked Him for an explanation. "What was the connection between the spinal surgeries, the back brace and the metal rods that forbade him to move? I don't get it, I must admit. Thinking of Your passion, Your suffering, Your life, I'm truly stumped on this one."

In an instant, He answered me, "It was the cross. The back brace was the cross that prevented his movement just as I was prevented from movement. The metal rods were never removed to serve as a reminder of the cross. He would carry it to his death." It was clear to me that Charlie was a good servant to Our Lord. Once again I was astounded at the great magnitude of God's love for me. He shared the answer to my question because I asked it of Him. I was in such awe that I could hardly take my eyes off of His eyes.

A CALL TO MOTHERHOOD

Through my newfound nursing career, I was led to work in the Mother/Baby Unit at Baptist Hospital East. Ironically, it was my one desire when I first considered nursing that I could some day be available to new mothers. I longed to have the opportunity to give hope to new parents facing medical trauma with their newborn. It is often a time of shock and disappointment when a baby is not born completely healthy. It is a time of fear and uncertainty and a time of many questions for God. It has been through these moments that I have witnessed my most important role in life.

It turns out that God did indeed have plans for me to "mother" the people in my world. As with any patient in the hospital, my new mothers are in a vulnerable position and at the mercy of those who care for them. A patient is like a child, dependent on a mother. She needs someone to understand, to listen, and to show emotional support during this time. She often needs guidance, wisdom and knowledge. My sharing of these gifts will enlighten her to the awe of God in her life. To mother someone is to share joy and hope and respond to those in need with kindness and compassion.

Each and every day that I work, I am given the opportunity to share the gifts of God with my patients, not only for the mothers who experience trauma, but for every new mother facing new experiences. It doesn't matter whether it's a first baby or seventh baby. Whether she's a teenager, single, married, American, foreigner, Christian or non-Christian, she is a child of God and she appreciates His love through me. Each patient has her own unique and special need. It is a privilege for me to say "yes" to God and to be used in whatever capacity He desires.

Our Blessed Mother has not abandoned me, nor has God. They have made it clear that I am to be a mother forever. A mother loves unconditionally and guides the souls of her children to eternal life in heaven. If I can merely plant the seeds for the people put on my path, then I will know that I am following the will of God by being a mother figure to all.

THE SPIRIT MOVES ON

The following comment is from a woman whom I have known only a short time. She never knew Charlie, but was aware that I had lost a son to heart disease. She has agreed to share a personal experience that is directly related to the story that you have just read.

While I have known Mary Jo for some two and one-half-years, the two of us have shared spiritual happenings in our lives. As I knew Mary Jo was writing the book about Charlie, I've never read any of it nor have I been told what was in the book. I opted to wait until it was published.

In the fall of 1997 I had a dream. It's the most exceptional, vivid and clear dream I've ever had. In this dream was revealed to me the Sacred Host, round and white. Then the same host was seen with three drops of blood in it. Next, I saw the host bend completely without breaking, for it was pliable. All of a sudden it went back to its original shape and started quivering and pulsating.

457

Then I saw the Sacred Host rest on the front cover of a book. The Host then penetrated through every page of the book. In this dream it was made clear to me that it was the book that Mary Jo was writing about Charlie.

After I had awakened, I realized the pulsating and quivering of the Sacred Host was the Flesh of Jesus. I feel that not only was it a dream, it was a miracle given to me. For you see, at the consecration of the Mass, the Holy Eucharist is the true presence of the body and blood of Christ.

Betty Fenwick
(Friend)

SUMMARY

A cross does not consist of a single trial; rather, it is a road of suffering. We are each invited to carry our cross and die to ourselves. For it is in dying that we are resurrected into a new life with Jesus Christ. The union makes us one with God. Once we have achieved this unity, the Holy Spirit is free to work through us. It is then that we are given true inner peace and joy to carry us into eternal life.

A FINAL FACT

Let it be known that the depth of my faith did not eliminate a fraction of my pain, nor did the depth of my pain diminish a fraction of my faith.

ABOUT THE AUTHOR

Mary Jo Stopher is an LPN at Baptist Hospital East, working on the Mother-Baby Unit. As a strong believer, a Christian, she practices the holistic approach in her nursing career, using personal experiences to offer hope to her patients dealing with difficult circumstances. Married to Charles since 1972, Stopher resides in Louisville, Kentucky, where she enjoys her roles as wife, mother and grandmother.

Printed in the United States
202196BV00001B/1-63/A

9 781588 204776